GOD, SCHOOLS, AND GOVERNMENT FUNDING

In recent years, a conservative majority of the U.S. Supreme Court, over vigorous dissents, has developed circumventions to the Establishment Clause of the First Amendment that allow state legislatures unabashedly to use public tax dollars increasingly to aid private elementary and secondary education. This expansive and innovative legislation provides considerable government funds to support parochial schools and other religiously-affiliated education providers. That political response to the perceived declining quality of traditional public schools and the vigorous school choice movement for alternative educational opportunities provokes passionate constitutional controversy. Yet, the Court's recent decision in *Arizona Christian School Tuition Organization v. Winn* inappropriately denies taxpayers recourse to challenge these proliferating tax funding schemes in federal courts. Professors Winer and Crimm clearly elucidate the complex and controversial policy, legal, and constitutional issues involved in using tax expenditures—mechanisms such as exclusions, deductions, and credits that economically function as government subsidies—to finance private, religious schooling. The authors argue that legislatures must take great care in structuring such programs and set forth various proposals to ameliorate the highly troubling dissention and divisiveness generated by state aid for religious education.

About the authors

Laurence H. Winer is Professor of Law and Faculty Fellow, Center for Law, Science, & Innovation at the Sandra Day O'Connor College of Law at Arizona State University. After graduating from Yale Law School, Professor Winer practiced with a Boston law firm before joining A.S.U. Before law school, he taught mathematics at Boston University where he earned his Ph.D. degree.

Nina J. Crimm is Professor of Law and the Frank H. Granito, Jr., Faculty Scholar at St. John's University School of Law, New York. Before entering academia, Professor Crimm was a law clerk for Judge Irene F. Scott, United States Tax Court and later an Attorney-Advisor/Senior Attorney in the Office of the Chief Judge of the Tax Court; she also practiced tax and nonprofit law with a Washington, D.C. law firm.

Professors Winer and Crimm are co-authors of POLITICS, TAXES, AND THE PULPIT: PROVOCATIVE FIRST AMENDMENT CONFLICTS (Oxford Univ. Press 2011), as well as related works co-authored and written separately.

In celebration of our fruitful and ongoing collaborations.

God, Schools, and Government Funding

First Amendment Conundrums

LAURENCE H. WINER
Sandra Day O'Connor College of Law,
Arizona State University, USA

NINA J. CRIMM
St. John's University School of Law, USA

Routledge
Taylor & Francis Group
LONDON AND NEW YORK

First published 2015 by Ashgate Publishing

Published 2016 by Routledge
2 Park Square, Milton Park, Abingdon, Oxon OX14 4RN
711 Third Avenue, New York, NY 10017, USA

Routledge is an imprint of the Taylor & Francis Group, an informa business

British Library Cataloguing in Publication Data
A catalogue record for this book is available from the British Library

The Library of Congress has cataloged the printed edition as follows:
Winer, Laurence H., author.
God, schools, and government funding : first amendment conundrums / By Laurence H. Winer and Nina J. Crimm.
pages cm
Includes bibliographical references and index.
ISBN 978-1-4094-5031-3 (hardback)
1. Federal aid to private schools--United States. 2. Church schools--Law and legislation--United States. 3. Church and state--United States. I. Crimm, Nina J., 1952- author. II. Title.
KF4124.W56 2014
344.73'072--dc23

2014018

ISBN 9781409450313 (hbk)

Contents

Acknowledgements *vii*

Introduction 1

1 Alternatives to Traditional Public Schools and Their Funding 17

2 The Establishment Clause and School Aid 69

3 Tax Expenditures and School Financing 149

4 Establishment Clause Standing and Challenges to School Aid 185

5 Where States Are and Proposals for Reform 227

Index *273*

Acknowledgements

We wish to thank our respective academic institutions, the Sandra Day O'Connor College of Law at Arizona State University and the St. John's University School of Law, for their support in our writing this book.

Introduction

> Plainly hostile to the Framers' understanding of the Establishment Clause, and *Flast*'s enforcement of that understanding, the Court vents that hostility under the guise of standing, "to slam the courthouse door against plaintiffs who [as the Framers intended] are entitled to full consideration of their [Establishment Clause] claims on the merits."[1]

I. The Legal and Constitutional Setting for School Choice

On June 10, 1968, the U.S. Supreme Court upheld a New York statute requiring local school boards to purchase textbooks and loan them without charge to students in grades 7–12 in all schools, including private, secular and parochial schools. This case, *Board of Education v. Allen*,[2] involved an early, unsuccessful challenge under the Establishment Clause of the First Amendment to government aid for religious education. Three Justices dissented, including William O. Douglas who graphically demonstrated how these textbooks, even in ostensibly secular subjects, could be used to promote highly sectarian ends of religious indoctrination.[3]

The same day that he dissented in *Allen*, Justice Douglas joined the Court's opinion in *Flast v. Cohen* holding that federal taxpayers had the legal right ("standing") to bring an Establishment Clause challenge to the expenditure of federal funds for instruction, books, and other educational and library materials in religious and sectarian schools.[4] Justice Douglas clearly was dismayed by what he considered the improper erosion of separation of church and state. "The mounting federal aid to sectarian schools is notorious and the subterfuges numerous."[5] To this sentence he appended without comment the following contemporaneous editorial:

> Tuition grants to parents of students in church schools is [sic] considered by the clerics and their helpers to have possibilities. The idea here is that the parent

1 Valley Forge Christian Coll. v. Ams. United for Separation of Church & State, Inc., 454 U.S. 464, 513 (1982) (Brennan, J., dissenting) (quoting Barlow v. Collins, 397 U.S. 159, 178 (1970) (Brennan, J., concurring in result and dissenting)) (alterations in original).

2 392 U.S. 236 (1968).

3 *Id.* at 257–65 (Douglas, J., dissenting). Justice Hugo Black, who 21 years earlier had written the first Court opinion allowing inroads on state aid for parochial schools, also dissented calling the New York statute a "flat, flagrant, open violation" of the Constitution. *Id.* at 250 (Black, J., dissenting).

4 392 U.S. 83 (1968).

5 *Id.* at 113 (Douglas, J., concurring).

> receives the money, carries it down to the school, and gives it to the priest. Since the money pauses a moment with the parent before going to the priest, it is argued that this evades the constitutional prohibition against government money for religion! This is a diaphanous trick which seeks to do indirectly what may not be done directly.
>
> Another one is the "authority." The state may not grant aid directly to church schools. But how about setting up an authority—like the Turnpike Authority? The state could give the money to the authority which, under one pretext or another, could channel it into the church schools.
>
> Yet another favorite of those who covet sectarian subsidies is "child benefit." Government may not aid church schools, but it may aid the children in the schools. The trouble with this argument is that it proves too much. Anything that is done for a school would presumably be of some benefit to the children in it. Government could even build church school classrooms under this theory because it would benefit the children to have nice rooms to study in.[6]

Justice Douglas then said he would be "liberal in allowing taxpayers standing to object to these violations of the First Amendment."[7]

These two simultaneous cases perfectly encapsulate the debate raging today that is the subject of this book. For a variety of reasons the past few decades have seen a deep, broad, and rapidly growing dissatisfaction with kindergarten through twelfth grade ("K–12") education in American public schools. Indeed, the perceived inadequacies of our nation's schools and what to do about them are among the most controversial and debated political, policy, and social issues of the day.[8] Well-publicized international comparisons of student performance on standardized tests suggest American students' educational achievements are mediocre at best despite far greater spending on education per student than in most other countries.[9] Some assert that America in effect is committing cultural

6 *Id.* at 113 n.9 (*Editorial*, Church & State, June 1968, at 5).

7 *Flast*, 392 U.S. at 114.

8 "Educational failure puts the United States' future economic prosperity, global position, and physical safety at risk." Council on Foreign Relations, Independent Task Force Report No. 68, U.S. Education Reform and National Security 4 (2012), *available at* http://www.cfr.org/united-states/us-education-reform-national-security/p27618. While not contending that "schools are fine just as they are," Professor Diane Ravitch recently ascribed the main problems of American public education to poverty and *de facto* segregation and maintains "[t]he public schools are working well for most students." Diane Ravitch, Reign of Error: The Hoax of the Privatization Movement and the Danger to America's Public Schools xii, 4 (Alfred A. Knopf 2013).

9 Results from the 2012 Program for International Student Assessment (PISA), released in late 2013, show U.S. teenagers slipped further in math, science, and reading compared to students in other countries. OECD, PISA 2012 Results, *available at* http://

and economic suicide as a result of the decline in our public schools. For others the perceived crisis in American education is rooted more in the lack of "values" that public schools are willing or able to instill in children. These concerns extend well beyond parents and educators seeking quality education for all children. Business leaders increasingly are worried about the future global competitiveness of the United States and the need for well-educated and highly skilled employees in a complex technological age. Military personnel have similar concerns. And politicians wishing to meet these needs in fiscally difficult circumstances forcefully address these issues, especially in election years.

So, under the rubrics of school choice and competition, demand for alternatives to traditional public schools, and therefore the financing of such options, is growing and will continue to expand. There is, in particular, a rich history and tradition in America of religiously-affiliated, private schools providing educational opportunities for those inclined toward such a setting. As the country became more religiously diverse, disputes over sectarian aspects of public schools fostered development of parochial schools of various denominations. Today, numerous alternative schools are religious in nature, and many tout smaller classes, greater discipline, and lower expenditures per student than traditional public schools. These attributes appeal to parents' senses that such alternative schools provide better and more effective educational opportunities for their children, as well as safer and morally compatible environments.

But among the various constituencies debating the merits of public versus private education there is an intensifying, realistic anxiety. An increasing number of children—who are particularly susceptible to ideological indoctrination and peer pressure—may leave a diverse, pluralistic public school environment that traditionally has promoted assimilation and unity by exposing students to diverse people and ideas, thereby instilling appreciation for, and tolerance of, difference. Upon exiting, those children then may enter a more insular, sectarian setting less welcoming of nonconformity or dissent that in the extreme could foster disregard of others, intolerance, or even radicalism, perhaps supported by public tax dollars. Such student migration, if too extensive, also may weaken public education systems, on which many parents and students depend and which broad constituencies are committed to preserve. The potential mass exodus and its ramifications accentuate the question of whether private schools, especially parochial schools, rightfully may claim financial assistance from the state for their educational missions.

Public schools today are financed by tax revenues, largely through local property taxes, but also by some state and federal funds. Taxpayer-parents of parochial school students share in this public financial burden but then also pay private school tuition to educate their own children as they wish. In doing so they arguably relieve some financial strain on the public fisc, as fewer students are

www.oecd.org/pisa/keyfindings/pisa-2012-results.htm (last visited Dec. 10, 2013). *See* Stephanie Banchero, *U.S. High-School Students Slip in Global Rankings*, Wall St. J., Dec. 4, 2013, at A8.

educated at government expense. Parents and the parochial schools their children attend therefore naturally seek various forms of government assistance for their educational programs.

Yet the debate over government financing of religious education predates the Constitution. In the mid-1780s, James Madison and Thomas Jefferson were able to defeat Patrick Henry's proposal in Virginia for a surtax to support religious teachers; they substituted a bill that Jefferson had drafted establishing religious freedom. Madison, who would become the "architect of the First Amendment," campaigned against Henry's proposal through his famous *Memorial and Remonstrance Against Religious Assessments*. For many, this episode reflects a key component of the concept of separation of church and state embodied in the Free Exercise and Establishment Clauses of the First Amendment. By the middle of the twentieth century, cases under these Religion Clauses began to reach the Supreme Court regarding both religious influences in public schools, especially prayer, and government financial support for parochial schools. On the latter issue the Court started down a 65-year path of confusing, controversial, and often inconsistent decisions that seem to depend more on the composition of the Court than on any coherent constitutional theory.

These developments culminated, first, in the 2002 *Zelman v. Simmons-Harris* Supreme Court case in which, by a 5–4 vote, the Court approved a state government tuition voucher plan for private schools that overwhelmingly supported parochial schools.[10] The voucher program approved in *Zelman* was very narrow and designed to aid educationally and economically disadvantaged students facing a truly dire failure of Cleveland's inner city school system. Many jurisdictions, however, interpreted *Zelman* as substantially lessening constitutional constraints on government aid to private, secular and parochial schools and began experimenting with educational alternatives and various tax expenditure mechanisms and other methods of supporting them. Arizona was in the forefront of this movement and, as its initial foray, developed a broad-based tax credit program for tuition scholarships for students attending private, predominantly parochial schools. The initiative led to a decade-long legal battle. Finally in 2011, with sharply divided opinions in *Arizona Christian School Tuition Organization v. Winn*,[11] the Court's conservative five-Justice majority restricted the ability of taxpayers opposed to public financing of private, parochial schools even to challenge in federal court such tax-based programs as violating the Establishment Clause. By denying such taxpayer-plaintiffs standing, the Court made clear that federal courts now generally lack jurisdiction to rule on the substantive constitutionality of a state's skillfully camouflaged method of funneling money to private, parochial schools such as the tax credit approach at issue in *Winn*.

But the standing limitation on federal judicial review does not mean states have *carte blanche* in how they channel tax monies to private, parochial schools.

10 536 U.S. 639 (2002).
11 131 S. Ct. 1436 (2011).

As both the majority and dissent in *Winn* suggested, innovative financing schemes might be more amenable to future federal court challenges that do not depend on plaintiffs' standing simply as taxpayers. Moreover, state legislators and executive branch officials have their own obligations to evaluate and conform to constitutional strictures. And the ruling in *Winn* does not preclude challenges in state courts to government aid to religion under the First Amendment, state anti-establishment analogues, or state constitutions' anti-funding provisions.[12] State legislatures therefore need informed guidance in exercising the increased freedom they enjoy after *Winn* to direct tax dollars to private, parochial schools so they may properly address the many relevant concerns in a constitutionally compliant and politically acceptable manner.

II. Relating the Constitutional and Policy Issues

This book focuses on legal and constitutional issues, mainly those under the First Amendment's Establishment Clause. But we initially should take note of the primary policy issues regarding the kinds of schools that should be supported with public tax dollars. Everyone, of course, wants safe, effective, and quality education for the nation's children. And there also is general agreement, confirmed by the Supreme Court, that even under compulsory education laws parents enjoy considerable discretion to educate their children as they wish, at least at their own expense.[13] But consider two generic cases. Country Day School ("CDS") is a private, secular, highly selective K–12 educational institution located in an affluent community. It boasts a modern, technologically advanced facility, hand-picked non-unionized teachers (many holding advanced degrees), small classes, and a progressive curriculum. Its prestigious college admissions record is a major draw for parents. It also charges a high tuition beyond the means even of many middle-class families. CDS may offer some scholarship assistance in an effort to increase diversity and attract some students truly deserving of the many attributes it has to offer. Still, its student body is largely socio-economically homogeneous and perhaps along racial, religious, and ethnic dimensions as well.

Pervasively Sectarian Academy ("PSA") on the other hand may be very different.[14] It is a parochial school affiliated with, and run by, a religious organization, often under the supervision and control of a religious leader. In addition to providing a secular education, its mission unabashedly is religious indoctrination to inculcate and propagate the faith. And this religious mission

12 Indeed, the initial iteration of the *Winn* case, *Kotterman v. Killian*, 972 P.2d 606 (Ariz. 1999), *cert. denied* 528 U.S. 921 (1999), was just such an unsuccessful claim in Arizona state court.

13 *See* Pierce v. Soc'y of Sisters, 268 U.S. 510, 535 (1925).

14 We discuss the somewhat controversial phrase "pervasively sectarian" in this context in Chapter 2.

may pervade all aspects of the educational experience, both secular subjects and specifically religious ones. PSA may have strict religious requirements for its faculty and may limit student admissions on the basis of religion, either explicitly or implicitly by requiring all students to participate in religious exercises, thereby discouraging applicants for whom this is unacceptable. Some parents may welcome the religious education while others merely accept it because PSA otherwise offers an overall better education for their children than is available in the area public schools. PSA may be more affordable for parents who have no other, realistic private school alternatives. But we do not intend to caricaturize; some PSAs will rival any CDS in the overall quality of the educational experience.

Should public tax dollars be used to support either CDS or PSA? Posed this way the question is a bit misleading. For both CDS and PSA most likely already receive considerable financial support from state and federal government. Each almost certainly is organized as a tax-exempt nonprofit entity under § 501(c)(3) of the Internal Revenue Code ("I.R.C."). Like CDS, PSA qualifies as a nonprofit simply as an educational organization quite apart from its religious character. Indeed, from Congress's first attempts at enacting a comprehensive federal income tax in the late nineteenth century, the triumvirate of charitable, religious, and educational organizations has always been afforded tax-exempt status.[15] As § 501(c)(3) organizations, both CDS and PSA are exempt from federal income taxation and, pursuant to I.R.C. § 170, their donors are entitled to a deduction on their federal tax returns if they itemize deductions. This is an important incentive to donate. Moreover, many states mirror these tax benefits with respect to their state income taxes, and CDS and PSA also may be exempt from property, sales and use taxes.[16] So, tax-exempt status is a considerable financial benefit for a private, secular or parochial school.

In addition, if PSA is affiliated sufficiently closely with a house of worship it may benefit from some of the additional tax and other accommodations extended to such entities.[17] These religion-based tax benefits and accommodations, which may be constitutionally permissible but are not constitutionally required,[18] can easily translate into financial assistance. In particular, in a separate context the Supreme Court recently ruled that the First Amendment entitles a church school

15 For the history of this exemption, now extended to several other types of entities, *see* Nina J. Crimm & Laurence H. Winer, Politics, Taxes and the Pulpit: Provocative First Amendment Conflicts 95–103 (Oxford Univ. Press 2011). Tax relief for religious entities was justified on the basis of their financial and social utility in fulfilling social welfare functions and not because of their religious nature *per se* or First Amendment considerations. *Id.* at 99–100.

16 *See id.* at 53–54.

17 *See id.* at 43–66, 373–79. For example, a primary or secondary parochial school that is affiliated with a house of worship within the meaning of Treasury regulation § 1.6033–2(h)(2) is not required to undertake the burden of filing an annual federal income tax return. Treas. Reg. § 1.6033–2(g)(1)(vii)(2013).

18 *See* Crimm & Winer, *supra* note 15, at 149–86.

to a ministerial exception that shields it from a lawsuit for terminating certain teachers allegedly in violation of employment discrimination laws.[19] This is another obvious advantage enjoyed by parochial schools but not by private, secular schools.

So, in the debate over providing government assistance for private alternatives to public schools, it must be emphasized that private schools—both secular and parochial—already receive a great deal of support from government, that is from taxpayers generally. The question properly put, then, is: Should they receive anything more, whether the additional assistance takes the form of in-kind educational materials, instructional support, vouchers, or especially tax mechanisms to relieve the burden of tuition payments? The argument for extending such aid is stronger to the extent public schools are perceived as providing sub-standard education. In this event, promoting private alternatives potentially not only satisfies the understandable desires and legitimate needs of students and parents but also, through competition, may spur improvement in the public schools. The argument, however, becomes weaker as public schools themselves improve and as better public education alternatives to traditional schools become available. New public education options have begun to proliferate in the forms of magnet schools, new charter schools started by independent groups, charter schools created from previously traditional public schools when triggered by sufficient parent discontent, and a home schooling movement invigorated and facilitated by advent of the internet and a plethora of sites geared to assist home schooling.[20] Ironically, then, state legislatures are developing broader and more inventive programs to funnel increasing amounts of state money into private schools, most of it going to parochial schools, thereby draining money from public education and dangerously threatening to encroach on church-state separation, even as the more compelling justifications for such programs are perhaps diminishing.

At any rate, as to CDS the policy issue is whether the elite education it offers generally to those with private resources who can afford to pay its tuition deserves additional financial assistance from the public that already is supporting the public schools. If in principle the answer is no, then one way to evaluate the various schemes that are emerging to direct taxpayer funds to private schools is to ask if the programs are narrowly tailored to help only those educationally and economically disadvantaged students who truly need it. We take account of this basic policy in fashioning our suggestions for how legislatures should proceed in accommodating the current movement toward increased public funding for alternatives to traditional public education.

---

19 Hosanna-Tabor Evangelical Lutheran Church & Sch. v. E.E.O.C., 132 S. Ct. 694 (2012).

20 Home schooling as alternative education raises a particular set of issues that we address in Chapters 1 and 5, including its treatment by states variously as the equivalent of public schooling, private schooling, or something different from either.

As to PSA, the question may be somewhat reversed. For many students PSA may provide the only feasible alternative to a public educational system that is not meeting their needs. If so, one easily can sympathize with the plight and financial bind of the students and their parents. Here, helping to provide choice and competition among schools seems quite appealing. But unlike with secular CDS, in addition to the private versus public policy issues, valid and weighty constitutional concerns constrain the wisdom and legitimacy of providing governmental assistance to PSA in addition to that which it already receives. As is well accepted with thorny issues of freedom of speech or press, there often are significant social costs of preserving First Amendment freedoms. And especially in the context of primary and secondary education we should heed the Supreme Court's admonition in its first substantive ruling on the constitutionality of school prayer that "a union of government and religion tends to destroy government and to degrade religion."[21]

Indeed, the fact that PSA already enjoys tax-exempt status and the many benefits that flow from it exacerbates, rather than mitigates, the problem. These basic tax advantages could derive simply from PSA's status as an educational entity, apart from its religious character, and are enjoyed in common and equal measure with a great many other tax-exempt entities both secular and religious. Any debate over including religious organizations within these broadly defined tax-preferred categories has largely dissipated over the 100 years since they were first created. Any proposal at this late date to deny organizations their long-standing and well-accepted tax status because of their religious character would be wholly unrealistic politically and likely seen as reflecting anti-religious animus. Moreover, as we discuss in Chapter 3, the income tax exemption for § 501(c)(3) organizations is simply a legislative determination that this class of entities lies outside the natural tax base. Tax expenditures on the other hand, like tuition tax credits and other school aid programs that states now are developing, are clearly state subsidies targeted for private education, the large majority of which support parochial education. These major, additional measures of state financial assistance for parochial education starkly raise the fundamental constitutional question affecting PSAs that does not arise for CDSs.

Furthermore, a state policy of fostering diversity and pluralism in education to prepare students to live and thrive in an increasingly heterogeneous world may be frustrated by promoting private K–12 education. At one time, many private schools in some parts of the country arose essentially as "segregation academies" in response to desegregation of public schools. Today, the homogeneity of many

21 Engel v. Vitale, 370 U.S. 421, 431 (1962). For a more recent statement on the "corrupting effect of government support" for religion, *see Rosenberger v. Rector & Visitors of the Univ. of Va.*, 515 U.S. 819, 891 (1995) (Souter, J., dissenting) (noting that the Establishment Clause "was meant not only to protect individuals and their republics from the destructive consequences of mixing government and religion, but to protect religion from a corrupting dependence on support from the Government.").

CDSs may be largely along socio-economic lines. PSAs, however, may be discriminatory by their very religious nature, and this discrimination may extend beyond religion, which itself may be problematic, to sexual orientation, ethnicity, or race.[22] Some also may promote an a-scientific, totally faith-based view of the world that will ill equip their students for life in the twenty-first century, with adverse societal consequences.[23] At the extremes, some parochial schools could instill in their students intolerance, chauvinism, or xenophobia and undermine cohesive civil society. With two ecumenically polar examples there is at least the realistic concern, if not the reality, that the overly insular, narrow-minded environment of a vigorously religious Orthodox yeshiva or Islamic madrassa could nurture students who reject assimilation and withdraw from the pluralistic, secular, democratic society that comprises America's strength.[24] Our proposals regarding government funding of religious education address and seek to ameliorate both constitutional and policy issues.

To be very clear, these questions and concerns do not reflect an anti-religious attitude. The point is not that private schools with strict doctrines and worldviews should be forbidden or that parents should not be free to choose such an education for their children. Rather, the Free Exercise Clause protects such schools as *private* entities offering individual parents options at their own expense. If such choices entail potential detrimental as well as beneficial social consequences, that is the price of free exercise, just as freedom of speech (and adherence to

22 Bob Jones University and a K–12 Christian school lost their tax-exempt status because, for religious reasons, they had racially discriminatory admissions or other policies. Bob Jones Univ. v. United States, 461 U.S. 574 (1983). *See* Brumfield v. Dodd, 2014 U.S. Dist. LEXIS 106541 (E.D. La. Aug. 4, 2014) (alleging Louisiana's new statewide educational voucher program results in racially segregated schools); SOUTHERN EDUCATION FOUNDATION, GEORGIA'S TAX DOLLARS HELP FINANCE PRIVATE SCHOOLS WITH SEVERE ANTI-GAY POLICIES, PRACTICES, & TEACHINGS (Jan. 2013) (asserting Georgia's "program of educational tax credits is providing public financing to a large number of private schools in Georgia that have draconian anti-gay policies and practices.").

23 *See* Stephanie Simon, *Taxpayers Fund Creationism in the Classroom*, POLITICO (Mar. 24, 2014), *available at* http://www.politico.com/story/2014/03/education-creationism-104934.html. *See, e.g.*, Bd. of Educ. of Kiryas Joel Vill. Sch. Dist. v. Grumet, 512 U.S. 687, 690 (1994) (describing Kiryas Joel, "a religious enclave of Satmar Hasidim" in New York, and the limited secular education their children receive in private schools); Wisconsin v. Yoder, 406 U.S. 205, 218, 245 (1972) (allowing an Amish community in Wisconsin to withdraw their children from school after eighth grade, in violation of a compulsory school attendance law, because secondary schooling "contravenes the basic religious tenets and practice of the Amish faith, both as to the parent and the child," despite Justice Douglas' partial dissent expressing concern for the potential adverse effect on students denied a full education).

24 *But see* Jay P. Greene, *Vouching for Tolerance at Religious Schools*, WALL ST. J., July 12, 2013, at A11 (describing social science evidence purporting to show greater political tolerance among private rather than public school students).

the Establishment Clause) often impose various public costs which we tolerate for good reasons. But the four dissenting Justices in *Zelman* well illustrated the constitutional problem:

> Religious teaching at taxpayer expense simply cannot be cordoned from taxpayer politics, and every major religion currently espouses social positions that provoke intense opposition. Not all taxpaying Protestant citizens, for example, will be content to underwrite the teaching of the Roman Catholic Church condemning the death penalty. Nor will all of America's Muslims acquiesce in paying for the endorsement of the religious Zionism taught in many religious Jewish schools, which combines a nationalistic sentiment in support of Israel with a deeply religious element. Nor will every secular taxpayer be content to support Muslim views on differential treatment of the sexes, or, for that matter, to fund the espousal of a wife's obligation of obedience to her husband, presumably taught in any schools adopting the articles of faith of the Southern Baptist Convention.[25]

The issue is not one of the free exercise of religion but of a state establishment of religion: Who can be made to pay for private parochial education; what tax monies, in what forms, and through what mechanisms can be used to support parochial schools or their students?

Direct state grants to parochial schools—in the sense of funds flowing from government treasury to the schools without passing through any intermediary, such as parents, choosing where to send the money—at least still seem to be precluded. Even Justice Clarence Thomas, the member of the Court with, as we shall see, the most constrained view of the meaning and scope of the Establishment Clause with its feeble application to state aid for parochial schools, may not support direct grants, nor would the other Justices.[26] But if outright state grants to parochial schools are unconstitutional, why are other forms of state financial aid permissible? Money after all is a perfectly fungible commodity; any state money that flows into a parochial school supports religious education. All such money is a government subsidy, so how can the method, mechanism, or intermediary used to transfer those funds make any constitutional difference?

Here the Court has created and indulged three related fictions. The first is that a state program of aid to private schools is "neutral," neither favoring nor disfavoring religion, and largely immune from Establishment Clause challenge if it does not explicitly promote religion and admits of the possibility that some

---

25 *Zelman*, 536 U.S. at 715–16 (Souter, J., dissenting) (internal citations omitted).

26 Justice Thomas is somewhat equivocal. *Compare Mitchell v. Helms*, 530 U.S. 793, 810, 818–20 & n.8 (2000) (Thomas, J., plurality opinion), *with Rosenberger*, 515 U.S. at 859–63 (Thomas, J., concurring). For other positions, *see Rosenberger*, 515 U.S. at 842 ("we have recognized special Establishment Clause dangers where the government makes direct money payments to sectarian institutions"); *Mitchell*, 530 U.S. at 855–56 (O'Connor, Breyer, JJ., concurring in judgment); *id.* at 890–93 (Souter, Stevens, Ginsburg, JJ., dissenting).

of the aid will go to private, secular schools even though it is well-known and expected that the vast majority will go to parochial schools, including pervasively sectarian ones. This blinks reality, ignoring the real-world consequences of state action in a way that the Court eschews doing in many other contexts.[27]

The second fiction the Court often relies upon is that when government funds reach a parochial school only through the "genuine and independent choices of private individuals"—the tuition vouchers in *Zelman*, for example—the entire program created and administered by the state for the use of taxpayer money in fact is just a "program of true private choice" that likely does not violate the Establishment Clause.[28] And third, to deny taxpayer standing to challenge Arizona's scholarship tax credit program in *Winn*, the majority adopted a disconcerting "untouched by government hands" approach. If money such as this tax expenditure never actually flows through the hands of a government official it somehow isn't really state taxpayers' money, even though without the tax credit it would be an indisputable debt owed to the state. These instances of judicial legerdemain, however, are no panacea for the substantial, substantive Establishment Clause issues raised by these programs.[29]

If they were, a state could use a simple subterfuge to fund all private schools and other education providers. For example, a state could apportion $X dollars per pupil for that pupil's education at any qualified school, public or private, secular or parochial. The money would follow the student to the school selected by his or her parents through an exercise of independent private choice. If necessary, the mechanics could be arranged so that the state money could be "laundered" through the parents to create an artificial element of indirectness in the state funding of schools. Checks could be sent to parents who then would be obliged to endorse them over to the selected school. If such elements of apparent neutrality, private choice, and indirectness are enough to insulate such a program from Establishment Clause challenge, regardless of how much government money in absolute or percentage terms actually supports religious education, there is no constitutional

---

27 *Compare Zelman*, 536 U.S. at 651–52 *with id.* at 694–709 (Souter, J., dissenting); *see* Santa Fe Indep. Sch. Dist. v. Doe, 530 U.S. 290, 315 (2000) (refusing to "turn a blind eye" to the actual context of a school prayer policy); Town of Greece v. Galloway, 134 S. Ct. 1811, 1824–25, 1838, 1851 (2014) (plurality and dissenting opinions) (the constitutionality of the practice of opening hybrid, legislative and adjudicative town board meetings with a prayer, ostensibly neutral among religions because it theoretically allowed for participation by representatives of all faiths, still depended on a "fact-sensitive" analysis, including whether a "pattern" of government conduct "betray[s] an impermissible government purpose."). Disparate impact analysis in discrimination cases is a prime example in another context of the importance of a focus on the actual effects of ostensibly neutral programs. *See generally* Charles A. Sullivan, *Disparate Impact: Looking Past the Desert Palace Mirage*, 47 Wm. & Mary L. Rev. 911 (2005).

28 *See Zelman*, 536 U.S. at 649, 653, 662.

29 *See* Justice Breyer's dissent in *Zelman*, discussed in Chapter 2, and Justice Kagan's dissent in *Winn*, discussed in Chapter 4.

impediment left to what has always been a cardinal principle of separation of church and state. This scenario is neither fanciful nor alarmist. In 2011 Arizona established a similar program of Empowerment Scholarship Accounts that can be used by parents to send their children to a qualified nongovernmental K–12 school in the state. The program initially provided education scholarships just for students with disabilities, but for academic year 2013–2014, Arizona expanded the initiative to include children in foster care, of active military members, and those in certain low-performing or failing public schools. The state deposits funds into an account from which parents may draw to purchase one or more of 11 permissible educational services. On state constitutional grounds, taxpayers unsuccessfully challenged in Arizona's lower courts the initial iteration of the law. Now that the Arizona Supreme Court has denied review, one easily can imagine yet wider expansion of the program and other jurisdictions following suit, with federal judicial review likely precluded by *Winn*.[30]

III. The Chapters Ahead

To elucidate how our country has arrived at the current constitutional moment regarding the application of the Establishment Clause to government aid to parochial schools and other private, religiously-affiliated education providers, we begin in Chapter 1 by describing the circumstances of K–12 education in the U.S. over the last several decades and the perceived decline in the substance and quality of the overall educational experience in traditional public schools. We largely leave to others the merits of the debate over the actual state of public education, the causes of any decline, and, especially, how to reform or at least improve primary and secondary education for children of the twenty-first century. Instead, we discuss the consequences from the rise of the movement for school choice and alternative educational opportunities. We survey the currently fashionable alternatives and the opportunities they present but focus on the constitutional issues these raise, prominently including potential violations of the Establishment Clause.

While conflicts over religion and schools arose in the nineteenth century as our public school system developed, they took on new dimensions as the Supreme Court in the mid-twentieth century began to apply the Religion Clauses of the First Amendment to the states. We chronicle these developments in Chapter 2, beginning with a discussion of the dispute over original and contemporary meanings of the Establishment Clause and especially its relevance in educational settings. We argue that various manifestations of the liberty of conscience

30 Niehaus v. Huppenthal, 310 P.3d 983 (Ariz. Ct. App. 2013), *review denied* CV-13–0323-PR (Ariz. Mar. 21, 2014). *See* Howard Fischer, *Supreme Court Deems Voucher-Like Program Legal*, Arizona Capitol Times, Mar. 21, 2014, *available at* http://azcapitoltimes.com/news/2014/03/21/supreme-court-deems-voucher-like-program-legal/ (describing plans for vast program expansion).

protected by the Religion Clauses should be given especially stringent application in the context of sensitive, impressionable, and vulnerable children in primary and secondary schools. In a number of instances we also suggest that the other main "side" of the First Amendment—the theory and implementation of freedom of expression—should inform the application of Establishment Clause principles in the context of primary and secondary education in a manner and to an extent that has not been fully appreciated. It is no accident, after all, as Madison observed, that both aspects of liberty of conscience—freedom of expression and of religion—are enshrined in the same constitutional provision, each reinforcing the other.[31]

By reviewing in depth the progression of the Supreme Court's disjointed jurisprudence in the state aid to education cases, culminating in *Zelman* and *Winn*, we demonstrate the dramatic shift in the Court's positions and reasoning as membership on the Court changed.[32] We contend that, in the crucial context of school aid, the Court recently has veered away from an appropriate constitutional vision of separation of church and state as embodied in the Establishment Clause, both as originally enacted and as evolved over the nation's history. Thus, we often are sharply critical of the Court and indicate some missed opportunities to reach more copacetic results. But our critique informs the proposals advanced in our last chapter as to how states should proceed under the current legal regime.

To avoid the more obvious constitutional difficulties direct government grants to parochial schools and other private, religiously-affiliated education providers would present, state legislatures have attuned to signals in Supreme Court decisions and have devised various, arguably indirect tax mechanisms to fund private education, even though the great majority of such state aid usually reaches parochial schools or other sources of religious instruction. To understand the intense controversy over these programs, Chapter 3 first explains these tax expenditure mechanisms and the relevant differences among tax exemptions, exclusions, deductions, and credits. We comprehensively examine the notion of tax expenditures—that economically function essentially as government subsidies—in the context of financing private, parochial schools and other religiously-affiliated education providers. We address multi-dimensional policy issues and complex constitutional problems these mechanisms raise, especially those implicating core values embodied in the Religion Clauses of the First Amendment.

A legislature's resort to some of these tax expenditure systems might make a difference for the constitutional analysis of government aid to parochial education. By its decision in *Winn*, however, a bare majority of the Supreme Court now has circumvented this central issue for all federal courts. Chapter 4 first provides a general introduction to the doctrine of federal court standing under the cases or

31 James Madison, *Report on the Virginia Resolutions*, *reprinted in* 5 The Founders' Constitution 141 (Philip B. Kurland & Ralph Lerner eds., Univ. Chicago Press 1987).

32 *But see* Douglas Laycock, *Why the Supreme Court Changed Its Mind About Government Aid to Religious Institutions: It's a Lot More Than Just Republican Appointments*, 2008 B.Y.U. L. Rev. 275 (2008).

controversies requirement of Article III of the Constitution. We then explain a long line of cases involving taxpayer standing to challenge government use of taxpayer dollars to support religion. Of particular note is the long-standing exception under *Flast* allowing taxpayer-plaintiffs to raise Establishment Clause challenges to government spending in aid of religion, expenditures that otherwise would be immune from federal judicial review. Indeed, in a good number of cases prior to *Winn*, and the predecessor case to *Winn* itself when it first reached the Court, the Court posed no barrier to adjudicating the validity of government aid to parochial schools. We argue that the majority's about-face in *Winn* stems from a perplexingly obtuse understanding of proper tax expenditure analysis, reflects a growing hostility to appropriate restraints of the Establishment Clause, therefore greatly compounds the Court's misdirection in minimizing Establishment Clause problems in recent school aid cases, and is profoundly mistaken.

Following vague hints in the majority and dissenting opinions in *Winn*, we also suggest in Chapter 4 how the Court might allow standing by some more innovative plaintiffs asserting somewhat different objections to palpable state financing of parochial schools. Given the Court's jurisprudential turbulence in this area over many years, there is no assurance that the Court's current positions, either as to school aid that is compatible with the Establishment Clause or the impediments to standing to challenge such programs, are settled or constitutionally sacrosanct. But unless and until the Court changes direction, unlikely with its current membership, *Winn* precludes federal courts as available fora for Establishment Clause challenges. We therefore describe how these issues could be handled at the state level.

The current abdication of federal courts in this area does not give states *carte blanche*. The Supreme Court's previous, substantive decisions on school aid remain effective and set limits that may not be as expansive as some may think or wish. More fundamentally, state legislatures and governors have their own obligations to act within constitutional boundaries, represent the interests of an increasingly heterogeneous population, and minimize religious discord and dissention. Nonetheless, we recognize the reality of the trend toward school choice and proliferating private, secular and parochial schools and other education providers with increasing government support. In Chapter 5, therefore, we draw upon the considerable social and legal history of the dispute over government financing of parochial schools to offer a number of suggestions as to how states should proceed as they seek to accommodate the various, and weighty, legitimate interests at stake. We first urge legislatures and state courts to liberally accord plaintiffs standing to initiate lawsuits in their capacity simply as taxpayers. We also set forth what we believe are reasonable parameters for tax financing that would be constitutionally compatible under current doctrine, politically and socially palatable to a large extent, and effective to provide appropriate financial support for needy parents who seek alternatives to public education for their educationally disadvantaged children while continuing to contribute general tax dollars for support of traditional public schools.

Our proposals no doubt will be controversial and to some may seem unfeasible, idealistic, improbable, misguided, or some combination of all of these. More optimistically, they may be reasonable and largely acceptable (albeit not perfect) for a broad segment of the engaged public. But most of all, while providing some critical touchstones as an increasing number of states experiment with charter schools and a variety of tax financing methods for private K–12 schools, we hope our informed, if opinionated, suggestions are provocative. Ultimately we want to stimulate debate by promoting an understanding of the complex, sensitive, and often emotional controversy over government support for parochial education and the considerable potential it poses for increased public divisiveness along religious lines. As George Washington once observed, "[r]eligious controversies are always productive of more acrimony and irreconcilable hatreds than those which spring from any other cause."[33] Echoing the first president, in a recent case invalidating courthouse display of the Ten Commandments, Justice Sandra Day O'Connor wisely cautioned: "At a time when we see around the world the violent consequences of the assumption of religious authority by government, Americans may count themselves fortunate: Our regard for constitutional boundaries has protected us from similar travails, while allowing private religious exercise to flourish. … Why would we trade a system that has served us so well for one that has served others so poorly?"[34] Legislatures, therefore, should take great care in structuring financial support for private education; we provide some modest contours for their deliberations and those of the concerned public.

---

33 Letter from George Washington to Edward Newenham, 22 June 1792, Founders Online, National Archives (http://founders.archives.gov/documents/Washington/05–10–02–0324, ver. 2013-06-26). Source: *The Papers of George Washington*, Presidential Series, vol. 10, *1 March 1792–15 August 1792*, ed. Robert F. Haggard and Mark A. Mastromarino. Charlottesville: University of Virginia Press, 2002, pp. 493–95.

34 McCreary Cnty., Ky. v. A.C.L.U., 545 U.S. 844, 882 (O'Connor, J., concurring).

Chapter 1
Alternatives to Traditional Public Schools and Their Funding

> Today, education is perhaps the most important function of state and local governments. ... It is the very foundation of good citizenship. Today it is a principal instrument in awakening the child to cultural values, in preparing him for later professional training, and in helping him to adjust normally to his environment. In these days, it is doubtful that any child may reasonably be expected to succeed in life if he is denied the opportunity of an education.[1]

I. Introduction: Perceived Inadequacies of Public Schools

These penetrating words of Chief Justice Earl Warren, penned approximately 60 years ago as the Supreme Court formally desegregated the nation's schools, capture the undeniably critical role of education in all aspects of children's lives. Indeed, George Washington, whom elementary school children learn to revere as the "father of our country," had a passionate commitment to promoting education as a fundamental and essential pillar to individual and national welfare. He and other founding fathers extolled education as foundational for instilling children with the proper values, knowledge, and skills to become good citizens.[2]

Yet, despite these men's recognition of education's importance and their formative roles in this nation, neither the U.S. Constitution nor the Bill of Rights guarantees a right to education, unlike many other countries' constitutions.[3] Forty years ago, the Supreme Court confronted the significance of that omission:

---

1 Brown v. Bd. of Educ., 347 U.S. 483, 493 (1954).

2 Addressing Congress on December 7, 1796, President George Washington spoke of the value of common education for "our youth from every quarter ... [t]he more homogenous our citizens can be made in these particulars the greater will be our prospect of permanent union; and a primary object of such a national institution should be the education of our youth in the science of government." George Washington, *Eighth Annual Message* (Dec. 7, 1976), *available at* http://avalon.law.yale.edu/18th_century/washs08.asp. Thomas Jefferson was equally enthusiastic: "If the condition of man is to be progressively ameliorated, as we fondly hope and believe, education is to be the chief instrument in effecting it." Thomas Jefferson to M.A. Jullien, 1818, *available at* www.famguardian.org/Subjects/Politics/ThomasJefferson/jeff1350.htm (citing The Writings of Thomas Jefferson, Memorial Edition 15:172 (Lipscomb & Bergh, eds. 1903–1904)).

3 *See* Cynthia Soohoo & Jordan Goldberg, *The Full Realization of Our Rights: The Right to Health in State Constitutions*, 60 Case W. Res. L. Rev. 997, 1004 (2010) (reporting 187 countries' constitutions guarantee rights to education).

"Education, of course, is not among the rights afforded explicit protection under our Federal Constitution. Nor do we find any basis for saying it is implicitly so protected."[4] So, even while acknowledging the undisputed "'grave significance of education both to the individual and to our society,'"[5] a bare majority ruled that there is no federal fundamental right to education.[6]

Matters are different at the state level in keeping with Justice William J. Brennan's observation "that state constitutions … are a font of individual liberties, their protections often extending beyond those required by the Supreme Court's interpretation of federal law."[7] Education is one such individual right enshrined in all 50 states' constitutions. Although varying in language, each such constitution establishes the obligations of the state government to provide some type of public education system.[8] Moreover, all 50 states have compulsory school attendance laws.[9] But, that education is an essential, critical responsibility of state—and

4 San Antonio Indep. Sch. Dist. v. Rodriguez, 411 U.S. 1, 35 (1973). The Equal Protection Clause, however, does protect undocumented children from being denied a free public education offered to other children. Plyler v. Doe, 457 U.S. 202 (1982).

5 *Rodriguez*, 411 U.S. at 30 (quoting the federal district court three-judge panel in Rodriguez v. San Antonio Indep. Sch. Dist., 337 F. Supp. 280, 283 (1971), *rev'd*, San Antonio Indep. Sch. Dist. v. Rodriguez, 411 U.S. 1 (1973)).

6 Still, some scholars invoke a "slowly and conservatively evolutionary" process of interpreting the U.S. Constitution common to judges and lawyers to assert that "it turns out there is a federal right to an adequate education—at least to a minimally adequate one. The right [under the Fifth and Fourteenth Amendments' Due Process clauses] has emerged over time, and thus its precise contours are not clear…." Barry Friedman & Sara Solow, *The Federal Right to an Adequate Education*, 81 Geo. Wash. L. Rev. 92, 96 (2013).

7 William J. Brennan, Jr., *State Constitutions and the Protection of Individual Rights*, 90 Harv. L. Rev. 489, 491 (1976–1977). *See* Clint Bolick, *Brennan's Epiphany: The Necessity of Invoking State Constitutions to Protect Freedom*, 12 Tex. Rev. L. & Pol. 137–38, 140 (2007) ("[S]tate constitutions provide an additional layer of constitutional rights and in many cases more expansive protection for those rights.").

8 *See* Paul L. Tractenberg, *Education Provisions in State Constitutions: A Summary of a Chapter for the State Constitutions for the Twenty-First Century Project, available at* http://camlaw.rutgers.edu/statecon/subpapers/tractenberg.pdf; Molly A. Hunter, *State Constitution Education Clause Language*, Educ. Law Ctr., *available at* http://pabarcrc.org/pdf/Molly%20Hunter%20Article.pdf (last visited June 30, 2013). Yet, as of 2008, only 19 states and the District of Columbia required students to attend high school until they are age 18 or graduate. *See* Grover J. "Russ" Whitehurst & Sarah Whitfield, *Compulsory School Attendance: What Research Says and What It Means for State Policy* 12–13, Brown Ctr. on Educ. Pol'y, Brookings Inst. (2012), *available at* http://www.brookings.edu/~/media/research/files/papers/2012/8/01%20education%20graduation%20age%20whitehurst%20whitfield/0801_education_graduation_age_whitehurst_whitfield.pd. The right to free education is also a fundamental right under Art. 26(1) of the U.N. Universal Declaration of Human Rights, which the U.S. ratified in 1948.

9 Nonetheless, four states provide explicit religious exemptions regarding the education of children. *See* Samantha Koon, *Study: Religious Exemption Doesn't Require*

local—government does not refute the "liberty of parents and guardians to direct the upbringing and education of children under their control."[10]

These basic legal principles are well established. The *quality* of K–12 education provided by the states is another matter entirely. Here the debate is contentious and intensifying. Polar positions are well represented in new books by Professor Diane Ravitch, a prominent education historian and critic whose own views have shifted dramatically in recent years, and Michelle Rhee, the divisive former Chancellor of the Washington, D.C. school system.[11] The controversy, however, is not new. Indeed, the 1983 report *A Nation at Risk* ominously began: "If an unfriendly foreign power had attempted to impose on America the mediocre educational performance that exists today, we might well have viewed it as an act of war. As it stands, we have allowed this to happen to ourselves."[12]

One recent barometer of the commonly perceived current crisis in American public education is the controversial 2010 "documentary," *Waiting for "Superman,"* which methodically purports to dissect the public education system and its intractable problems. This film has enjoyed extensive mainstream popularity for highlighting the disastrous plight of many urban and suburban school-age children and the public schools they attend. It uses "a patchwork of interviews with talking heads, vignettes of ambitious young students from large urban areas hoping to win entry into charter schools via lotteries, and statistics that paint a dismal picture of American public schools."[13] For example, it depicts dramatic scenes and delivers doomsday messages in bold to describe many public schools as "drop-out factories" and "academic sinkholes" from which children "are getting a crappy education" and are "eight times" more likely to go to prison, and where they and future generations "are on the bridge of the Titanic and everybody is going to drown."[14]

Numerous commentators have sharply criticized the film even while acknowledging public education has numerous systemic problems, including racial

---

Mandatory Child Education, THE DAILY PROGRESS, Sept. 11, 2012, *available at* http://www.dailyprogress.com/newsvirginian/news/study-religious-exemption-doesn-t-require-mandatory-child-education/article_4307066d-9695-58b3-8649-e2a8ca916000.html.

10 Wisconsin v. Yoder, 406 U.S. 205, 233, 235–36 (1972). For further discussion of *Yoder*, *see infra* note 171. The U.S. is bound by Article 26(3) of the U.N. Universal Declaration of Human Rights, which provides that parents have a choice of the "kind of education that shall be given to their children."

11 DIANE RAVITCH, REIGN OF ERROR: THE HOAX OF THE PRIVATIZATION MOVEMENT AND THE DANGER TO AMERICA'S PUBLIC SCHOOLS (Alfred A. Knopf 2013); MICHELLE RHEE, RADICAL: FIGHTING TO PUT STUDENTS FIRST (Harper 2013).

12 TERREL BELL, NAT'L COMM'N OF THE SENATE EDUC. COMM., A NATION AT RISK: THE IMPERATIVE FOR EDUCATIONAL REFORM 8 (1983), *available at* http://datacenter.spps.org/uploads/sotw_a_nation_at_risk_1983.pdf.

13 Katy Swalwell & Michael W. Apple, *Starting the Wrong Conversations: The Public School Crisis and "Waiting for Superman,"* 25 EDUC'L. POL'Y 368, 370 (2011).

14 WAITING FOR "SUPERMAN" (Paramount Vantage 2010).

and socio-economic achievement gaps among students.[15] Two academics suggest "the movie paints an overly simplistic picture of what ails American public schools and suggests equally naïve solutions for what should fix them."[16] They also are appalled by the film's failure to fully expose and explain the web "between charter schools, neoliberal venture capitalists, and neoconservative think tanks [that] forms an increasingly powerful, interconnected force intent on influencing votes on policies supporting the expansion of charter schools and even running candidates for office."[17]

As these criticisms indicate, in addition to various initiatives from state legislatures to create and fund alternatives to traditional public schools, which are the main focus of this book for the constitutional issues they raise, *Waiting for "Superman"* engendered new attention for an already active corporate school reform faction largely representing philanthropic interests, Wall Street, and the high-technology sector. Bill Gates (Microsoft and the Bill & Melinda Gates Foundation), Mark Zuckerberg (Facebook), and the Walton family (Wal-Mart), among others, have provided significant education grants to reform some troubled public school systems, to develop new public education initiatives and models, to support public charter schools, or to underwrite vouchers for use in private schools.[18] These private efforts provide some context for the state legislative initiatives. Still, the strategically targeted funds from these venture philanthro-

15 *See* Ravitch, Reign of Error, *supra* note 11, at 40–41; Diane Ravitch, *The Myth of Charter Schools*, N.Y. Rev. of Books (Nov. 11, 2010), *available at* http://www.nybooks.com/articles/archives/2010/nov/11/myth-charter-schools/?pagination=false; Barbara Miner, *Ultimate $uperpower: Supersized Dollars Drive "Waiting for Superman" Agenda*, Not Waiting For Superman (Oct. 20, 2010), http://www.notwaitingforsuperman.org/Articles/20101020-MinerUltimateSuperpower; Swalwell & Apple, *supra* note 13, at 368.

16 *Id.* at 370. Professors Swalwell and Apple assert the film "ignores decades of educational research" and "neglects the impact of No Child Left Behind and other educational policies that have cut off funding to schools labeled as failing, shifted curricula toward test preparation, mechanized teaching, and further marginalized children who are predicted to drag down test scores." *Id.* at 372, 373. Moreover, "[t]he roots of the gap [between aims and outcomes of public education], the movement toward privatization and marketization of increasing parts of our public life and institutions, the demonization and defunding of the public sector, the racializing dynamics of the larger society, the structural inequalities in the economy, the fundamentally unfair systems of taxation—all of these are elided." *Id.* at 376.

17 *Id.* at 373.

18 These philanthropists have promoted charter schools as a "market-based approach to education typified by common standards, pay for performance, data-driven decision making, and consumer choice" customary in the corporate culture. *See* Diane Ravitch, The Death and Life of the Great American School System ("Death and Life") 278 (Basic Books 2010); Dale Russakoff, *Schooled*, The New Yorker, May 19, 2014, at 58; Janelle Scott, *The Politics of Venture Philanthropy in Charter School Policy and Advocacy*, 23 Ed. Pol'y 106, 115 (2009). Over time these private funders have promoted higher curriculum standards, longer school days and years, and better teacher quality, and have given significant sums for teacher training programs, the development of charter school provider

capitalists, who Professor Ravitch derides as a "billionaire boys' club,"[19] to date have been no match for the widespread, systemic ills and inadequate performance riddling K–12 traditional public school education throughout the nation or the deep and broad dissatisfaction these have provoked.

Differing philosophical, religious, and political ideologies promoted by parents, education experts, and government decision-makers have driven—and have burdened—several decades of a seemingly perpetual work-in-progress to reform education. Those experiments, carried out through targeted government programs, broader government projects, private investment strategies, and parental initiatives, have attempted to mitigate or eliminate the various educational deficiencies of traditional public primary and secondary schools in the hope of, at least eventually, leaving them vastly improved. Still, it is easy to appreciate the frustration of students and parents and the need that state legislators feel to respond ever more comprehensively.

Despite the various reform efforts of recent years, today the U.S. remains a nation where many do not graduate from high school. There is, in particular, great disparity in graduation rates among the country's wide ethnic and racial mix of students, who often reside in cities with large populations of poor families.[20] And while our urban areas also encompass "[t]he world's richest places ... dense ...

organizations, pro-charter research and advocacy groups, and even to put school reform on the presidential campaign agenda in 2008. *Id.* at 106, 120–21.

19 Ravitch, Death and Life, *supra* note 18, at 276–79. Professor Ravitch escalated her criticisms in *Reign of Error*, decrying the corporate reform movement as attempting to broadly privatize education and endangering public schooling. *See* Ravitch, Reign of Error, *supra* note 11, at 19–43. Other educational policy intellectuals suggest that, under the rubric of "altruism," the philanthropists essentially have thrust charter schools onto communities, especially those of color, in order to achieve misguided, self-interested educational policy goals and pragmatic outcomes that have forced communities, particularly urban locales, to relinquish their interests in, and power over, their public schools. *See, e.g.*, Scott, *supra* note 18, at 106; Andrew J. Coulson, *Are Philanthropists Backing the Best Charter Schools?*, *Commentary*, Cato Inst., *available at* http://www.cato.org/publications/commentary/are-philanthropists-backing-best-charter-schools (last visited Oct. 16, 2013). Some, however, support pushing philanthropic strategies and more private money to continue to advance the charter school movement. *See, e.g.*, Philanthropy Roundtable, *Quality + Scale = Charter Schools 2.0*, Philanthropy Roundtable, *available at* http://www.philanthropyroundtable.org/site/print/quality_scale_charter_schools_20 (last visited Oct. 16, 2013). More neutral commentators observe that the venture philanthro-capitalists and their powerful private foundations have close ties to businesses and politicians and so wield significant influence over federal education policy and education reform agendas. Michael Fabricant & Michelle Fine, Charter Schools and the Corporate Makeover of Public Education: What's at Stake? 19–20, 63–66 (Teachers College Press 2012). *See also supra* note 18 and accompanying text.

20 Although approximately 80 percent of White and Asian high school students graduate, just 55 percent of African-Americans and Hispanics do. Only approximately 70 percent of ninth graders are expected to receive high school diplomas. *See* Henry M. Levin & Cecilia E. Rouse, *The True Cost of High School Dropouts*, N.Y. Times, Jan., 26, 2012, at A31.

with well-educated residents and a free-market [economic] orientation …,"[21] they generally have not been free-markets for primary and secondary education structures. Rather, these locales, as well as low-income suburban districts, essentially have been monopolized by underperforming public schools that produce high school dropouts who likely will not realize job and economic successes. In other words, these children, often living in readily identifiable zip codes, are being left behind by quality- and equality-deficient public education systems.

Quality education of course costs money, and "more money" is central in the heated debate about how to improve public schools.[22] According to Joel Klein, former Chancellor of the New York City public school system, two major and polarized groups engaged in the discourse differ as to how to wisely apply financial resources. He summarizes the debate between traditionalists—teachers and their union officials—and reformists—policy analysts, some parents, certain corporate interests, and educational idealists. Traditionalists want to spend more public money on traditional public schools and argue that reformers' ideas of

> … expending taxpayer funds on alternative school choices … [with] greater accountability … will essentially destroy the public schools and consign the children of low-income families to a dire fate. The reformers argue that, without the kind of major changes in school structure and teacher performance that they advocate, the crisis of the schools will get worse and worse—until America ends up as a country with a small, educated upper class and a vast, uneducated underclass, with few between.[23]

Such an inequitable division between the "haves" and "have-nots" has extremely deleterious ramifications for individuals' welfare and disquieting impacts for the nation's broader civil society and economic well-being.[24] So education is far more than a social issue; it is a political and economic one also, both domestically and globally.

Indeed, many engaged in the education debate draw attention to issues that extend well beyond our nation's borders. They are acutely troubled by the underperformance of U.S. primary and secondary schools as compared to the educational systems of

---

21 Ryan Avent, Opinion, *One Path to Better Jobs: More Density in Cities*, N.Y. Times, Sept. 4, 2011, at 7.

22 *See, e.g.*, Gannon v. Kansas, 2014 Kan. LEXIS 110 (despite recessionary financial stresses, the state's constitutional obligation to provide a "suitable" public education system across school districts must be satisfied through adequate and equitable funding formulae and distributions).

23 *See* Joel Klein, *Learning the Hard Way*, Wall St. J., Aug. 20, 2011, at C5.

24 *See* Robert J. Gordon, *The Great Stagnation of American Education*, N.Y. Times, Sept. 8, 2013, at Sunday Review 5 (summarizing some harmful ramifications for individuals).

numerous industrialized countries.[25] They note with great trepidation the negative impact our education system will have on the nation's job, trade, and economic competitiveness and opportunities in our now-globalized world, especially as other countries, such as Singapore,[26] put greater emphasis on children's educations. Like many countries that offer free primary and secondary educations, the backbone of revenues permitting states in the U.S. to fulfill their obligation to educate youths comes from various sources of taxation. Depending upon the state, money may be raised from imposing taxes on income, property,[27] sales, amusement and entertainment, tobacco, alcohol, gasoline, mineral productions and leases, timber, financial institutions, vehicles, occupational licenses, and utilities.[28] But despite

25 America's education system recently was ranked seventeenth in the world. Pisa Envy, *The Economist* (Jan. 19, 2013), *available at* http://www.economist.com/news/international/21569689-research-comparing-educational-achievement-between-countries-growing-drawing. *See* Introduction chapter, n.9 (describing the 2012 Program for International Student Assessment (PISA), released in late 2013). Two Hoover Institute fellows who studied data across various countries recently commented: "According to our calculations, raising student test scores in this country [a math proficiency rate of 32%] up to the level in Canada [a math proficiency rate of 49%] would dramatically increase economic growth. We estimate that the additional growth dividend has a present value of $77 trillion over the next 80 years." Paul E. Peterson & Eric A. Hanushek, *The Vital Link of Education and Prosperity*, Wall St. J., Sept. 12, 2013, at A19.

26 *See, e.g.*, Lee Hsien Loong, Prime Minister of Singapore, Yale-NUS College Groundbreaking Ceremony (July 6, 2012) *available at* http://www.news.gov.sg/public/sgpc/en/media_releases/agencies/micacsd/speech/S-20120706–2.html (explaining that education is one of Singapore's top priorities because it is essential for good jobs, "is an important pillar of social mobility and a means for our people to achieve our aspirations").

27 Daphne A. Kenyon, Lincoln Inst. of Land Pol'y, The Property Tax—School Funding Dilemma ("Policy Focus Report") 4 (2007), *available at* http://www.lincolninst.edu/pubs/1308_The-Property-Tax-School-Funding-Dilemma. Almost one-half of all property tax dollars now collected in the United States are used for public elementary and secondary education, and much of that money is attributable to local government levies. *Id.*

28 *See* Michael Griffith, Educ. Comm'n of the States, Full-Day Kindergarten: An Exploratory Study of Finance and Access in the United States, Education Commission of the States, Taxation and Spending Policies (June 2004), *available at* http://www.ecs.org/clearinghouse/52/94/5294.htm. Additionally, some states, such as South Carolina, have dedicated lotteries for public schools. *See Education Wins*, S.C. Educ. Lottery, *available at* http://www.sceducationlottery.com/lottery/lottery.aspx (last visited Oct. 13, 2013). Other states also may fund charter schools with lottery money. Moreover, charter schools may be eligible for federal discretionary grants, such as those under the federal Race to the Top ("RTT") program. Joy Resmovits, *Race to the Top 2012 Invites School Districts to Compete*, Huffington Post (May 22, 2012, 6:02 AM), *available at* http://www.huffingtonpost.com/2012/05/22/race-to-the-top-2012-school-districts_n_1534517.html. In contrast to traditional public schools, charter schools also commonly may receive private contributions, which may be tax-deductible by the contributor under federal and state tax laws. *See, e.g.*, Ariz. Rev. Stat. Ann. § 15–185 (2012); Colo. Rev. Stat. § 22–30.5–112 (2012); Mo. Rev. Stat. § 160.415 (2012).

recognizing the need to use their revenues wisely to prepare children adequately for the globalized world, financial stresses and other pressures over time have led state and local governments to reduce school budgets and resources, leaving school programs and children victims of the retrenchments.

Concerns about the unmet educational needs of children and the nation have driven the federal government to increasingly inject itself into primary and secondary education, traditionally a local affair. The federal government's insertion of its policies supported by taxpayer monies typically has had specific aims. The first such substantial federal effort, Title I of the Elementary and Secondary Education Act of 1965 ("ESEA"), granted "financial assistance ... to local educational agencies serving areas with concentrations of children from low-income families to expand and improve their educational programs ... which contribute particularly to meeting the special educational needs of educationally deprived children."[29] The primary beneficiaries of the remedial education services were public school students, but "educationally deprived children ... enrolled in private elementary and secondary schools," including parochial schools, were not precluded from benefiting through the provision of audio-visual devices, television and radio programs, and mobile teaching units.[30] And, interestingly for our purposes, because the federal funds were administered by local public school systems and directed to benefit students, rather than to parochial schools themselves, Congress hoped to avoid First Amendment Establishment Clause issues.[31]

The most recent version of the ESEA, the No Child Left Behind Act ("NCLB"), proposed by President George W. Bush in 2001 and enacted in 2002, granted federal aid to states "to ensure that all children have a fair, equal, and significant opportunity to obtain a high-quality education and reach, at a minimum, proficiency on challenging State academic achievement standards and state academic assessments."[32] Sparked by public school failures as evaluated by children's test scores on mandatory

29 Elementary and Secondary Education Act of 1965 ("ESEA"), Pub. L. No. 89–10, § 201, 79 Stat. 27, 27 (1965) (replaced by the general revision of ESEA Title I in the enactment of the No Child Left Behind Act of 2001, Pub. L. No. 107–110, 115 Stat. 1440, § 101 (2002)). The ESEA increased the financial role of the federal government in primary and secondary education relative to state and local funding. *See Table 180: Revenues for Public Elementary and Secondary Schools, by Source of Funds: Selected Years, 1919–20 through 2008–09* ("NCES, *Revenues for Public Schools*"), U.S. Dep't of Educ., Nat'l Ctr. for Educ. Statistics, *available at* http://nces.ed.gov/programs/digest/d11/tables/dt11_180.asp (last visited Oct. 24, 2013).

30 ESEA, § 205(a)(2) (1965).

31 *See* Joseph P. Viteritti, *The Federal Role in School Reform: Obama's "Race to the Top,"* 87 Notre Dame L. Rev. 2087, 2089 (2012). Moreover, the funding structure of the ESEA could be used as a weapon to force recalcitrant school districts to dismantle segregated public schools. Ravitch, Death and Life, *supra* note 18, at 116.

32 Pub. L. No. 107–110, 115 Stat. 1440, § 101 (2002). The No Child Left Behind Act has needed reauthorization since 2007.

standardized math and reading tests under the NCLB Act, Congress passed the American Recovery and Reconstruction Act of 2009. Important education-specific provisions in this legislation included competitive grant programs to states, such as the Race to the Top ("RTT"),[33] to "incentivize excellence and spur reform."[34] And rather than abandon NCLB, President Barack Obama's effort, led by Secretary of Education Arne Duncan, imposed new, more rigorous standards on many public schools in addition to requirements that states and districts evaluate individual teachers.[35] Reformers generally applaud RTT's aggressive accountability standards and encouragement for the further development of charter schools. Another targeted federal funding program of the Obama administration is the American Creating Opportunities to Meaningfully Promote Excellence in Technology, Education, and Science (CREATES) Act of 2010.[36] This legislation reauthorized aid to encourage educational improvements in science, technology, engineering, and math.

While these various targeted education initiatives have been lauded by some as valuable for reforming schools, they also have been subjected to much criticism. As one critique noted: "[T]he federal government is simply not well situated to make schools and teachers improve. … [It] can make states, localities and schools do things—but not necessarily do them well."[37] And, if the federal government cannot insist on quality or effectiveness, questions arise as to the worth of the financial cost to federal taxpayers as "[m]ost American schools [on a nationwide basis] derive 10% or more of their budgets from the federal government."[38]

---

33 American Recovery and Reinvestment Act of 2009, Pub. L. No. 111–5, 123 Stat. 115 (2009). As of October, 2012, 19 states had been awarded RTT grants. *See* Motoko Rich, *Loopholes Seen at Schools in Obama Get-Tough Policy*, N.Y. Times, Oct. 6, 2012, at A10.

34 Remarks by the President on Education, July 24, 2009, The White House, http://www.whitehouse.gov/the-press-office/remarks-president-department-education (last visited June 26, 2013). One initial RTT strategy was to increase the supply of high quality charter schools, and criteria for reform included the linking of student standardized test score results and teacher performance. *See* Joy Resmovits, *Race to the Top 2012 Invites School Districts to Compete*, Huffington Post (May 22, 2012, 6:02 AM), *available at* http://www.huffingtonpost.com/2012/05/22/race-to-the-top-2012-school-districts_n_1534517.html; Viteritti, *supra* note 31, at 2102–03. Funding for 2012 was given directly to school districts or clusters of them rather than to the states. *See, e.g.*, Mary Ann Giordano, *New Race to the Top Money Will Support Individualized Teaching, SchoolBook*, WNYC (May 22, 2012, 8:13 AM), *available at* http://www.schoolbook.org/2012/05/22/new-race-to-the-top-money-will-support-individualized-teaching.

35 Rich, *Loopholes Seen at Schools in Obama Get-Tough Policy*, *supra* note 33, at A10. Nonetheless, the Obama administration has provided waivers to 33 states to relieve them from satisfying the No Child Left Behind requirement of making all students proficient in reading and math by 2014.

36 Pub. L. No. 111–358, 124 Stat. 3998 (2011).

37 Frederick M. Hess & Linda Darling-Hammond, *How to Rescue Education Reform*, N.Y. Times, Dec. 6, 2011, at A29.

38 Eric Smith, Op.-ed, *"No Child Left Behind" Gets Left Behind*, Wall St. J., Apr. 29, 2013, at A17. *See* Brian Gottlob, Found. for Educ. Choice, Nat'l Research, School

II. School Choice—The Accelerating Response

Despite their education reform objectives, the above federal funding programs—perhaps valuable in their own right—were not intended to address the growing desire for alternatives to traditional public schools among educational theorists, policy experts, and parents who wish to direct the education of their children.[39] So, facilitated over the past half-century by decisions of the U.S. Supreme Court discussed in Chapter 2, state and local experimental education initiatives have multiplied rapidly in recent decades. An expansive array of educational opportunities, now provided at taxpayers' expense under the rubric of "school choice," purportedly enables parents to select instruction that best serves their children's individual educational needs and enhances competition among K–12 institutions with the aim of decentralizing government power while improving traditional public schools.[40] Within this context, "school choice" excludes private, secular and parochial schooling alternatives supported almost

---

PASSPORTS: MAKING THE STIMULUS PAY OFF FOR STUDENTS AND STATE BUDGETS (2011), *available at* http://www.edchoice.org/CMSModules/EdChoice/FileLibrary/617/School-Passports---Making-the-Stimulus-Pay-Off-for-Students-and-State-Budgets.pdf, at 6.

39 The ESEA "approach [actually] was the very opposite of [Milton] Friedman's goal of maximizing individual freedom through school choice." RAVITCH, DEATH AND LIFE, *supra* note 18, at 116. For a discussion of Professor Friedman's education proposal, *see infra* note 75 and accompanying text.

40 Former Judge Michael W. McConnell captured the widespread sentiment in writing that "when public schools are given a monopoly on public funding, making alternatives economically infeasible for most of the population, they come to exhibit the ever-present vices of monopolies: inefficiency and unresponsiveness on the one hand, and homogeneity and coercion on the other. Introducing competition and choice will have both the economic effect of improving quality and the political effect of decentralizing power." Michael W. McConnell, *Governments, Families, and Power: A Defense of Educational Choice*, 31 CONN. L. REV. 847, 851 (1999).

The school choice movement's stated premise is that "the quality of schools will improve if parents are permitted to act as consumers in an educational marketplace [that maximizes individual freedom]. ... [C]ompetition of this kind would give rise to new and diverse schools that better meet students' educational needs." Helen Hershkoff & Adam S. Cohen, *School Choice and the Lessons of Choctow County*, 10 YALE LAW & POL'Y REV. 1, 2 (1992). Ostensibly "[t]he philosophy of school choice is simple: If the government is going to spend money on public education, then it should be done in a way that maximizes parental choice and minimizes government monopolization. Parents know better than bureaucrats what kind of educational environment best suits their children's needs, and choice-driven competition between schools is essential to any education reform effort that seeks to ensure that public schools perform at acceptable levels." Tim Keller, *Another Big Year for the First Amendment: Arizona Christian School Tuition Organization v. Winn: Does the Government Own the Money in Your Pocket?*, CATO SUP. CT. REV. 149, 151 (2010–2011).

exclusively by private donations, religiously-affiliated institutions,[41] and parents' tuition payments, even though they constitute a popular parental choice for those who can afford them. What "school choice" does encompass are various public school alternatives to traditional public schools, as well as private schooling options based at least partially on assorted tax-supported tuition mechanisms. These several alternatives allow parents opportunities to educate their children in either secular or religiously-imbued environments, the latter of which raise constitutional concerns at the heart of this book.

In the realm of public school alternatives offering a level of choice, during the late 1970s some school systems—predominantly those in urban areas with large enrollments of African-American, Hispanic, and other ethnic group students—opened magnet schools. Magnet schools were designed around specialized curricular themes, like the sciences, math, foreign languages, or performing arts, and were intended to attract a racially and ethnically diverse and balanced population of students from outside their normal attendance sector. They were developed in good measure to provide an incentive for parents to enroll their children in integrated public schools as one method of complying with the Supreme Court's mandate in *Brown v. Board of Education* and the Civil Rights Act of 1964.[42] Between 1972 and 1981, the federal government, under the Emergency School Aid Act, provided magnet school funding to school districts in the process of voluntary or court-ordered school desegregation, resulting in the close identification of magnet schools and desegregation.[43] Since then, federal funding for magnet schools has waxed and waned, supplemented by state and

41 For example, most Catholic schools receive financing from the parishes in which they are located in addition to private donations and parents' tuition payments.

42 In *Green v. County School Board of New Kent County*, 391 U.S. 430 (1968), the Supreme Court held that a school board's "freedom of choice" plan that permitted students to choose annually to attend one of two schools, one of which remained all Black and the other 85 percent White, did not satisfy the board's duty under *Brown* to dismantle its dual system of racially segregated schools and take the steps necessary to develop a unitary education system. As it became abundantly clear that students' and parents' voluntary choices would not achieve integrated schools, school systems began to adopt mandatory student assignments and busing to effectuate school desegregation. The Supreme Court upheld one such desegregation plan in *Swann v. Charlotte-Mecklenburg Board of Education*, 402 U.S. 1 (1971). *See* Molly Townes O'Brien, *Desegregation and the Struggle for Equal Schooling: Rolling the Rock of Sisyphus*, *in* Our Promise: Achieving Educational Equality for America's Children 3, 13–15 (Maurice R. Dyson & Daniel B. Weddle, eds. 2009); Lauri Steel & Roger Levine, Educational Innovations in Multiracial Contexts: The Growth of Magnet Schools in American Education (prepared for the U.S. Dep't of Educ. 1994) 13–14, *available at* http://files.eric.ed.gov/fulltext/ED370232.pdf. The use of magnet schools to accomplish intra- and inter-district racial balance through reliance on race as an explicit factor in students' public school assignments ceased in 2007. *See* Parents Involved in Cmty. Sch. v. Seattle Sch. Dist. No. 1, 551 U.S. 701 (2007).

43 Steel & Levine, *supra* note 42, at 91–92.

local funding and some private financial support.[44] The numbers and enrollments of magnet schools increased dramatically into the 1990s but more recently have tapered off. As of 2010–2011, 2,722 magnet schools existed in various locales supported largely by school districts with funding allocations slightly greater than for traditional public schools.[45] Today, although magnet schools are experiencing renewed support in some cities and continue to draw a diverse student population from across school districts, they are eclipsed by charter schools.[46]

The popularity of charter schools as alternative public schools is heightened by their "quasi-public" or "hybrid" nature. They are directly funded by government but have certain characteristics of private schools, in particular private nonsectarian or sectarian operators.[47] Some also receive support from private venture philanthro-capitalists. Charter schools, created under state legislation, typically are organized without parental action, but one variant enacted by seven states (with California as the first) to further empower disgruntled parents is a "parent trigger law." These statutes permit a critical mass of parents to use specific processes to trigger conversions of targeted, poorly performing traditional public schools into charter schools.[48] There were 5,274 charter schools in 2010–2011 influencing the lives of many children, parents,

44 *Id.* at 15, 38–39, 92–95; *Magnet School Assistance*, U.S. Dep't of Educ., *available at* http://www2.ed.gov/programs/magnet/index.html (last visited Oct. 20, 2013).

45 *Numbers and Types of Public Elementary and Secondary Schools from the Common Core of Data: School Year 2010–2011, Table 2* ("NCES, *Numbers and Types of Public Schools*"), U.S. Dep't of Educ., Nat'l Ctr. for Educ. Statistics (2012), *available at* http://nces.ed.gov/pubs2012/pesschools10/tables/table_02.asp. *See also A Review of the Research on Magnet Schools*, Information Capsule, Jan. 2012, at 1–2, *available at* http://files.eric.ed.gov/fulltext/ED536516.pdf.

46 *See* Motoko Rich, *For New Urban Trend, Look Back 50 Years*, N.Y. Times, Feb. 17, 2014, at A9.

47 Brick-and-mortar charter schools are largely operated by nonprofit corporations, and some cyber-charter schools, including elite high schools such as Stanford University's Education for Gifted Youth, are managed by nonprofits. *See* Alan Schwarz, *Online High Schools Attracting Elite Names*, N.Y. Times, Nov. 20, 2011, at A24. Yet, as of 2011, there also were nine for-profit corporations operating cyber-charter schools, some of which were quite profitable, receiving tuition payments from states that far exceeded their costs. *See* Stephanie Saul, *Profits and Questions at Online Charter Schools*, N.Y. Times, Dec. 13, 2011, at A1.

48 *See* Parent Trigger Laws in the States, Nat'l Conference of State Legislatures, *available at* http://www.ncsl.org/issues-research/educ/state-parent-trigger-laws.aspx (last visited Oct. 17, 2013) (listing the jurisdictions having such laws); Stephanie Banchero, *School's Twist on Going Private*, Wall St. J., Jan. 16, 2013, at A2; Stephanie Banchero, *School Vouchers Gain Ground: Louisiana's New Statewide Program Will Expand the Concept to Apprenticeships*, Wall St. J., Apr. 12, 2012, at A3. Professor Ravitch is quite critical of "parent trigger laws." Ravitch, Reign of Error, *supra* note 11, at 203 (questioning parents' suitability to run schools and exercise privatization powers over public schools that belong to the broader public whose taxes support schools).

and educators.[49] Charter schools now exist as brick-and-mortar entities, as well as in cyber-forms often used in home schooling settings. As of 2009–2010, 40 states and the District of Columbia had charter schools, 55 percent of which were located in cities and 21 percent in suburban areas.[50] At that time, the vast majority of charter schools (approximately 54 percent of which were elementary schools) served low-income children entitled to free or reduced price lunches.[51] These enrolled approximately 1.6 million students, quadruple the number from 10 years earlier, over 60 percent of whom were African-American, Hispanic, or Asian.[52] By 2012, charter schools had wait lists totaling approximately 60,000 children despite a total enrollment of more than 2 million students.[53] One year later, 42 states and the District of Columbia had charter school laws that governed 6,000 charter schools attended by 2.3 million students.[54]

As in some foreign countries,[55] several states have increased exponentially opportunities to combine the centuries-old educational approach of home schooling

---

49 NCES, *Numbers and Types of Public Schools*, *supra* note 45, at Table 2. Originally charter schools tended to be single, stand-alone institutions with scarce resources. More recently, networks of charter schools have arisen with shared educational visions and missions, common financial resources, and charter management organizations such as Knowledge is Power Program (KIPP), Uncommon Schools, and Aspire as the private operators. Nat'l Res. Ctr. on Charter Sch. Fin. & Gov., Mapping the Landscape of Charter Management Organizations: Issues to Consider in Supporting Replication 1–3, *available at* http://www.charterresource.org/files/MappingTheLandscape-SupportingReplication.pdf. (last visited Oct. 19, 2013).

50 *Fast Facts: Charter Schools* ("NCES, *Fast Facts: Charter Schools*"), U.S. Dep't of Educ., Nat'l Ctr. for Educ. Statistics (2012), *available at* http://nces.ed.gov/fastfacts/display.asp?id=30; U.S. Dep't of Educ., Nat'l Ctr. for Educ. Statistics 2011, Table 103, http://nces.ed.gov/programs/digest/d11/tables/dt11_103.asp (May 2011).

51 NCES, *Fast Facts: Charter Schools*, *supra* note 50.

52 *Id.* This enrollment data reflects in part how parents determine and exercise school choice for their children. According to one commentator, in 2011, "[j]ust above 10 percent of Americans exercise[d] school choice by sending their K–12 children to private school. Many more exercise[d] school choice by moving to neighborhoods with (what they believe to be) good public schools. But most Americans lack the financial means to do either of those things and must instead accept whatever public schools happen to serve the neighborhood they can afford to live in." Keller, *supra* note 40, at 151 (footnotes omitted). *See also* James E. Ryan, Five Miles Away, A World Apart 217–19 (Oxford Univ. Press 2010) (indicating that many African-American children and those of ethnic heritage living in urban areas may reject vouchers for private schools, favoring attendance at nearby public schools, including charter schools).

53 *See* Bruno V. Manno, *Education Reform Gets a Hollywood Boost*, N.Y. Times, Sept. 29, 2012, at A15.

54 Friedman Found. for Educ. Choice, The ABCs of School Choice 4 (2013) ("Friedman Found., The ABCs"), *available at* http://www.edchoice.org/CMSModules/EdChoice/FileLibrary/965/The-ABCs-of-School-Choice---2013-edition.pdf.

55 Germany, for example, takes a relatively liberal approach to home schooling, whereas Sweden has been criticized for its illiberal attitude. Indeed, a 2010 Swedish law

(treated by many, but not all, states as private schooling) and the quite contemporary methods of cyber-instruction, sometimes by religiously-based providers, that have joined the stable of experimental programs. With over 1.5 million children home schooled in 2007 and this number presumably growing,[56] the reach of contractual online secular and religiously-affiliated providers undoubtedly will gain significance, especially as more states adopt and expand tax deductions or tax credits for parents of home-schooled children for qualified education expenses, including tuition for courses offered by such providers.

In the private sector, choices for attending brick-and-mortar private, parochial and secular schools, with tuition payments enabled by government financing mechanisms, are burgeoning. These innovative approaches include vouchers,[57] "plain vanilla" individual and corporate tax deductions and tax credits, more complex tax credit structures involving nonprofit § 501(c)(3) organizations

---

makes it possible to criminally charge parents who home-school their children, unless for "exceptional circumstances," such as autism. *Swedish Family Fined $15,700 for Home-Schooling Heads to European Court*, TARGETED NEWS SERV., Apr. 22, 2013; Erin Roach, *German Homeschoolers Case Has Implications for Religious Freedom in America*, BAPTIST PRESS (Apr. 9, 2013), *available at* http://www.bpnews.net/bpnews.asp?id=40036.

56 *Fast Facts: Homeschooling* ("NCES, *Fast Facts, Homeschooling*"), U.S. DEP'T OF EDUC., NAT'L CTR. FOR EDUC. STATISTICS, *available at* http://nces.ed.gov/fastfacts/display.asp?id=91 (last visited Oct. 17, 2013) (giving 2007 as the latest year for which statistics are available). Comparing the "percentage of homeschooled students from 1999 to 2007 represents a 74 percent relative increase [in the number of home-schooled students] over the 8-year period and a 36 percent relative increase since 2003." *Id.* And, as with other alternative schooling options, racial and ethnic heritage are notable factors. "More White students were homeschooled than Black or Hispanic students or students from other racial/ethnic groups, and White students constituted the majority of homeschooled students (77 percent). White students (3.9 percent) had a higher homeschooling rate than Blacks (0.8 percent) and Hispanics (1.5 percent) …." *Id.*

57 Twelve states have at least one voucher plan. Additionally, the District of Columbia has a congressionally enacted voucher program. As of January 2013, more than 104,000 students were benefitting from 18 voucher programs of varying natures and with varying numerical caps. FRIEDMAN FOUND., THE ABCS, *supra* note 54, at 5. The expansion of school voucher programs over their 30-plus year history has inured largely to the advantage of parochial schools, even recently breathing new life into some urban Catholic schools in financially- or scandal-troubled parishes, such as in Chicago. *See* Stephanie Banchero & Jennifer Levitz, *Vouchers Breathe New Life into Shrinking Catholic Schools*, WALL ST. J., June 9–10, 2011, at A1. Several scholars have promoted the growth in school choice as an opportunity for Catholic schools, but, of course, such private, parochial schools must be willing to contend with the regulatory burdens and obligations associated with being eligible to participate in a state's voucher or other school choice program. *See, e.g.*, John Schoenig, *Parental Choice, Catholic Schools, and Educational Pluralism at the Dawn of a New Era in K–12 Education Reform*, 27 NOTRE DAME J. L. ETHICS & PUB. POL'Y 513, 536–38 (2013).

generally known as scholarship tuition organizations ("STOs"),[58] and education savings accounts ("ESAs"). As of 2013, 17 states and the District of Columbia established one or more such government-funding initiatives; most, but not all, limit student eligibility to those who are economically disadvantaged.[59] Six states have launched "plain vanilla" tax deduction and credit programs,[60] and 11 states now have instituted more complex STO-tax credit programs. Furthermore, in 2011, Arizona, a leading innovator in this area, introduced ESAs as a new financing vehicle. ESAs are directly funded with taxpayer dollars that are set aside for parents to draw from in order to pay their children's qualified private education expenses. Although initially limited in scope, some commentators have ventured that ESAs will revolutionize school choice across the nation.[61]

Statistics regarding these programs are impressive. In 2012, more than 1.1 million students benefitted from these various publicly funded approaches.[62] The number of students whose full or partial private school tuition has been supported by these initiatives jumped an astronomical 748 percent between 2000 and 2013.[63]

---

58 Publicly funded scholarships through voucher programs and STO-tax credit initiatives served 210,000 eligible students in 2012. *See* Manno, *supra* note 53, at A15. Student eligibility criteria often, but not always, include low-income requirements. Additionally, states may impose limits on scholarship assistance, caps on tax-preference amounts that can be claimed, and restrictions on the number of eligible students. For discussion of details of such programs and policy issues they raise, *see* Stephen D. Sugarman, *Tax Credit School Scholarship Plans*, 43 J.L. & Educ. 1 (2014).

59 Some initiatives base student eligibility on special needs and disabilities rather than economic disadvantages, but these programs are not the focus of this book. For discussion of such programs, *see* Wendy S. Hensel, *Recent Developments in Voucher Programs for Students with Disabilities*, 59 Loyola L. Rev. 323 (2013). There also are several programs that are available to affluent children. *See infra* note 70 and accompanying text.

60 Friedman Found., The ABCs, *supra* note 54, at 5 (one applies only to children with disabilities).

61 *See, e.g.*, Matthew Ladner, Friedman Found. for Educ. Choice, The Way of the Future: Education Savings Accounts for Every American Family 19 (2012), *available at* http://www.edchoice.org/CMSModules/EdChoice/FileLibrary/925/The-Way-of-the-Future--Education-Savings-Accounts-for-Every-American-Family.pdf. In June, 2014, Florida became the second state to create ESAs. *See* Mary C. Tillotson, *Florida's New School Choice Law Likely to Spark Others*, June 23, 2014, *available at* http://watchdog.org/155758/florida-school-choice/.

62 Friedman Found., The ABCs, *supra* note 54, at 5. No state provides a constitutional right to government-funded private education for children.

63 *See* Jonathan Butcher, *The Evidence on School Choice Is Out There, Let's Use It*, Goldwater Inst. (Apr. 4, 2013), *available at* http://goldwaterinstitute.org/blog/evidence-school-choice-out-there-lets-use-it (referencing Malcom Glenn & Randan Swindler, School Choice Now: The Power of Educational Choice—School Choice Yearbook 2012–2013 (2013), *available at* http://goldwaterinstitute.org/blog/evidence-school-choice-out-there-lets-use-it). The huge increase in students receiving tax-supported funding has occurred despite the overall decline in total enrollment in private, secular and parochial schools between

Nationally the majority of tax-supported financing from the various school choice initiatives presumably benefits the 76 percent of private schools that are parochial.[64] And parochial schools—Catholic, conservative Christian-affiliated, and schools with a "more general religious orientation or purpose"—include a large percentage of students from racial and ethnic minority groups.[65]

School choice initiatives are profoundly significant not only for their increasing magnitude and reach. They have generated much literature and engaged theorists, instructors, and parents in debate on educational philosophy and pragmatics, such as comparative teacher quality and student achievement levels among racial and ethnic groups in traditional public schools versus alternative schooling venues.[66] They also have fostered the introduction of

---

2001–2002 and 2009–2010. *The Condition of Education: Private School Enrollment* ("NCES, *Private School Enrollment*"), U.S. Dep't of Educ., Nat'l Ctr. for Educ. Statistics, *available at* http://nces.ed.gov/programs/coe/indicator_cgc.asp (last visited Oct. 17, 2013).

64 *See Education Options in the States: State Programs that Provide Financial Assistance for Attendance at Private Elementary or Secondary Schools*, U.S. Dep't of Educ. (2007), *available at* http://www.ed.gov/parents/schools/choice/educationoptions/educationoptions.pdf. *See generally* Martha McCarthy, *Determining the Legality of School Vouchers: Are State Courts the New Venue?*, 32 J. Educ. Fin. 352, 369–72 (2007) (discussing the future implications of state voucher programs in funding private school choice); Lynn Bosetti, *School Choice: Public Education at a Crossroad*, 111 Am. J. Educ. 568, 568–95 (2005) (critiquing the use of public resources to support private schools); Jeff Archer, *Private Schools Learn Benefits of Bond Issues*, Educ. Week, at 1 (May 20, 1998). The latest relevant statistics from 2003–2004 indicate: 28,384 total private schools, of which 7,919 (28 percent) were Catholic, 13,659 (48 percent) were affiliated with other religions, and 6,806 (24 percent) were nonsectarian. U.S. Dep't. of Educ., Nat'l Center for Educ. Statistics, A Brief Profile of America's Private Schools 2 (2007), *available at* http://nces.ed.gov/pubs2007/2007380.pdf (*citing* E.D. Tab, U.S. Dep't of Educ., Nat'l Center for Educ. Statistics, Characteristics of Schools, Districts, Teachers, Principals, and School Libraries in the United States 2003–2004: Schools and Staffing Survey (2007)).

65 NCES, *Private School Enrollment*, *supra* note 63, at 1. And while a larger percentage of Hispanics and Asians were enrolled in Catholic schools than other private, parochial or secular schools, the percentage of African-Americans attending Catholic schools was lower than for other private schools. *Id.* at 2. One researcher has noted that African-Americans "disproportionately [were] more likely to leave the private [school] sector, as were students in schools serving proportionally more voucher students. … [A]lthough these results indicate that a large voucher program may provide an educational home for some students, it may not provide a long-term solution to those who are among the most disadvantaged." Joshua M. Cowen, et al., *Going Public: Who Leaves a Large, Longstanding, and Widely Available Urban Voucher Program?*, 49 Am. Educ. Research J. 231, 231–32 (2012).

66 For instance, there is considerable controversy over school effectiveness and student achievement levels attained as a result of school choice opportunities, and studies show varying outcomes. *See* Ravitch, Death and Life, *supra* note 18, at 138–44 (reporting on several studies between 2007 and 2009); Melissa A. Clark, et al., *Do Charter Schools*

myriad new state legislation,[67] referenda, ballot measures,[68] and local school

---

Improve Student Achievement? Evidence from a National Randomized Study 2 (Mathematica Pol'y Research, Working Paper, 2011), *available at* http://www.mathematica-mpr.com/publications/pdfs/education/charterschools_WP.pdf (Dec. 2011) (finding: "no evidence that, on average, attending charter schools had a positive impact on student achievement;" a large and positive "average impact [from] attending charter schools in large urban areas or those serving lower achieving or more disadvantaged students;" and a large and negative "average impact of charter schools in non-urban areas or those serving higher achieving or more advantaged students"); FABRICANT & FINE, *supra* note 19 at 37–60 (discussing a range of national and local empirical studies on the impacts of charter schools based on numerous factors, and concluding that in the aggregate charter schools do not outperform traditional public schools); CTR. FOR RESEARCH ON EDUC. OUTCOMES, STANFORD UNIV., NATIONAL CHARTER SCHOOL STUDY 2013 85 (2013), *available at* http://credo.stanford.edu/documents/NCSS%20 2013%20Final%20Draft.pdf (studying 27 states; showing charter school enrollment had expanded among students living in poverty, African-Americans, and Hispanics; comparing African-American, Hispanic, Asian, and White students' math and reading achievements in traditional public schools and charter schools; and warning that "[o]nly when the annual learning gains of these [economically disadvantaged] student subgroups exceeds that of white students or non-poverty students can progress on closing the achievement gap be made.").

With respect to vouchers used by children to attend private (mostly parochial) schools, some critics, including those in President Barack Obama's administration, have suggested that the evidence generally does not support that students receiving vouchers perform better on standardized tests than students in public schools. *See, e.g.*, Matthew M. Chingos & Paul E. Peterson, *A Generation of School-Voucher Success*, WALL ST. J., Aug. 23, 2012, at A13; Trip Gabriel, *Budget Deal Fuels Revival of School Vouchers*, N.Y. TIMES, Apr. 15, 2011, at A18. *See also* RYAN, *supra* note 52, at 218–28 (discussing academic achievement among students who utilize school choice).

Yet, education experts suggest that private, parochial schools, perhaps particularly Catholic schools, currently and historically may be especially successful in educating African-American and other low-income minority students. *See, e.g.*, RAVITCH, DEATH AND LIFE, *supra* note 18, at 127; JOSEPH P. VITERITTI, CHOOSING EQUALITY 82–86 (Brookings Institution 1999). With respect to studies focused on voucher programs themselves where the vast majority of students attended parochial schools, mostly Catholic, *see* PATRICK J. WOLF, THE COMPREHENSIVE LONGITUDINAL EVALUATION OF THE MILWAUKEE PARENTAL CHOICE PROGRAM: SUMMARY OF FINAL REPORTS, SCDP MILWAUKEE EVALUATION, REPORT #36 4 (Feb. 2012), *available at* http://www.uark.edu/ua/der/SCDP/Milwaukee_Eval/Report_36.pdf; Patrick Wolf, et al., *Evaluation of the D.C Opportunity Scholarship Program, Final Report, Executive Summary*, at v, xvii (June 2010), *available at* http://ies.ed.gov/ncee/pubs/20104018/pdf/20104019.pdf.

67 *See, e.g.*, Geoff Mulvihill, *Chris Christie's Budget Proposes Support for School Choice Programs in New Jersey*, HUFFINGTON POST (Feb. 27, 2013, 2:50 AM), *available at* http://www.huffingtonpost.com/2013/02/27/christie-budget-school_n_2772967.html; *see infra* note 70 (describing several other legislative initiatives not targeted to low-income families).

68 One ballot measure debate played out recently in Florida. Voters in 2012 defeated a legislatively-referred constitutional amendment (Florida Religious Freedom, Amendment 8) that some alleged had been designed to make more difficult the denial of financing by the

board actions[69] seeking to further school choice opportunities. New tuition voucher programs available even to affluent children have been created, thus controversially expanding the freedom of choice notion beyond the traditional "income-disadvantaged" voucher plans.[70]

School quality and teacher and student performance at traditional public schools, as well as the proliferation of educational alternatives, are challenging topics of utmost concern. We note the importance and controversial nature of these matters but leave the substance of these arguments to others as we concentrate on the highly provocative and even divisive financial, legal, and constitutional issues surrounding the modern school choice movement. To set the stage for our focus on the Establishment Clause, however, we first consider the historical background involving alternative schools and equal protection for the insights it may provide for the current debate.

III. Education, Racial and Ethnic Heritage, and Equal Protection Under the Fourteenth Amendment

To set the matters of education, racial and ethnic heritage, and equal protection under the Fourteenth Amendment into historical context, we return to the early 1900s. In his influential book *Democracy and Education*, American philosopher and educational reformer John Dewey argued that education must be built upon democratic principles of equality and individuality and must facilitate the

---

state for tuition vouchers for use at parochial schools. *See* Aaron Deslatte, *Failed Amendments Too Confusing, Too Controversial, Some Critics Say*, Orlando Sentinel, Nov. 12, 2012, at A1.

69 For school years 2002/2003 through 2009/2010, due to budget cutbacks the Jefferson County, Tennessee, school board contracted with, and outsourced to, a private, parochial school, Kingswood School, Inc., the instruction of children suspended or expelled from traditional public schools. A lawsuit alleged that the outsourcing violated the First Amendment's Establishment Clause because Kingswood, a Christian institution, deliberately maintained a "religious character." A federal district court noted that students attended secular classes, but listed a litany of religious elements of Kingswood and ruled that the school board violated the Establishment Clause because it appeared to endorse religion. Kucera v. Jefferson Cnty. Bd. of Sch. Comm'rs, No. 3:03-CV-593, 2013 U.S. Dist. LEXIS 95108 (E.D. Tenn. July 9, 2013).

70 In 2011, Douglas County, Colorado, a school district outside of Denver composed largely of affluent families, launched school vouchers for use at private, secular and parochial schools. Friedman Found., The ABCs, *supra* note 54, at 15. And in February 2013, the Indiana House Education Committee voted to provide vouchers to children from wealthier families (those families of four earning up to $128,000 annually) that could cover up to 50 percent of the cost of children's private school expenses. Tim Grimes, *House Committee Approves Expansion of Indiana's School Voucher Program*, CourierPress.com, Feb. 7, 2013, *available at* http://www.courierpress.com/news/2013/feb/07/48pt-hed1-15-inches-of-02/?print=1.

"breaking down of … barriers of class, race, and national territory …."[71] Demand slowly increased for states to satisfy their perceived obligation of providing equal education opportunities to all students, stimulating a great movement to desegregate America's schools.

Several decades later, Linda Brown, an African-American student in Topeka, Kansas, was forced to walk six blocks through a dangerous railroad switchyard to board a bus to the Monroe public elementary school, which enrolled African-American children. Segregation laws barred her from attending the nearby New Summer School reserved for White children. She brought a lawsuit in federal court contending that every child in America, regardless of race, has an equal constitutional right to a decent education and that segregated public schools are "not equal and cannot be made equal."[72] On May 17, 1954, the U.S. Supreme Court issued its unanimous decision in *Brown v. Board of Education*, ruling that racial "segregation [in public schools] … is ["inherently unequal" and] a denial of the equal protection of the laws guaranteed by the Fourteenth Amendment."[73] One year later the Court instructed district courts to implement a remedy for the constitutional violation "with all deliberate speed."[74] In response, droves of White children fled public school systems, mostly in urban areas, leaving in their wake *de facto* segregated schools.

The inequalities and deficiencies of the public schools in serving all broad groups of racially- and economically-disadvantaged children, as laid bare in *Brown*, gave rise to the school choice movement. Groups of racial-justice promoters, educators, and others coalesced to find bold approaches to improve education and make a quality learning experience accessible to all children, regardless of race or socio-economic status. Economist and Nobel laureate Milton Friedman, recognizing the imperfections of government having a virtual monopoly over K–12 education, envisioned fostering equality in education for all children through a free market approach. He formulated his "equal-justice" concept to provide a competitive and diversified education marketplace with a system of publicly financed, privately managed schools, thus presumably enhancing the quality of education while reducing government's role.[75] Professor Friedman's ideas of government funded

---

71 John Dewey, *Democracy and Education, reprinted in* S. Cahn, Classic and Contemporary Readings in the Philosophy of Education 288–93 (1997).

72 *Brown*, 347 U.S. at 489.

73 *Id.* at 495.

74 Brown v. Bd. of Educ., 349 U.S. 294, 301 (1955). But "all deliberate speed" in reality was meaningless. Even where school districts made efforts to desegregate, state legislatures made desegregation difficult, if not impossible. For example, in 1959, Virginia took the unusual step of repealing its earlier compulsory attendance law, thus making it a matter of local option, purportedly to further segregation. Va. Code Ann, §§ 22–275.1 to 22–275.25 (1959).

75 Milton Friedman considered the growth of government responsibility for financing and administering schools unbalanced and unjustifiable in a "predominantly free enterprise society." Milton Friedman, Capitalism and Freedom: Fortieth Anniversary 85 (Univ. Chicago Press 2002). He suggested de-coupling governmental financial and administrative

tuition assistance for attendance at private schools caught the attention of many education specialists and parents who wanted to maximize their control in selecting a school for their children.

But Professor Friedman's suggestions were seized upon and, ironically, actually used "to evade complying with the *Brown* decision against segregation."[76] "The massive withdrawal of white students [from public schools in Southern states to avoid integration after *Brown*] to … [attend] private academies was initially funded by state tuition grants,"[77] an act that essentially turned Professor Friedman's idea on its head.[78] So as Professor Martha Minow summed up the unsavory outcome that stemmed from Professor Friedman's brainchild, "'freedom-of-choice' plans in education became a euphemism for resurgent racial segregation."[79] Similarly today, some may suggest that school choice is a means, at least in part, of rejecting the secularization of public schools and promoting alternative religious education at public expense. The bitter battles over prayer, as well as teaching evolution versus "intelligent design," in public schools reflects this reaction.

At any rate, *Brown* accelerated the flight from cities to suburban areas of middle-income Whites with resources to pay taxes to support schools. This, together with state and local governments' continued virtual monopoly over the primary and

---

responsibilities to reduce government's role in education. Fundamental to Professor Friedman's vision were economic, political, and philosophical beliefs, the latter of which were informed by such luminaries as Thomas Jefferson, Alexis de Tocqueville, and John Stuart Mill. Professor Joseph P. Viteritti, a political science and education policy scholar, wrote of Professor Friedman's proposal, "Friedman understood, as the authors of *Brown* did, that without fostering equality in educational outcomes, there could be no real equality of opportunity in a larger social context." Viteritti, Choosing Equality, *supra* note 66, at 54–55.

76 Ravitch, Death and Life, *supra* note 18, at 116. For the efforts of Prince Edward County, Virginia, to avoid court-ordered desegregation after *Brown* by closing its public schools and instead supporting segregated, private, White schools, *see* Griffin v. Cnty. Sch. Bd., 377 U.S. 218 (1964).

77 Betsy Levin, *Race and School Choice*, *in* School Choice and Social Controversy: Politics, Policy, and Law 266, 267 (S.C. Sugarman & F.R. Kemerer, eds. 1999) (noting that seven states in the South enacted state tuition grant laws). *See* Jerome C. Hafter & Peter M. Hoffman, *Segregation Academies and State Action*, 82 Yale L.J. 1436, 1440 (1973) (discussing enactment of tuition-grant legislation in seven Southern states).

78 Professor Friedman maintained that the *Brown* decisions did not prompt his proposal. One commentator summarizes Professor Friedman's position this way: He "deplored racial prejudice and initially thought that the risk of exacerbating 'class differences' would count against his proposal [but he] reasoned that government-forced desegregation was only slightly less objectionable than government-forced segregation, as both involved the use of government to force individuals to act in accordance with views not their own. Publicly funded parental choice of schools—including all-White, all-Black, and racially integrated schools—struck him as the best solution both for addressing racial segregation and improving the quality of schooling." Martha Minow, In Brown's Wake: Legacies of America's Educational Landmark 117 (2010) (footnotes omitted).

79 *Id.*

secondary education marketplace (a predominance enjoyed since the mid-nineteenth century), exacerbated the problems of school segregation. With fewer tax dollars available for public schools in urban and poor suburbs, the quality of those schools declined. Traditional public schools became stigmatized as inferior, and children attending them became isolated racially and economically.[80] These phenomena were reinforced by the influx of Latino immigrants after the U.S. government removed ethnic immigration quotas in the mid-1960s. Largely due to settlement patterns, income levels, and language barriers, Latinos also were relegated to inferior urban and suburban public schools.[81] Hence, despite the Supreme Court's recognition of the rights of Latinos to attend desegregated schools,[82] and of undocumented children to attend free public schools,[83] Latinos joined African-Americans in the unrelenting public schools' "resegregation" problem.[84]

Despite *Brown*, the "equal-justice" concept, and the 1964 Civil Rights Act, subsequent Supreme Court decisions became major setbacks for urban public school desegregation. In 1984, the Court in *Milliken v. Bradley*[85] ruled that the "fault line of public education"[86]—school district boundaries, including those between urban districts containing mostly unsuccessful schools with minority and low-income students and those suburban districts with reasonably successful schools enrolling White, middle-income students—must be honored unless actually drawn with discriminatory intent. And beginning in the early 1990s, the Court further relaxed desegregation standards, which essentially permitted a renewal of *de facto* segregated public schools.[87] According to some, this "resegregation" prompted a

80 *See* Levin, *supra* note 77, at 267. "By 1986, only 3 percent of the nation's white school-aged children were enrolled in the twenty-five largest urban districts." *Id.* at 268. Moreover, "[e]ven in the remaining integrated schools in the large urban districts, gifted and talented within-school programs [were populated] predominantly [with] white and middle class [children] ...." *Id.*

81 *See* Gary Orfield & Chungmei Lee, Civil Rights Project, Harvard Univ., Racial Transformation and the Changing Nature of Segregation (2006) *available at* http://www.swannfellowship.org/research/files07/racialtransformation.pdf.

82 Keyes v. Sch. Dist. No. 1, 413 U.S. 189, 247–48 (1973).

83 *Plyler*, 457 U.S. at 207–08.

84 Orfield & Lee, *supra* note 81, at 4 (coining the term "resegregation" and noting that segregation is not just by or about race or ethnicity because "[i]t is almost always double or triple segregation, involving concentrated poverty and, increasingly, linguistic segregation, and this multiple segregation is almost always related to many forms of tangible inequality in educational opportunity on multiple dimensions.").

85 418 U.S. 717, 745 (1984) (setting the bar high for showing racially discriminatory intent).

86 Ryan, supra note 52, at 3.

87 Bd. of Educ. of Okla. City Pub. Sch. v. Dowell, 498 U.S. 237 (1991) (authorizing school districts to return to segregated neighborhood schools); Freeman v. Pitts, 503 U.S. 467 (1992) (permitting districts to dismantle desegregation plans despite failure to achieve integration); Missouri v. Jenkins, 515 U.S. 70 (1995) (emphasizing local control

select group of school choice promoters to advocate taxpayer support for public and private schooling alternatives for low-income and minority children.[88] Yet, their efforts seemed to accomplish little; the school choices available to those students as a result of new government-financed initiatives still largely confined the students to intra-district schools, namely public charter schools or private schools but each still within a particular city or suburban area.[89]

---

over desegregation as a primary goal to achieve quality educational programs); *Parents Involved in Cmty. Sch.*, 551 U.S. at 701 (holding that school districts, which did not operate legally segregated schools but attempted, through a broad race-based reliance, to racially balance student assignments among intra-district schools, denied students equal protection; racial imbalance in the schools, without more, was not unconstitutional).

88 *See* James Forman, Jr., *The Rise and Fall of School Vouchers: A Story of Religion, Race, and Politics*, 54 UCLA L. Rev. 547, 551 (2007).

89 Many critics assert that, as a whole, the design, locations, and advertising methods of numerous charter schools could promote cream-skimming, could fail to foster racial and ethnic integration and instead affirmatively facilitate segregation, and thus could prompt a lack of diversity even in comparison to traditional public schools. *See, e.g.*, Saul, *supra* note 47, at A1; Aaron Saiger, *Charter Schools, the Establishment Clause, and the Neoliberal Turn in Public Education*, 36 Cardozo L. Rev. 1163, 1173 (2013); Wendy Parker, *From the Failure of Desegregation to the Future of Choice*, 40 Wash. U. J.L. & Pol'y 117, 127–35 (2012); Genevieve Siegel-Hawley & Erica Frankenberg, *Does Law Influence Charter School Diversity? An Analysis of Federal and State Legislation*, 16 Mich. J. Race & L. 321 (2011); *Church, Choice, and Charters: A New Wrinkle for Public Education?* ("*Church, Choice, and Charters*"), 122 Harv. L. Rev. 1750, 1755 (2009); Suhid S. Gajendragadkar, *The Constitutionality of Racial Balancing in Charter Schools*, 106 Colum. L. Rev. 144 (2006).

Some charter schools purposely are dedicated to a specific racial, ethnic, or culture orientation and thus attract a homogenous student population. For example, several schools in Hawaii focus on the Hawaiian language and a Hawaiian way of life connected to nature, including the Mokai Charter School, the Koa Public Charter School, and the Hilo Charter School. *See* Nina K. Buchanan & Robert A. Fox, *Back to the Future: Ethnocentric Charter Schools in Hawaii, in* The Emancipatory Promise of Charter Schools: Toward Progressive Politics of School Choice ("The Emancipatory Promise of Charter Schools") 77 (Eric E. Rofes and Lis M. Stulberg, eds., State Univ. of N.Y. Press 2004). Native American charter schools exist in several states, some of which heavily emphasize local Native American languages and cultures. *See* Mary Jiron Belgarde, *Native American Charter Schools: Culture, Language, and Self-Determination, in* The Emancipatory Promise of Charter Schools 107, *supra*. One is the Walatowa Charter High School, formerly a Catholic school, located on a reservation in Jemez Pueblo, New Mexico. Afro-centric curriculum charter schools also are found in several states. *See* Milton L. Flynt, *The New Generation of Civil Rights Advocacy: The Charter School Movement in African American Communities in the South*, 4 S. Regional Black L. Students Ass'n L.J. 100 (2010) (commenting on the appeal of charter schools to African-Americans, the role of Black churches in South Carolina's charter school movement, and that state's laws requiring charter schools to reflect the racial composition of the school districts in which they are located); *Charter Schools Growing in South Carolina*, Voice for Sch. Choice (Jan. 20, 2009), http://thevoiceforschoolchoice.wordpress.com/2009/01/20/charter-schools-growing-in-south-carolina/ (describing Achievement Academy located on

States' school choice programs continue to raise concerns about "resegregation." Quite recently, for example, the U.S. Department of Justice controversially sought initially to enjoin Louisiana from awarding vouchers under its Student Scholarships for Educational Excellence Program ("SSEEP") to public school students for academic year 2014–2015 in school districts under federal desegregation orders.[90] The Department primarily has argued that, based on data, the use of vouchers currently is disrupting or impeding the racial balance and desegregation progress of numerous schools in multiple public school systems protected by desegregation orders and is depriving students attending these schools of their right to an integrated education.

The poignant educational problems, school choice questions, and equal protection issues raised by the racial and ethnic heritage of students enrolled in traditional public and various alternative schools are extremely contentious and important. But the mix of education, religion, and anti-establishment safeguards also provokes intense and volatile controversies, which are at the heart of this book. The equal protection concerns provide some valuable parallels and cautions for the Establishment Clause issues, and indeed inform our non-discrimination proposal presented in Chapter 5. But to fully appreciate the complex conundrums involved with respect to the Establishment Clause dilemmas, we present some historical context for that provision.

---

the grounds of the primarily African-American, Christian Pentecostal, Miracle Deliverance Temple in South Carolina as focusing on college at an early age); *Church, Choice, and Charters*, *supra*, at 1755–56 (commenting on the Betty Shabazz International Charter School in Illinois); Patty Yancey, *Independent Black Schools and the Charter Movement*, *in* The Emancipatory Promise of Charter Schools 125, *supra* (describing the Umoja Charter School founded in Michigan with the help of the Episcopal Ministry).

90 Brumfield v. Dodd, 2014 U.S. Dist. LEXIS 106541 (E.D. La. Aug. 4, 2014). This case arises from a 1975 lawsuit that challenged the state's practice of providing aid (textbooks, supplies, funding for transportation) to all-White, segregated and racially discriminatory private schools. The federal court ruled that, as implemented, the state aid violated the Equal Protection Clause. Brumfield v. Dodd, 405 F. Supp. 338 (E.D. La., 1975). The court permanently enjoined the State from providing aid to any racially discriminatory or segregated private school. SSEEP statutorily is "subject to any court-ordered desegregation plan in effect for the school system in which the public school is located." The voucher program allows Louisiana students who (a) have family incomes below 250 percent of the poverty line, and (b) are enrolled in a public school that received a grade of "C" or lower on the State's accountability scale (where public schools are given grades of A, B, C, D, or F) to attend a participating private school or certain high-performing public schools. *See* Clint Bolick, Op.-ed, *Will Minority Children Be Barred from Southern Schoolhouses Again?*, Wall St. J., Mar. 1–2, 2014 at A13 (a prominent proponent of vouchers involved in the litigation opposes the Justice Department's position).

IV. Education, Religion, the Establishment Clause, and State Constitutions' Anti-Funding Provisions

As discussed in more detail in Chapter 2, the First Amendment's famous clause, "Congress shall make no law respecting an establishment of religion …," is something of an anomaly. "The use of the word 'establishment' in the First Amendment is unique to constitutions of this period. No state constitution used this particular term, instead making specific provisions which prohibited tax monies for churches, discrimination against minority sects, and other measures which might establish a church."[91] These state constitution provisions were restrictions on government powers, and the state constitutions served as models for the U.S. Constitution.[92] So it is enlightening that, in a majority of the 11 states that ratified the Bill of Rights in 1791 with its explicit limitations on government powers, either the state constitution had abolished tax assessments for the maintenance of religious establishments, the government "declined to adopt legal mechanisms necessary for their operation, causing the practice to die out,"[93] or the bulk of people believed government should not support religion.[94] Thus, a general contemporary consensus maintained that tax assessments for the support of religion—that is, houses of worship and spiritual leaders—were incompatible with government authority, as well as contrary to the rights of religious conscience of the people.

As for education, before and after ratification of the Bill of Rights, Thomas Jefferson advocated for public education systems, supported by taxes and open and free for children "regardless of wealth, birth or other accidental condition."[95] This

---

91 John K. Wilson, *Religion Under the State Constitutions, 1776–1800*, 32 J. Church & State 753, 766 (1990). Moreover, seven of the original 13 states still had various forms of religious establishment at the time the Bill of Rights was being drafted. *See* John Witte, Jr., *Introduction, in* No Establishment of Religion: America's Original Contribution to Religious Liberty ("No Establishment of Religion") 5 (T. Jeremy Gunn & John Witte, Jr., eds., Oxford Univ. Press 2012).

92 Robert F. Williams, The Law of American State Constitutions 37–38 (Oxford Univ. Press 2009). *See also* The Federalist No.1 6 (Modern Library ed. 1937) (Alexander Hamilton advising New Yorkers that the new U.S. Constitution was an "analogy to your own State constitution.").

93 Steven K. Green, *The "Second Disestablishment," in* No Establishment of Religion 280, 281, *supra* note 91 (noting that in 1775 only four colonies did not impose assessments for religious institutions, but by 1790 11 of the 14 states had no such assessment system).

94 *See* Leonard W. Levy, The Establishment Clause: Religion and the First Amendment 147 (Univ. N.C. Press 1994) ("Of the eleven states that ratified the First Amendment, New Hampshire and Vermont were probably the only ones in which a majority of the people believed that the government should support religion. In all the other ratifying states, a majority very probably opposed such support.").

95 In 1779, 1790, and 1813, Jefferson proposed that Virginia establish a three-tier local school system, including free elementary schools, 20 regional academies with free tuition for selected boys, and support for the best ten needy graduates of the academies

would have been a dramatic change. Since the colonial era, children largely of the rich and the merchant class had been educated and indoctrinated by private tutors or at private, sectarian academies or "subscription schools;" most youths of other socio-economic groups did not receive instruction and training because no formal educational structures existed.[96] In the subsequent gradual movement toward public schooling for all children in which government would have a role, Jefferson and others were inspired by the values and philosophies of such influential thinkers as Plato, Aristotle, John Locke, Baron de Montesquieu, and Jean-Jacques Rousseau.[97] Americans considered it essential that children be prepared with a "universal" knowledge base and republican values to ensure the children's liberty, moral well-being, self-determination, and financial security; they also perceived such an

---

to attend William and Mary College. His plan called for regional-level supervision of the education system and general oversight of a statewide curriculum by the College's faculty. Jefferson emphasized the importance of, and his commitment to, public education supported by public funds by commenting: "... establish & improve the law for educating the common people ... and ... the tax which will be paid for this purpose is not more than a thousandth part of what will be paid to kings, priests & nobles who will rise up among us if we leave the people in ignorance ...." Letter from Thomas Jefferson, U.S. Minister to France, to George Wythe, Professor of Law, Coll. of William & Mary (Aug. 13, 1786), *available at* http://teachingamericanhistory.org/library/index.asp?document=2219. Jefferson's failure in repeated attempts to have the Virginia legislature adopt his plan has been attributed in part to local citizens' skepticism of new forms of state taxation to support the school system and their devotion to local control and individual choice toward education and its regulation. *See* CARL F. KAESTLE, PILLARS OF THE REPUBLIC: COMMON SCHOOLS AND AMERICAN SOCIETY 1780–1860 6–9 (Hill & Wang 1983).

96 As early as 1642 Massachusetts colony required parents to attend to the literacy of their children, and in 1647 it passed an act requiring each town of at least 50 households to create a common school to teach local children reading and writing. But its compulsory attendance law would not be enacted for another 200 years. *See* VICTORIA J. DODD, PRACTICAL EDUCATION LAW FOR THE TWENTY-FIRST CENTURY 7 (Carolina Academic Press 2010) (*citing* Jenkins v. Andover, 103 Mass. 94, 97 (1869)); MARK D. YUDOF, ET AL., EDUCATION POLICY AND LAW 1 (2012). In addition, in efforts to convert African-Americans, free and slave, as well as Native Americans, to Christianity, some had been taught to read scriptures, often by missionaries and occasionally by masters. *See, e.g.*, L. DEAN WEBB, THE HISTORY OF AMERICAN EDUCATION: A GREAT AMERICAN EXPERIMENT 95–96 (2006); Marcus W. Jernegan, *Slavery and Conversion in the American Colonies*, 21 AM. HIST. REV. 504, 512 (1916).

97 These ideas embraced Plato's belief that education has the power to alter a person's instincts and to shape a particularized character that fosters a state's values, as well as Aristotle's wisdom that citizens should be molded to suit the particular form of government under which they live. As education is the instrument to sculpt the specific character of each citizen, education should be public. *See generally* Plato's *Republic Books I-X*, 1 THE DIALOGUES OF PLATO 591–879 (Benjamin Jowett, trans. 1920); Aristotle, *Politics, Book VIII*, *in* THE BASIC WORKS OF ARISTOTLE 1305–16 (Richard McKeon, ed., Benjamin Jowett, trans. 1941); Aristotle, *Nicomachean Ethics, Book VI*, *in* THE BASIC WORKS OF ARISTOTLE 1022–36, *supra*.

education critical for a self-governing democratic nation dependent upon disciplined and civic minded citizens, knowledgeable voters, and virtuous lawmakers.

In the initial wave of education reform, parts of New England and some eastern seaboard towns developed and often financially supported a "loose system of town or 'district' primary schools." These "involved a hybrid of public and private-religious cooperation, with the established or 'settled' town minister frequently serving as the teacher,"[98] or private charity schools operated with the support of religious denominations, such as Quakers, Methodists, and Lutherans.[99] In certain areas, the state legislature levied taxes to support and expand urban schools without distinguishing between public and private schools. For instance, in the late 1790s New York City officials allocated the City's share of state taxes appropriated for schools exclusively to private religiously-affiliated charity schools that operated in parallel with more secular and parochial private-pay schools.[100] So despite general sentiments against government funding of houses of worship and clergy, at the end of the eighteenth century some government officials still did not construe anti-establishment strictures to encompass schools with religious ties. The stage had been set for secular-public and religiously-affiliated private school systems to compete for, and quarrel over, finite public monies.

As immigration to America accelerated in the early and mid-nineteenth century from places such as Ireland and Germany, communities experienced significant increases in their Catholic population, many of whom were largely uneducated and unskilled. Animus of Protestants toward foreigners, and Catholics in particular, grew.[101] Catholic immigrant children often enrolled in Catholic charity schools rather than secular schools, and the parochial institutions then sought expanded allocations of limited government school funds. These phenomena triggered arguments over financing and exacerbated Protestants' bigotry.[102] At this time of rising Christian evangelicalism and nativism and accelerating Catholic immigration, Massachusetts became a beacon for education reform. In 1827, the Commonwealth enacted a law aimed at standardizing and secularizing education across the state's urban and rural areas and consolidating supervision under a

98 Steven K. Green, The Bible, the School, and the Constitution 46 (Oxford Univ. Press 2012). Teachers generally used texts that had religiously imbued content.

99 Edward Channing, 5 A History of the United States: A Period of Transition 1815–1848 249 (1921); Kaestle, *supra* note 95, at 3.

100 Green, *supra* note 98, at 46–47 (discussing briefly a five-year, $50,000 annual appropriation).

101 Soaring crime rates, America's bout with the economic depression of 1839–1843, and resentment toward Irish immigrants known to be under-represented in the Union military forces exacerbated the animus. *See* Mary Jane Morrison, *Dictionaries, Newspapers, and "Blaine Amendments in State Constitutions in the Twenty-first Century,"* 7 U. St. Thomas J.L. & Pub. Pol'y 204, nn.51–53 (2013).

102 *See, e.g.*, Green, *supra* note 98, at 18–22, 46–71. In reaction, some urban governments imposed restrictions on the allocation of public funding to charity schools, which fueled rising tensions and engendered charity school consolidations. *Id.* at 18–20.

centralized government authority. To diffuse potential for intra-Protestant sect disputes, the law forbade sectarian texts and the teaching of doctrines of particular religious denominations in the state's "common schools." It also prohibited the allocation of funds for any school that taught sectarian doctrine.[103] Thereafter in 1837, Horace Mann, a legislator, was appointed as the first secretary of the Massachusetts board of education. Mann firmly believed in public, common schooling for the masses and was committed to ensuring implementation of the 1827 law throughout the state.

Mann harbored an unrealistic notion of an ideal "nonsectarian" education program that should be acceptable to all people. His educational goal of building children's moral and civic character would be implemented in the public, common schools by inculcating students with "universal Christian morals" through the reading of the King James Bible "without note or comment,"[104] which some called "a stroke of genius"[105] for its quasi-ecumenical approach. But, not only was his exclusion of the Catholic Douay-Rheims Bible as an instructional tool and the use of the King James Bible with a non-interpretive approach offensive to Catholics, it also was criticized by Jews and many orthodox Protestants. So, "[a]lmost no one at the time supported secular public schools."[106] Yet to the Protestants, Mann asserted that to abandon nonsectarianism could create dissention among their very denominations, leading to the destruction of common schools, undermining republican democracy, and contravening the right of religious conscience in violation of the religious liberty provisions of the Massachusetts Constitution.[107] As for the financial support for these schools, Mann reasoned that because "nonsectarian" common schools were not "special religious institutions," taxing the property of wealthy residents was the appropriate means.[108] Apparently he did not fathom that taxation to fund school prayer and instruction utilizing the King James Bible itself could violate religious conscience, particularly that of religious minorities.

---

103 *Id.* at 20–21.

104 Noah Feldman, Divided by God: America's Church State Problem—and What We Should Do About It 61–62 (Farrar, Straus & Giroux, 1st ed. 2005).

105 Robert Michaelsen, Piety in the Public School 69 (Macmillan 1970).

106 Thomas C. Berg, *Disestablishment from Blaine to Everson*, *in* No Establishment of Religion 307, 315, *supra* note 91.

107 Michael J. Kaufman & Sherelyn R. Kaufman, Education Law, Policy, and Practice: Cases and Materials, 24–26 (2009).

108 *Id.* at 15–16 (citing Wayne J. Urban & Jennings L. Waggoner, Jr., American Education: A History 108–09 (Routledge 2009) and noting that Mann argued landowners had an interest in seeing all segments of society gain access to publicly financed education and a special obligation to fund such education in proportion to their ownership in land, which he considered a national asset entrusted to the wealthy for the common good). Taxpayers and the wealthy initially were not in favor of Mann's scheme of free, common schooling for the masses, perhaps particularly because it would impact their wallets. But over time, they acquiesced. Channing, *supra* note 99, at 253.

During the 1840s–1870s, proponents of common schools continued to perceive these institutions, despite their distinct Protestant orientation, as crucial institutions enabling social assimilation of children of all religions. The schools provided appropriate non-sectarian alternatives to religion-based private schools, and their "goals of moral training, discipline, patriotism, mutual understanding, formal equality, and cultural assimilation … [would be unachievable] if substantial numbers of children were in [private] independent schools."[109] So the movement concentrated on further developing public common school systems, adding post-elementary school education, increasing enrollments, extending school terms, and building new facilities, all of which financially strained local public school districts.[110] At the same time, Catholic leaders argued it was unconstitutional for government to use taxes to support only Protestant-oriented "nonsectarian" public schools without also funding the growing number of Catholic and other parochial schools.[111] And some taxpayer money continued to make its way into parochial schools' coffers.[112]

The "'[p]ublic support of private education [that] obtained quite generally until 1850,'" changed gradually over the next few decades.[113] By 1860 nine states had enacted laws or constitutional provisions prohibiting public financing of sectarian institutions, thereby excluding Catholic and other religiously-affiliated schools;[114] by 1876 nearly half of the states (17 of 36) had such anti-funding provisions.[115] So by that time, "the principle against funding parochial schools … was already installed in the laws and conditions of many states …."[116] Moreover, "[b]y the second third of the nineteenth century, the dominant practice [among the states, even those without anti-funding laws] was to restrict public funding to education [solely] under the control of public officials."[117] (As noted in Chapter 2, this is

109 Kaestle, *supra* note 95, at 116.

110 Northern and Southern states enacted laws to abolish private tuition that formerly helped support rural public school districts, exacerbating their financial stresses. *See id.* at 116, 122.

111 Meir Katz, *The State of Blaine: A Closer Look at the Blaine Amendments and Their Modern Application*, 12 Engage: J. Federalist Soc'y Prac. Groups 111, 112 (2011); Green, *supra* note 98, at 29 (*citing The School Question*, Catholic World 91–106 (Apr. 1870)). The Vatican at the time fueled religious tensions between Protestants and Catholics, and Catholic and American press reports stirred more Protestant-Catholic tensions in the U.S. Green, *supra* note 98, at 183–84.

112 *Id.* at 181.

113 Berg, *supra* note 106, at 317 (internal citation omitted).

114 *See* U.S. Comm'n on Civil Rights, School Choice: The Blaine Amendments & Anti-Catholicism 53–54 (2007), *available at* http://www.usccr.gov/pubs/BlaineReport.pdf.

115 *See* Green, *The "Second Disestablishment," supra* note 93, at 299.

116 *Id.*

117 Green, *supra* note 98, at 45. Sometimes Catholic priests developed plans to place their parochial schools under the control of local school officials. In Poughkeepsie, New York, two formerly private, parochial schools were redesigned in 1873 to be open to all children and to abstain from religious instruction, although voluntary religious exercises

the period in which the Fourteenth Amendment was ratified, pursuant to which the Establishment Clause later became incorporated and applicable to the states.) Occurrences in the federal political arena help to explain this transformation to prohibit public funding.

Indeed, Ulysses S. Grant generated significant religious controversy, both as General of the U.S. Army and later as President.[118] In the midst of an economic depression that had begun two years earlier, on September 30, 1875, President Grant addressed a convention of patriotic veterans, the Society of the Army of the Tennessee. Grant exhorted:

> Encourage free schools, and resolve that not one dollar, appropriated for their support, shall be appropriated to the support of any sectarian schools. Resolve that neither the State nor Nation, nor both combined shall support institutions of learning ... [that teach] sectarian, pagan, or atheistical dogmas. Leave the matter of religion to the family altar, the Church, and the private school, supported entirely by private contributions. Keep the Church and State forever separate.[119]

Two months later, President Grant's annual message to Congress asked legislators to pass a constitutional amendment

> ... [m]aking it the duty of each of the several States to establish and forever maintain free public schools adequate to the education of all the children ...; forbidding the teaching in said schools of religious, atheistic, or pagan tenets; and prohibiting the granting of any school funds or taxes, or any part thereof, either by the legislative, municipal, or other authority, for the benefit or in aid, directly or indirectly, of any religious sect or denomination ....[120]

---

were available to students. Purportedly, neither Protestants nor Catholics were content with this arrangement. *Id.* at 183.

118 Grant was widely known during the Civil War to have issued General Orders No. 11, "the most notorious anti-Jewish official order in American history." Jonathan D. Sarna, *Ulysses S. Grant and General Orders No. 11: How the Infamous Order Changed the Lives of Jews in America*, SLATE (Mar. 13, 2012), *available at* http://www.slate.com/articles/news_and_politics/history/2012/03/ulysses_s_grant_and_general_orders_no_11_how_the_infamous_order_changed_the_lives_of_jews_in_america_.html. President Lincoln countermanded Grant's order, and later, as President, Grant tried to make amends to the Jewish population, rejecting calls for a "Christian nation" and promoting Jewish equality. *Id.*

119 *See* GREEN, *supra* note 98, at 187 (*quoting* N.Y. TRIB., Oct. 1, 1875, *reprinted in* THE INDEX, Oct. 28, 1875, at 513, *The President's Speech at Des Moines*, CATHOLIC WORLD, at 434–35 (Jan. 1876)).

120 4 CONG. REC. 175 (1875). *See* GREEN, *supra* note 98, at 193 (*citing Seventh Annual Message*, *in* ULYSSES S. GRANT, 1822–1885 92 (Philip P. Moran, ed., Oceana Pub. 1968); CHICAGO TRIB., Dec. 8, 1875, at 4; THE INDEX, Dec. 16, 1875, at 593).

The press largely suggested that President Grant's motives were political opportunism, perhaps to enhance his re-election possibilities, but at the very least to identify the Republican Party with educational reform aligned with a Protestant cause.[121]

With the presidential election only about a year away, the speeches were not lost on one potential candidate, James G. Blaine, then-Speaker of the House of Representatives. Because the First Amendment at that time was not applicable to states, Blaine perceived the states as "free to do as they pleased in regard to 'an establishment of religion'" and to tax citizens for the support of sectarian institutions.[122] As a perceived remedy, Blaine proposed that Congress enact an amendment to the U.S. Constitution, now known as the "Blaine Amendment," providing:

> No State shall make any law respecting an establishment of religion, or prohibiting the free exercise thereof; and no money raised by taxation in any State, for the support of the public schools or derived from any public fund therefore, shall ever be under the control of any religious sect, nor shall any money so raised ever be divided between religious sects or denominations.[123]

The House passed the bill by an overwhelming margin, but opponents of aid to religion "dismissed it as a 'fraud and a sham' because it applied only to funds earmarked for public schools" and not for other sectarian service-oriented institutions, such as orphanages.[124] In other words, the bill did not provide sufficient separation of religion from state. The Senate considered a significantly broader version, also referred to as the "Blaine Amendment," but it narrowly failed to garner the necessary two-thirds majority.[125]

With that defeat, Blaine and his supporters subsequently entreated states to pass anti-funding legislation,[126] and many slowly added their own counterparts to the failed Blaine Amendment. While the matter was for the states to address, Congress prompted the trend by enacting enabling legislation applicable to

121 *See* GREEN, *supra* note 98, at 188.

122 *Id.* at 189 (citing JAMES P. BOYD, LIFE AND PUBLIC SERVICES OF HON. JAMES G. BLAINE 353 (Publishers Union 1893)).

123 GREEN, *supra* note 98, at 189–90 (citing BOYD, *supra* note 122, at 353). *See also* KENT GREENAWALT, 2 RELIGION AND THE CONSTITUTION: ESTABLISHMENT AND FAIRNESS 37 (Princeton Univ. Press 2008); Joseph P. Viteritti, *Blaine's Wake: School Choice, the First Amendment, and State Constitutional Law*, 21 HARV. J.L. & PUB. POL'Y 657, 670 (1998).

124 Berg, *supra* note 106, at 312.

125 *See id.* (noting the Senate vote was 28 to16 and explaining that opponents made such alternative arguments as schools should be entirely nonsectarian so as to be fully inoffensive to all religions, or public funding should be available equally to religious and nonreligious service providers, including those providing education).

126 *See, e.g.*, 19 CONG. REC. 4615 (1888); 20 CONG. REC. 433–34 (1889); 33 CONG. REC. 97 (1900); 33 CONG. REC. 6121 (1900).

territories seeking admission to statehood. This legislation stipulated that constitutions of these new states must forbid the use of tax revenues for religious institutions, including sectarian schools. As a result, 10 new states adopted anti-funding constitutional provisions between the 1890s and early 1900s.[127] For those states, the condition under which such provisions were implemented arguably accentuates the "shameful pedigree" some associate with the Blaine Amendment because of its partial origins in anti-Catholic sentiment.[128] At any rate, "[i]n the thirty-five years following the debate over the [Blaine] [A]mendment, twenty-one states would adopt express non-funding provisions in their constitutions to bolster existing language,"[129] leading eventually to the current status of nearly all states having one or multiple anti-funding provisions applicable either specifically to parochial schools or more generally to religious institutions, or to both.[130]

Many of these various state anti-funding provisions, sometimes referred to as "Blaine Amendments" or "Aid Clauses," clearly had a genesis partly in anti-Catholic prejudice.[131] Some scholars have gone so far as to suggest that anti-Catholic animus was the primary or sole reason that states enacted their anti-funding provisions.[132] But more recently, other researchers are offering an enhanced, nuanced view,[133] attributing their enactments to a combination of factors: the practical considerations of the government's need to satisfy its responsibility of securing the

---

127 *See* Joseph P. Viteritti, The Last Freedom: Religion From the Public School to the Public Square 82 (Princeton Univ. Press 2007); United States Commission on Civil Rights, School Choice: The Blaine Amendments & Anti-Catholicism 53–54 (2007), *available at* http://www.usccr.gov/pubs/BlaineReport.pdf.

128 Mitchell v. Helms, 530 U.S. 793, 828 (2000) (Thomas, J., plurality opinion).

129 Green, *The "Second Disestablishment," supra* note 93, at 299.

130 A list of states' current anti-funding provisions is part of the book authors' files.

131 While the rule for no state funding of private, parochial schools originated in the mid-nineteenth century largely as a principle of church-state separation rather than purely out of anti-Catholic bias, "Protestant educators and public officials refused to apply the same notion of church-state separation to the public schools where Protestant-oriented values and religious doctrines were taught to children." Green, *The "Second Disestablishment," supra* note 93, at 297.

132 *See, e.g.*, Katz, *supra* note 111, at 111–12; Mark Edward DeForrest, *An Overview and Evaluation of State Blaine Amendments: Origins, Scope, and First Amendment Concerns*, 26 Harv. J.L. & Pub. Pol'y 551, 565–73 (2003); Viteritti, *supra* note 123, at 659.

133 *See, e.g.*, Green, *The "Second Disestablishment," supra* note 93, at 297 ("the origin of the no-funding rule, as a component of church-state separation, was not motivated by anti-Catholic animus"); Steven K. Green, *"Blaming Blaine": Understanding the Blaine Amendment and the "No-Funding" Principle*, 2 First Amend. L. Rev. 107, 152 (2004) ("Although nativist groups used the no-funding principle to advance their bigoted goals, not all supporters of the principle were nativists or equated church-state separation with anti-Catholicism."); John Witte, Jr., *Facts and Fictions About the History of Separation of Church and State*, 48 J. Church & St. 15, 35 (2006) ("[A] good number of American Catholic clergy saw separation of church and state as an essential principle of religious liberty and embraced the doctrine without evident cavil or concern.").

success of common public schools sustained entirely by tax monies; anti-Catholic enmity leading Protestants to attempt to counteract Catholic influence; and such constitutional considerations as guaranteeing religious liberties and enforcing anti-establishment safeguards.[134] Viewed from a modern vantage, free of the historical bias, the state anti-funding provisions now find considerable legitimate support, especially among those with strong separationist views. Like the notion of "states' rights" born of a segregationist past, which today has gained a far more respectable, if still controversial, basis in federalism, state anti-funding provisions deserve to be considered on their contemporary merits free of their less savory historical vestiges. Their rehabilitation, like that (for some) of the *Lochner* doctrine,[135] has evolved over many years. In this regard they are a reminder of the evolution of Sunday Closing laws, of which the Supreme Court noted that "through the centuries, and [in light] of their more or less recent emphasis upon secular considerations, it is not difficult to discern that as presently written and administered, most of them, at least, are of a secular rather than of a religious character ...."[136]

However portrayed, school choice proponents currently perceive the state anti-funding provisions as "the most substantial legal hurdle to school choice."[137] During the 1970s, the religious right, particularly conservative evangelical Christians, became committed school choice supporters. This attitude was provoked by strong discontent with the 1962 and 1963 Supreme Court rulings in *Engel v. Vitale* and *School District of Abington Township v. Schempp* that prayer and bible reading in public schools amount to unconstitutional establishments of religion.[138] These religious groups disdained the forced secularization of public education and the amorality they believed it advanced, which they viewed as hostile to their fundamental values and beliefs. Evangelical Christians wanted their religious values and belief systems

134 *See, e.g.*, GREEN, *supra* note 98, at 46; Green, *The "Second Disestablishment," supra* note 93, at 286–98; Berg, *supra* note 106, at 316–28; Jill Goldenziel, *Blaine's Name in Vain?: State Constitutions, School Choice, and Charitable Choice*, 83 DENV. U.L. REV. 57, 64 (2005); Noah Feldman, *Non-Sectarianism Reconsidered*, 18 J.L. & POL. 65, 115 (2002).

135 *See generally* DAVID E. BERNSTEIN, REHABILITATING LOCHNER: DEFENDING INDIVIDUAL RIGHTS AGAINST PROGRESSIVE REFORM (Univ. Chicago Press 2011) (explaining why *Lochner v. New York*, 198 U.S. 45 (1905), should not be reviled).

136 McGowan v. Maryland, 366 U.S. 420, 444 (1961) ("[D]espite the strongly religious origin of these laws, beginning before the eighteenth century, nonreligious arguments for Sunday closing began to be heard more distinctly and the statutes began to lose some of their totally religious flavor."). *Id.* at 433–34.

137 Nicole Stelle Garnett, *A "Winn" for Educational Pluralism*, 121 YALE L.J. ONLINE 31, 37 (2011), http://yalelawjournal.org/2011/05/26/garnett.html. *See* LADNER, *supra* note 61, at 14 (commenting on state anti-funding provisions being an impediment to the school choice movement).

138 Engel v. Vitale, 370 U.S. 421 (1962); Sch. Dist. of Abington Twp. v. Schempp, 374 U.S. 203 (1963). *See* Forman, *supra* note 88, at 557–60 (noting activism of conservative evangelical Christians prompted debate and disputes over the control and content of public school education).

represented in and integrated into the K–12 public school curriculum, textbooks, and life.[139] In the late 1970s, convinced that the continued secularization of the public schools virtually constituted the unconstitutional establishment of the religion of secularism, some conservative and evangelical Christians progressively became more engaged in the school choice movement.[140] Moreover, by this time, conservative Christian children who remained in public schools after desegregation—many had withdrawn and moved to private Christian schools, perhaps especially in the South—increasingly experienced multicultural curricula and instructional materials. This added to the level of parents' resentment of secularism and opposition to the near monopoly that public schools had for educating K–12 grade children, increasing their advocacy for tax-supported school choice options.[141]

After Ronald Reagan's election as President and into the 1990s, school choice, broadened to include both public and private options, became increasingly acceptable throughout the country.[142] Some conservatives and evangelical Christians forged alliances with libertarians and free-market enthusiasts to actively pursue school choice, incentivized to do so by the added appeal that

139 Non-doctrinal teaching of religion and morals in public schools, even using the bible in courses on history or comparative world religions, was not considered sufficient. By the 1980s, litigation abounded by evangelical Christians asserting that the secularization of public school textbooks and curricula violated their First Amendment religious freedoms. *See, e.g.*, Mozert v. Hawkins Cnty. Bd. of Educ., 827 F.2d 1058 (6th Cir. 1987). *See also* James E. Wood, Jr., *Religion and Public Education in Historical Perspective*, 14 J. Church & St. 397, 401 (1972) ("While most Protestants in America did eventually come to oppose the use of public funds for parochial schools, Protestants generally have not been reticent to favor Protestant influences, including Protestant religious exercises, in the public schools.").

140 *See* Forman, supra note 88, at 561 (citing James C. Carper, *The Christian Day School Movement*, 47 Educ. F. 135, 139–40 (1983) and John W. Whitehead & John Conlan, *The Establishment of the Religion of Secular Humanism and Its First Amendment Implications*, 10 Tex. Tech L. Rev. 1, 29 (1978)).

141 *See* Forman, *supra* note 88, at 561–62.

142 Ravitch, Death and Life, *supra* note 18, at 116. Directly influenced by Milton Friedman's ideas, in the early 1980s President Reagan proposed private school vouchers for low-performing students. Pressured by teachers unions, he later withdrew his proposal in favor of public school choice exclusively. *Id.* at 117. Now public school choice obtained support among politicians, teachers unions, and others.

Public and private schooling options to traditional K–12 public schools aimed primarily (but not always solely) at socio-economically disadvantaged children gained footing in many states as well as the District of Columbia. *See* Forman, *supra* note 88, at 565 (noting that some programs, such as several federal voucher programs, did not apply family income limits for student eligibility). *See also supra* notes 85–88 and accompanying text (discussing the Supreme Court cases beginning in the 1980s and 1990s that motivated school choice proponents to advocate for equal justice to justify taxpayer support for public and private schooling alternatives for low-income and minority children).

these alternative forms of education were largely unregulated.[143] Not only were participating private schools relatively free from non-discrimination restrictions and other typical limitations imposed by governmental grantors, but private educators and institutions were not accountable to government officials for reporting data on student academic achievement levels, graduation rates, or test scores.[144] The relative absence of accountability and the lack of regulatory requirements and oversight later would change significantly, with some exceptions such as the frequently continued freedom of private schools to maintain religion-based student admission policies. Such initial government regulatory forbearance partly accounts for the explosion of alternative private schooling options and the proliferating forms of state financial support, including vouchers, "plain vanilla" tax deductions and tax credits, complex structures involving tax deductions and tax credits, and later, education savings accounts.

V. Where We Are Today: Religion and School Choice

The continuing expansion of school choice opportunities funded by taxpayer dollars raises important policy and constitutional questions as old as the country's founding. Without violating the First Amendment's Establishment Clause, state anti-establishment analogues, and state anti-funding provisions, how can states devote increasing amounts of public funds to these educational alternatives when religiously-affiliated institutions and their students are the primary beneficiaries? And how can states fulfill their responsibilities to provide quality public K–12 education for an increasingly pluralistic society while diverting significant portions of taxpayer funds to subsidize private, mainly parochial schools and other religiously-based education providers?

In addressing these issues, we should be mindful that it is the students who are the most direct beneficiaries of the values instilled through religious instruction and indoctrination. As with all education, the knowledge and skills students acquire and the ideals they adopt fundamentally affect their future wellbeing, including employment opportunities, incomes, and upward mobility.[145] Parents who wish a parochial school education for their children also benefit when they are relieved of

143 *But see* Forman, *supra* note 88, at 552, 565. While initially charter schools shared similarities with private schools—less bureaucratic structure and subject to weaker governmental regulation than traditional public schools—regulatory powers over charter schools increasingly strengthened, imposing robust recordkeeping requirements, mandates covering curriculum, and student and teacher assessment standards intended to ensure and enhance education quality.

144 *Id.*

145 *See* Jason DeParle, *For Poor, Leap to College Often Ends in a Hard Fall*, N.Y. Times, Dec. 22, 2012, at A1 (discussing the growing role that poor education plays in limiting children's upward mobility).

paying that portion of their children's private school tuition supported by a state's voucher, tax deduction or credit mechanisms, or education savings accounts. And parochial schools themselves profit both intangibly and financially by being more available to wider groups of students. Those schools have the opportunity to further their religious missions by inculcating in the hearts and minds of children specific religious doctrine, beliefs, and values, thereby encouraging youths to form lifetime habits of worshiping and engaging in other religious practices, thus promoting individuals' long-term relationships with particular denominations and religious institutions.[146] On a financial level, when parents of school children receive government subsidies, normal economic forces may permit private, parochial schools to increase tuition for all students or may enable under-enrolled schools to receive tuition funds otherwise unavailable, thus either way resulting in increased gross revenues.[147] And those parochial schools that often enjoy waiting lists for prospective students may be able to diversify their student bodies racially and ethnically by accepting students whose tuition becomes affordable because it is at least partially tax-supported.

In these ways government financing of children's religious education seems to blatantly conflict with James Madison's and Thomas Jefferson's notions that individuals should not be compelled to support religion, whether their own faith or that of others. And their basic principle arguably is a fundamental component of the First Amendment's Establishment Clause. The pressures and tensions here obviously are problematic,[148] but through a series of cases discussed in Chapter 2 the Supreme Court has come to rule certain forms of, and financial structures for, government aid to private, parochial schools constitutionally permissible under the Establishment Clause. Moreover, state courts often have determined government funding for private schooling alternatives to traditional public schools do not violate state anti-establishment and anti-funding provisions. While religiously-

146 *See* Patrick J. Wolf, *Civics Exam: Schools of Choice Boost Civic Values*, 7 Educ. Next 66, 71 (2007) (finding the impact of Catholic schools as compared with other alternative schooling arrangements, including private, evangelical Protestant schools and secular schools, more effective in infusing political and social ("civic") tolerance in students). This research suggests that parochial schools can be similarly effective in implanting religious doctrines, beliefs, values, and practices in students. So while alternative schooling choices supported by taxpayer dollars may foster civic values, they also may advance the cultivation and indoctrination of religion.

147 As pointed out with respect to higher education, increased government subsidies "gives every incentive and every opportunity for colleges to raise their fees." Allysia Finley, *The Real Reason College Costs So Much*, Wall St. J., Aug. 24, 2013, at A9. Similarly, when "[p]oliticians subsidize the purchase of a good or service, prices inevitably rise in response to this pumped-up demand …." Editorial, *Obama State University*, Wall St. J., Aug. 24, 2013, at A10.

148 *See, e.g.*, Paul Finkelman, *School Vouchers, Thomas Jefferson, Roger Williams, and Protecting the Faithful: Warnings from the Eighteenth Century and the Seventeenth Century on the Danger of Establishments to Religious Communities*, 2008 BYU L. Rev. 525 (2008).

imbued charter schools would seem to conjure the same constitutional concerns, to date they largely have escaped litigation in this regard. As we consider how states constitutionally may structure taxpayer-financed school choice initiatives now and in the future, an appreciation of current opportunities and possibilities is imperative.

A. Public Charter Schools

Charter schools emerged, first in Minnesota in 1991, promising something for everyone across the political spectrum.[149] Parents would have a choice of quality-enhanced, tuition-free education for their children within their school districts funded directly by taxpayer dollars.[150] Because most states statutorily define these hybrid schools as "public schools," they operate within public school systems and, accordingly, directly receive allocations of taxpayer funds based on their share of the per-pupil dollars available from local school districts.[151] Hence, charter schools arguably divert funds from, and operate at the financial expense of, traditional public schools, an issue harking back to the 1800s when the funding controversy was between early public, common schools and private, sectarian schools.

By reason of the First Amendment's Establishment Clause and state anti-establishment analogues, this diversion of public money may be problematic in several contexts. "Public schools face one set of constitutional rules about religion

149 Liberals purportedly perceived charter schools as a means of impeding the undesirable voucher option for schooling and potentially improving public education; conservatives and libertarians supposedly viewed them as a way to deregulate public education, circumvent some bureaucratic rules applicable to traditional public schools through conferral of a significant degree of autonomy on charter schools, and increase competition within public education systems. *See* Ravitch, Death and Life, *supra* note 18, at 124; *Church, Choice, and Charters*, *supra* note 89, at 1753. *See also* Saiger, *supra* note 89, at 1166, 1171, 1173–74 (describing charter schools as "neoliberal at their heart").

For some initial charter school proponents, heightened school quality for all students, particularly those underserved, unmotivated, and at-risk in traditional public schools, was of utmost importance. But some original charter school supporters, such as Albert Shanker, a former president of the American Federation of Teachers, withdrew their endorsements after realizing that charter schools were not admitting certain disadvantaged students, were not collaborating with traditional public schools to solve education quality issues, or were moving toward further privatization viewed as incompatible with public education. *See* Ravitch, Death and Life, *supra* note 18, at 122–24; Ravitch, Reign of Error, *supra* note 11, at 157.

150 Three jurisdictions, however, permit charter "schools to charge tuition under the same conditions as traditional public schools, such as when a student who resides outside of the school district seeks to attend the school." Julie F. Mead, *Devilish Details: Exploring Features of Charter School Statutes that Blur the Public/Private Distinction*, 40 Harv. J. on Legis. 352, 367 (2003). *See also supra* note 28 (indicating some types of public funding charter schools may receive).

151 Nonetheless, there is no single definition of "public school." *See* Saiger, *supra* note 89, at 1170–71; Mauren Hulden, *Charting a Course to State Action: Charter Schools and § 1983*, 111 Colum. L. Rev. 1244, 1255 (2011).

and private schools another. … [T]he Supreme Court's cases interpret the First Amendment to bar much religious activity in 'public schools' while leaving private schools free to pursue religious missions."[152] So if charter schools—either in brick-and-mortar or cyber form[153]—are created and operated by religiously-affiliated § 501(c)(3) nonprofit entities and directly supported by taxpayer funds,[154] their religious nature may conflict with their ostensible public character.

Perhaps especially troubling are brick-and-mortar charter schools that have religiously-based culture-oriented specialties. An ecumenical spectrum of four examples—Minnesota's now-defunct Tarek ibn Ziyad Academy (TiZA),[155] Florida's The Ben Gamla Charter School, a chain of charter schools founded by followers of a Turkish Islamic cleric, and a chain of 13 Christian evangelical schools—illustrates purportedly public institutions operating with characteristics of private schools free of First Amendment prohibitions against inculcating students with particular religious doctrine and engaging students in religious practices. TiZA, sponsored by Islamic-Relief, USA, shared space in a mosque, was named for two imams, and claimed to impart only a respect for Muslim culture and knowledge of the Arabic language. Students attended "Islamic studies" classes after school hours, with buses leaving the premises only thereafter.[156] Students prayed daily, participated with teachers in Friday prayer services, ate only halal food prepared in the school cafeteria, and studied Arabic.[157] Female students and teachers typically wore headscarves, although these were not required, and school vacations coincided with Islamic holidays.[158] The brick-and-mortar charter school, The Ben Gamla Charter School, operates under the direction of an Orthodox rabbi with a stated mission

---

152 Saiger, *supra* note 89, at 1173.

153 *See* Weintana Abraha, *Online Charters May Fail Students and Reduce Public School Funding*, *in* Charter Schools—Opposing Viewpoints Series (Greenhaven Press 2012); Kevin P. Brady, et al., *Unchartered Territory: The Current Legal Landscape of Public Cyber Charter Schools*, 2010 BYU Educ. & L. J. 191 (2010). For a discussion of cyber-charter schools used in connection with home schooling, see *infra* notes 179–81 and accompanying text.

154 *See supra* note 47.

155 Minnesota changed its charter laws to preclude charter schools operated by a supporter based out of state. Tarek ibn Ziyad Academy was sponsored by such an organization, Islamic-Relief, USA.

156 *See* Katherine Kersten, *Blurring the Lines between Mosque and State: Public Education in the Twin Cities* ("*Blurring the Lines*"), 24 Acad. Questions 32, 34 (2011).

157 *See id.* at 35.

158 *See id.*; Benjamin Siracusa Hillman, *Is There a Place for Religious Charter Schools?*, 118 Yale L.J. 554, 564–65 (2008). The A.C.L.U. brought an action against TiZA, alleging it unconstitutionally promoted Islam and that the government's entanglement with TiZA violated the First Amendment's Establishment Clause. *See* Kersten, *Blurring the Lines*, *supra* note 156, at 33–34, 38–39; Katie Humphrey, *ACLU Settles Dispute with Former TiZA School Leaders*, Star Trib., Aug. 4, 2012, at 5B; Katherine Kersten, *TiZA Is Gone, but Lawsuit and Questions Remain*, Star Trib., Oct. 9, 2011, at 30P.

of preparing students for "global competition," but some assess its purpose as the indoctrination of children with "Jewish culture and values" and religion.[159] All students study Hebrew as a second language, even those for whose parents it is their native language. Some students and teachers wear yarmulkes, and a minority of students wears clothing distinguishing them as strictly Orthodox.[160]

Finally, two chains of brick-and-mortar charter schools might be considered at least quasi-religious. One chain, founded by followers of the Turkish Islamic cleric Fethulla Gulen, who stresses that studying math and science are a form of "worshipping God," touts a focus on academic success for underserved populations of children.[161] Another pre-K through 12 school chain, the Shekinah Learning Institute schools, is headed by an evangelical Christian. Some of these federally and state financed Shekinah schools are located in churches and share their names.[162] A promotional video, formerly on the chain's website, portrayed students' parents describing how chapel services teach their children "about all the wonderful things God is doing for them in their lives."[163]

While government institutions—state actors—must be neutral in their treatment of religions, and between religion and non-religion, as demanded by the Establishment Clause and state anti-establishment analogues, several academicians assert that charter schools may be distinguished from traditional public schools for this purpose.[164] Basically their contention is that, because charter schools are

---

159 *See* Hillman, *supra* note 158, at 569 n.81.

160 *See id.* at 568 n.73.

161 *60 Minutes: Gulen Movement: U.S. Charter Schools Tied to Powerful Turkish Imam* (CBS television broadcast May 13, 2012). The Gulen chain of 130 charter schools operates in several states and is the largest charter school chain in the U.S., outnumbering the purely secular KIPP chain. Some critics have expressed worry over the Gulen schools' religious, as well as foreign, affiliation. *See id.* In Texas, these schools operate under the Harmony School banner. *See, e.g.*, *Our Mission*, Harmony Sch. of Excellence, *available at* http://hsehouston.org/?midframe=/AboutUs/ourmission.htm (last visited Oct. 19, 2013). Some commentators have noted concern that these and other Muslim-affiliated culture schools could be incubators of Islamic radicalism. *See, e.g.*, M. Zuhdi Jasser, *Islamic Schools and American Civic Culture*, 24 Acad. Questions 24 (2011).

162 *See* Howard Friedman, *Controversy Continues Over Whether Texas Charter Schools Are Promoting Religion*, Religion Clause (June 21, 2012), *available at* http://religionclause.blogspot.com/2012/06/controversy-continues-over-whether.html. For a link to the schools' website, *see* http://www.shekinah-edu.com/shekinah/site/default.asp.

163 Simon Brown, *Showdown at Shekinah: A Church, A Charter School and Church-State Chicanery*, Church-State (2012), *available at* https://www.au.org/church-state/june-2012-church-state/featured/showdown-at-shekinah.

164 As a result of the hybrid nature of charter schools, the academic literature notes that charter schools may be treated as "public schools" for some statutory and constitutional purposes and as "private schools" for other such purposes. Whether charter schools are state actors, rather than private actors, constrained by the First Amendment's Establishment Clause, state anti-establishment analogues, or other constitutional provisions, may be heavily context-dependent. For various analyses, *see* Saiger, *supra* note 89, at 1190–92

so similar to private parochial schools that teach religious doctrine and practice, they too should be treated as private actors for such constitutional purposes. But this approach would create striking anomalies. For example, both charter and traditional public schools receive direct government funding, but prayers in any charter schools—even highly sectarian ones—would be permissible while prayers in traditional public schools are not. This approach also would produce the incongruity that government constitutionally is prohibited from directly funding private, parochial schools but would be allowed to directly fund religiously-affiliated charter schools, even those overtly promoting a religious mission. And, on the other hand, aside from the Establishment Clause, religiously-affiliated charter schools could suffer under state anti-funding provisions that prohibit money raised for the support of public schools to be appropriated to, or used for, the support of any private, sectarian or denominational school. If religiously-affiliated charter schools are treated as private, under their own requirements states might need to cease funding them, a grave financial implication for such charter schools indeed.

Finally, all of these issues regarding religiously-affiliated charter schools might be particularly problematic when private, parochial schools convert to hybrid charter schools receiving direct government funding.[165] Catholic parochial schools have comprised the nation's largest system of alternative schools, with student enrollment outnumbering those attending all other private schools.[166] Yet, the recent national trend of large-scale closings of financially pressed Catholic schools, to the considerable consternation of Catholic and non-Catholic supporters of parochial education,[167] makes the possibility of conversion of greater import. Nine states and

(contending that charter schools are so similar to private schools, which can accept vouchers and teach and practice religion, that especially after *Zelman v. Simmons-Harris* they should be treated as private; charter schools essentially act merely as contractors and not government agents, and therefore should not be considered state actors subject to Establishment Clause constraints); *Church, Choice, and Charters*, *supra* note 89, at 1752 (suggesting the constitutional feasibility of religious charter schools); Hillman, *supra* note 158, at 554 (asserting that there might well be a place for religious charter schools without violating the Establishment Clause); Preston C. Green, III, *Charter Schools and Religious Institutions: A Match Made in Heaven?*, 158 Educ. Law Rep. 1 (2001) (indicating religious charter schools may pass constitutional review under the Establishment Clause); Lawrence D. Weinberg, Religious Charter Schools: Legalities and Practicalities 124–30 (2007) (commenting that whether charter schools are state actors must be determined state by state, but concluding that they likely should be considered so). *See also* Caviness v. Horizon Cmty. Learning Ctr., Inc., 590 F.3d 806 (9th Cir. 2010) (holding an Arizona charter school was not a state actor for purposes of 42 U.S.C. § 1983 when a fired teacher sued).

165 *See, e.g.*, Mead, *supra* note 150, at 349; Green, III, *supra* note 164, at 1.

166 Viteritti, Choosing Equality, *supra* note 66, at 82.

167 *See* David Gonzalez, *A Lifeline for Minorities, Catholic Schools Retrench*, N.Y. Times, June 21, 2013, at A16 (reporting that since 2011 New York's Archdiocese closed 56 Catholic, mostly elementary, schools; New York Catholic elementary and secondary school enrollments dropped from 95,837 students in 2006 to 75,875 in 2013; and although

the District of Columbia permit private schools to convert to charter school status; 27 states prohibit private schools in general from converting to charter schools; while only two—Wisconsin and Utah—specifically prohibit sectarian private schools from so converting.[168] If instead of closing, strained Catholic schools were allowed to convert to charter schools but allowed to retain significant elements of their religious character, charges of government establishment of religion may be inescapable.

B. Home Schooling and Taxpayer Funding

In one respect home schooling is the most ancient and religiously prescribed method of teaching. Of the laws and commandments Moses is about to convey to the Israelites, he entreats, "Take to heart these instructions with which I charge you this day. Impress them upon your children."[169] In keeping with this tradition, after its many years as the original form of schooling in this country, home schooling turned into the first "alternative" to established common schools. Although the vast majority of parents—often libertarians, academicians, or cultural dissidents—who chose to home school their children before the 1980s did so chiefly for academic reasons,[170] thereafter more parents began home schooling their children for religious reasons.[171] The 1980s and 1990s brought an increased

---

Latino student enrollments rose, African-American student enrollment precipitously declined from 31 percent in 2006 to 17 percent in 2013); Cardinal Timothy Dolan, Op.-ed, *The Plan to Save Catholic Schools*, WALL ST. J., Feb. 1, 2013, at A11 (noting that between 2000 and 2013 Catholic school enrollment declined 23.4 percent, a loss of 621,583 students, leading to some closures). *But see* Schoenig, *supra* note 57, at 533 (estimating approximately 460,000 empty seats in Catholic schools nationwide despite the closings).

168 *See* Mead, *supra* note 150, at 356; 382 nn.246–47; Appendix, Table 2.

169 Deuteronomy, 6: 6–7. This is one "source of the halakhic requirements that one must study the Torah and teach it to one's children." THE JPS TORAH COMMENTARY: DEUTERONOMY 78 n.7 (The Jewish Publication Society 1996).

170 These parents found the bureaucracies and quality of traditional public schools inappropriate for their children and the arrogant elitism of many private schools off-putting. *See* URBAN & WAGGONER, *supra* note 108, at 400; Courtenay E. Moran, *How to Regulate Homeschooling: Why History Supports the Theory of Parental Choice*, 2011 U. ILL. L. REV. 1061 (2011).

171 In 1972, the Supreme Court addressed a certain type of home schooling in *Yoder*, 406 U.S. at 205. Amish parents argued that being compelled by the state to send their children, aged 14 and 15, to public secondary school rather than providing them at home with a vocational education would expose the children to worldly influences—attitudes, goals, and values—contrary to their sincere religious beliefs. This would substantially interfere with the children's religious training and their integration into the way of life of the Amish community at the crucial adolescent developmental stage, and contravene the basic religious tenets and practice of their own and their children's Amish faith. The Court ruled that Wisconsin's interest in universal compulsory education of children could not prevail as balanced against the First Amendment Free Exercise rights of Amish parents to control the upbringing, and hence the education, of their children. A religious accommodation to the generally applicable

interest in home schooling by fundamentalist, evangelical Christians discontent with the secularization of traditional public schools. Accommodating that interest, 34 states in those two decades adopted state statutes or regulations permitting home schooling.[172] Dissatisfaction with the quality of education in public schools grew, safety in public schools declined, financial resources for public schools waned, and an industry of commercial and nonprofit educational service providers developed instructional materials and assessment measures facilitating home schooling. But, at least as of 2007, the "most common reason parents gave as the most important [for home schooling their children] was a desire to provide religious or moral instruction."[173]

States allow home schooling, despite its broad decentralizing effect, by acknowledging its compliance with compulsory attendance laws. But states take various statutory approaches that impact the degree and conditions of government regulation imposed, the category of education to which home schooling is assigned—that is, whether statutorily it is considered the equivalent of public school instruction, private schooling, or something entirely different than either—and funding available for home schooling.[174] But as home schooling has

---

state compulsory attendance law for this rather unique religious group was warranted. Justice William O. Douglas, dissenting in part, disagreed with the majority's disposition of the case based on parental rights. He argued that religious liberty rights are personal, and are those of the children. Thus, their religious rights, not those of the parents, were at stake; all such students involved should have been heard on the matter. *Id.* at 421–29 (Douglas, J., dissenting in part). *See generally* Jeffrey Shulman, The Constitutional Parent: Rights, Responsibilities, and the Enfranchisement of the Child (Yale Univ. Press 2014).

172 *See* Summary of Home School Laws in the Fifty States, Home Sch. Legal Defense Ass'n iv, *available at* http://www.hslda.org/laws/Summary_of_Laws.pdf. Before the 1980s, only Nevada had adopted home school laws. *Id.* A unique Virginia statute, § 22.1–254(b)(1), may have been adopted with home schooling in mind; it provides that school boards "shall excuse from attendance at school … any pupil who, together with his parents, by reason of bona fide religious training or belief, is conscientiously opposed to attendance at school."

173 NCES, *Fast Facts: Homeschooling*, *supra* note 56, reporting that according to the U.S. Department of Education, 36 percent of students were home schooled for religious or moral reasons. This dropped to only 21 percent by the 2011–12 school year. National Center for Education Statistics, *Parent and Family Involvement in Education, from the National Household Education Surveys Program of 2012*, Table 8, "Number and percentage of school-age children who were homeschooled, by reasons parents gave as important and most important for homeschooling: 2011–12," *available at* http://nces.ed.gov/pubs2013/2013028/tables/table_08.asp. *See also* Clive R. Belfield, *Home-Schooling in the U.S.* 6–8 (Nat'l Ctr. for the Study of Privatization in Educ., Colum. Univ., Occasional Paper No. 88, Jan. 2004), *available at* http://ncspe.org/publications_files/OP88.pdf (last visited May 13, 2013); Urban & Waggoner, *supra* note 108, at 400.

174 State statutes include those that expressly regulate home schools, those that treat home schooling the same as any private schools without regulatory distinctions, and those with equivalency provisions that regulate the actual content of the home schooling curriculum. *See* Christina Sim Keddie, Note, *Homeschoolers and Public School Facilities:*

proliferated, states have faced increasing controversy. Debates have focused on various regulatory, financing, educational, and societal impacts,[175] but they may be at their greatest intensity when taxpayer dollars might be used to support religion in the home schooling environment.[176]

Parents of home-schooled children are not exempt from paying taxes to support public schools, and most parents do not receive government funding for expenses associated with home schooling their children. But several states do specially permit government aid for home schooling under certain conditions. For example, Arizona, Illinois, Kentucky, and Minnesota provide some restricted financial assistance in the form of reimbursements, tax credits, or educational savings accounts for qualified educational expenses.[177] While some states, such as Kentucky and Alaska, do not provide public funding for home schooling if the education is considered religiously-affiliated,[178] other states, such as Arizona,

---

Proposals for Providing Fairer Access, 10 N.Y.U. J. Legis. & Pub. Pol'y 603 (2006/2007). The approach can impact such matters as qualifications of instructors, student assessments, curriculum submissions for approval, and students' ability to participate in a state's virtual-education resources and classes or activities at brick-and-mortar public school facilities.

175 Some argue that home schooling may dilute or defeat children's ability to acquire basic civic values and the means to acclimate within a pluralistic society. Additionally, debates focus on the personal welfare and social well-being of students isolated to a good extent from their peers, the possible reduction in family and educational efficiencies, inadequate transparency issues, the insufficiency of accountability, and inequities created among socio-economic, racial, and ethnic groups. *See, e.g.*, Belfield, *supra* note 173, at 9–16.

176 *See, e.g.*, Chester E. Finn Jr., *Do Home Schoolers Deserve a Tax Break?*, *Room for Debate*, N.Y. Times (Jan. 4, 2011), *available at* http://www.nytimes.com/roomfordebate/2011/01/04/do-home-schoolers-deserve-a-tax-break.

177 *See, e.g.*, Minn. Stat. §§ 290.0674; 123B.41; Curtis Ophoven, *What Tax Advantages Are Available to Homeschoolers?*, Save Money Homeschooling (Sept. 15, 2008), *available at* http://www.savemoneyhomeschooling.com/pp/public/Articles.aspx?aid=9; *Publication 119: Education Expense Credit General Rules and Requirements for Home Schools*, Ill. Dep't of Revenue (2009), *available at* http://tax.illinois.gov/Publications/Pubs/Pub-119.pdf. Qualified education expenses vary depending upon the state. For example, they may include tuition and textbooks or other teaching materials, such as enrollment in cyber-classes and fees for virtual instruction materials.

178 In Kentucky, home schooling can be considered a "church school," a type of private school, and if so categorized cannot receive government funding. *See* Ky. Rev. Stat. Ann. § 159.030 (West 2010). Alaska gives financial support for home schooling but only if the home school is not considered a "religious or private school." Ak. Stat. §§ 14.45.200; 14.30.010(b); 14.17.430 (2012) (providing a student's school district an amount approximately 80 percent of the funding normally allotted to a public school student and regulating the disbursement of the funds for the purchase of secular texts and course materials for student use). *See* Memorandum from Scott J. Nordstrand, Deputy Attorney Gen., Ala. Dep't of Law, to Hon. Fred Dyson, Chair, Senate Health, Educ. & Soc. Servs. Comm., Ala. State Senate & Hon. Lyda Green, Co-Chair, Finance Comm., Ala. State Senate (Sept. 20, 2005), *available at* http://www.eed.state.ak.us/news/AG_Memo.pdf.

have no such restriction. So in Arizona, parents who home school a child may be able to use government funds to support teachings centered on religious doctrines and tenets, such as those from cyber-providers whose curricular materials and programming content reflect religious values and aim to inculcate impressionable children.[179] Liberty University Online Academy, for instance, provides courses for grades 3–12 and advertises that its curriculum adopts a "Christian perspective."[180] Another cyber-provider touts that "[t]he primary objective and purpose of A Beka Academy is to provide a traditional distance-learning program for students in kindergarten, elementary, and high school. This innovative program of study gives students an excellent academic education taught from a Christian perspective."[181]

Just because parents affirmatively and independently choose to educate their children with such religious orientation does not ameliorate or eliminate the thorny constitutional concerns triggered by taxpayer funds being used to support such educational providers and instructional content. Indeed, one might ask how such government support for religiously-imbued home schooling differs in any meaningful way from state aid for parents to enroll their children in a house of worship's traditional "Sunday school," which presumably would be impermissible. Parents' interests in providing a religious education to their children in their home with government financial support involves a sensitive balancing. On the one hand is the freedom of religious belief protected by the Free Exercise Clause and corresponding state guarantees and, on the other hand, are prohibitions against government establishment of religion under the Establishment Clause and state anti-establishment analogues. And while that calculus may be impacted by whether a state considers home schooling to be equivalent to public school instruction, part of the private school system, or something entirely different,

179 Despite Arizona's categorizing home schooling as non-private education, state statutes permit parents to claim tax credits, capped in amount, for expenditures for extracurricular instruction and activities and "character education programs," the latter of which does not appear to preclude religiously-based teachings. ARIZ. REV. STAT. ANN. §§ 15–802; 15–719 (2012); *see* ARIZONA DEP'T OF REV., PUB. 707: SCHOOL TAX CREDITS 1–2 (2013), *available at* https://www.azdor.gov/LinkClick.aspx?fileticket=lyMlhtowOpw%3D&tabid=240. Character fitness programs must include "instruction in the definition and application of at least six of the following character traits: truthfulness, responsibility, compassion, diligence, sincerity, trustworthiness, respect, attentiveness, obedience, orderliness, forgiveness and virtue." ARIZ. REV. STAT. ANN. § 15–719 (2012). Additionally, under ARIZ. REV. STAT. ANN. § 15–2402, Arizona's Empowerment Accounts (education savings accounts) can be spent simultaneously for multiple education providers associated with home schooling, including those religiously affiliated. For further discussion, *see supra* note 174; *infra* notes 202–12 and accompanying text.

180 Online Academy, LIBERTY UNIV., *available at* http://www.luonlineacademy.com/?&acode=D80538&gclid=CNWvyfqd3LYCFUp66wodFC4A9A (last visited Oct. 19, 2013).

181 Home School Distance Learning, A BEKA ACAD., *available at* http://www.abekaacademy.org/HomeSchool/Default.aspx (last visited Oct. 19, 2013).

such categorization cannot solve the constitutional dilemma.[182] Moreover, the constitutional complexity grows in states with anti-funding provisions, where diverting public funds to private sectarian institutions ostensibly is impermissible on that basis alone.

C. Private Schools and Tuition Voucher Programs

Most tuition voucher programs share similar features. Vouchers, representing taxpayer funds, are provided by the government to parents. Parents choose to enroll their children in programmatically-qualified private, sectarian and non-sectarian schools and pay the balance of any tuition not covered by the government voucher. Those children "eligible" to receive vouchers traditionally were socio-economically disadvantaged minority students, often attending "failing" or "failed" segregated urban schools.[183] Today, however, bolder and more controversial efforts seek to expand voucher programs to make them more widely available to middle-income and affluent children.[184] For all such programs, taxpayer monies represented by the vouchers flow indirectly through parental choice, rather than directly,[185] from government to a student's selected qualifying private school or education provider. The parents thus choose the school and act as intermediaries to whom the government makes the tuition assistance check payable, and then the parents endorse the check to the chosen private school.[186]

---

182 For consideration of how the classifications might complicate the balancing of government interest and parental interest, *see* Memorandum from Scott J. Nordstrand, *supra* note 178.

183 There is no one measure to discern what constitutes a "failing" or "failed" school. Achievement test scores of children and teacher performance evaluations often are relied upon. But some researchers promote "impact measures" of school quality. *See* Jeff Grabmeier, *Many "Failing" Schools Aren't Failing When Measured on Impact Rather Than Achievement*, Research News (Aug. 1, 2008), *available at* http://researchnews.osu.edu/archive/failschool.htm (last visited Apr. 30, 2013) (referring to Douglas B. Downey, et al., *Are "Failing" Schools Really Failing? Removing the Influence of Non-School Factors from Measures of School Quality*, 81 Sociology of Educ. 242 (2008)).

184 *See supra* note 70 (discussing the Douglas County, Colorado and Indiana initiatives).

185 Under Milwaukee's original voucher plan of 1989, only private, secular schools could participate, and the government paid them directly for children's tuition, amounting to approximately $2,500 per child. Wis. Stat. § 119.23(4). That plan withstood constitutional challenge. Davis v. Grover, 480 N.W.2d 460 (Wis. 1992). In 1995, the Wisconsin legislature amended the law to extend participation to private, parochial schools and required the financial aid to be paid to the parent or guardian for endorsement to the selected private school. 1995 Wis. Act 27, § 4006(m) (1995). The Wisconsin Supreme Court upheld the modified voucher plan as constitutional under the state and federal constitutions. Jackson v. Benson, 578 N.W.2d 602 (Wisc. 1998), *cert. denied*, 119 S. Ct. 466 (1998).

186 *See, e.g.*, Zelman v. Simmons-Harris, 536 U.S. 639, 646 (2002).

It is this feature—taxpayer funds funneled through independent parental choice to parochial schools—that superficially removes government from direct financing of religion, thereby ostensibly blunting the imprimatur of government support. But often the largest proportion of the voucher money goes to parochial schools, some of which may have admissions policies that discriminate based on religion, sexual orientation, or disability. This accentuates that it is far from clear why merely a particular payment mechanism through which government funds reach parochial schools should insulate government from what almost certainly would be an unconstitutional establishment of religion if accomplished more directly. Nonetheless, in *Zelman v. Simmons-Harris* five Justices of the Supreme Court embraced this independent private choice theory to reject an Establishment Clause challenge to Ohio's limited voucher plan.[187] Moreover, it is the *Zelman* ruling, further discussed in Chapter 2, that subsequently has driven many litigation successes of the school choice movement when vouchers have been challenged under the Establishment Clause and state anti-establishment analogues. These wins, consequently, have emboldened the movement to expand private school choice opportunities through various, innovative tax-supported mechanisms.

Nevertheless, as further discussed in Chapter 5, vouchers continue to meet with resistance as they siphon taxpayer funds away from public schools in contravention of state anti-funding provisions, state uniformity clauses (that compel states to provide a uniform system of public schools), "local control provisions" (that delegate public school control to local authorities), or other constitutional provisions.[188] So voucher programs based upon parental choice remain very prevalent and controversial not only for their use of taxpayer dollars for parochial private school tuition. And depending upon the particular state and its constitution's multiple relevant provisions, state court decisions on the merits of challenges to these programs vary.

D. Tax Deduction and Tax Credit Programs for Private Education

Perhaps the hottest current debates involve the use of tax mechanisms—deductions and tax credits—to support children's tuition and expenses associated with private parochial schooling. "Plain vanilla" tax deduction and credit initiatives permit parents to claim a tax deduction or tax credit on their state income tax returns for their child's qualified educational expenses, such as private, parochial (or secular) school tuition, textbooks, lab fees, software, and the like. Each state places annual maximums on the tax deduction or credit to which parents are entitled, but, as further discussed in Chapter 3, such a tax deduction or tax credit reduces the

187 *Id.* at 639.

188 For a fuller discussion of constitutional issues that can be triggered by vouchers under state anti-funding provisions, uniformity clauses, and "local control" provisions, *see* Preston C. Green, III & Peter L. Moran, *The State Constitutionality of Voucher Programs: Religion Is Not the Sole Determination*, 2010 BYU Educ. & L. J. 275 (2010).

individual's amount paid in state income taxes. So, as indicated above, such a state tax concession lessens the state's tax revenues and benefits the child and parents directly and a private, parochial (or secular) school or other education provider intangibly and financially. There is, however, as numerically illustrated in Chapter 3, a small associated financial detriment for those parents who itemize deductions on their federal income tax returns. These straightforward tax initiatives preceded newer, more complicated structures designed to operate through nonprofit § 501(c)(3) entities created for the purpose.

Pat Rooney, the chairman of Golden Rule Insurance Company, apparently was the innovator of the more complex structured tax mechanisms. In 1991, he started the country's first § 501(c)(3) private foundation scholarship tuition organization ("STO"), supported by tax-deductible contributions from Golden Rule, to provide tuition scholarships that permitted 500 low-income students in Indianapolis, Indiana to attend private schools.[189] Upon reading a *Wall Street Journal* story about Mr. Rooney's program, Jack and Isabelle McVaugh, retirees in Arizona, decided to establish an STO to implement a similar private tuition scholarship program in Phoenix.[190]

These two private citizen endeavors soon took on a life of their own, stimulating numerous states—11 states as of March, 2013—to enact specific legislation and launch similar but larger-scale tax-supported scholarship programs. Transforming private initiatives into government programs, however, more blatantly implicates constitutional concerns. The details of the caps on contributors' permissible dollar-for-dollar tax credits for donations to STOs, student eligibility requirements for scholarships, qualifications of schools that can participate,[191] schools' anti-discrimination policy requirements, and the like vary among states. The tax credit feature, however, is available to all taxpayers, and thus has broad appeal. Contributions to STOs may be given by parents of students for whom the scholarships will be used. Nonetheless, parents may not earmark their donations for their own child or for another child under a reciprocal arrangement.

The underlying tax approach of these statutory plans is fairly consistent. Each generally permits either individual or corporate taxpayers annually to donate funds to STOs, which are formed to qualify as § 501(c)(3) entities under federal income tax laws. Under the broader state programs would-be contributors to STOs

---

189 Editorial, *Education Reform Breakout*, Wall St. J., Dec. 17, 1993, at A14; Editorial, *The Choice Divide*, Wall St. J., Aug. 11, 1992, at A14.

190 Dan Lips, Goldwater Inst., The Impact of Tuition Scholarships on Low-Income Families: A Survey of Arizona School Choice Trust Parents: Policy Report, No. 187 2 (2003), *available at* http://goldwaterinstitute.org/sites/default/files/The%20Impact%20of%20Tuition%20Scholarships%20on%20Low-Income%20Families-%20A%20Survey%20of%20Arizona%20School%20Choice%20Trust%20Parents.pdf.

191 In some states, such as Arizona, a similar plan may permit the scholarship money to be used at charter schools to pay for extra-curricular activity fees. Most often, however, the scholarship funds are used for tuition for private schooling.

(as well as non-contributors) apparently can establish the STOs. The STOs can be religiously-affiliated and limit the scholarships they grant to parochial schools, and, at least in Arizona, most STOs in fact are sectarian.[192] The contributors experience dual tax effects. First, annually they can claim the allowed state dollar-for-dollar tax credit for their donations. Additionally, because there is no "child benefit" earmarking permitted, the contribution is a legitimate gift for which there is no *quid pro quo*.[193] So, corporate contributors and individual itemizing taxpayer-contributors can claim a charitable contribution deduction under § 170 of the federal income tax laws. But this deduction is offset by a reduced federal deduction for state taxes paid, with a net neutral effect.

Many states, such as Indiana, Iowa, Louisiana, New Hampshire, Oklahoma, Pennsylvania, Rhode Island, and Virginia have enacted tuition tax credit scholarship programs, with the contributor's state tax credit capped at between 50 percent and 95 percent of the amount contributed to STO-type organizations.[194] Several, however, provide an even more generous tax benefit. In 1997, Arizona implemented a program providing a 100 percent income tax credit for each dollar individuals donate to state approved STOs, up to a current cap of about $500 per individual taxpayer.[195] In 2006, it launched a similar dollar-for-dollar tax credit

---

192 *See* Ariz. Dep't of Revenue, Private School Tuition Organization Income Tax Credits in Arizona: A Summary of Activity FY 2012 ("Private School Tuition Organization Income Tax Credits") 2, 42–51 *available at* http://www.azdor.gov/Portals/0/Reports/FY2012%20private%20schl%20tuition%20org%20crdt%20rept.pdf (last visited Oct. 19, 2013).

193 *See* Hernandez v. Commissioner, 490 U.S. 680, 680 (1989) (limiting deductible gifts and contributions under Internal Revenue Code § 170 to "unrequited payments" to a § 501(c)(3) organization); Sklar v. Commissioner, 549 F.3d 1252, 1257 (9th Cir. 2008) and Sklar v. Commissioner, 282 F.3d 610 (9th Cir. 2002) (denying parents' deductibility of a payment to a § 501(c)(3) parochial school for any portion that would represent their child's school tuition, and finding parents failed to prove the amount paid for religious and secular instruction and thus to show the amount of a contribution transferred without return consideration).

194 For example in Indiana, a taxpayer who contributes $100 to a Scholarship Granting Organization is entitled to claim as a tax credit $50, reducing his state tax liability by that amount.

195 To promote greater transparency and accountability, in 2010 the Arizona legislature amended the state's individual tax credit scholarship program. The alterations, effective January 2011, included: prohibitions against STOs restricting scholarships solely on the basis of donor recommendations and taxpayers claiming tax credits when swapping donations with other taxpayers to benefit their own children; requiring STOs to certify that they allocate at least 90 percent of their annual revenues to scholarships; suggesting STOs consider financial need (statutorily defined) in awarding scholarships; and mandating STOs report the amount of scholarships paid to low-income students. Additionally, the definition of an STO, which had required the entity to be a "charitable organization," was amended to require it to be a "nonprofit organization exempt from income taxation under § 501(c)(3) of the Internal Revenue Code." The statutes do not prevent an STO from

program for corporate contributors to STOs. These two Arizona income tax credit programs have been hugely successful in attracting contributions, and Arizona reports that the amount of money flowing into the STOs, especially contributions by individuals, has increased greatly since the programs began. Indeed, total donations to Arizona STOs from 1998 through 2012 were almost $581 million.[196] Georgia and Florida also enacted a 100 percent tax credit for each dollar given to an STO, but Florida limits contributor eligibility to corporations.

Although popular, these complex STO-tax credit schemes have generated considerable litigation despite their short history. Challenges have been asserted under state anti-funding provisions, as well as under the First Amendment's Establishment Clause and state anti-establishment analogues because often the great majority of money raised by these programs goes to religiously-affiliated STOs that support tuition at parochial schools.[197] This litigation is discussed in subsequent chapters.

E. Schooling Alternatives and Education Savings Accounts

In 2011, one media commentator asserted that "[t]o date, none of the[] valuable school-choice policies have provided parents with full control over their children's share of school funding. But that will now change with the newest (and most aggressive) school-choice policy ever enacted."[198] Indeed, ESAs, touted as "designed to produce fiscal savings for taxpayers"[199] and as "open[ing] doors to

---

accepting donations apart from those received through the tax credit program. Also, the definition of "qualified school" was changed; a qualified school now cannot include a charter school, nor can it accept a scholarship or tuition grant in an amount exceeding the school's total cost of educating the student receiving the scholarship or grant. For a summary of the changes, see *HB 2664: Tax Credit Requirements*, ARIZ. STATE LEGISLATURE (March 5, 2010), *available at* http://www.azleg.gov//FormatDocument.asp?inDoc=/legtext/49leg/2r/summary/h.hb2664_03–05–10_houseengrossed.doc.htm&Session_ID=93 (last visited Oct. 5, 2013).

196 *See* PRIVATE SCHOOL TUITION ORGANIZATION INCOME TAX CREDITS, *supra* note 192, at 2.

197 Just two sectarian STOs, Catholic Education Arizona and Arizona Christian School Tuition Organization, the latter of which was the named party in *Winn*, have received nearly $231 million (39.7 percent) of the more than $580 million contributed since 1998. *Id.* at 42–51.

198 Carrie Lukas, *The Future of School Choice: Arizona's New ESA Program*, NAT'L REVIEW ONLINE (Apr. 21, 2011), *available at* http://www.nationalreview.com/content/future-school-choice-arizona%E2%80%99s-new-esa-program.

199 Lindsey Burke, *Education Savings Accounts: A Promising Way Forward on School Choice*, The HERITAGE FOUND. 2 (Oct. 4, 2011), *available at* http://thf_media.s3.amazonaws.com/2011/pdf/wm3382.pdf (last visited Oct. 20, 2013).

the free market of schooling options,"[200] practically can support an even broader spectrum of parochial schools and other religiously-affiliated education providers, and in greater amounts. Unlike school vouchers or scholarship grants from STOs that fund a student's tuition at a single school, ESAs are promoted as opportunities for parents personally to decentralize, tailor, and individualize their child's education by using taxpayer funds simultaneously to purchase supplies or services from multiple education providers.[201]

In 2012 Arizona's Governor signed into law the first ESA, legislatively labeled "Arizona Empowerment Accounts," to fund schooling for primary and secondary age children who qualified for the program. As currently constructed, the Arizona statute enables the state annually to redirect 90 percent of the money that it otherwise would have spent on a child in the public school system and deposit it into the participating child's ESA.[202] The parents are exempt from state income taxation on the deposited money.[203]

The student cannot attend a public or charter school and cannot simultaneously receive an STO scholarship at a private school.[204] Beyond these restrictions, the student's parents are entitled to spend the ESA money not only for school tuition at a qualified school (including private, parochial schools), but additionally for tutors, online learning programs, public school extracurricular programs, and other specified education expenses.[205] Technically, students who receive Arizona's ESA aid cannot qualify for home schooling status.[206] But there may be means of complying with the statute while schooling a child at home through contracting

200 Brittany Corona, *Education Savings Accounts: Empowering Parents*, The Foundry, The Heritage Found (Feb. 12, 2013), *available at* http://blog.heritage.org/2013/02/12/education-savings-accounts-empowering-parents/.

201 In this respect ESAs also are intended to limit the government's control over private schools. *See* Ariz. Rev. Stat. Ann. § 15–2404 (2012).

202 Ariz. Rev. Stat. Ann. § 15–2402(C) (2012). *See Empowerment Scholarship*, Ariz. Dep't of Educ., *available at* http://www.azed.gov/esa/ (last visited Oct. 19, 2013); Friedman Found., The ABCs, *supra* note 54, at 13.

203 Ariz. Rev. Stat. Ann. § 15–2402(J) (2012). The parents also may be exempt from taxation under federal tax laws if such deposit is considered a gift for purposes of I.R.C. § 102, or a § 117 scholarship for their child, or if their dependent child's annual unearned income is under the threshold of I.R.C. § 1(g) for taxing the amount at the parents' highest maginal rate. For further discussion, *see* Chapter 3, n.26.

204 Ariz. Rev. Stat. Ann. § 15–2402(B)(2), (3) (2012).

205 Ariz. Rev. Stat. Ann. § 15–2401(5); § 15–2402(B)(4) (2012). Parents are issued use-restricted debit cards to access the funds. Ladner, *supra* note 61, at 1. The funds cannot be expended, however, for charter school purposes, transportation, or computer hardware. Ariz. Rev. Stat. Ann. § 15–2402(B)(6) (2012).

206 Ariz. Rev. Stat. Ann. § 15–2402(B)(5) (2012) (prohibiting a parent from filing an affidavit with the government that a child is to be home schooled).

with education providers.[207] In its initial phase, many Arizona parents apparently either find the ESA money more than adequate for their children's immediate educational needs or are accumulating the ESA funds for later use, such as to pay for a child's post-secondary school education.[208] As of academic year 2012–2013, the average Arizona ESA was valued at $13,500, approximately $5,000 more than Arizona's total per-student spending of $7,968,[209] thus indicating some ESA financial assistance was being saved within accounts.

The Arizona ESA program initially was limited to special needs children, but, beginning in academic year 2013–2014, eligibility expanded to include children in foster care, of active military members, and in certain low-performing or failing public schools and school districts.[210] The expansion means that 20 percent of Arizona's school children qualify for ESAs.[211] And, consonant with the position of several think tanks,[212] the Arizona legislature, which already has demonstrated how highly it favors school choice programs, may consider a broader role for ESAs in the future.

To date, only one other state, Florida, has adopted ESAs.[213] But, as the school choice movement shows no sign of abating, more states might seize upon ESAs as an alternative school choice funding mechanism. Under a broad ESA regime, taxpayer funds may be diverted from the public school system and distributed to parents who then could use the money for their children's religiously-oriented educations provided by parochial primary and secondary schools, religiously-affiliated cyber-providers, and even religiously-affiliated universities and colleges. So, like other tax-supported school choice programs, the ESA mechanism is open

207 *See* Holly Craw, *Arizona Empowerment Scholarships Are Not the Same as Homeschooling*, Examiner.com (May 30, 2012), http://www.examiner.com/article/arizona-empowerment-scholarships-are-not-the-same-as-homeschooling.

208 There is no "use it, or lose it" provision in the statute, at least until graduation from a post-secondary institution or four consecutive years after non-enrollment in high school. Ariz. Rev. Stat. Ann. § 15–2402(I) (2012). Thus, there may be a built-in financial incentive for parents to retain money in ESAs for use at a time that a larger cumulative sum can, in their eyes, buy greater educational value. Indeed, Ariz. Rev. Stat. Ann. § 15–2402(B)(4)(h-j) (2012) contemplates that the funds can be used as seed money for 529 college savings accounts and for post-secondary school educational purposes, such as community college or other post-secondary school tuition and textbooks.

209 Friedman Found., The ABCs, *supra* note 54, at 13.

210 *See id.*

211 *Education Savings Accounts Expand Opportunities for Families*, Goldwater Inst. (Oct. 30, 2012), *available at* http://goldwaterinstitute.org/article/education-savings-accounts-expand-opportunities-families.

212 *See, e.g.*, Carona, *supra* note 200; Ladner, *supra* note 61, at 1; Burke, *supra* note 199, at 3–4.

213 *See* Tillotson, *supra* note 61 (noting qualification under the 2014 law currently is limited to children with certain disabilities, who will receive approximately $10,000 each (90 percent of what the state would have expended for public school education)).

to similar challenges under the Establishment Clause, state anti-establishment analogues, and state anti-funding provisions. Yet, tracking the jurisprudential developments described in Chapter 3, The Friedman Foundation for Educational Choice suggests that because ESAs are framed to be neutral and designed so that parents can use government funds for a broad array of educational services by secular and sectarian providers, ESAs may be more invulnerable to constitutional challenge than vouchers.[214] As short-lived and geographically narrow as ESAs are, however, they already have been challenged in state court. This litigation is discussed in Chapter 5.

VI. Conclusion

The *Wall Street Journal* hailed 2011 as "The Year of School Choice."[215] With the continuing expansion of interest in, and possibilities for, more creative tax-related funding schemes to support a growing and wider array of alternatives to traditional public schools, it is conceivable that this decade may be saluted as "The Decade of School Choice." As throughout the history of this country, the transformations that may emerge for primary and secondary school education and its financing are likely to be influenced and shaped by competing, and not always harmonious, racial, ethnic, socio-economic, political, and religious interests. So, it is imperative that, as policymakers and legislators work toward enlarging current initiatives and developing new ones, they eschew the political pressures of the moment and maintain scrupulous purpose and rigorous attention to complying completely with the First Amendment's Establishment Clause, state anti-establishment analogues, state anti-funding provisions, and other state constitutional safeguards. Some proponents of school choice seem to perceive these fundamental constitutional principles as mere annoying impediments to be worked around. Nonetheless, it is inevitable that lawsuits, perhaps particularly as initiated by taxpayers, will continue to challenge the constitutionality of inventive funding approaches and innovative school choice plans. After *Arizona Christian School Tuition Organization v. Winn*, most such litigation will be relegated to state courts for the foreseeable future. In recent years some state courts have interpreted the various restrictions narrowly. As bolder and more sweeping programs proliferate, it would be most regrettable and troubling if these courts minimize the intrusion on the liberty of conscience of all citizens that government financial support for religion necessarily presents.

---

214 Ladner, *supra* note 61, at 14 ("Education savings accounts have constitutionally meaningful differences with school vouchers. In some states, they may prove more durable to court challenge under state Blaine Amendments than a school voucher program.").

215 Editorial, *The Year of School Choice*, Wall St. J., July 5, 2011, at A14.

Our nation's constitutional relationship with religion is unlike that of other countries;[216] accordingly, our debates and litigation over the propriety of government funding of religious education and institutions assume a unique hue. Thus to impart a greater appreciation for the constitutional complexities and the sensitivities at stake here, the next chapter looks at core values embodied by the First Amendment's Establishment Clause and the significant U.S. Supreme Court jurisprudence on state aid for private parochial schools.

---

216 This is true even in countries, such as Australia, which has its own establishment clause. Section 116 of Australia's constitution provides that "[t]he Commonwealth shall not make any law for establishing any religion …." AUSTRALIAN CONSTITUTION § 106. For the Australian High Court's interpretation in the education context, *see* Attorney General (Vic); Ex. Rel. Black v. Commonwealth (1981) HCA 2, 146 CLR 559.

Chapter 2
The Establishment Clause and School Aid

> The "establishment of religion" clause of the First Amendment means at least this: Neither a state nor the Federal Government can set up a church. Neither can pass laws which aid one religion, aid all religions, or prefer one religion over another. ... No tax in any amount, large or small, can be levied to support any religious activities or institutions, whatever they may be called, or whatever form they may adopt to teach or practice religion.[1]

I. Introduction

The First Amendment begins with the familiar language mandating that "Congress shall make no law ...." With respect to freedom of expression—speech and press—the textual prohibition on government abridgement is complete. This of course does not mean that the freedom is absolute. The Supreme Court long has recognized several categorical exceptions to free speech, such as obscenity or incitement,[2] and questions arise over what constitutes expressive conduct more subject to regulation than pure speech—erotic nude dancing or burning an American flag as a political protest, for instance.[3] Moreover, varying levels of judicial scrutiny apply for reviewing different regulations of speech—namely, those that are content-based restrictions on the one hand, versus those that are non-content-based limitations that focus merely on the time, place, or manner of speech[4]—and these produce different degrees of protection. But unlike other formulations in many state constitutions, such as a provision that guarantees freedom of speech conditioned upon one "being responsible for the abuse of that right,"[5] the First Amendment itself contains no express limitation upon, or inherent tension within, the freedom of expression it guarantees.

---

1 Everson v. Bd. of Educ., 330 U.S. 1, 15–16 (1947).

2 *See* United States v. Stevens, 559 U.S. 460, 468–69 (2010).

3 *See, e.g.*, City of Erie v. Pap's A.M., 529 U.S. 277 (2000) (nude dancing); Texas v. Johnson, 491 U.S. 397 (1989) (flag burning).

4 *See, e.g.*, Ward v. Rock Against Racism, 491 U.S. 781 (1989) (volume control at an outdoor concert).

5 Regarding state constitutional provisions, *see* Justice Robert F. Utter, *The Right to Speak, Write, and Publish Freely: State Constitutional Protection Against Private Abridgment*, 8 U. Puget Sound L. Rev. 157, 171 (1985). Blackstone's Commentaries on the Laws of England stated a similar restriction on freedom of the press, one that the Supreme Court rejected under the First Amendment in *Near v. Minnesota*, 283 U.S. 697, 713–15 (1931).

The situation, however, is quite different with the First Amendment's Religion Clauses. The Establishment Clause prevents government from making any law "respecting an establishment of religion," terminology that by itself raises a host of questions as to its meaning, some of which we explore. The Free Exercise Clause is next, as the First Amendment continues, "or prohibiting the free exercise thereof." As is well recognized, the immediate juxtaposition of these two phrases creates often irreconcilable tension between the two fundamental rights. How can government avoid impinging on the free exercise of religion unless it sometimes grants religious persons and institutions special accommodations, including perhaps exceptions from otherwise generally applicable laws and regulations that on their face are neutral towards religion? But how can government extend such accommodations and exceptions without making laws respecting religion, singling it out for special treatment, and therefore arguably running afoul of the Establishment Clause?

One much publicized and contested current example of this conundrum is the requirement of the 2010 Patient Protection and Affordable Care Act ("ACA") that certain employers provide their employees with health insurance that covers women's "preventive health services," which include a full range of contraceptive methods. Certain "religious employers," such as houses of worship, are exempt from this requirement, but some other nonprofit and for-profit entities that do not qualify for this exemption object on religious grounds to having to pay, even indirectly, for all contraceptive methods, or just for those they consider to be abortifacients. And several have challenged the selective nature of the religious exemption that excludes them, raising the issue of how far government accommodation of religion may or should go. An underlying question is particularly relevant by analogy to the themes of this book. As discussed below, the Supreme Court has ruled that the indirect manner in which some state aid is provided to parochial schools, reaching them through the independent, private choices of parents, is sufficient to insulate government from establishment problems. So in the parallel context of the ACA regulation, one question is whether the sole and independent, private choices of employees to use contraceptives similarly might be sufficient to eliminate impingement on the free exercise of their employers by rendering the employer's argument of "complicity with evil" too attenuated in these circumstances. Not surprisingly, reflecting the difficulties inherent in reconciling the competing legal and constitutional principles, lower courts that considered the issue took widely divergent approaches, leaving it to the Supreme Court to decide the issue.[6]

---

6 *See* Burwell v. Hobby Lobby Stores, Inc., 134 S. Ct. 2751 (2014), consolidating two cases involving for-profit employers asserting that statutory free exercise rights should exempt their corporations from the contraception regulation under the ACA. The Court's five-Justice conservative majority ruled, over a vigorous dissent, in favor of the companies while largely eliding the actual attenuation argument—one that should depend on a legal conclusion and not on religious belief—and never attempting to distinguish its contrary position in the school aid context. *Compare id.* at 2777–79 (majority opinion) *with id.* at 2797–99 (Ginsburg, J., dissenting).

The Supreme Court unabashedly has acknowledged that the Free Exercise and Establishment Clauses "are not the most precisely drawn portions of the Constitution,"[7] and they "often exert conflicting pressures."[8] Justice William Rehnquist once criticized the Court for its too expansive interpretations of both clauses that "has constantly narrowed the channel between the Scylla [of what the Free Exercise Clause demands] and Charybdis [of what the Establishment Clause forbids]."[9] The Court often resolves this conflict in an *ad hoc* manner by finding "room for play in the joints" between the clauses.[10]

The first case in which the Court incorporated the Establishment Clause (pursuant to the Due Process Clause of the Fourteenth Amendment) and applied it against the states involved the issue of interest here, namely state aid to private, parochial education, and perhaps seemed innocuous enough at the time. The Court in *Everson v. Board of Education* pronounced that the Establishment Clause prohibits government from "aid[ing] one religion, aid[ing] all religions, or prefer[ing] one religion over another,"[11] but it still upheld a New Jersey statute that reimbursed parents from general tax funds for the cost of bus transportation for their children commuting to parochial schools, though not to other private schools. After all, one might think, what was the great threat to First Amendment values from the state simply paying to bus children to schools, even schools where they might receive religious training? In fact the danger arguably was palpable, for from this inauspicious beginning we now have reached an emotional, political, and constitutional quagmire.

II. The Establishment Clause: Enactment, Incorporation, and Interpretation

There always has been considerable debate over the meaning and appropriate applications of the Establishment Clause, but the controversy has only sharpened lately, driven in part by disputes over increased government funding for parochial schools. Addressing specifically the context of religious imagery on government property, but with more general implications, Justice Clarence Thomas recently

---

7 Walz v. Tax Comm'n of the City of New York, 397 U.S. 664, 668–69, 673 (1970).

8 *See* Hosanna-Tabor Evangelical Lutheran Church & Sch. v. E.E.O.C., 132 S. Ct. 694, 702 (2012) (quoting Cutter v. Wilkinson, 544 U.S. 709, 719 (2005)).

9 Texas Monthly, Inc. v. Bullock, 489 U.S. 1, 42 (1989) (Scalia, J., dissenting) (quoting Thomas v. Review Bd. of the Ind. Employ. Sec. Div., 450 U.S. 707, 721 (1981) (Rehnquist, J., dissenting) and supplying the bracketed explanations).

10 *Walz*, 397 U.S. at 669; *see also* Locke v. Davey, 540 U.S. 712, 718 (2004); *Cutter*, 544 U.S. at 713.

11 330 U.S. at 15. The Court previously had incorporated the Free Exercise Clause applying it to the states under the Fourteenth Amendment. *See* Cantwell v. Connecticut, 310 U.S. 296, 303 (1940). The Court in effect determined that both Clauses are so "implicit in the concept of ordered liberty" as to come within the Court's then developing incorporation doctrine. Palko v. Connecticut, 302 U.S. 319, 325 (1937). For a current formulation of the incorporation standard, *see McDonald v. City of Chicago*, 130 S. Ct. 3020, 3036 (2010).

pronounced the Supreme Court's "Establishment Clause jurisprudence in shambles."[12] His views, although idiosyncratic, are not without justification.

The difficulty is engendered, appropriately enough, first by considerable uncertainty about what the Framers and ratifiers of the First Amendment intended and the original public meaning of its provisions.[13] James Madison initially was ambivalent about the need for a Bill of Rights to the Constitution but campaigned for election to the first House of Representatives on a pledge to work for such enactment, specifically including protection for religious liberties ("the rights of Conscience in the fullest latitude").[14] Good to his word, Madison introduced his first draft in the House on June 8, 1789, and earned renown as the "leading architect of the religion clauses of the First Amendment."[15] Madison's language referred to protection for "the full and equal rights of conscience," but the final text of the First Amendment that emerged as a consensus from successive congressional committees omitted the more generic reference to conscience and spoke instead in terms specifically of religion.[16]

---

12 Utah Highway Patrol Ass'n v. American Atheists, Inc., 132 S. Ct. 12, 13 (2011) (Thomas, J., dissenting from denial of certiorari); Rosenberger v. Rector & Visitors of the Univ. of Va., 515 U.S. 819, 861 (1995) (Thomas, J., concurring) (relatively new in his Court tenure describing Establishment Clause jurisprudence as "in hopeless disarray").

13 As many have noted, the Framers, ratifiers, and those with political power were overwhelmingly White, male, Protestant property holders, which makes any reliance on their views with respect to religious matters particularly problematic for modern day America. *See generally* Alan Brownstein, *The Reasons Why Originalism Provides a Weak Foundation for Interpreting Constitutional Provisions Relating to Religion*, 2009 Cardozo L. Rev. De Novo 196 (2009).

14 Richard Labunski, James Madison and the Struggle for the Bill of Rights 162–64 (Oxford Univ. Press 2006) (quoting Madison's letter to Reverend George Eve, Jan. 2, 1789).

15 *Hosanna-Tabor*, 132 S. Ct. at 703 (quoting Ariz. Christian Sch. Tuition Org. v. Winn, 131 S. Ct. 1436, 1446 (2011) (quoting Flast v. Cohen, 392 U.S. 83, 103, (1968))).

16 Madison perhaps was long enamored of his particular phraseology, expressing his hope for a revival of "Liberty of Conscience" to counteract religious intolerance in a letter to a college friend William Bradford. *Letter from James Madison to William Bradford* (Jan. 24, 1774), *reprinted in* 5 The Founders' Constitution 60 (Philip B. Kurland & Ralph Lerner eds., Univ. Chicago Press 1987). On the possible significance of the change from "conscience" to "religion," *see* Michael W. McConnell, *The Origins and Historical Understanding of Free Exercise of Religion*, 103 Harv. L. Rev. 1409, 1488–1500 (1990). On liberty of conscience compared to religious liberty, *see* Nathan S. Chapman, *Disentangling Conscience and Religion*, 2013 U. Ill. L. Rev. 1457 (2013). For a detailed chronological survey of the drafts of, and debates over, the Religion Clauses, *see* Carl H. Esbeck, *The First Federal Congress and the Formation of the Establishment Clause of the First Amendment* ("*The First Federal Congress*"), *in* No Establishment of Religion: America's Original Contribution to Religious Liberty ("No Establishment of Religion") 208, 232–33 (T. Jeremy Gunn & John Witte, Jr. eds., Oxford Univ. Press 2012).

The "specialness" of religion under the Constitution is the subject of much discussion and debate. *See, e.g.*, Micah Schwartzman, *What If Religion Is Not Special?*, 79 U. Chi.

The terminology perhaps is more significant with respect to the prohibition on the federal government from making any law "respecting an establishment of religion." The text does not say more simply, but perhaps more comprehensively, Congress shall make no law "respecting religion;" that phrasing might overlap considerably with the guarantee of free exercise.[17] But "respecting" has broad connotation and could be understood to mean any law positively or negatively "impinging upon" an establishment of religion. The prohibition's use of the term "respecting" (especially considering the honorific sense of the word) thus likely includes a ban on affirmative government action in aid or support of religion and does not merely preclude government action that is negative toward religion.[18]

Yet the text refers not just to a law "respecting religion" but, in accord with Madison's original draft, one "respecting" an *establishment* of religion.[19] This leads

---

L. Rev. 1351, 1354 nn.13, 14 (2012) (collecting sources). For a more philosophical argument, *see* Brian Leiter, Why Tolerate Religion? (Princeton Univ. Press 2013). For a critical review of Professor Leiter's book, *see* Michael W. McConnell, *Why Protect Religious Freedom?*, 123 Yale L. J. 770 (2013). As a legal matter, in *Hosanna-Tabor*, 132 U.S. at 706, a unanimous Court rejected what it termed the "remarkable view" that the First Amendment does not accord "special solicitude to the rights of religious organizations" compared to secular groups.

17 Professor Akhil Amar describes the resulting Establishment Clause language as most closely tracking the New Hampshire proposal that "Congress shall make no laws touching religion." Akhil Reed Amar, The Bill of Rights 33 (Yale Univ. Press 1998); *see also* Mark D. McGarvie, *Disestablishing Religion and Protecting Religious Liberty in State Laws and Constitutions (1776–1833)*, *in* No Establishment of Religion, *supra* note 16, at 70, 77 ("Implicitly, law was reconceived in the Constitutional Convention—from supporting the social good through communitarian ideals consistent with Christian morality to serving ideals of individual liberty. … The new legal framework addressed two distinct but interrelated concerns: religious freedom and the separation of church and state.").

18 *See* Amar, The Bill of Rights, *supra* note 17, at 248 (comparing the use of the word "respecting" in Article IV of the Constitution); *see also* Cnty. of Allegheny v. A.C.L.U., 492 U.S. 573, 649 (1989) (Stevens, J., concurring and dissenting in part); Esbeck, *The First Federal Congress*, *supra* note 16, at 233–34 (speculating on federalist or grammatical reasons for addition of the word "respecting").

19 Madison's draft included the phrase "nor shall any national religion be established." 1 Annals of Cong. 451 (Joseph Gale ed., 1834), *available at* http://lcweb2.loc.gov/ammem/amlaw/lwac.html. In his reflections during retirement, in the course of noting his objection to Congress' appointment of legislative chaplains, Madison made it clear that, in his view, "The Constitution of the U.S. forbids everything *like* an establishment of religion." James Madison, *Detached Memoranda*, *reprinted in* 5 The Founders' Constitution, *supra* note 16, at 103, 104 (emphasis added).

Some scholars contend that at the time of the Bill of Rights "virtually every American" knew what the Establishment Clause meant. Michael W. McConnell, *Establishment at the Founding*, *in* No Establishment of Religion, *supra* note 16, at 45, 45. Professors John Witte, Jr., and T. Jeremy Gunn, however, write that "we look in vain for the eighteenth century meaning of the term 'establishment of religion' for it served more as a term of opprobrium to some scholars to the position that the Establishment Clause was meant merely to prohibit the federal government from forming its own established religion and, at the same time, to prevent it from interfering in any respect with the established state churches that existed then and for some time into the nineteenth century.[20] Viewing the Establishment Clause at least initially as only a limited, anti-establishment provision at the federal level, and then also as a states-rights, federalism provision, makes rather ironic and perhaps inappropriate its later incorporation and application against the states. But there are strong contrary views.[21]

Justice William J. Brennan addressed this debate in his opinion concurring in the Court's 1963 decision in *School District of Abington Township v. Schempp* that

---

insult a disfavored church-state arrangement rather than as a term of art whose meaning was shared by everyone." John Witte, Jr., *Introduction, in* No Establishment of Religion, *supra* note 16, at 3, 6, 24; T. Jeremy Gunn, *The Separation of Church and State Versus Religion in the Public Square, in* No Establishment of Religion, *supra* note 16, at 15, 24. Professor Gunn further challenges Professor McConnell's statement: "[T]he First Congress considered many alternate ways to express their intent rather than adopt a term that was widely shared or universally understood." *Id.* at 24; *see also*, Daniel L. Dreisbach, *Defining and Testing the Prohibition on Religious Establishment in the Early Republic, in* No Establishment of Religion, *supra* note 16, at 252, 252, 271 ("[T]he search for a fixed, discernible original understanding of the First Amendment may be an impossible undertaking. … There was no national consensus in the days following ratification of the Constitution and Bill of Rights on the scope and application … of the First Amendment prohibition on laws 'respecting an establishment of religion.'"); Steven K. Green, *The "Second Disestablishment," in* No Establishment of Religion, *supra* note 16, at 280, 281 (referring to the "diversity of views concerning disestablishment and religious liberty that existed during the founding period, views that were dynamic and unfolding"); Robin Charlow, *The Elusive Meaning of Religious Equality*, Wash. U.L.Q. 1529, 1544 (2005) ("[I]t could be argued that, with regard to religion, the American people as a collective entity have never actually had a common understanding about what the clauses would or should mean ….").

20 See Amar, The Bill of Rights, *supra* note 17, at 32–34, 41–42. Madison had proposed an addition to the Constitution's Article I limitations on the powers of the states (Section 10) that "No State shall violate the equal rights of conscience." 1 Annals of Cong. 452 (Joseph Gales ed., 1834). He thought this explicit restriction of state power would be the "most valuable amendment." *Id.* at 783–84.

21 *See* Esbeck, *The First Federal Congress*, *supra* note 16, at 241 ("[T]he primary focus of the Establishment Clause was to limit the power of Congress, *not* to uniquely protect the states.") (emphasis in original); Steven K. Green, *Federalism and the Establishment Clause: A Reassessment*, 38 Creighton L. Rev. 761, 767–68 (2005) ("Although the ultimate phrasing of the Establishment Clause may indicate the presence of federalism concerns, such was not [sic] primary or overriding impetus behind the call for or drafting of the First Amendment. … [T]he federalism aspect … has been overstated; by far, the clause is not 'purely jurisdictional in nature.'"). *See also* John Witte, Jr., God's Joust, God's Justice: Law and Religion in the Western Tradition 229 (Wm. B. Eerdmans Publ'g Co. 2006) (noting the federalist reading of the Establishment Clause is "plausible … though the evidence for this reading is very thin").

the Establishment Clause prohibits officially prescribed bible reading or prayer in public schools.[22] Justice Brennan finessed the issue of original interpretation as of 1791 by focusing instead on the 1868 adoption of the Fourteenth Amendment, for it is pursuant to that Reconstruction Era Amendment that the guarantees of the First Amendment bind state governments as well as the national government. As Justice Brennan noted, as of 1868 there had been no established state church for several decades, so the Fourteenth Amendment's absorption of the Establishment Clause could not have been predicated on protecting this anachronism. Rather, as Justice Brennan put it:

> It is … plain … that the Fourteenth Amendment created a panoply of new federal rights for the protection of citizens of the various States. And among those rights was freedom from such state governmental involvement in the affairs of religion as the Establishment Clause had originally foreclosed on the part of Congress.[23]

Moreover, "the role of the Establishment Clause [is] as a coguarantor, with the Free Exercise Clause, of religious liberty[ ]," part of the individual "liberty" protected against state infringement by the Fourteenth Amendment.[24] To be quite clear Justice Brennan added a footnote:

> There is no doubt that, whatever "establishment" may have meant to the Framers of the First Amendment in 1791, the draftsmen of the Fourteenth Amendment three quarters of a century later understood the Establishment Clause to foreclose many incidental forms of governmental aid to religion which fell far short of the creation or support of an official church.[25]

In support of his position Justice Brennan cited not only an 1853 report of a senate committee but also Thomas M. Cooley's acclaimed treatise contemporaneous with ratification of the Fourteenth Amendment:

> Those things which are not lawful under any of the American constitutions may be stated thus:—
>
> 1. Any law respecting an establishment of religion. …
> 2. Compulsory support, by taxation or otherwise, of religious instruction. Not only is no one denomination to be favored at the expense of the rest, but all support of religious instruction must be entirely voluntary.[26]

---

22 374 U.S. 203 (1963).

23 *Id.* at 255 (Brennan, J., concurring).

24 *Id.* at 256.

25 *Id.* at 258 n.24.

26 *Id.* (quoting Cooley, Constitutional Limitations 469 (1868)). Justice Brennan also refuted the notion that the unsuccessful Blaine Amendment, discussed in Chapter 1,

Justice Brennan is hardly alone in suggesting that a modern court interpreting the Fourteenth Amendment's substantive protections, such as due process, and applying these to the states by incorporating fundamental provisions of the Bill of Rights, prominently including the First Amendment, should consider the 1868 Reconstruction Era understanding of those provisions and not just that of 1791. As one prominent scholar observes: "Much recent scholarship has suggested that originalist analyses of Bill of Rights provisions applied to the states via the Fourteenth Amendment should consider the original understanding as of 1868 in addition to that of 1791."[27] Originalism, in other words, as an interpretive theory, has at least these two chronological baselines, as well as "'the accumulated product of judicial interpretation.'"[28]

Specifically with regard to incorporation of the Establishment Clause, Professor Kurt T. Lash accepts the federalism principle of the 1791 ratification but argues that "there is *no less reason* to incorporate the Establishment Clause than any other provision in the First Amendment."[29] Through his comprehensive examination of the evolution of non-establishment principles from the Bill of Rights through Reconstruction in terms of personal freedom from state-imposed religious establishments, Professor Lash concludes:

> By Reconstruction, the common interpretation of the Establishment Clause and its "counterparts" in the states was that no government had any legitimate

---

was somehow inconsistent with his argument. For a review of the Blaine Amendment's "complicated" effect on incorporation of the Establishment Clause, *see, e.g.*, Thomas C. Berg, *Disestablishment from Blaine to Everson*, *in* No Establishment of Religion, *supra* note 16, at 307, 312–15; Ira C. Lupu & Robert W. Tuttle, *Federalism and Faith*, 56 Emory L.J. 19, 47–48 (2006); Steven K. Green, *The Blaine Amendment Reconsidered*, 36 Am. J. Legal Hist. 38, 68–69 (1992).

27 Eugene Volokh, *Freedom for the Press as an Industry, or for the Press as a Technology? From the Framing to Today*, 160 U. Pa. L. Rev. 459, 464 (2012) (listing additional sources). *See* Amar, The Bill of Rights, *supra* note 17, at 41–42, 246–54.

28 Regents of Univ. of Mich. v. Ewing, 474 U.S. 214, 226 (1985) (unanimous opinion) (internal citation omitted); *see, e.g.*, Ryan C. Williams, *The One and Only Substantive Due Process Clause*, 120 Yale L. J. 408, 416 (2010) ("Between 1791 and 1868, when the Fourteenth Amendment was ratified, due process concepts evolved dramatically through judicial elaboration of due process and similar provisions in state constitutions .... As a result, by 1868 'due process of law' had developed additional, well-established substantive connotations as both a prohibition of legislative interference with vested rights and as a guarantee of general and impartial laws.").

29 Kurt T. Lash, *The Second Adoption of the Establishment Clause: The Rise of the Nonestablishment Principle*, 27 Ariz St. L.J. 1085, 1088, 1154 (1995). When a lower federal court ruled that the Supreme Court had "erred" in applying the Establishment Clause to the states, the Court did not hesitate to confirm "how firmly embedded in our constitutional jurisprudence" is its incorporation via the Fourteenth Amendment. Wallace v. Jaffrey, 472 U.S. 38, 45 n.25, 48 (1985).

> power over religion as religion: the state could neither establish a preferred religion, nor could it visit "disadvantages or penalties" upon disfavored religious beliefs. Citizens by right were immune from such religious-based persecutions.[30]

This position is supported by an historical study of state constitutional law to assess the fundamental rights guaranteed among the 37 states in 1868 when the Fourteenth Amendment was adopted. The authors found "a broad consensus [over 70 percent of states comprising over 70 percent of the population] in 1868 ... had clauses in their state constitutions prohibiting the establishment of religion and implying that freedom from an establishment was an individual fundamental right and not a collective-federalism state right against the national government."[31] Another study asks more specifically whether at the time of ratification of the Fourteenth Amendment a principle of non- or anti-establishment among the states included the idea that government could not "endorse" religion in the sense of the approach Justice Sandra Day O'Connor proposed as an "analytical device" in the perhaps forlorn hope of clarifying the Court's twentieth-century Establishment Clause jurisprudence.[32] For Justice O'Connor, state action with the purpose or objective effect of endorsing or disapproving of religion is likely unconstitutional.[33] For almost 30 years the endorsement test has proved highly controversial among the Justices, with some invoking and relying on it while others are dismissive of it.[34]

---

30 Lash, *supra* note 29, at 1135, 1141. Professor Lash discusses developments in the common law, conflicts between the Protestant majority and the Catholic minority (including the Blaine Amendment), and southern regulation of religion in relation to the Fourteenth Amendment; *see also* Green, *The "Second Disestablishment," supra* note 19, at 289, 292 ("[T]he meaning of disestablishment to Americans from 1776 to 1865 was varied and evolving. ... [A]s the [nineteenth] century progressed, judges and lawyers were increasingly open to more expansive interpretations of the religion clauses contained in the various state constitutions.").

31 Steven G. Calabresi & Sarah E. Agudo, *Individual Rights Under State Constitutions When the Fourteenth Amendment Was Ratified in 1868: What Rights are Deeply Rooted in American History and Tradition?*, 87 Tex. L. Rev. 7, 32 (2008). *See* McGarvie, *supra* note 17; Esbeck, *The First Federal Congress, supra* note 16, at 246 (arguing that Lash, as well as Calabresi and Agudo, do not sufficiently distinguish between a federalist Establishment Clause focused on national/state structure and a jurisdictional Establishment Clause about church/government structure).

32 For this study, *see* E. Duncan Getchell, Jr. & Michael H. Brady, *How the Constitutions of the Thirty-seven States in Effect When the Fourteenth Amendment Was Adopted Demonstrate that the Governmental Endorsement Test in Establishment Clause Jurisprudence Is Contrary to American History and Tradition*, 17 Tex. Rev. L. & Pol. 125 (2012).

33 Lynch v. Donnelly, 465 U.S. 668, 688–91 (1984) (O'Connor, J., concurring). For discussion of the endorsement test, *see infra* notes 131–33 and accompanying text.

34 *See* Getchell & Brady, *supra* note 32, at 128–38.

The second study, a recent historical review of all the relevant state constitutions, concludes that when the Fourteenth Amendment was ratified "nonestablishment principles and values included no concern about governmental endorsement."[35] But this conclusion is quite ambiguous and immaterial for many current issues because of what the reviewers broadly interpret as "endorsement" of religion in the language of the state constitutions. It could be as simple as a preamble that, unlike the U.S. Constitution, acknowledged God or divine provenance, or a provision regarding religious conscientious objection. What is most notable for present purposes is that the vast majority of state constitutions contained language that fairly could be construed to preclude government financial aid, through taxation or otherwise, for religious institutions, including parochial schools.[36] This is not surprising because, even when the First Amendment was being formulated, the "formal state establishments of religion, particularly the controversial practice of state funding and tax collections for religion, were eroding in support."[37] Thus, as one scholar concludes,

> whatever the understanding of the Establishment Clause was in 1789, there is good reason to believe that by the time of the Fourteenth Amendment, nonestablishment had come to be seen as an essential liberty of citizens. ...

35 *Id.* at 184.

36 This assessment is based on Getchell's and Brady's study that early state constitutions included general statements such as "no man can of right be compelled to attend, erect, or support any place of worship, or to maintain any ministry against his consent," and more specific provisions such as "[n]o money shall be drawn from the treasury, for the benefit of any religious or theological institution," or "no religious sect, or sects, shall have exclusive right to, or control of, any part of the school funds of the State, nor shall sectarian principles be taught in the public schools." *Id.* at 139–76 (referencing various state constitutions). We say in the above text "fairly could be construed" because any definitive conclusion would depend on judicial constitutional interpretation in a particular adjudicative context.

37 Witte, Jr., *supra* note 19, at 5. Precluding tax-supported financial aid for religion, even on a non-preferential basis, was a core purpose of the Establishment Clause. *See* Douglas Laycock, *The Origins of the Religion Clauses of the Constitution: "Nonpreferential" Aid to Religion: A False Claim about Original Intent*, 27 Wm. & Mary L. Rev. 875, 878 (1986); Noah Feldman, Divided by God: America's Church State Problem—and What We Should Do About It 48 (Farrar, Straus and Giroux 2005). Indeed, the role of government in promoting religion more generally was waning by the 1780s. Gunn, *supra* note 19, at 17. *See also* Arlin M. Adams & Charles J. Emmerich, *A Heritage of Religious Liberty*, 137 U. Pa. L. Rev. 1559, 1568–82 (1989) (noting "the period between 1776 and the Constitutional Convention witnessed heightened efforts in the struggle against the remaining establishments"); Carl H. Esbeck, *Dissent and Disestablishment: The Church-State Settlement in the Early American Republic*, 2004 BYU L. Rev. 1385, 1395 (2004) (observing "the conventional argument" favoring "material government support for religion and religious institutions" was in decline during the War of Independence and the early republic).

> [T]he Establishment Clause was a full partner with the Free Exercise Clause in the dual protection of religious liberty.[38]

This does not mean, however, that principles of the founding era, including especially canonical writings of Madison and Jefferson, are irrelevant to the contemporary meaning of an Establishment Clause declared incorporated in the twentieth century via a transformative nineteenth-century amendment.[39] Rather, the individual liberties that the Establishment Clause protects arise from a cumulative interplay and accretion over time of values recognized and adopted at both state and federal levels.[40]

Naturally there are some opposing positions, notably those of Justice Thomas. In the school voucher case, *Zelman v. Simmons-Harris*, Justice Thomas suggested that government action that raises Establishment Clause issues might be evaluated differently at the state and federal levels. In particular, he would allow states "greater latitude in dealing with matters of religion and education."[41] Subsequently, when the Court dismissed for lack of standing a challenge to a public school district's policy requiring teacher-led recitation of the Pledge of Allegiance including the words "under God," Justice Thomas concurred only in the Court's judgment because he wanted to use the case to begin "the process of rethinking the Establishment Clause" as a federalism clause which "resists incorporation."[42] Without engaging any of the arguments about the import of incorporation via ratification of the Fourteenth Amendment, Justice Thomas asserted that "any sensible incorporation of the Establishment Clause ... would probably cover little more than the Free Exercise Clause."[43] Thus, Justice Thomas

---

38 Berg, *supra* note 26, at 312. Professor Berg cites developments in state constitutions to reinforce the view that "by mid-[nineteenth] century the Establishment Clause was not a mere federalism provision, but a model for individual rights at the state level." *Id.* at 327. *See also* Getchell & Brady, *supra* note 32, at 127–28; Cameron A. VanSant, *From Opportunity to Right: Constitutional Change and the Establishment Clause*, 25 YALE J.L. & HUMAN. 149, 163–64 (2013) (noting that state constitutional conventions "sometimes drafted provisions modeled on the Federal Clause, underlining the connection between the Establishment Clause and a new '(substantive) nonestablishment rule' that had come to protect citizens' individual liberty.").

39 *Cf.* Lash, *supra* note 29, at 1088.

40 *See* McCreary Cnty., Ky. v. A.C.L.U., 545 U.S. 844, 877 (2005) (comparing the historical record as to endorsements of religion with 60 years of precedent applying a neutrality principle).

41 536 U.S. 639, 680 (2002).

42 Elk Grove Unified Sch. Dist. v. Newdow, 542 U.S. 1, 45 (2004) (Thomas, J., concurring in the judgment).

43 *Id.* at 46. More recently, adhering to his singular view that the Establishment Clause "resists incorporation," Justice Thomas termed "mixed" the historical argument on this point regarding the Fourteenth Amendment. Town of Greece v. Galloway, 134 S. Ct. 1811, 1836 (2014) (Thomas, J., concurring in part and in the judgment). Justice Thomas

would limit prohibited state establishments of religion to state action that involves "actual legal coercion," though he acknowledged that this might include coercive taxation in aid of religion.[44] Justice Thomas maintains that returning to what he considers the "original meaning" of the Establishment Clause would resolve the "incoherence of the Court's decisions in this area [that] renders the Establishment Clause impenetrable and incapable of consistent application."[45]

While interesting and provocative, Justice Thomas' idiosyncratic and stringent, originalist approach to constitutional interpretation in a variety of contexts has little influence, particularly with regard to the First Amendment. For example, Justice Thomas was clearly an outlier in a case involving a high school sponsored and supervised social event where a group of students attracted attention by unfurling a banner that read, "Bong Hits 4 Jesus." Although rather nonsensical, the principal took this message as promoting illegal drug use. She immediately ordered the banner removed and subsequently suspended one student who refused to comply. When the student's suit for infringement of his freedom of speech reached the Supreme Court, the Court acknowledged its long-standing principle that "students do not 'shed their constitutional rights to freedom of speech or expression at the schoolhouse gate.'"[46] Nonetheless, a five-Justice majority accepted as reasonable an interpretation of the banner not simply as "offensive" but as encouraging illegal drug use and therefore upheld the school's right to discipline the student. Justices Anthony Kennedy and Samuel Alito joined the majority on the explicit understanding that it did not encompass a school's broader right to censure political or social commentary.[47] All dissenters were concerned about the implications of the majority's opinion for restraining students' speech. Only Justice Thomas rejected the Court's underlying premise that public school students enjoy freedom of speech under the First Amendment.[48] No other Justice—not even Justice Antonin Scalia who broadly supports originalism as an interpretative tool—thought it necessary even to address Justice Thomas' extraordinary conclusion that, "[a]s originally understood, the Constitution does not afford students a right to free speech in

---

also inexplicably opined that the "Clause *probably* prohibits Congress from establishing a national religion." *Id.* at 1835 (emphasis added).

44 *Elk Grove*, 542 U.S. at 52–54; *see also Town of Greece*, 134 S. Ct. at 1837 (Thomas, Scalia, JJ., concurring in part and in the judgment); Lee v. Weisman, 505 U.S. 577, 641 (1991) (Scalia, J., dissenting).

45 Van Orden v. Perry, 545 U.S. 677, 694 (2005) (Thomas, J., concurring). A majority of the Court, however, is not likely to conclude "that incorporation of the Establishment Clause under the Fourteenth Amendment was erroneous." *Lee*, 505 U.S. at 623 n.5 (Souter, J., concurring).

46 Morse v. Frederick, 551 U.S. 393, 396 (2007) (quoting Tinker v. Des Moines Indep. Cmty. Sch. Dist., 393 U.S. 503, 506 (1969)).

47 *Morse*, 551 U.S. at 422 (Alito, Kennedy, JJ., concurring).

48 *Id.* at 411 (Thomas, J., concurring).

public schools."[49] There is no more reason to take account of Justice Thomas' extreme Establishment Clause originalism than there is to be concerned about his radical view of the limits of free speech protected by the First Amendment.[50]

Justice Scalia, formerly a self-described "faint-hearted" originalist,[51] stops short of fully embracing the limited federalism interpretation of the Establishment Clause, but with little different consequence. He

> ... would prefer to reach the same result by adopting an Establishment Clause jurisprudence that is in accord with our Nation's past and present practices, and that can be consistently applied—the central relevant feature of which is that there is nothing unconstitutional in a State's favoring religion generally, honoring God through public prayer and acknowledgment, or, in a nonproselytizing manner, venerating the Ten Commandments.[52]

With regard at least to "public acknowledgment of religious belief," Justice Scalia's Establishment Clause however embraces only mainstream monotheism, as the Clause allows "disregard of polytheists and believers in unconcerned deities, just as it permits the disregard of devout atheists."[53] Nonetheless, Justice Scalia

---

49 *Id.* at 418–19. Similarly, when California restricted the sale or rental of violent video games to minors the Court cited another of its well established principles: "[M]inors are entitled to a significant measure of First Amendment protection." Brown v. Entm't Merchs. Ass'n, 131 S. Ct. 2729, 2735 (2011) (quoting Erznoznik v. City of Jacksonville, 422 U.S. 205, 212–23 (1975)). Only Justice Thomas ignored the Court's premise in favor of his peculiar version of originalism: "'the freedom of speech,' as originally understood, does not include a right to speak to minors (or a right of minors to access speech) without going through the minors' parents or guardians." *Entm't Merchs. Ass'n*, 131 S. Ct. at 2751 (Thomas, J., dissenting). Writing for the majority striking down the California law, Justice Scalia dismissively noted that there was absolutely no judicial precedent for this position and that, if taken seriously, Justice Thomas' approach also would interfere with the religious liberty of youths and those who wish to proselytize them. *Id.* at 2736 n.3 (majority opinion).

50 Thirty years ago even a conservative majority acknowledged that "[i]t is far too late in the day to impose a crabbed reading of the [Establishment] Clause on the country." *Lynch*, 465 U.S. at 687.

51 Antonin Scalia, *Originalism: The Lesser Evil*, 57 U. Cin. L. Rev. 849, 864 (1989); *cf.* Randy E. Barnett, *Scalia's Infidelity: A Critique of "Faint-Hearted" Originalism*, 75 U. Cin. L. Rev. 7 (2006). Justice Scalia has since recanted the qualification in his self-description. Marsha Coyle, The Roberts Court 165 (Simon & Schuster 2013).

52 *Van Orden*, 545 U.S. at 692 (Scalia, J., concurring).

53 *McCreary*, 545 U.S. at 893 (2005) (Scalia, J., dissenting). The majority disavowed this "remarkable view." *Id.* at 879–81 (majority opinion). Indeed, when Thomas Jefferson composed the 1779 draft of his Bill for Establishing Religious Freedom, drawing on "principles ... which had, to a certain degree, been enacted before," he "had drawn [it] in all the latitude of reason and right." Thomas Jefferson, *Autobiography* (1821), *reprinted in* 5 The Founders' Constitution, *supra* note 16, at 85. He therefore opposed changing the language of the Bill's preamble that, as drafted, referred to "the holy author of our religion"

also may accept that the original nonestablishment principle precluded, as a form of legal coercion, government taxation to provide financial support for religion.[54]

Thus Justices Thomas and Scalia are the strongest proponents on the Court of an accommodationist position whereby little government action in acknowledgement or aid of religion will be found to violate the Establishment Clause. But now that Justice Alito has replaced Justice Sandra Day O'Connor, he and Chief Justice John G. Roberts, Jr., and Justice Kennedy complete a majority of

---

to read instead, "Jesus Christ, the holy author of our religion." *See* Thomas Jefferson, *A Bill for Establishing Religious Freedom* (1779), and *Virginia, Act for Establishing Religious Freedom* (1785), each *reprinted in* 5 The Founders' Constitution, *supra* note 16, at 77, 84–85. Jefferson noted that this change to the Bill "was rejected by a great majority, in proof that they meant to comprehend, within the mantel of its protection, the Jew and the Gentile, the Christian and Mahometan, the Hindoo, and Infidel of every denomination." Jefferson, *Autobiography*, *supra*, at 85; *see also* Madison, *Detached Memoranda*, *supra* note 19, at 103.

54 *See Lee*, 505 U.S. at 641 (Scalia, J., dissenting). In his jurisprudence involving the Religion Clauses, Justice Scalia may fall into the error he has acknowledged as "the hardest part of being a conscientious judge," namely that "judges will mistake their own predilections for the law." Scalia, *supra*, note 51, at 863. *See generally* Bruce Allen Murphy, Scalia (Simon & Schuster 2014). *Salazar v. Buono*, 130 S. Ct. 1803 (2010), involved a challenge to a Latin cross erected on federal land as a memorial to soldiers slain in World War I and Congress' attempt to circumvent the constitutional difficulties by transferring title to the small parcel of land containing the cross to a private entity. During oral argument, in a colloquy with plaintiff's counsel, Justice Scalia tried to suggest that the cross was erected as a war memorial and so honored *all* the war dead. Counsel responded that the cross is the "predominant symbol of Christianity … the most common symbol to honor Christians" and is never found in a Jewish cemetery. Justice Scalia took umbrage at this, terming it an "outrageous conclusion" that the cross honors only the Christian war dead. *Salazar*, Transcript of Oral Argument, 2009 U.S. Trans. LEXIS 46, at *36 (Oct. 7, 2009). *Compare Salazar*, 130 S. Ct. at 1820 (plurality opinion) ("a Latin cross is not merely a reaffirmation of Christian beliefs"), *with id.* at 1822 (Alito, J., concurring in part and in the judgment) ("[t]he cross is of course the preeminent symbol of Christianity"), *and id.* at 1836 n.8 (Stevens, J., dissenting) ("The cross is not a universal symbol of sacrifice. It is the symbol of one particular sacrifice, and that sacrifice carries deeply significant meaning for those who adhere to the Christian faith."); *see also* Trunk v. San Diego, 629 F.3d 1099, 1113 (9th Cir. 2011), *cert. denied*, 132 S. Ct. 2535 (2012) ("The cross … has never been used to honor all American soldiers in any military cemetery, and it has never been used as a default gravestone in any national cemetery in the United States."). On another occasion, Justice Scalia tried to attribute his universalist, Pollyannaish view of government promotion of religious exercise to the Founders who, he simply asserted, "knew that nothing, absolutely nothing, is so inclined to foster among religious believers of various faiths a toleration—no, an affection—for one another than voluntarily joining in prayer together, to the God whom they all worship and seek." *Lee*, 505 U.S. at 646 (Scalia, J., dissenting). Remarkably, he made this unsupported assertion in a case in which the majority upheld an Establishment Clause claim by a public middle-school student who objected to the inclusion of a prayer in her school's graduation ceremony.

five with a predilection toward that accommodationist position. And as discussed in Chapter 4, this position can be advanced either by rejecting an Establishment Clause claim directly through a substantive decision on the merits or, perhaps more elusively, by denying federal court standing to persons (particularly for our purposes, taxpayers *qua* taxpayers) objecting to government action, thereby according state actors greater freedom in religious matters.

Still, government accommodation of religion is tempered by the rich tradition in this country of separation between church and state that imputes a persistent and foundational individual rights dimension to the Establishment Clause. This extra-constitutional metaphor is often credited to Thomas Jefferson's 1802 letter to the Baptist Association of Danbury, Connecticut, but can be traced to a 1643 letter of Roger Williams.[55] Justice Hugo Black's majority opinion in *Everson* enshrined the concept in modern constitutional and popular thought,[56] though not without substantial criticism. In particular, Professor Philip Hamburger asserts that the notion of separation of church and state has been employed by many, including nativists and anti-Christian secularists, in support of anti-Catholic bias.[57] Some proponents of separation of church and state well may have been so motivated. But Professor T. Jeremy Gunn and other scholars have refuted Professor Hamburger's basic thesis: "Hamburger and those who challenge the deep American roots of separating church and state are fundamentally mistaken."[58]

---

55 *See* Thomas Jefferson, *Letter to Danbury Baptist Association* (Jan. 1, 1802), *reprinted in* 5 THE FOUNDERS' CONSTITUTION, *supra* note 16, at 96; MARK DEWOLFE HOWE, THE GARDEN AND THE WILDERNESS: RELIGION AND GOVERNMENT IN AMERICAN CONSTITUTIONAL HISTORY 5 (1965) (Williams' letter); *but see* David Little, *Roger Williams and the Puritan Background of the Establishment Clause*, *in* NO ESTABLISHMENT OF RELIGION, *supra* note 16, at 100, 112, 119 (challenging Howe's interpretation of Williams' image of a "wall of separation" and maintaining that "[f]or Williams, 'freedom of religion' and 'no establishment of religion' were concepts that were inextricably connected, and these concepts, which he shared with Madison, ultimately would become hallmarks of the U.S. Constitution."). Jefferson's wall of separation as manifested in his refusal to issue religious proclamations as president, but not earlier as governor of Virginia, likely reflected federalism principles. *See* Dreisbach, *supra* note 19, at 262; Daniel L. Dreisbach, *Mr. Jefferson, a Mammoth Cheese, and the "Wall of Separation Between Church and State": A Bicentennial Commemoration*, 43 J. CHURCH & ST. 725, 738–40 (2001); J. Clifford Wallace, *The Framers' Establishment Clause: How High the Wall*, 2001 BYU L. REV. 755, 768 (2001).

56 *Everson*, 330 U.S. at 15–18.

57 *See, e.g.*, PHILIP HAMBURGER, SEPARATION OF CHURCH AND STATE 2–10, 251, 359, 391, 497–83 (Harvard Univ. Press 2002).

58 Gunn, *supra* note 19, at 27. "The 'separation of church and state' was not a term used exclusively by Republicans as a code word against Catholics: it also was used by Democrats, and indeed by Catholics as well. In other words, it was used across the political spectrum as a broadly and widely accepted term that was, as stated by Professor Diman 'a fundamental maxim of our body politic.'" *Id.* at 32; *see also* Green, *The "Second Disestablishment," supra* note 19, at 293–301 (acknowledging that "an illiberal version of church-state separation emerged in the mid-century in conjunction with Protestant and Catholic clashes over parochial

More recently the Supreme Court has scaled back its references to *Everson*'s "high and impregnable" wall of separation, deeming the phrase a mere "figurative illustration," "a useful signpost," and a "reminder" of the Establishment Clause.[59] Still influential, the concept of separation of church and state perhaps is best thought of as what Professor Jack Balkin refers to as an "underlying principle" that "support[s] and illuminate[s] the [constitutional] text."[60] Despite, therefore, the strong and growing accommodationist tendencies among a number of the current Justices, Professor Balkin synthesizes principles of the First and Fourteenth Amendments and nicely summarizes the compelling argument for an energetic Establishment Clause jurisprudence:

> [D]oes the constitutional guarantee of nonestablishment create an individual right of citizens that could be applied to the states? Yes. The guarantee of nonestablishment has two elements: one concerns civil liberty, and the other civil equality. The establishment clause protects individual liberty because it prevents the federal government from coercing anyone to adhere to or participate in a favored religious belief or to contribute money toward the maintenance of a church or religion. The establishment clause also protects civil equality because it prohibits government from designating a preferred religion or a preferred set of religious beliefs, and therefore it prohibits government from making distinctions among citizens depending on whether they agree or disagree with the government's religious viewpoint. The establishment clause bans practices that convey the message that there is a favored group of citizens, or "real" Americans, who share the government's stated religious views and other citizens whose religious beliefs are merely tolerated. The idea that government may not create first- and second-class citizens when it comes to matters of religion is strongly connected to the Fourteenth Amendment's general purpose of securing equal citizenship. These principles of liberty and equality belong to all United States citizens, and states may not violate them.[61]

III. Establishment Clause Controversies: History, Custom, and Tradition

Establishment Clause issues, often in conjunction with Free Exercise claims, arise in a variety of contexts including tax benefits or other accommodations for religious institutions and individuals, religious displays on public property, Sunday closing

---

school funding," *id.* at 298, but stating that "it is still inaccurate to associate it chiefly with Protestant efforts to subjugate Catholic interests." *Id.* at 295).

59 *Everson*, 330 U.S. at 18; Larkin v. Grendel's Den, Inc., 459 U.S. 116, 123 (1982); *Lynch*, 465 U.S. at 673.

60 Jack M. Balkin, Living Originalism 203–04 (Belknap Harvard 2011).

61 *Id.* at 204–05 (citations omitted).

laws, equal access to public facilities and resources, and government involvement in house of worship internal matters. In particular with respect to K–12 education, prayer or other religious exercises in public schools, and which subjects can or cannot be taught (and from what perspectives), raise high-profile controversies. And with declining confidence in the quality of public education and the concomitant rise in alternative education, much of which is religiously affiliated, government aid in one form or another to religious education, the specific subject of this book, has become increasingly prevalent and controversial. When faced with claims in this context, and given the indeterminacies of the bare constitutional text, courts often resort to examinations of history, custom, and tradition for rough analogues to extrapolate support or opposition for the particular issues at hand. As these controversies tend to recur, before analyzing our specific subject of government financial or other aid for parochial schooling it is instructive to survey the litany of more general arguments and counter-arguments.[62]

A. General Arguments and Counter-Arguments

Prior to ratification of the Constitution, religion played a more significant role in the proceedings and official acts of the Continental Congress and then, to a lesser degree, the Confederation Congress. Especially while the difficult war with Britain was raging, it is not surprising that the emerging country's leaders, and the populace generally, looked to religion for solace and guidance. Official congressional invocations of God's grace, assembled legislative prayer, appointment of legislative and military chaplains, and proclamation of national days of fasting (up to 1784) and thanksgiving were all common.[63] Three-quarters of the delegates to the Constitutional Convention of 1787 had served in at least one of the previous Congresses. But in the words of Thomas Paine, with independence from England, "[w]e have it in our power to begin the world over again,"[64] and separationist ideas were emerging.

Beginning anew—a *novus ordo seclorum*—the Constitution proclaims that there shall be no religious test to hold an office of the United States.[65] Beyond this, however,

62 Supreme Court opinions prominently discuss and debate these matters. *See, e.g.*, *Lee*, 505 U.S. at 577 (school graduation prayer); *Wallace*, 472 U.S. at 91–108 (Rehnquist, J., dissenting) (school moment of silence); Engel v. Vitale, 370 U.S. 421, 446–50 (1962) (Stewart, J., dissenting) (school classroom prayer); *Lynch*, 465 U.S. at 668 (city Christmas display including crèche); Marsh v. Chambers, 463 U.S. 783, 784–92 (1983) (legislative prayer).

63 *See generally* Derek H. Davis, *The Continental Congress and Emerging Ideas of Church-State Separation, in* No Establishment of Religion, *supra* note 16, at 180, 180–207; David E. Steinberg, *The Myth of Church-State Separation*, 59 Clev. St. L. Rev. 623, 625–30 (2011).

64 Thomas Paine, Common Sense 57 (Peter Eckler Publishing Co. 1914).

65 *See* Dreisbach, *supra* note 19, at 254–57; Adams & Emmerich, *supra* note 37, at 1575.

and unlike other founding era documents including the Declaration of Independence and the Articles of Confederation, the Constitution strikingly omits any reference to God or divine provenance.[66] The president's oath of office, for example, need not be taken on a bible, although George Washington initiated the tradition, which subsequent presidents followed almost uniformly. President Washington also included a prayer in his first inaugural address as did both Presidents Jefferson and Madison, and this tradition also persists to modern times.[67] But, while imbued with the official aura of the auspicious occasion, these are individual decisions reflecting individual choice and discretion of the president or president-elect.[68]

The fast days proclaimed by the Continental Congress ended with the war, but President Washington, with Congress' approval, initiated Thanksgiving Proclamations with distinctly religious themes. As the first Congress was approving the final wording of the First Amendment, at least one member objected to the religious nature of the custom.[69] Most, but not all, presidents have issued thanksgiving or prayer proclamations.[70] President Jefferson and later President Andrew Jackson thought the Constitution precluded these customs, at least at the national level.[71] President Madison was of like mind, although as a wartime president he acquiesced in the practice at the urging of a joint congressional resolution.[72] Moreover, he later noted that he always took care to make his proclamations "absolutely indiscriminate, and merely recommendatory."[73]

---

66 On the conspicuous omission of any reference to God in the U.S. Constitution, *see* Akhil Reed Amar, America's Unwritten Constitution 70–79 (Basic Books 2012).

67 *See Lee*, 505 U.S. at 631 (Scalia, J., dissenting); *Engel*, 370 U.S. at 444 (Stewart, J., dissenting).

68 *See* Newdow v. Roberts, 603 F.3d 1002, 1006–13 (D.C. Cir. 2010) (dismissing constitutional challenge to certain religious aspects of presidential inauguration); *Van Orden*, 545 U.S. at 706–35 (Stevens, J., dissenting).

69 Davis, *supra* note 63, at 189–90. *See also* Akhil Reed Amar, *Some Notes on the Establishment Clause*, 2 Roger Williams U. L. Rev. 1, 5 (1996).

70 Davis, *supra* note 63, at 189–90.

71 *Id.*; Thomas Jefferson, *Letter to Rev. Samuel Miller*, *reprinted in* 5 The Founders' Constitution, *supra* note 16, at 98–99; *see also* Ian Bartrum, *Constitutional Canon as Argumentative Metonymy*, 18 Wm. & Mary Bill Rts. J. 327, 331–32 (2009); Dreisbach, *supra* note 19, at 259–64 (describing Jefferson's alleged atheism as a "critical issue" in the highly contested 1800 presidential campaign, with public opposition to presidential religious proclamations helping to defeat John Adams).

72 Davis, *supra* note 63, at 190; James Madison, *Proclamation* (Nov. 16, 1814), *reprinted in* 5 The Founders' Constitution, *supra* note 16, at 102–03. A modern Establishment Clause challenge to a congressional statute calling for a presidential proclamation for a national day of prayer was dismissed for plaintiffs' lack of standing. Freedom from Religion Foundation, Inc. v. Obama, 641 F.3d 803, 808 (7th Cir. 2011).

73 James Madison, *Letter to Edward Livingston* (1822), *reprinted in* 5 The Founders' Constitution, *supra* note 16, at 105 (concluding with his "lesson" that "Religion flourishes in greater purity, without than with the aid of Gov't."). *See also* Madison, *Detached Memoranda*, *supra* note 19, at 103.

As one of its first acts, the Continental Congress also began the practice of opening its daily sessions with prayer, although not without debate over the propriety of doing so among a group with diverse religious beliefs. For a time, Sunday church services of various Christian denominations were held in the hall of the House of Representatives (and in other government buildings), and even Jefferson began attending services at the House immediately after he wrote his Danbury letter, perhaps as a "master of using the symbolic act" to counterbalance his perceived anti-religious sentiments.[74] The tradition of legislative prayer continues in Congress under the Constitution, as does the practice of appointing and paying out of the public fisc legislative chaplains as well as chaplains for members of the armed forces.[75] Again, this was over the objection of Madison and others: "[I]t was not with my approbation, that the deviation from [non-establishment] took place in Congs., when they appointed Chaplains, to be paid from the Nat'l Treasury."[76] As for military chaplains, although similarly problematic there is more reason for government to provide for the religious needs of service men and women who, by reason of their military service, might both be in particular need of spiritual succor and otherwise precluded from obtaining it for themselves. Failing to fill this need under these circumstances well might be considered interference with the free exercise of religion.[77] As Madison later reflected, rather than look to such minor deviations from strict nonestablishment as legal precedents, "better to apply … the legal maxim 'de minimis non curat lex.'"[78]

The matter of the Northwest Ordinance, first adopted by the Confederation Congress in 1787 to provide for governance of the federal territories northwest of the Ohio River, is perhaps somewhat more significant and relevant to our topic. Article 1 of the Ordinance protected religious conscience, but Article 3 provided

---

74 James H. Hutson, Religion and the Founding of the American Republic 84–93 (Library of Congress 1998).

75 Davis, *supra* note 63, at 188, 197–98. As is often noted, the Supreme Court's own sessions long have opened with the invocation "God save the United States and this Honorable Court." *Lee*, 505 U.S. at 635 (Scalia, J., dissenting).

76 Madison, *Letter to Edward Livingston, supra* note 73, at 105. In his *Detached Memoranda, supra* note 19, at 104, Madison made clear that he thought this practice amounted to an establishment of religion in violation of the Constitution.

77 Madison appreciated that his concerns about government provision of military chaplains might be lessened in the "case of navies with insulated crews." *Id.*

78 *Id.*; Davis, *supra* note 63, at 191 (noting that chaplaincies and prayer proclamations were traditions from the Continental Congress inherited by the First Congress, and concluding that: "[V]ery little attention seems to have been given to the relationship of these practices to the First Amendment. Thus, one must be careful not to read too much into the framers' purposes by an overemphasis on the early chaplaincy and prayer practices of Congress."). One can imagine that Madison likely would take the same pragmatic approach to later sentimental manifestations such as adoption of the national motto "In God We Trust" and its use on U.S. coins. *See also Engel*, 370 U.S. at 440 n.5 (Douglas, J., concurring in opinion ruling schoolroom prayer unconstitutional).

in relevant part: "'Religion, Morality, and knowledge being necessary to good government and the happiness of mankind, Schools and the means of education shall forever be encouraged.'"[79] Simultaneously with consideration of early drafts of what became the First Amendment, the First Congress reenacted the Ordinance. Both Justices Rehnquist and Thomas have relied on what they view as the Ordinance's support for religion, enacted by the same representatives (though before they approved and were bound by the First Amendment), for a narrow construction of the Establishment Clause that does not restrict even-handed government aid for religion.[80] Yet Professor Akhil Amar notes that Congress' simultaneous action is consistent with an original federalism-based reading of the Establishment Clause under which it could not interfere with state establishments but still had plenary legislative authority over federal territories pursuant to Article IV of the Constitution. This reading then "faded from view, replaced by a substantive anti-establishment interpretation."[81]

Even more to the point, Professor Carl Esbeck points out that the final version of Article 3 was the product of an amendment that "eliminated any suggestion that the new territorial governments should offer direct financial support for religion." Thus, "[a]lthough 'religion' was acknowledged as one of the necessary prerequisites to good government, the objects that affirmatively were to 'be encouraged' by government had been pared down to 'schools and the means of education.' That left the encouragement of 'religion' and 'morality' to the private sector." Professor Esbeck therefore concludes that "the evolution of Article 3 demonstrates an early example in the attitude of American continental government turning away from financial support for religion. The final Article 3 dropped the authority to provide affirmative financial support for religion thereby embracing voluntary private support."[82]

There also is a striking First Amendment parallel to these early congressional and presidential actions that urges additional caution in attributing much weight to them in interpreting the Establishment Clause as allowing broad government support for religion even on a non-preferentialist basis. In the politically contentious atmosphere of the late 1790s the Federalist party of President John Adams controlled Congress as well. But Vice President Jefferson and his "French Party" Republicans

79 As quoted in Carl H. Esbeck, *Religion During the American Revolution and the Early Republic*, *in* Law & Religion (Silvio Ferrari, ed., Ashgate 2013) (manuscript at 18, *available at* http://ssrn.com/abstract=2154443).

80 *Rosenberger*, 515 U.S. at 862–63 (Thomas, J., concurring); *Wallace*, 472 U.S. at 100 (Rehnquist, J., dissenting).

81 Amar, The Bill of Rights, *supra* note 17, at 249. Until 1845, some schools receiving land grants pursuant to the Ordinance may have been sectarian, after which time Congress limited the grants to nonsectarian schools. *Wallace*, 472 U.S. at 100 (Rehnquist, J., dissenting).

82 Esbeck, *Religion During the American Revolution and the Early Republic*, *supra* note 79, at manuscript 18.

were gaining strength anticipating the election of 1800. In the summer of 1798 the Federalists pushed through their highly partisan Sedition Act that made criminal any "false, scandalous and malicious" criticism with intent to defame Congress or the President, but notably omitted protecting the Vice President. The Federalists acted in defiance of strenuous arguments that the Act was unconstitutional as both beyond the power of Congress and specifically in violation of the speech and press clauses of the First Amendment.[83] Madison and Jefferson both campaigned anonymously against the Act, arousing opposition to it among the states. In particular, they debunked the Federalist argument that the freedom of press protected by the First Amendment was nothing more than freedom from prior restraint as set forth in Blackstone's *Commentaries on the Laws of England.*[84]

The Sedition Act was not inconsequential; a number of prominent individuals were prosecuted and convicted at trials presided over by individual Supreme Court Justices riding circuit.[85] The Court itself, however, never passed on the constitutionality of the Act, which expired on its own terms when Jefferson became president. President Jefferson then pardoned all those convicted, explaining to Abigail Adams that he considered "that law to be a nullity."[86] Later, in 1840, removed from the political controversy of the earlier day, Congress reimbursed some fines that had been paid, stating that the Act was "unconstitutional, null, void."[87] And, ultimately in 1964, Justice Brennan repudiated the Sedition Act in his landmark opinion for the Court in *New York Times Company v. Sullivan*, which held that alleged libel of government officials could not claim "talismanic immunity" from protection under the First Amendment.[88]

83 The story of the history and politics of the Sedition Act is colorfully recounted in Anthony Lewis, Make No Law: The Sullivan Case and the First Amendment (First Vintage Books 1991).

84 *See* James Madison, *Virginia Resolutions* (Dec. 21, 1798), *reprinted in* 5 The Founders' Constitution, *supra* note 16, at 135–36 (protesting against the "palpable and alarming infractions of the Constitution … leveled against … free communication among the people …"); James Madison, *Report on the Virginia Resolutions* (1800), *reprinted in* 5 The Founders' Constitution, *supra* note 16, at 141–47; *Kentucky Resolutions* (1798–99), *reprinted in* 5 The Founders' Constitution, *supra* note 16, at 131–35. *See supra* note 5 (noting that the Supreme Court firmly rejected the Blackstone approach in *Near*, 283 U.S. at 713–15).

85 *See* Amar, America's Unwritten Constitution, *supra* note 66, at 154 & n.19 (collecting cases). *See, e.g.*, Case of Fries, 9 Fed. Cas. 826, 829 (C.C.D.Pa. 1799), *reprinted in* 5 The Founders' Constitution, *supra* note 16, at 140–41.

86 Lewis, *supra* note 83, at 65 (quoting Jefferson's letter to Mrs. Adams in 1804).

87 Amar, America's Unwritten Constitution, *supra* note 66, at 169 (quoting House committee report).

88 New York Times Co. v. Sullivan, 376 U.S. 254, 269, 276 (1964) (denouncing the Sedition Act as condemned in the "court of history").

So how did Congress in 1798, less than 10 years after approving the First Amendment, go so far astray in enacting the Sedition Act?[89] This rhetorical question makes a considerable cautionary tale for imputing too much of current consequence to other, analogous early lapses in official and semi-official actions arguably at odds with the import of the Establishment Clause. Madison was wise enough to appreciate the limited effect that enumeration of a bill of rights might have in the face of shifting and impassioned public sentiment. In explaining to Jefferson his somewhat ambiguous attitude toward adding a bill of rights to the Constitution, Madison noted that "overbearing majorities in every state" have wrought "[r]epeated violations of these parchment barriers," proving "the inefficacy of a bill of rights on those occasions when its control is most needed." In particular, Madison was "sure that the rights of Conscience" would be narrowed "if submitted to public definition." But, Madison concluded, a bill of rights might be useful because "political truths declared in that solemn manner acquire by degrees the character of fundamental maxims of free government, and as they become incorporated with the National sentiment, counteract the impulses of interest and passion."[90]

But this is an imperfect process. It is an "obvious fact that leaders who have drafted and voted for a text are eminently capable of violating their own rules."[91] The Framers undoubtedly were men of great principle but also were politicians who "could raise constitutional ideals one day and turn their backs on them the next."[92] Justice Brennan made the point somewhat more charitably:

> Legislators, influenced by the passions and exigencies of the moment, the pressure of constituents and colleagues, and the press of business, do not always pass sober constitutional judgment on every piece of legislation they enact, and this must be assumed to be as true of the Members of the First Congress as any other.[93]

---

89 One might note that, "[o]f the ninety-five senators and representatives who served in the First Congress, only eighteen remained when the Sedition Act was enacted in July 1798, and of those only ten voted 'aye.'" David A. Anderson, *The Origins of the Press Clause*, 30 UCLA L. Rev. 455, 517 (1983). Still, one would think members of the founding generation would not so ignore the guarantee Madison termed "the only effectual guardian of every other right" that had just been enshrined in the First Amendment. Madison, *Report on the Virginia Resolutions*, *supra* note 84, at 146.

90 James Madison, *Letter to Thomas Jefferson* (Oct. 17, 1788), *in* James Madison, Writings 418, 420, 421–22 (Jack N. Rakove, ed., The Library of America 1999).

91 *Van Orden*, 545 U.S. at 706 (Stevens, J., dissenting).

92 *Lee*, 505 U.S. at 626 (Souter, J., concurring).

93 *Marsh*, 463 U.S. at 814–15 (Brennan, J., dissenting). In 1954, during the second red scare and the cold war with "godless communism," Congress added the words "under God" to the Pledge of Allegiance. The religious motivation for this was fairly palpable, raising substantial constitutional issues, especially when the Pledge became part of a state-mandated and teacher-led daily recitation in public schools. The proposed addition was uniformly praised in the House, and this apparently overcame any initial hesitation in the Senate over Establishment Clause issues. Both Houses then passed the bill by unanimous voice vote. *See*

In short, sometimes even Homer nods.[94] And this phenomenon is hardly unique to the founding era. Rather, "public officials, no matter when they serve, can turn a blind eye to constitutional principle,"[95] even with regard to First Amendment freedoms.

B. The Specific Case of the Virginia Tax Assessment

Beyond various isolated episodes, for present purposes it certainly is best to focus the historical and constitutional inquiry on the types of governmental practices at issue and therefore most relevant. With regard to tax assessments and public funding for the support of religious institutions, including schools, perhaps the best and most pertinent historical evidence is the well-known controversy sparked by Patrick Henry's proposed *Virginia Tax Assessment*. Madison's and Jefferson's successful opposition to this measure provides what arguably should be canonical principles for interpreting and applying the Establishment Clause in this context. Indeed, Justice Wiley B. Rutledge invoked the Virginia history in his dissent for himself and three other Justices in *Everson*. Yet, the Court's current jurisprudence is striking in its departure from this paradigm.

Henry's 1784 proposal to the Virginia General Assembly, entitled *A Bill Establishing a Provision for Teachers of the Christian Religion*, likely was designed to support Henry's preferred Protestant Episcopal Church, but was written more generally in support of various Christian denominations.[96] It imposed a property surtax, but a taxpayer could designate the "society of Christians" to which his levy would be paid; the recipients were to use the funds for a "Minister or Teacher of the Gospel" or to provide for places of worship.[97] In the absence of such taxpayer designation, the taxes collected would be used "for the encouragement of seminaries of learning," and these seminaries apparently could have included nonsectarian schools.[98] Thus Henry's *Bill* had all the elements of many modern

---

Newdow v. Rio Linda Union Sch. Dist., 597 F.3d 1007, 1056 (9th Cir. 2010) (Reinhard, J., dissenting). Which member of Congress would have dared vote against it? As Justice Brennan further observed: "Legislators, by virtue of their instinct for political survival, are often loath to assert in public religious views that their constituents might perceive as hostile or non-conforming." *Marsh*, 463 U.S. at 798 n.5 (Brennan, J., dissenting).

94 *Lee*, 505 U.S. at 624 n.5 (Souter, J., concurring). One prominent scholar nicely makes the point: "Our task is not to perpetuate the Framers' blind spots, but to implement their vision." Laycock, *supra* note 37, at 923.

95 *Lee*, 505 U.S. at 616 n.3.

96 *See* Donald O. Dewey, *Virginia Statute for Religious Freedom*, *in* James Madison and the American Nation, 1751–1836, An Encyclopedia 428–29 (Simon & Schuster 1994). The text of the Bill is attached as a Supplemental Appendix to Justice Rutledge's dissenting opinion in *Everson*, 330 U.S. at 72–74.

97 Mennonites and Quakers could use their funds to best promote "their particular mode of worship." *Id.* at 74.

98 *Id. See Rosenberger*, 515 U.S. at 869 n.1 (Souter, J., dissenting); *Winn*, 131 S. Ct. at 1461 nn.11–12 (Kagan, J., dissenting).

schemes for funding parochial schools. It proposed not a direct legislative grant from general taxpayer funds to such schools but a special tax mechanism that relied on the individual, private choices of taxpayers to direct money to a religious school. And, although the great majority of tax funds so raised might in fact have gone to (Christian) sectarian schools, the opt-out provision allowed an objecting taxpayer to avoid use of his money to support religious education.[99]

Henry's proposed assessment provoked immediate opposition,[100] including Madison's famous, though at the time anonymous, encomium to religious liberty, his *Memorial and Remonstrance Against Religious Assessments*.[101] In 15 numbered paragraphs Madison advanced compelling reasons why the tax assessment was an affront to religious freedom and violated the liberty of conscience. "Who does not see that … the same authority which can force a citizen to contribute three pence only of his property for the support of any one establishment, may force him to contribute to any other establishment in all cases whatsoever?" Madison's language throughout the *Memorial and Remonstrance* demonstrates his view that even a small tax in support of religion favors an establishment of religion and lends weight to such a prohibition being implicit in the Establishment Clause.[102] And as a basic tenet of equality, Madison specifically supported a person's right to believe in no religion at all.

Madison's arguments expanded on Jefferson's earlier drafted *Virginia Bill for Establishing Religious Freedom*, which pronounced that "to compel a man to furnish contributions of money for the propagation of opinions which he disbelieves and abhors, is sinful and tyrannical." While Jefferson here used the more general word "opinions," he clearly was talking about religious beliefs, which, after all, is the subject of his proposed *Bill*. Jefferson's next sentence makes this clear: "That even the forcing him to support this or that teacher of his own religious persuasion" improperly compromises one's religious liberty.[103]

99 The only difference is that Henry's *Bill* provided that a public accounting be made of all assessments collected, including each taxpayer's name and his designated recipient.

100 *See* Adams & Emmerich, *supra* note 37, at 1573 ("The public … responded [to Henry's Assessment Bill] with a flood of critical petitions and memorials."); Dreisbach, *supra* note 19, at 253 ("The use of general assessments, which taxed all residents for the support of religion, was an especially contentious policy."). Professor Steven K. Green notes that in the late 1700s "[t]he emerging consensus was that tax assessments for churches and 'public worship' were inconsistent with rights of conscience and beyond the authority of government." Green, *The "Second Disestablishment," supra* note 19, at 281. But the application of this no-funding principle to religious education is perhaps more uncertain. *Compare id.* at 296 *with* Berg, *supra* note 26, at 317.

101 James Madison, *Memorial and Remonstrance Against Religious Assessments* (June 20, 1785), *reprinted in* 5 The Founders' Constitution, *supra* note 16, at 82.

102 Ralph Ketcham, *James Madison, Thomas Jefferson, and the Meaning of "Establishment of Religion" in Eighteenth-Century Virginia, in* No Establishment of Religion, *supra* note 16, at 158, 170.

103 Jefferson, *A Bill for Establishing Religious Freedom, supra* note 53, at 77.

Once Patrick Henry was elected governor and therefore no longer a member of the Virginia legislature, Madison was able to substitute Jefferson's *Bill* for Henry's, and the legislature enacted the essence of Jefferson's proposal, declaring "the rights hereby asserted are of the natural rights of mankind."[104]

The vigorous and ultimately successful opposition to Henry's proposed assessment provides an explicit and powerful argument that public financing of religious schools is not consistent with the later prohibitions of the Establishment Clause. In *Everson*, despite the outcome, the Court acknowledged that it "has previously recognized that the provisions of the First Amendment, in the drafting and adoption of which Madison and Jefferson played such leading roles, had the same objective and were intended to provide the same protection against governmental intrusion on religious liberty as the Virginia statute."[105] The majority of the Court in *Committee for Public Education & Religious Liberty v. Nyquist* termed the Virginia experience "one of the greatest chapters in the history of this country's adoption of the essentially revolutionary notion of separation between Church and State."[106] The four dissenting Justices in *Rosenberger v. Rector & Visitors of the University of Virginia* reiterated this historical reliance and cited support for this proposition by several prominent scholars.[107] In short, the renowned defeat of Henry's proposed *Virginia Tax Assessment* is a principal, edifying episode within the "'historical practices and understanding'" that the Court heavily relies upon in interpreting the Establishment Clause.[108]

The Madisonian and Jeffersonian position is also reflected in developments in the states. Professor Steven K. Green notes that between 1776 and 1830 most state constitutions outside New England precluded tax assessments generally for the support of religious institutions. More specifically, "the idea that public funding of religious schooling violated church-state separation went back to at least the 1820s," and the Michigan Constitution of 1835 included the "first express constitutional provision prohibiting the public funding of religious institutions, including parochial schools, in any state constitution." Michigan's anti-funding provision then served as a model for anti-funding provisions in several other new state constitutions.[109]

---

104 *Virginia, Act for Establishing Religious Freedom*, *supra* note 53, at 84–85.

105 *Everson*, 330 U.S. at 13. The Court was unanimous on the significance of the Virginia assessment controversy, as the four dissenters agreed that "[a]ll the great instruments of the Virginia struggle for religious liberty thus became warp and woof of our constitutional tradition...." *Id.* at 39 (Rutledge, Frankfurter, Jackson, Burton, JJ., dissenting).

106 413 U.S. 756, 770 n.28 (1973).

107 *Rosenberger*, 515 U.S. at 871–72 (Souter, Stevens, Ginsburg, Breyer, JJ., dissenting).

108 *Town of Greece*, 134 S. Ct. at 1819 (citation omitted). *See supra* note 37.

109 Steven K. Green, *The Insignificance of the Blaine Amendment*, 2008 BYU L. Rev. 295, 313 (2008); Green, *The "Second Disestablishment," supra* note 19, at 287–88, 299. Professor Green, however, notes that "[d]ivining a common understanding of these

Thus, just as we celebrate Madison's and Jefferson's interpretation of the free speech and press clauses in their fight against the Sedition Act, and in particular their refutation of the crabbed Blackstonian approach to freedom of expression, we also should credit their prevailing opposition to tax support for religious education as later reflected in the Establishment Clause. One historian makes the point this way:

> Americans sometimes focus undue attention on the radical libertarianism of Virginia in order to argue that the conceptions of religious freedom proposed by Jefferson and Madison are anomalistic. Yet, the same separation between church and state that Virginia sponsored in 1786 took place everywhere else by 1833, albeit without most of the language used in Virginia challenging religious belief.[110]

C. The Unique Context of Children and Schools

The issue of public financing of private, parochial schools, ultimately through some form of taxation, therefore has its own highly skeptical history and enhanced importance as a central feature of separation of church and state under the Establishment Clause. This alone should render state aid to religious education highly suspect. The constitutional restraint then should be heightened by the very special situation of children within primary and secondary schools, as context often is critical for First Amendment issues. Children generally must be treated with particular sensitivity under the First Amendment. In particular, the Supreme Court has long recognized that First Amendment rights must be analyzed "in light of the special characteristics of the school environment."[111] The contextual specialness of schools and children combined thus makes religious establishment issues in K–12 education, especially increasingly pervasive government funding, of virtually *sui generis* significance, justifying exacting judicial scrutiny and legislative discretion. Certainly, the primary and secondary school setting is at least as sensitive with regard to matters of religion as it is with respect to freedom of speech.

Even when children are not impacted directly, context generally is critical with regard to many First Amendment speech issues, and there is nothing unusual about

---

early constitutional provisions is all but impossible" as "the meaning of disestablishment to Americans from 1776 to 1865 was varied and evolving." *Id.* at 289. For further discussion of state anti-funding provisions and the Blaine Amendment, *see* Chapter 1, Section IV.

110 McGarvie, *supra* note 17, at 94. Other scholars also argue for giving great consideration and weight to the nonestablishment views of Jefferson and Madison. *See, e.g.*, Kent Greenawalt, *Some Reflections on Fundamental Questions about the Original Understanding of the Establishment Clause*, *in* No Establishment of Religion, *supra* note 16, at 341, 344–48; Jonathan K. Van Patten, *In the End Is the Beginning: An Inquiry into the Meaning of the Religion Clauses*, 27 St. Louis U. L.J. 1, 34 (1983).

111 *Tinker*, 393 U.S. at 506 (commenting in the context of students' free speech rights).

this. Professor Robert Post offers a classic example. A men's urinal normally is just a men's urinal, which no one would consider imbued with First Amendment protection from government control. But if incorporated into a museum's art exhibit, it may well become a medium for the communication of ideas and thereby warrant protection.[112] A person who burns an American flag also may enjoy constitutional protection if his action is part of a political protest. And what may be said with immunity inside a courtroom as part of a judicial proceeding may entail liability if repeated to the public outside on the courthouse steps.

As for children, the Supreme Court always has shown special concern for possible adverse effects from some expressive material to which children may be exposed. Early in its struggle to define material that is "obscene" and therefore not covered by the First Amendment, the Court established a broader classification of "variable obscenity," sexually explicit material that is not obscene for adults but may be restricted because it is nonetheless harmful to minors. Although an inherently ambiguous category, the idea that children are more vulnerable and therefore must be more protected than adults from the content of certain speech remains viable.[113] Indeed, the Federal Communications Commission's somewhat anachronistic campaign against "indecency" in broadcasting is premised on shielding children, or at least on assisting parents in controlling the material to which their children are exposed.[114] On the other hand, "'minors are entitled to a significant measure of First Amendment protection,'" and a legislature cannot protect them from any ideas and images it simply deems unsuitable.[115] While in 1969 the Court grandly proclaimed that students do not "shed their constitutional rights to freedom of speech or expression at the schoolhouse gate,"[116] in subsequent cases the Court has allowed school authorities substantial leeway to restrict student freedom of expression, again because of the "special characteristics of the school environment."[117]

---

112 Robert Post, *Recuperating First Amendment Doctrine*, 47 Stan. L. Rev. 1249, 1253–54 (1995) (describing Marcel Duchamp's "The Fountain," which he submitted as a sculpture to the Exhibition of Independent Painters in New York in 1917, and explaining: "This transformation is made possible because artists and spectators share conventions that establish the medium of art exhibitions, and these conventions can by themselves generate forms of human interaction that are acknowledged as 'ideas' within the jurisprudence of the First Amendment.").

113 Ginsberg v. New York, 390 U.S. 629, 631, 635 n.4 (1968); *Entm't Merchs. Ass'n*, 131 S. Ct. at 2729; *see* L.A. Powe, Jr., *The Obscenity Bargain: Ralph Ginzburg for "Fanny Hill,"* 35 J. of Supr. Ct. History 166 (2010).

114 F.C.C. v. Fox Television Stations, Inc., 132 S. Ct. 2307 (2012).

115 *Entm't Merchs. Ass'n*, 131 S. Ct. at 2735 (internal quotation omitted).

116 *Tinker*, 393 U.S. at 506, reiterated in *Morse*, 551 U.S. at 397.

117 *Id.* at 393, 396–97 (quoting Hazelwood Sch. Dist. v. Kuhlmeier, 484 U.S. 260, 266 (1988), and *Tinker*, 393 U.S. at 506). Students' Fourth Amendment rights against searches by public officials also are constrained in the school setting. *See Morse*, 551 U.S. at 406.

The importance of careful, nuanced, and particularized consideration of the unique context of children and schools is thus well recognized with respect to First Amendment issues of freedom of speech. The nature of religious interests and sensibilities toward which the Establishment Clause demands that government be solicitous is of course different, but the idea that applying First Amendment principles requires distinctive consideration of the full range of pertinent circumstances is the same.

It is hardly surprising that the general social setting in which a controversy arises can be highly consequential with respect to Establishment Clause issues. In two challenges to different displays of the Ten Commandments on public property, for example, Justice Stephen Breyer relied heavily on the facts and contexts of the displays in reaching his divergent positions. Justice Breyer joined a five-Justice majority opinion holding the displays in county courthouses improper. A manifestation of government favoritism of one religion over another, or even of religion generally, sends a message of partiality that is particularly inappropriate in a venue dedicated to equal justice for all.[118] But the same day, Justice Breyer switched sides to join the four previous dissenters in finding no Establishment Clause violation in a long-standing display, donated by a private civic organization, on the grounds of a state capitol. This "borderline case" was different for him because the circumstances of the display evidenced a predominantly secular message of civic morality. Notably, in his separate opinion concurring in the judgment in the capitol display case, Justice Breyer specifically distinguished the situation of the Ten Commandments displayed on public school grounds "where, given the impressionability of the young, government must exercise particular care in separating church and state."[119] Venue matters; indeed, the Court had prohibited such school displays some years earlier.[120]

D. School Classroom Prayer

Prayer conducted pursuant to government auspices is another especially relevant example of the Supreme Court distinguishing, based in large part on the pertinent social context involving children and schools, the constitutionality of religious practices in the face of Establishment Clause claims. With regard to a state's practice of opening each legislative day with a prayer by a paid chaplain, the Court looked to the long history and tradition of legislative prayer in the country, including in Congress. Doing so, the Court found that this historically accepted practice was not compromised by government proselytizing or official endorsement of a particular religion because legislators are adults "not readily susceptible to

118 *McCreary*, 545 U.S. at 860.

119 *Van Orden*, 545 U.S. at 703 (Breyer, J., concurring in judgment).

120 Stone v. Graham, 449 U.S. 39 (1980) (per curiam).

'religious indoctrination' ... or peer pressure."[121] Legislators also may avoid the religious exercises entirely with impunity.[122] The Court's approach to legislative prayer, however, contrasted sharply with its previous disapproval of mandated prayer or Bible reading in public schools in two earlier decisions, "a pair of cases that hang over this one [legislative prayer] like a reproachful set of parents."[123]

Distinguishing school prayer from legislative prayer was not difficult for a majority of the Justices. The Court dealt first with a nondenominational prayer composed by the New York State Board of Regents that was to be recited daily in all classes. Even though objecting students could remain silent or be excused from the classroom, the Court found this to be a "practice wholly inconsistent with the Establishment Clause." The "indirect coercive pressure" on students to conform was inappropriate.[124] The following year the Court similarly invalidated state requirements for daily reading of Bible verses, without comment, and recitation of the Lord's Prayer. Again, students could leave the classroom during these opening exercises or otherwise not participate, but this did not insulate the practice from constitutional challenge.[125] This was explained by Justice Brennan's separate concurrence in which he expounded upon his reasons for fully joining the Court's opinion and judgment. The devotional exercises were held on school property, under official school auspices, and injected a religious ceremony into the school day, so excusing an objecting student could not cure the establishment violation. Moreover, the ritual infringed the free exercise rights of an objecting student by requiring a public expression of disbelief, or at least non-conformity, thus inhibiting the student from asserting his or her conscience for fear of being stigmatized and shunned by peers. The public school setting presented a "unique problem" in this regard.[126]

The Court then invalidated Alabama's attempt to reintroduce school prayer by authorizing a moment of silence for "meditation or voluntary prayer." Just a moment of silence, truly unmotivated by or directed toward promoting prayer, is not constitutionally problematic, even if an individual student chooses to use it for silent prayer. But Alabama went too far because, as the Court found, the state's intent was to endorse religion and its statute had no secular purpose.[127] When she

121 *Marsh*, 463 U.S. at 792. Justice Brennan, in dissent, noted that he earlier had been less concerned about the effect on mature adults but now viewed that as an error. *Id.* at 795–96, 798 n.5 (Brennan, J., dissenting) (citing *Schempp*, 374 U.S. at 299–300 (Brennan, J., concurring)). *See also Town of Greece*, 134 S. Ct. at 1823, 1827 (majority and plurality opinions).

122 *Schempp*, 374 U.S. at 299–300.

123 *Marsh*, 463 U.S. at 806 (Brennan, J., dissenting).

124 *Engel*, 370 U.S. at 424–25, 431.

125 *Schempp*, 374 U.S. at 203.

126 *Id.* at 287–94 (Brennan, J., concurring). "[N]onconformity is not an outstanding characteristic of children." McCollum v. Bd. of Educ., 333 U.S. 203, 227 (1948) (Frankfurter, J., concurring).

127 *Wallace*, 472 U.S. at 38.

concurred in the judgment, Justice O'Connor emphasized the important difference between the state promoting school prayer and simply providing a moment of silence. She did so by invoking the endorsement test she had proposed the previous year in *Lynch v. Donnelly* to modify the Court's *Lemon* test. Justice O'Connor's endorsement approach is particularly helpful in evaluating government aid programs for private religious schools.

E. State Endorsement of Religion in Schools

Lemon v. Kurtzman provides the backdrop to Justice O'Connor's endorsement analysis. In that case, the Court articulated and applied a three-part test to strike down several state statutes granting various kinds of aid to parochial schools.[128] The Court "gleaned" its *Lemon* test from previous cases: "First, the statute must have a secular legislative purpose; second, its principal or primary effect must be one that neither advances nor inhibits religion; finally, the statute must not foster 'an excessive government entanglement with religion.'"[129] Then, 13 years later in *Lynch*, the Court upheld a municipality's annual Christmas display, including a nativity scene. The display was in a park owned by a nonprofit organization, but the city owned the components of the display, including the crèche, and spent a modest sum on the display each year. Still, a five-Justice majority ruled that the *Lemon* test was satisfied. Although she joined the majority opinion, Justice O'Connor wrote separately to suggest a "'clarification' of [the Court's] Establishment Clause doctrine."[130]

For Justice O'Connor, "government endorsement or disapproval of religion" is a "direct infringement" of the Establishment Clause.[131] Her reasoning, articulated in *Lynch*, a religious display case, nonetheless has particular resonance for the school aid cases: "Endorsement sends a message to nonadherents that they are outsiders, not full members of the political community, and an accompanying message to adherents that they are insiders, favored members of the political community. Disapproval sends the opposite message."[132] A majority of the Court soon explicitly adopted Justice O'Connor's approach, noting:

---

128 Lemon v. Kurtzman, 403 U.S. 602 (1971).

129 *Id.* at 612–13 (citations omitted). *See infra* notes 210–14 and accompanying text. The *Lemon* test retains some vitality despite considerable criticism and attempts to deem it moribund.

130 *Lynch*, 465 U.S. at 687 (O'Connor, J., concurring).

131 *Id.* at 688.

132 *Id.* The Christmas display in *Lynch* passed Justice O'Connor's test because, in her view, in the context of celebrating a public holiday with "very strong secular components," it was not intended to, nor objectively in fact did it, convey a message of endorsement of religion. *Id.* at 692. As Justice O'Connor explained the following year, government cannot "make[] adherence to religion relevant to a person's standing in the political community.... The endorsement test does not preclude government from acknowledging religion or from taking religion into account in making law and policy. It does preclude government from

> [W]e have paid particularly close attention to whether the challenged governmental practice either has the purpose or effect of "endorsing" religion, a concern that has long had a place in our Establishment Clause jurisprudence ... [T]he essential principle remains [that the] Establishment Clause, at the very least, prohibits government from appearing to take a position on questions of religious belief ....[133]

The importance that Justice O'Connor's focus on government endorsement has for the school aid cases can be appreciated by first considering the Court's two variations on the issue of classroom prayer. In 1992, in *Lee v. Weisman*, the Court held that clergy invocations and benedictions—even "nonsectarian" ones, if such is possible, which seems unlikely[134]—at public secondary school graduation exercises violate the Establishment Clause. Although attendance at, and participation in, the graduation ceremony were not diploma requirements, the Court sensibly said they were "in a fair and real sense obligatory."[135] It would be "formalisitc in the extreme" to rely on the voluntary nature of attending "one of life's most significant occasions."[136] Thereafter the Court extended its approach to other, more discretionary though still official, school events. In *Santa Fe Independent School District v. Doe*,[137] following the principles it had articulated eight years earlier in *Lee*, the Court held that a school policy permitting student-led, student-initiated prayer over the public address system at high school football games also violates the Establishment Clause. The student speaker for the season was elected by majority student vote, in a two-step process, to deliver an appropriate "statement or invocation."[138] This government policy, intended and understood to encourage a religious message, authorized and enabled the invocations on government property and at regularly scheduled, government-sponsored, school events. So the invocations were public, not private, religious speech that disregarded minority views. This amounted to "both perceived and actual endorsement of religion."[139]

The classroom prayer cases *Schempp*, *Engel v. Vitale*, and *Wallace v. Jaffrey*, though highly controversial politically, are comparatively straightforward as a matter of constitutional principle, similar to one of the great free speech episodes

---

conveying or attempting to convey a message that religion or a particular religious belief is favored or preferred." *Wallace*, 472 U.S. at 69–70 (O'Connor, J., concurring).

133 *Cnty. of Allegheny*, 492 U.S. at 592–93.

134 *See* Geoffrey R. Stone, *In Opposition to the School Prayer Amendment*, 50 U. Chi. L. Rev. 823, 829 (1983) ("[T]he very concept of a 'nondenominational prayer' is self-contradictory.").

135 *Lee*, 505 U.S. at 586.

136 *Id.* at 595.

137 530 U.S. 290 (2000).

138 *Id.* at 303.

139 *Id.* at 305.

of the mid-twentieth century. In a remarkable about-face over just three years, the Court reversed itself to protect Jehovah's Witnesses public school children who refused to recite the Pledge of Allegiance because doing so contravened their religious tenets.[140] It is always heartening to recall Justice Robert H. Jackson's eloquence: "If there is any fixed star in our constitutional constellation, it is that no official, high or petty, can prescribe what shall be orthodox in politics, nationalism, religion, or other matters of opinion or force citizens to confess by word or act their faith therein."[141] But the Court's reasoning in the more difficult *Lee* and *Santa Fe* cases in terms of coercion, endorsement, and divisiveness is particularly relevant to the school aid issue.[142]

Prayer in the classroom or at other school functions surely places considerable coercive pressure on a dissident student, regardless of voluntary or mandatory attendance. The Court rightly acknowledged that this coercive effect was exacerbated by the fact that it involved adolescents in a school setting. In both *Lee* and *Santa Fe* the Court reiterated its often expressed "heightened concerns with protecting freedom of conscience from subtle coercive pressure in the elementary and secondary public schools."[143]

But while the sort of coercion imposed on students in these cases may be sufficient to create an Establishment Clause violation, it is not a necessary component.[144] Some members of the Court, however, unfortunately do not grasp the central concern. Justice Scalia, for example, would recognize as coercive establishments of religion only what government imposes "by force of law and threat of penalty."[145] Similar to his approach to standing in some Establishment Clause cases, as presented in

140 W. Va. State Bd. of Educ. v. Barnette, 319 U.S. 624, 633–34 (1943) (*overruling* Minersville Sch. Dist. v. Gobitis, 310 U.S. 586 (1940)).

141 *Barnette*, 319 U.S. at 642.

142 In his majority opinion in *Lee*, 505 U.S. at 584, Justice Kennedy termed the case "difficult." Indeed, one commentator reports, based on Justice Blackmun's now public personal records, that Justice Kennedy initially was assigned to write a majority opinion for the "conservative" position upholding the graduation prayer. But, he apparently switched his vote as he appreciated the nature of the coercive pressure involved and wrote the majority opinion the other way. R. Randall Kelso, *Justice Kennedy's Jurisprudence on the First Amendment Religion Clauses*, 44 McGeorge L. Rev. 103, 144–45 (2013).

143 *Lee*, 505 U.S. at 592–93 (citing psychological research that "supports the common assumption that adolescents are often susceptible to pressure from their peers towards conformity, and that the influence is strongest in matters of social convention"); *Santa Fe*, 530 U.S. at 311–12.

144 *See id.* at 317; *Lee*, 505 U.S. at 604–06 (Blackmun, J., concurring), 618–26 (Souter, J., concurring). This is not a new principle: "The Establishment Clause, unlike the Free Exercise Clause, does not depend upon any showing of direct governmental compulsion and is violated by the enactment of laws which establish an official religion whether those laws operate directly to coerce nonobserving individuals or not." *Wallace*, 472 U.S. at 60 n.51 (quoting *Engel*, 370 U.S. at 430).

145 *Lee*, 505 U.S. at 640 (Scalia, J., dissenting).

Chapter 4, Justice Scalia denigrated as "incoherent" the psychological coercion invoked by the majority in *Lee*—"ersatz, 'peer-pressure' psycho-coercion," as he termed it.[146] He professed not to understand how a student objecting to a graduation prayer was compelled to do anything other than stand, or even remain sitting, in respectful silence. And for Justice Scalia, this neither compelled actual participation in the prayer nor gave the appearance of participation.

What Justice Scalia did not appear to comprehend is what five other Justices stressed, consistent with Justice O'Connor's concept of endorsement and its special meaning for students. Justice Kennedy wrote for the majority in *Lee*:

> What to most believers may seem nothing more than a reasonable request that the nonbeliever respect their religious practices, *in a school context* may appear to the nonbeliever or dissenter to be an attempt to employ the machinery of the State to enforce a religious orthodoxy. … The undeniable fact is that *the school district's supervision and control of a high school graduation ceremony* places public pressure, as well as peer pressure, on attending students to stand as a group or, at least, maintain respectful silence during the invocation and benediction. This pressure, though subtle and indirect, can be as real as any overt compulsion. … For *the dissenter of high school age*, who has a reasonable perception that she is being forced by the State to pray in a manner her conscience will not allow, the injury is no less real. … It is of little comfort to a dissenter, then, to be told that for her the act of standing or remaining in silence signifies mere respect, rather than participation. What matters is that, given our social conventions, *a reasonable dissenter in this milieu* could believe that the group exercise signified her own participation or approval of it.[147]

Thus it is important to consider the nature of the injury that results when a school puts its imprimatur on an explicit religious exercise in this manner. Justice Harry Blackmun's concurrence in *Lee*, and the majority in *Santa Fe*, articulated this explicitly in terms of the message Justice O'Connor first identified in *Lynch* and then reiterated in *Wallace*, a message that results when "the government makes adherence to religion relevant to a person's standing in the political community."[148] Such government action "'sends a message to nonadherents that they are outsiders, not full members of the political community, and an accompanying message to adherents that they are insiders, favored members of the political community.'"[149]

---

146 *Id.* at 636, 641 (Scalia, J., dissenting). Justice Scalia showed more concern for the emotional well-being of a religiously devout and distinctive group of students in *Bd. of Educ. of Kiryas Joel Vill. Sch. Dist. v. Grumet*, 512 U.S. 687, 738 (1994) (Scalia, J., dissenting).

147 *Lee*, 505. U.S. at 592–93 (emphasis added).

148 *Wallace*, 472 U.S. at 69 (O'Connor, J., concurring in judgment).

149 *Id.* (quoting *Lynch*, 465 U.S. at 688 (O'Connor, J., concurring)); *see Lee*, 505 U.S. at 606 n.9 (Blackmun, J., concurring); *Santa Fe*, 530 U.S. at 309–10.

As most of the Court recognized, this stigmatizing effect is particularly acute and worrisome when the "political community" in fact is a school.

It is clear that the religious content of prayer at a school event is what makes the message constitutionally problematic; it is not just the fact that students are a captive audience. A public school graduation speech that is simply boring unfortunately must be politely endured, but thereafter can be, and frequently is, freely criticized and spoofed. A public school graduation speech that is explicitly partisan politically—for example, endorsing or opposing a particular candidate or even a contentious ballot issue—likely would be inappropriate and offensive to the occasion despite the speaker's couching her remarks in some plausible context of exhorting the graduates regarding their obligations of good citizenship and civic duty to participate in the democratic process. Giving such a speech would be wrong as a matter of etiquette even if not giving rise to a viable legal claim; the speaker likely would not soon be invited to address another graduating class. But such a school speech that seeks to proselytize or indoctrinate on a religious basis, let alone a prayer—even one that some consider nonsectarian—does violate the Establishment Clause as it "creat[es] a state-sponsored and state-directed religious exercise in a public school."[150]

Consider an analogous situation. A non-Jewish student enrolled in a public middle school attends her classmate's bar mitzvah. She expects to observe appropriate dress and behavioral decorum at the synagogue, and perhaps she even chooses to rise with the congregation as a further show of respect. She views the service and helps to celebrate an important occasion in her friend's life, but she in no sense participates in the religious exercise or feels any coercion in that regard. This is because her presence at the service is truly voluntary, simply a matter of friendship; the synagogue is a private institution, not a state (*her* government's) entity; the synagogue is not *her* church; and the service is not *her* ritual. The school graduation, and even the football game or other public school-sponsored event, is entirely different in all these respects. The public school is *her* school, part of *her* government, and the graduation (or other event) is *her* graduation or event. She belongs to the public school community, perhaps the most significant organization in her life, and she is entitled to be a full participant in that community, attending all community events she chooses without being pressured to abstain by being subjected to an unwanted religious exercise.

Another classmate who welcomes the prayer at graduation might complain that it is *his* graduation as well, and he, and his many classmates who agree with him, are entitled to the religious component to solemnize the occasion. But as the Court recognized, to argue that "it is the objector, not the majority, who must take unilateral and private action to avoid compromising religious scruples … turns conventional First Amendment analysis on its head."[151] The Establishment Clause

150 *Lee*, 505 U.S. at 587.
151 *Id.* at 596.

emphatically rejects balancing majority religious views against minority ones.[152] "A majority [cannot] use the machinery of the State to practice its beliefs."[153] Or, as Justice O'Connor put it in *McCreary County, Kentucky v. American Civil Liberties Union*, "we do not count heads before enforcing the First Amendment."[154] Even if no person present at the event objects, the state cannot violate the Constitution by promoting a religious exercise. Just as a public school student who wishes to pray during the school day can do so privately in a quiet moment, those students who wish to invest an occasion with religious meaning are free to do so, individually or with a privately organized group, before or after the official government event. What they cannot do, however, is invoke the power of the state to enforce conformity and endorsement of their spiritual viewpoint.[155]

F. Avoiding Religious Divisiveness

Mixing government support for religion with schools, creating an inevitable and inappropriate effect on vulnerable and impressionable students, also accentuates the social, political, and religious divisiveness the Establishment Clause is specifically meant to avoid. George Washington's observation, noted in this book's Introduction, that "[r]eligious controversies are always productive of more acrimony and irreconcilable hatreds than those which spring from any other cause," is an apt warning.[156] Even in the relative American homogeneity of the founding era, Madison recognized the value and security of a society with a multiplicity of religious sects.[157] Largely because of our religious freedom and absence of government involvement with religion, we have since become incredibly diverse

---

152 *Id.* Justice Jackson invoked this basic principle to protect Jehovah's Witnesses children, at the height of nationalist fever, from being forced to recite the Pledge of Allegiance in school: "The very purpose of a Bill of Rights was to withdraw certain subjects from the vicissitudes of political controversy, to place them beyond the reach of majorities and officials and to establish them as legal principles to be applied by the courts." *Barnette*, 319 U.S. at 638.

153 *Schempp*, 374 U.S. at 226.

154 545 U.S. 844, 884 (O'Connor, J., concurring). The classic statement of this principle as to free speech is John Stuart Mill's: "If all mankind minus one, were of one opinion, and only one person were of the contrary opinion, mankind would be no more justified in silencing that one person, than he, if he had the power, would be justified in silencing mankind." John Stuart Mill, On Liberty 35 (Henry Holt & Co. 1874).

155 *See Lee*, 505 U.S. at 629–30 (Souter, J., concurring). This is why the complaint that the Court has "taken God out of our schools" (as though a secular authority had the power to do so) is a misconception. Rather, the state appropriately simply leaves religious matters to individual conscience and initiative, not government sponsorship or promotion. *See also Schempp*, 374 U.S. at 226; *but see Lee*, 505 U.S. at 645–46 (Scalia, J., dissenting).

156 *See* Introduction chapter, n.33 (regarding and citing George Washington's Letter to Edward Newenham).

157 The Federalist No. 51, at 351–52 (James Madison) (Jacob E. Cooke, ed., 1961).

along a broad religious spectrum. Indeed, "[o]ur country has become strikingly multireligious as well as multiracial and multiethnic."[158] But as a recent study notes, our tremendous religious pluralism, "including growing ranks of the nonreligious," is coexisting with growing religious polarization.[159] Emotional and sometimes vitriolic controversies over various religious activities in schools are very real and persistent.[160] A sure way to exacerbate religious divisiveness, an often expressed concern among members of the Court,[161] is to widen, rather than to curtail, government promotion of religion within schools.

Although religious discord clearly is detrimental to civil society, the potential for divisiveness alone may be too uncertain a basis for invalidating government action that supports religion. But when Justice O'Connor concurred with this proposition in *Lynch*, even while acknowledging divisiveness as an "evil addressed by the Establishment Clause," she focused the "constitutional inquiry ... ultimately on the character of the government activity that might cause such divisiveness, not on the divisiveness itself."[162] The Court implicitly agreed with her approach by distinguishing the religious display at issue in *Lynch* from direct government

158 Edwards v. Aguillard, 482 U.S. 578, 607 n.6 (Powell, J., concurring). We are "exponentially more diverse" in the twenty-first century even compared to the mid-twentieth century when the Court began fashioning its Establishment Clause jurisprudence. Zelman v. Simmons-Harris, 536 U.S. 639, 723 (2002) (Breyer, J., dissenting).

159 Robert D. Putnam & David E. Campbell, American Grace 3–4 (Simon & Schuster 2010).

160 *See, e.g.*, Schultz v. Medina Valley Indep. Sch. Dist., 2012 U.S. Dist. LEXIS 37130, at *1, *9 (W.D. Tex. Mar. 19, 2012) (court issued what it termed a "Non-Kumbaya Order" after previously finding in *Schultz v. Medina Valley Indep. Sch. Dist.*, 2012 U.S. Dist. LEXIS 19397, at *5 (W.D. Tex. Feb. 9, 2012) and *Schultz v. Medina Valley Indep. Sch. Dist.*, 2011 U.S. Dist. LEXIS 126969, at *5 (W.D. Tex. Nov. 2, 2011), profound harassment, threats, intimidation, fear, and the use of demagoguery by the parties and toward the court in a case involving claims that in allowing various religious practices at school events a local school board was proselytizing or promoting particular religious views with taxpayer funds); Matthews v. Kountze. Indep. Sch. Dist. (TX Dist. Ct., May 8, 2013) (discord over allowing high school cheerleaders to display banners with religious messages at football games), *available at* https://www.oag.state.tx.us/newspubs/releases/2013/050813_kountze_s_jorder.pdf. *See also* Abby Goodnough, *Student Faces Town's Wrath in Protest Against a Prayer*, NY Times, Jan. 26, 2012, at A12 (describing harassment of a high school student who sued to remove a large Prayer Mural from the wall of her school, which was ordered removed in *Ahlquist v. City of Cranston*, 840 F. Supp. 2d 507 (D.R.I. 2012)).

161 In *Santa Fe*, 530 U.S. at 294 & n.1, 311, 317, the Court noted that the lower courts permitted the plaintiffs to litigate anonymously to protect them against persistent attempts at intimidation and harassment. *See McCreary*, 545 U.S. at 876, 881; *Van Orden*, 545 U.S. at 698 (Breyer, J., concurring in judgment) (stating that one of the "basic purposes" of the religion clauses is "to avoid that divisiveness based upon religion that promotes social conflict, sapping the strength of government and religion alike" (citing *Zelman*, 536 U.S. at 717–29 (Breyer, J., dissenting))); *Lee*, 505 U.S. at 587–88.

162 *Lynch*, 465 U.S. at 689 (O'Connor, J., concurring).

subsidies to parochial schools, which are more likely to raise the troubling prospect of fostering religious discord.[163]

Indeed, Justice Breyer's dissent in *Zelman,* joined by Justices John Paul Stevens and David Souter, was prompted by his unease over the "religiously based social conflict" inherent when "government becomes involved in religious education."[164] This concern applies equally with regard to religious practices in public school, such as prayer, or government aid to parochial schools, even the "well-intentioned school voucher program" at issue in *Zelman.*[165] Justice Breyer concluded that the Establishment Clause therefore required separation of church and state, and not an "equal opportunity" approach to government aid "at least where the heartland of religious belief, such as primary religious education, is at issue."[166] In particular, unrestricted financial aid for religious instruction through vouchers or other tuition subsidies differs in kind and degree from the more limited provision of secular teaching materials.

There are good reasons for special concern over government involvement in religious education. First, children inherently are less mature than adults, more impressionable and susceptible to peer pressure, and prone to coercion to conform as the Court repeatedly noted in the school prayer cases.[167] Their vulnerability is especially acute with regard to religious matters. When the state puts its power, prestige, and influence behind support for religious education the message is not lost on children or their parents, either those who avail themselves of a government-funded religious education or those who do not for whatever reason. The message is exactly the one Justice O'Connor identified as constitutionally inappropriate—favored status and inclusion as opposed to exclusion. The effect arguably is far greater than simply momentarily viewing a religious display on public property. From the child's perspective, if the state pays for her religious schooling it must mean that such education is considered a good thing officially,

---

163 *See id.* at 684–85; Bowen v. Kendrick, 487 U.S. 589, 617 n.14 (1988). Both cite *Mueller v. Allen*, 463 U.S. 388, 403–04, n.11 (1983), for the particular danger of political divisiveness posed by financial subsidies for parochial schools.

164 *Zelman*, 536 U.S. at 717–18 (Breyer, Souter, Stevens, JJ., dissenting).

165 *Id.* at 717.

166 *Id.* at 722–23.

167 *Santa Fe*, 530 U.S. at 312; *Lee*, 505 U.S. at 592; *Wallace*, 472 U.S. at 81 (O'Connor, J., concurring); *Schempp*, 374 U.S. at 299 (Brennan, J., concurring). The immaturity of school children is not just a modern concern. In discussing his ideas for a precursor of public schools, Jefferson proposed that secular subjects be stressed and "'the Bible and Testament [not be put] into the hands of the children, at an age when their judgments are not sufficiently matured for religious inquiries.'" *Id.* at 235 (Brennan, J., concurring) (quoting 2 Writings of Thomas Jefferson 204 (Memorial ed. 1903)). Jefferson thought religious instruction at the university level was more appropriate, reinforcing the notion that government aid to parochial schools at the primary and secondary levels is a much more sensitive issue than at institutions of higher learning, an important difference the modern Court too often does not recognize.

and not just by her parents. The state in effect is endorsing the religious content and truth of what she is being taught. The subtlety of the fact that parents may direct the flow of government money, including some to secular schools, may well be lost on their children. The child's obvious perception is that a government program allows and facilitates her and her classmates receiving instruction at parochial schools through the allocation of funds that otherwise would be spent on public education. And if the vast majority of state money for private schools supports one denomination, or just Christian denominations generally, as is often the case, then this can only reinforce in the eyes of many school children the official "specialness" of their religion and the "outsider" status of others. The majority of the Supreme Court in *School District of the City of Grand Rapids v. Ball* and the dissenters in *Zobrest v. Catalina Foothills School District*, each discussed below, recognized exactly this danger from the "symbolic union of church and state" in the context of primary and secondary schools.

In short, there is something very distinctive about the confluence of religion, children, and schools. For comparison, consider the idea of direct government financial support for houses of worship. Nothing could be more axiomatic than Establishment Clause prohibition here, whether or not the aid is to be available evenhandedly among religions and directed by individual private choice. Yet, in the wake of damage caused by natural disasters like 2012's Hurricane Sandy, the question arises whether a house of worship is entitled to federal assistance for rebuilding on the same basis as secular entities.[168] Should it matter that government money is used to repair structural damage to a sanctuary where religious worship will take place? One might distinguish this case on the basis of entitlement to a form of taxpayer supported social insurance to restore the *status quo ante* rather than support for creating a house of worship. However persuasive this approach may be, the assistance is somewhat secular in nature—a new roof by itself (without any religious symbol) has no religious content, and lost prayerbooks or other purely religious items presumably would not be replaced with public funds. Moreover, such financial assistance is aiding adults who already have chosen a particular religious life. I may not agree with, or even like, my neighbor's choice, but I can at least respect his right to that choice.

By contrast, religious issues involving children in schools are essentially *sui generis*, as the Court's dramatically disparate treatment of school prayer and legislative prayer demonstrates. This uniqueness applies on several levels. First, religion itself is different. A taxpayer's natural aversion to being forced to financially support political views he or she philosophically opposes may be particularly acute when those subsidized views stem from someone else's religious traditions, beliefs, and doctrines that are perceived to be incompatible with, if not antagonistic toward, one's own. Those existential traditions, beliefs, and doctrines, after all, operate at the most intimate, transcendent level of individual conscience.

168 Tax exemptions for religious entities are discussed in Chapter 3, and that discussion also applies to the present question of disaster relief as a form of social insurance.

Second, this general abhorrence then is greatly accentuated when it comes to the education of children. An individual may not like helping to pay for a new roof for his neighbor's house of worship but viscerally objects to helping pay for his neighbor's child to be indoctrinated into a "false" religion, or perhaps any religion at all for that matter. An adult is free and competent to make his own decisions about religion; he is not subject to the same influences and pressures with which children attending school must deal. A choice an adult makes for himself is not the business of other individuals, nor are the choices he makes for his children expending his own resources.[169] Invoking the power of the state to compel support for the religious education of other people's children, however, is an entirely different, far more offensive matter.

Most people are willing to pay for what Justice Brennan described as the "uniquely *public* function" that American public schools serve: "the training of American citizens in an atmosphere free of parochial, divisive, or separatist influences of any sort—an atmosphere in which children may assimilate a heritage common to all American groups and religions. This is a heritage neither theistic nor atheistic, but simply civic and patriotic."[170] Indeed, Justice Felix Frankfurter once praised teachers as "the priests of our democracy" whose "special task … [is] to foster those habits of open-mindedness and critical inquiry which alone make for responsible citizens, who, in turn, make possible an enlightened and effective public opinion."[171]

All Americans, parents or not, should be willing to support the considerable common public good derived from this kind of education. But many people understandably object to subsidizing religious education that well may include indoctrination and proselytizing of impressionable and susceptible children before they are mature enough to make their own reasoned decisions. Many, and perhaps most, parochial schools do a fine job of providing a solid secular education as well as inculcating moral and spiritual values that greatly enrich the lives of their students in the best spirit of American pluralism. But if based in explicit sectarian doctrine, such education should be entirely independent from government support or encouragement. And other, less enlightened parochial schools may reject the free inquiry that should exemplify sound education; they instead may instill just one version of the "truth," perhaps fostering in more extreme instances intolerance and disdain for others.

---

169 This presumes parents enjoy a considerable measure of freedom to direct the upbringing and education of their children. *See* Pierce v. Soc'y of Sisters, 268 U.S. 510 (1925); Meyer v. Nebraska, 262 U.S. 390 (1923).

170 *Schempp*, 374 U.S. at 241–42 (Brennan, J., concurring) (internal citations omitted).

171 Wieman v. Updegraff, 344 U.S. 183, 196 (1952) (Frankfurter, J., concurring). *See McCollum*, 333 U.S. at 216–17 (extolling public schools as the "symbol of our secular unity" and "the most powerful agency for promoting cohesion among a heterogeneous democratic people").

Of course, there are many secular subjects and ideas to which parents also may not want their children exposed in school, and there are many ideological and cultural battles over school curricula and related issues. But, again, inculcation of religion is different, and it is the one area the Constitution puts off-limits for government funding. This presents no impediment for parents who want a religious education for their children because parents are always free to provide, on their own initiative, moral and religious training for their children either in the home or through more formal, private instruction that either supplants or supplements public schooling. In particular, parents can present alternative views on matters to which their children have been exposed in public school, through the media, or otherwise, and which they consider objectionable. On the other hand, for children who receive only a narrow sectarian education in an ideologically rigid parochial school there may be no counter influence—either from parents or others influential in a child's life—to stimulate reflective, independent thinking.[172] The Constitution gives parents this basic choice regarding their children but also should preclude general taxpayer support for the sectarian choice. "The Establishment Clause prohibits precisely … the government's lending its support to the communication of a religious organization's religious message."[173]

IV. The Establishment Clause and Government Aid to Parochial Schools

With the above background on the Establishment Clause generally, and its application in particular to issues of religion in public schools, we now survey chronologically the most pertinent, major Supreme Court cases regarding government financial aid to private schools, predominantly including parochial schools. The 65-year evolution of this jurisprudence has hardly been linear; it has proceeded in back and forth, jagged movements, often changing with the Court's composition, sometimes with simply plurality decisions or later majorities overruling earlier decisions over vigorous dissents. The review demonstrates how, from modest though perhaps inappropriate beginnings, the current Court has altered dramatically the constitutional analysis to the point where one must ask not what aid a state constitutionally *may* provide to a parochial school but what may it *not* do in this regard. As described in the Introduction chapter, a direct government monetary subsidy to a religious school still likely is problematic.[174] If a state cannot make an outright grant of funds to a parochial school, can it achieve the same result through only slightly indirect means? If so, is exalting form over

172 Sufficiently mature children might have their own interests in the character and quality of their education even apart from their parents' wishes. *See Yoder*, 406 U.S. at 242 (Douglas, J., dissenting); *Elk Grove*, 542 U.S. at 15; Roger J.R. Levesque, Not By Faith Alone 166 (NYU Press 2002).

173 *Cnty. of Allegheny*, 492 U.S. at 601.

174 *See* Introduction chapter, n.26.

substance in this blatant way consistent with modern notions of the Establishment Clause and the cardinal principle of separation of church and state it embodies? Does such jurisprudence enjoy coherent integrity entitled to respect? Whatever the normative answers to these questions, can a state now act largely with legal impunity because the Supreme Court's 2011 decision denying standing in *Arizona Christian School Tuition Organization v. Winn* greatly has curtailed federal courts in their adjudicatory role of interpreting and applying the Establishment Clause?

A. Everson v. Board of Education

Everson is a truly seminal case because it not only applied the Establishment Clause to the states for the first time, but it did so in the context of allowing government taxpayer support for private religious education in the face of the clearly contrary historical lesson of the early *Virginia Tax Assessment*.[175] Moreover, in *Everson*, the Court ignored the most flagrant, facial aspect of the New Jersey ordinance at issue that, even today, might condemn such an approach.

A New Jersey statute allowed a school district to provide for transportation of students to any public or nonprofit private school. If a school district did provide transportation for public school students, it had to allow any eligible student to use that transportation to attend any school along an established school route. The Ewing Township Board of Education provided bus transportation by using the regular public transit system and reimbursing parents for the cost of their children's bus tickets, about $40 per pupil per year. But the reimbursement covered only public school students and, explicitly, students at Catholic schools where religion was part of the curriculum. Because it underwrote a student's very attendance at a Catholic school, the reimbursement, like a tuition subsidy, could not be attributed only to secular, rather than religious, components of education. So, in the dissent's view, the Board's program could not be distinguished from paying for transportation to Sunday school.[176] The Court, however, ignored the patent denominational preference because there was no indication there were any non-Catholic private school students seeking transportation.

Referencing Jefferson's "wall of separation," Justice Hugo Black's opinion for the Court first expressed the grand and expansive view of the Establishment Clause

---

175 Prior to *Everson*, *Cochran v. La. State Bd. of Educ.*, 281 U.S. 370 (1930), allowed Louisiana to use taxpayer funds to purchase and supply nonsectarian textbooks free to schoolchildren, including those attending private schools. But that case involved only a challenge to the program as an unconstitutional taking, not any First Amendment issue. And, in *Quick Bear v. Leupp*, 210 U.S. 50 (1908), some members of the Sioux Indian Tribe were allowed to attend religious schools with fees paid by federal trust and treaty funds. But this was the Tribe's own money, not general tax revenues, as it came from payments for termination of certain land and treaty rights. *See* Comm. for Pub. Educ. & Religious Liberty v. Nyquist, 413 U.S. 756, 781 n.37 (1973).

176 *Everson*, 330 U.S. at 47 (Rutledge, J., dissenting).

that introduces this chapter. From Justice Black's broad statement one might think the opinion quickly would invalidate the Board's reimbursement program as applied to Catholic school students, especially as availability of the bus subsidy could have made the difference as to whether a student attended Catholic rather than public school, thereby benefiting both the student and the Catholic school. As the program used regular public buses, any student—attending public school, Catholic school, or other private school whether for-profit or nonprofit—could ride the bus. But to avoid aiding religion the Board could have chosen to reimburse only public school students and presumably those attending any nonprofit, secular private schools if such existed. For reasons that have never been entirely clear, the Court declined to rule that the First Amendment prevents using state money to pay for the bus fares of parochial school students when government also pays for public school students.

Not all students were covered by the transportation program. But all who were covered rode the same public buses, and the issue in the lawsuit was one of money, not conditions of transport.[177] Nonetheless, the Court rationalized that the Board's program was for the safety and welfare of children going to and from school. Importantly, although the state subsidy went to parents and assisted them in procuring a religiously-imbued education for their children, the Court maintained that "the State contributes no money to the schools. It does not support them." This, however, ignores the dual benefit to students and schools. So, even though the First Amendment erects a "high and impregnable" wall of separation between church and state of which the Court "could not approve the slightest breach," and the state was operating at the "verge" of its constitutional power, it had not crossed the line.[178]

Justice Jackson's dissent is interesting because he wrote that his first impression was to join the majority, indicating the intuitive but superficial reaction that there can't be much of a problem with government simply paying for all students attending parochial schools as well as public schools to ride a bus, a form of government aid the majority considered "separate and … indisputably marked off from the religious function."[179] But, focusing on the denominational preference of the Board's approach, Justice Jackson recognized the majority's legerdemain and the discord between its First Amendment theory and its conclusion, famously calling to mind Byron's Julia who "whispering 'I will ne'er consent,'—consented."[180] Considering the talismanic reliance the Court would come to place on the formal manner in which government funds flow to private, parochial schools and the constitutional difference it created in this regard based

177 Although not stated, the Court might have imagined that, without the bus subsidy, some students who wanted to attend Catholic school would have been forced to find other, less safe, means of transport. *See* Mark Strasser, Religion, Education and the State 10 (Ashgate 2011).

178 *Everson*, 330 U.S. at 16, 18.

179 *Id.* at 18. *See id.* at 18–19 (Jackson, J., dissenting).

180 *Id.* at 19. Justice Scalia could not have done better rhetorically.

on intervening, independent private choice, Justice Jackson's discrediting such an approach in this initial case is especially noteworthy:

> It is of no importance in this situation whether the beneficiary of this expenditure of tax-raised funds is primarily the parochial school and incidentally the pupil, or whether the aid is directly bestowed on the pupil with indirect benefits to the school. … The prohibition against establishment of religion cannot be circumvented by a subsidy, bonus or reimbursement of expense to individuals for receiving religious instruction and indoctrination.[181]

Justice Jackson also joined Justice Rutledge's dissent for four Justices, which began by quoting Jefferson's *Virginia Bill for Religious Freedom* and relied heavily on Madison's *Memorial and Remonstrance Against Religious Assessments*. Denominational neutrality benefiting all faiths equally would not have mattered to the dissenters who presciently feared that the Court's initial breach of the wall of separation would lead to "continuing corrosive decision[s]," just as Madison had feared any "'first experiment on our liberties.'"[182] In this initial school aid case, four Justices thus rejected any notion that ostensible government neutrality among religions could cure the problem with government assistance to religion that the Constitution forbids. The dissenters voiced sympathy with the plight that drives the search for government support for alternative schools today. Parents must pay taxes to support public schools while many of them, for a wide variety of reasons, wish to send their children elsewhere despite the financial burden. But financial hardship incurred due to individual choice cannot alter the separation called for by the Constitution.[183]

The dissent in *Everson* recognized that the controversy was not "just a little case over bus fares."[184] Again referencing Madison, Justice Rutledge wisely appreciated that "[p]ublic money devoted to payment of religious costs, educational or other, brings the quest for more. It brings too the struggle of sect against sect for the larger share or for any."[185] This is a well-known phenomenon of which the Court always should be mindful. As Chief Justice Warren Burger wrote for the Court in *Lemon*:

---

181 *Id.* at 24.

182 *Id.* at 29, 41 (Rutledge, Jackson, Frankfurter, Burton, JJ., dissenting) (quoting Madison's *Memorial and Remonstrance*). In contrast to Justice Jackson's initial ambivalence, Justice Rutledge thought "'[w]e ought to stop this thing right at the threshold of the public school.' … there was 'no telling where the end [would] be.'" Roger K. Newman, Hugo Black: A Biography 361 (Pantheon Books 1994).

183 *Everson*, 330 U.S. at 58–60 (Rutledge, Jackson, Frankfurter, Burton, JJ., dissenting).

184 *Id.* at 57.

185 *Id.* at 53.

> [M]odern governmental programs have self-perpetuating and self-expanding propensities. … [I]n constitutional adjudication some steps, which when taken were thought to approach "the verge," have become the platform for yet further steps. A certain momentum develops in constitutional theory and it can be a "downhill thrust" easily set in motion but difficult to retard or stop.[186]

Indeed, Justice William O. Douglas, who was with the majority in *Everson*, realized from later developments that, while its extension of aid to needy children seemed appealing at the time, in fact it was "out of line with the First Amendment."[187]

B. McCollum v. Board of Education

Although differences over *Everson* persisted among the Justices, they coalesced a year later to hold in *McCollum v. Board of Education* that a program of release time from public school for religious education violated the Establishment Clause. Illinois had a compulsory school attendance law. The school board in Champaign, however, allowed teachers paid by private religious groups, but subject to approval and supervision by the superintendent of schools, to come into grades 4–9 in the public schools to teach religion for 30 to 45 minutes once a week during the regular school day. Parents had to give written consent for their children to attend the religious classes. Students without parental permission were required to move from their classrooms to elsewhere in the school for some type of secular offering while the classrooms were taken over for religious instruction. But all students had to attend either the religious or the secular program.[188]

This release time program had many of the elements the Court more recently has focused on in evaluating the constitutionality of government aid to religion in schools. No student was forced to participate in the religious instruction, but there well may have been subtle peer pressure on a student not to noticeably leave the classroom when it was devoted to religion. The Court found it unnecessary to consider this possible coercive effect, but Justice Frankfurter's separate concurring opinion noted the "obvious pressure" on students, the "feeling of separatism" engendered in non-participating students, and the overall effect of the program that "sharpens the consciousness of religious differences."[189] Similar consequences can result when the state financially supports not just limited release time in public schools but sending students full time to parochial schools.

---

186 *Lemon*, 403 U.S. at 624.

187 *Engel*, 370 U.S. at 443 (Douglas, J., concurring). In 1970, Douglas further repudiated his position in *Everson*. *Walz*, 397 U.S. at 703 (Douglas, J., dissenting). In the flag salute case Justice Jackson described a wiser approach when confronted with initial small steps that seem innocuous: "[T]he First Amendment to our Constitution was designed to avoid these ends by avoiding these beginnings." *Barnette*, 319 U.S. at 641.

188 *McCollum*, 333 U.S. at 207–09.

189 *Id.* at 227–28 (Frankfurter, J., concurring).

More importantly for the Court, although the religious teachers were privately paid, the public school system "assist[ed] and [was] integrated with the program of religious instruction."[190] Indeed, certainly in the minds of many students sitting in their regular classrooms, albeit with "private" teachers, any line distinguishing non-governmental religious instruction from their public secular education must have been hopelessly blurred. On the other hand, no students received religious instruction but for the private, independent choice of parents, a factor a majority of the Court recently has emphasized in upholding various forms of state aid. Equally important, the program was facially evenhanded in that different religious denominations could and did offer their own programs of instruction. This theoretical neutrality, however, depended in practice on whether any particular religious community was large enough and willing to participate.[191] Still, Justice Black, in his concise majority opinion, had little trouble in concluding that, "beyond all question," use of the "tax-established and tax-supported public school system to aid religious groups to spread their faith ... falls squarely under the ban of the First Amendment" as the Court had interpreted it in *Everson*.[192]

C. Zorach v. Clauson

Just four years later in *Zorach v. Clauson*, however, six Justices upheld a variation of the Champaign release time program. New York City had what is perhaps best called a "dismissed time program." Upon a parent's written request, a student could leave the public school grounds and go to a religious center for instruction or devotional exercises for one hour a week. A report of student attendance was sent to the schools, but the Court saw no evidence of coercion of students to participate, perhaps because the trial court denied plaintiffs the opportunity to present such.

---

190 *Id.* at 209 (majority opinion).

191 For example, while at some point a rabbi may have taught some classes in Judaism, the Court noted that appeared not to have been the case for the past several years. *Id.* at 209–10. Today, a majority of the Court does rely on the theoretical neutrality of voucher and other tax-supported programs even though the actual evenhandedness of such programs is belied by the vast proportion of funds going to parochial schools of mainstream denominations.

192 *Id.* at 210. Only Justice Stanley Reed dissented from this conclusion. Justice Frankfurter wrote a concurring opinion for himself and three other Justices to place the Champaign program in context in light of "[t]he evolution of colonial education, largely in the service of religion, into the public school system of today." *Id.* at 214 (Frankfurter, Jackson, Rutledge, Burton, JJ., concurring). Justice Frankfurter summarized this transition by saying "the prohibition of furtherance by the State of religious instruction became the guiding principle, in law and feeling, of the American people" long before passage of the Fourteenth Amendment. *Id.* at 215. This was not due to a waning of religious beliefs among the public but the needs of an increasingly heterogeneous democratic society, which contributed to the congressional effort to pass the Blaine Amendment. *Id.* at 218 n.6. For a discussion of the Blaine Amendment, *see* Chapter 1, Section IV.

Students not released remained in their public school classrooms for the balance of the school day. The majority distinguished *McCollum* because the public schools were not used for the religious program and no public funds were expended. Taxpayer-parents who challenged the program, however, argued that the public schools were putting their "weight and influence ... behind a program for religious instruction; public school teachers police it; ... [and] the school is a crutch on which the churches are leaning for support in their religious training."[193]

As in *Everson*, Justice Douglas' majority opinion here includes some absolutist if somewhat enigmatic language:

> There cannot be the slightest doubt that the First Amendment reflects the philosophy that Church and State should be separated ... the separation must be complete and unequivocal. The First Amendment within the scope of its coverage permits no exception; the prohibition is absolute. The First Amendment, however, does not say that in every and all respects there shall be a separation of Church and State.[194]

Justice Douglas, who had not yet come to perceive the difficulty that the result in *Everson* could engender, then applied "common sense" to conclude that it would be taking the constitutional principle to "extremes" to condemn the New York City program. The schools merely were adjusting their schedules to accommodate the religious needs of some students. Otherwise, for example, how could a student request an excused absence from school to observe an important religious holiday?[195]

Indeed, compared to the significant government involvement in the religious instruction of the *McCollum* release time program, one can ask what the harm is in instituting a dismissed time program. The participating students incur no additional burden of time during the week to receive the religious instruction their parents wish for them; the bit of secular education they forego is a trade-off their parents choose. Yet, to only a slightly lesser degree than in *McCollum*, the government puts its power, prestige, and endorsement behind the concept of religious education in a dismissed time program. Not only might students be pressured by school administrators, teachers, or peers to participate in the religious programming, but non-participants may experience the same stigma of difference and separateness from the larger school community, likely sending a message of inclusion and exclusion as in the school prayer controversies.[196]

---

193 Zorach v. Clauson, 343 U.S. 306, 309 (1952).

194 *Id.* at 312.

195 *Id.* at 312–14. Along the way, Justice Douglas gratuitously added a sentence that spawned subsequent controversy: "We are a religious people whose institutions presuppose a Supreme Being." *Id.* at 313.

196 On the other hand, there also may be substantial benefits if a fair number of students remain behind. They may enjoy some special, small-class time, interaction with teachers, and supplemental and enriched educational programs and activities. But if not

Although, as Justice Douglas said, the wisdom of the dismissed time program in *Zorach* was not within the province of the Court, the dissenting Justices had a better view of the program from a constitutional perspective. Justice Black, joined by Justices Frankfurter and Jackson, saw no meaningful difference from *McCollum* other than non-use of the public school buildings. The City still was employing "its compulsory education laws to help religious sects get attendants presumably too unenthusiastic to go unless moved to do so by the pressure of this state machinery. … This is not separation but combination of Church and State."[197] Justices Frankfurter and Jackson, each also writing separately, additionally focused on the compulsory nature of the New York scheme. The public schools could close early one day a week, dismissing *all* students, thereby freeing up some time for those who wished—actually, those whose parents provided them no choice—to attend religious school. But Justice Frankfurter identified the constitutional problem in the City's calling upon public schools to compel this attendance and also noted that invoking this compulsion "betrays a surprising want of confidence in the inherent power of the various faiths to draw children to outside sectarian classes."[198] Justice Jackson too commented that proponents of the dismissed time program wanted its compelled attendance feature because students would not attend religious school if attendance were solely voluntary and optional at the end of a school day.[199]

The majority's approach in *Zorach* is thus both bad constitutional law and a sad commentary on parental responsibility and authority. Parents have the right to direct the upbringing and education of their children and opt for parochial or other adequate private schooling in lieu of public schooling. But parents who choose parochial schools have the responsibility to enforce that choice (and, arguably, to fully pay for it as well) without relying upon government to control or coerce their children. Reverting to personal experience, one author vividly recalls seeing many public school classmates dismissed early for religious education one afternoon each week. Some other students who completed that regular school day, but then attended Hebrew school for an hour-and-one-half two afternoons a week and two hours Sunday morning, knew full well this was not because of a state mandate; their parents provided them no option. As discussed in Chapter 5, in evaluating a First Amendment challenge to a government restriction on the free exercise of religion, a court often inquires into the extent of the infringement on constitutional rights, the nature and strength of the government interest at stake in imposing the constraint, and whether less-restrictive, alternative methods of achieving that

---

within a copacetic environment, especially with just one or two students declining the dismissed time, the effect could be quite different.

197 *Id.* at 318 (Black, Frankfurter, Jackson, JJ., dissenting).

198 *Id.* at 323 (Frankfurter, J., dissenting).

199 The coercive nature of the program caused Justice Jackson to add: "The day that this country ceases to be free for irreligion it will cease to be free for religion—except for the sect that can win political power." *Id.* at 325 (Jackson, J., dissenting).

government interest are available. If we were to adopt the same balancing approach to a release or dismissed time school program, one that clearly raises substantial Establishment Clause problems, the governmental interest is simply to aid parents in compelling their children to attend religious school. This is not only an extremely weak governmental interest but, in fact, a constitutionally inappropriate one, as the dissenters in *Zorach* recognized even without analysis explicitly in these terms. In an excellent example of the constant, unseemly pressure for greater and greater aid for religion even in public schools, a school district in South Carolina and school districts in Ohio now not only allow release time for off-campus religious education, but permit students to receive public school academic credit for such coursework simply to accommodate the desire—"the genuine and independent choices"—of parents and students for private religious instruction.[200]

D. Board of Education v. Allen

Sixteen years after *Zorach*, when the next significant case of government aid to private schools, *Board of Education v. Allen*, came to the Court, the only Justices from the earlier era still sitting were Justices Black and Douglas. The prior cases involved state action that helped place students in religious school settings. In this sense, the government aid could not avoid facilitating overall sectarian, as well as secular, instruction, although it was not always directed at, and did not necessarily promote, the former. The government assistance in *Allen*, however, was narrower. It involved a New York state law that required local school boards to purchase textbooks and lend them without charge to students in grades 7–12 in all schools, including private secular and parochial schools. The law described the covered textbooks as those "which a pupil is required to use as a text for a semester or more in a particular class in the school he legally attends."[201]

Because "books are different from buses," the Court recognized that the support extended by the New York law was more specifically related to the instructional function. But, according to the majority, the books loaned had to be approved by public school authorities and could be only secular, not religious. Thus, on the "meager record" before it following summary judgment below, the Court blithely assumed that all loaned books would be "not unsuitable for use in the public schools because of religious content."[202] The Court therefore accepted the proposition that

---

200 Ohio Session Law No. 110 (June 12, 2014), effective Sept. 11, 2014; Moss v. Spartanburg Cnty. Sch. Dist. Seven, 683 F.3d 599, 611 (4th Cir. 2012) (citing *Zelman*, 536 U.S. at 649), *cert. denied* 133 S. Ct. 623 (2012). Such accommodation is hardly necessary, as Justice Brennan recognized in his concurrence in *Schempp*: "The student's compelled presence in school for five days a week in no way renders the regular religious facilities of the community less accessible to him than they are to others." 374 U.S. at 299 (Brennan, J., concurring).

201 392 U.S. 236, 239 (1968).

202 *Id.* at 245, 248.

the religious and secular components of education in a parochial school, and the textbooks used for each, could be distinguished adequately. Moreover, because most private schools did not furnish books to their students, the financial benefit of the New York law was to parents and children, not to schools. Still, as with the reimbursement of bus fares in *Everson*, the program here benefited parochial schools as well as it relieved some of the financial burden of children attending. Nonetheless, the aid program satisfied the Establishment Clause test—one "not easy to apply"—that the Court had developed to that point: "[T]here must be a secular legislative purpose and a primary effect that neither advances nor inhibits religion."[203]

Justice Douglas, however, took great exception to the majority's Panglossian view of the textbooks that might actually be used in private schools. While there is "nothing ideological about a bus," a "textbook goes to the very heart of education in a parochial school."[204] Examining more closely how the New York law would operate, Justice Douglas realized—and Justice Abe Fortas agreed—that requests for textbooks in fact would come not from an individual student but from a private school itself. So, these two Justices reasoned that a parochial school might well choose books that best promote its sectarian beliefs. This would infect the entire textbook approval process with powerful religious and political pressure because, as Justice Douglas noted, the very purpose of any parochial school "is to provide an education oriented to the dogma of the particular faith."[205] The books selected and actually used in parochial schools would not be limited to those adopted by the public schools. Rather, as Justice Fortas concluded, the program was "hand-tailored to satisfy the specific needs of sectarian schools."[206] As we shall see, the same might well be said of more recent tax funding mechanisms that channel a good deal of public money into parochial schools.

In particular, in a few devastating examples, Justice Douglas demonstrated that books that could be approved for use in a parochial school, even for ostensibly secular subjects, might include a science text that describes an embryo as having a "human soul infused into the body by God" because through parents' "cooperation with God souls are born for heaven." And an economics text that might be approved and adopted by some parochial schools asserted "Man's right to private property stems from the Natural Law implanted in him by God. … If Socialists do not deny Christ's message, they often ignore it."[207] Numerous other examples that Justice Douglas presented were less blatant, but they still were "liberally sprinkled with … creeping

203 *Id.* at 243.

204 *Id.* at 257 (Douglas, J., dissenting). Justice Black similarly distinguished the bus fares he had approved in *Everson* from state provision of textbooks because the latter "actively and directly assists the teaching and propagation of sectarian religious viewpoints." *Id.* at 253 (Black, J., dissenting).

205 *Id.* at 262 (Douglas, J., dissenting).

206 *Id.* at 271 (Fortas, J., dissenting).

207 *Id.* at 258–59 (Douglas, J., dissenting).

sectarianism," confirming Justice Jackson's earlier observation about the difficulty in determining "where the secular ends and the sectarian begins in education."[208]

Justice Douglas' dissent creates the context for understanding Justice Black's own strongly worded dissent that makes one wonder whether Justice Black had come to regret his opinion in *Everson*. Justice Black attributed the New York law in *Allen* to "powerful sectarian religious propagandists" whose "insidious" efforts "have succeeded in securing passage of the present law to help religious schools carry on their sectarian religious purposes … looking toward complete domination and supremacy of their particular brand of religion." The New York law was a "flat, flagrant, open violation" of the Establishment Clause because "tax-raised funds cannot constitutionally be used to support religious schools, buy their school books, erect their buildings, pay their teachers, or pay any other of their maintenance expenses, even to the extent of one penny."[209] Considering his emotionally laden language, one can only imagine what Justice Black would say about the proliferating present-day programs of substantial state tuition subsidies for parochial schools.

Indeed, *Allen* is a good example of how a program of state aid to religious education that seems evenhanded and relatively innocuous at first glance in fact can actually serve narrow sectarian purposes and promote religious polarization. Even if Justice Douglas' textbook examples were extreme, designed to emphasize his point, they illustrate the difficulty that arises from any program that creates the potential for abuse of state aid and the intractable constitutional and pragmatic problems of monitoring parochial school activities to prevent such abuse. Which state agency will tell a parochial school, and on what basis, that a textbook the school wants to adopt is too "religious"? The far better approach is to maintain the strict church-state separation the dissenters advocated.

E. Lemon v. Kurtzman

A few years later *Lemon* became a milestone in the Court's Establishment Clause jurisprudence for the controversial test a broad majority articulated.[210] *Lemon* involved two appeals of various state programs extending financial aid to parochial elementary and secondary schools. In one program, Rhode Island directly supplemented by up to 15 percent the salaries of teachers of secular subjects in certain nonpublic elementary schools. Eligible teachers could teach only courses taught in the public schools using public school instructional materials; they could not teach a course in religion. All teachers who received benefits taught at Catholic schools. Twenty-five percent of the state's elementary school population attended private schools, and 95 percent of these pupils enrolled in Catholic schools. In the other program, Pennsylvania imposed a specific tax to reimburse private schools

---

208 *Id.* at 260 n.9, 262 (quoting *McCollum*, 333 U.S. at 237–38 (Jackson, J., concurring)).

209 *Allen*, 392 U.S. at 250–51, 253–54 (Black, J., dissenting).

210 403 U.S. at 602.

for the costs of teachers' salaries and state-approved textbooks and instructional materials, but only for specified secular, not religious, subjects within the curricula of the public schools. More than 96 percent of the Pennsylvania pupils whose schools benefited attended church-related schools, mostly Catholic schools.[211]

In this "extraordinarily sensitive area of constitutional law" the Court articulated its three-prong test for analyzing Establishment Clause issues in terms of legislative purpose, effect, and entanglement.[212] The expressed legislative purpose of both the Rhode Island and Pennsylvania programs was to improve secular education in nonpublic schools, and this was not problematic. Recognizing that total separation between church and state is not possible, the Court "examine[d] the character and purposes of the institutions that are benefited, the nature of the aid that the State provides, and the resulting relationship between the government and the religious authority."[213] Whether or not the states effectively could separate secular educational components from religious ones, the Court found that the "cumulative impact of the entire relationship ... involves excessive entanglement between government and religion," and thus invalidated the two programs.[214]

One key factor in reaching this result was that each state supported teachers at parochial schools, either through direct payments, as in Rhode Island, or by reimbursing the schools in Pennsylvania. Moreover, an integral part of the mission of the parochial schools was to propagate and promote a particular faith. Subsidizing teachers is fundamentally different from the types of assistance the Court previously had allowed in the forms of "secular, neutral, or nonideological services, facilities, or materials."[215] Despite the difficulties described by the dissenters in *Allen*, textbooks for example can be examined once and approved or rejected. Teachers on the other hand are subject to the religious authorities in charge of parochial schools, whose control now is only strengthened by the Supreme Court's 2012 decision to uphold a ministerial exception that effectively exempts religious institutions, including many parochial schools, from employment discrimination laws.[216]

Even acting in the best of faith, teachers supported by state programs necessarily would have great difficulty in completely separating their secular and religious educational functions and remaining religiously neutral. Indeed, as he had in *Allen*, Justice Douglas now again described how religious indoctrination can be infused throughout the ostensibly "secular" curriculum.[217] The majority realized that Rhode Island would have to engage in "comprehensive, discriminating, and

---

211 *Id.* at 607–10.

212 *Id.* at 612. *See supra* note 129 and accompanying text (stating the three-prong *Lemon* test).

213 *Id.* at 615.

214 *Id.* at 614.

215 *Id.* at 616.

216 *Hosanna-Tabor*, 132 S. Ct. at 694.

217 *Lemon*, 403 U.S. at 634–37 (Douglas, J., concurring).

continuing … surveillance" to ensure, as it must under the Constitution, that teachers it subsidizes do not inculcate religion. Such "excessive and enduring entanglement between state and church" is impermissible.[218] Pennsylvania's direct payments to parochial schools compounded this problem. Moreover, allowing this type of financial aid to parochial schools would foster unacceptable political divisiveness along religious lines as pressure inevitably would build for ever increasing appropriations to benefit relatively few denominations, exactly what the First Amendment was designed to prevent.[219]

All of these compelling objections to states' financially aiding teachers apply *a fortiori* to current state programs that subsidize student tuition at parochial schools. Such tuition aid significantly helps students attend these schools where they are taught by teachers in both secular and religious classes without limitations, not even the restrictions deemed inadequate in *Lemon*. Salary subsidies help place teachers in front of students; tuition assistance helps place students in front of teachers. The end result is the same, and the palpable constitutional infirmities are very similar.[220]

F. Committee for Public Education & Religious Liberty v. Nyquist

Controversies over government aid to religious education did not abate, and on one day in June, 1973, the Court issued four opinions exemplifying "some of the most perplexing questions to come before [the] Court."[221] The most significant case

218 *Id.* at 619 (majority opinion).

219 *Id.* at 622–24. Justice Douglas elaborated on the historical conflict between Protestants and Catholics over education that gave rise to the now extensive system of Catholic parochial schools and the "hydraulic pressures" gradually leading to the "situation where vast amounts of public funds are supplied each year to sectarian schools." *Id.* at 628–30 (Douglas, J., concurring).

220 The same day that the Court decided *Lemon*, a plurality upheld a federal act providing construction grants to colleges and universities, some of which could be church-related, to build academic facilities used only for secular educational purposes. The plurality stressed the differences between higher education, on the one hand, and primary and secondary schooling on the other, and so distinguished *Lemon* because: the building aid was non-ideological in character; the inculcation of religious values is not the same central, permeating purpose of institutions of higher education as it is for elementary and secondary parochial schools; colleges and universities operate with some level of academic freedom so the religious influence on secular education is mitigated—student attendance at religious services was not required, for example; "college students are less impressionable and less susceptible to religious indoctrination;" and, with the institutions' broad constituencies, there is less potential for political divisiveness. Tilton v. Richardson, 403 U.S. 672, 686 (1971); *see also* Aguilar v. Felton, 473 U.S. 402, 411 (1985) (noting that many religiously affiliated colleges are not as pervasively sectarian as elementary and secondary parochial schools).

221 *Nyquist*, 413 U.S. at 760. In *Levitt v. Comm. for Pub. Educ. & Religious Liberty*, 413 U.S. 472 (1973), the Court struck down unrestricted state reimbursements to private schools, including parochial schools, for certain costs of testing and recordkeeping mandated by the state because the aid might support religious activities. In *Sloan v. Lemon*,

is *Committee for Public Education & Religious Liberty v. Nyquist*. New York had enacted three measures to assist education. To ensure the health, safety, and welfare of students, it provided direct grants for repair and maintenance of school facilities and equipment to nonprofit, private elementary and secondary schools serving a high concentration of pupils from low-income families. These families also could receive a small, unrestricted tuition reimbursement for each child enrolled in a private school. Finally, taxpayers who qualified for the tuition reimbursement were entitled to claim a "tax adjustment," a graduated subtraction from their adjusted gross incomes on their state tax returns, which the Justices saw as a "hybrid" tax benefit. The Court determined that pervasively religious private schools could benefit under all three provisions. These schools, for example, could discriminate on the basis of religion in admission of students and hiring of teachers. All, or almost all, of the schools receiving grants were Catholic institutions, but schools benefiting under the reimbursement and tax adjustment provisions included a "substantial" number of private schools affiliated with other faiths.[222]

New York had legitimate, nonsectarian interests in assisting a variety of pluralistic alternatives to public education. But the maintenance and repair grants could be used to support religious facilities and activities, and this was more than an incidental and indirect effect. The modest tuition reimbursement program similarly failed this effects aspect of the three-prong *Lemon* test. It was clear to the Court's majority in *Nyquist* that these subsidies could not be given directly to parochial schools, and the fact that they went instead to parents did not make a significant difference because they still subsidized religious education. In sharp contrast to a majority of Justices on the current Court, the Court in *Nyquist* was unwilling to open the door to any of the "ingenious plans for channeling state aid to sectarian schools" that periodically came before it, whether labeled "a reimbursement, a reward, or a subsidy" or whether the hybrid tax scheme was one based on deductions, credits, or another mechanism.[223] The Court was well aware of the potential for increasing political conflict over religion as "aid programs of any kind tend to become entrenched, to escalate in cost, and to generate their own

---

413 U.S. 825 (1973), more than 90 percent of the children attending private schools in the state enrolled in sectarian schools, and the Court invalidated a partial tuition reimbursement scheme constitutionally indistinguishable from the ones involved in *Nyquist*. But in *Hunt v. McNair*, 413 U.S. 734 (1973), the Court upheld a state's issuance of revenue bonds, explicitly not obligations of the state itself but with certain tax advantages in financing, for the benefit of a Baptist college because, among other matters, the college was not oriented significantly toward sectarian as opposed to secular education, and the project would not include any facilities for religious purposes or activities. *See also* Roemer v. Bd. of Pub. Works, 426 U.S. 736 (1976) (state allowed to make annual, unrestricted direct grants to private colleges, including religiously-affiliated institutions (found not to be pervasively sectarian), as long as the funds were not used for "sectarian purposes").

222 *Nyquist*, 413 U.S. at 768.

223 *Id.* at 785–86, 789–91.

aggressive constituencies."[224] Despite this strong majority position, in a portent of how a reconstituted Court soon would change direction, Chief Justice Burger and Justices Byron White and William Rehnquist issued their own dissents as to the aid to parents through the tuition and tax relief measures.

G. Meek v. Pittenger

These three Justices also dissented in the next major case, *Meek v. Pittenger*, in which Pennsylvania provided assistance to private schools in terms of auxiliary services, textbooks, and other instructional materials and equipment. The auxiliary services included such things as teaching and related assistance for exceptional and educationally disadvantaged students, counseling, testing, psychological services, and speech and hearing therapy. All services rendered under the program were supposed to be "secular, neutral, non-ideological" and were to be provided in the private schools by personnel from a unit of the public school system. Textbooks that were acceptable for use in the public schools could be loaned free of charge to students in private schools. Instructional materials and equipment that could be lent to private schools included printed and published items such as maps, photographs and films, and projection, recording and laboratory equipment.[225]

A majority of the Court agreed that *Lemon* supplied the appropriate guidelines, and the dissenters helped form a majority to uphold the loan of textbooks to students under the authority of *Allen*. The instructional materials and equipment, however, were lent directly to qualifying nonpublic schools, more than 75 percent of which were church-affiliated institutions. A majority therefore held that the predominantly religious character of these private schools rendered this "massive aid" loan program unconstitutional because its primary effect was to advance religion. This was so despite the nature of the materials and equipment, such as maps and laboratory apparatus, was purely secular and non-ideological. The Court realized that the provision of even this type of aid earmarked for neutral, secular educational functions could not be segregated from the predominant and pervasive religious purpose of the schools.[226] Finally, the ostensibly secular auxiliary services were provided directly to children with special needs but only

---

224 *Id.* at 797. The Court presciently continued: "Moreover, the State itself, concededly anxious to avoid assuming the burden of educating children now in private and parochial schools, has a strong motivation for increasing this aid as public school costs rise and population increases. In this situation, where the underlying issue is the deeply emotional one of Church-State relationships, the potential for seriously divisive political consequences needs no elaboration." *Id.* And in a footnote at the end of the first sentence of this passage the Court added: "The self-perpetuating tendencies of any form of government aid to religion have been a matter of concern running throughout our Establishment Clause cases." *Id.* at 797 n.56.

225 421 U.S. 349, 352 (1975) (*overruled* by Mitchell v. Helms, 530 U.S. 793 (2000)).

226 *Meek*, 421 U.S. at 364–66.

on the premises of the private, mainly parochial schools. The personnel providing these services were employed by the public school system and not by the private schools, but within the private school environment this assistance raised too much potential for the inadvertent advancement of religion for this aspect of the program to survive. Overall, the Court was troubled by the "successive opportunities for political fragmentation and division along religious lines" that private school aid programs inevitably create.[227] Indeed, this factor, as elaborated in *Lemon*, caused Justices Brennan, Douglas, and Thurgood Marshall to dissent from upholding the textbook loan program. It was "pure fantasy" to treat this aid as a loan to students rather than to the private schools themselves.[228]

H. Wolman v. Walter

Ohio then tried to conform to the holdings in *Meek* with its provision to private schools of textbooks, instructional materials and equipment, diagnostic and therapeutic services, field trip transportation, and services for standardized testing and scoring. This produced a fractured Court in *Wolman v. Walter*. Millions of dollars in assistance were at stake, and the usual disparities prevailed in the state. Of 720 chartered private schools, "all but 29 were sectarian. More than 96% of the nonpublic enrollment attended sectarian schools, and more than 92% attended Catholic schools."[229] A plurality of the Justices upheld both a textbook loan program similar to those in *Allen* and *Meek* and the provision of standardized tests and scoring services as were used in the public schools. The latter services were not problematic because private school personnel were not involved with them. A majority of the Court also upheld the provision of speech, hearing, and psychological diagnostic services provided in the private schools but by personnel from the public school system. The limited contact these public employees had with students, even within the private schools, posed little risk of fostering religious instruction. Therapeutic, guidance and remedial services for children with special needs were more problematic in this regard. But these services were provided by public employees and only at public facilities, not on private school premises. Still, there was concern that a facility, such as a mobile unit, might be seen as an adjunct of a parochial school. The Court determined, however, that the program authorized services to be provided only "on sites that are 'neither physically nor educationally

227 *Id.* at 372.

228 *Id.* at 374–80 (Brennan, Douglas, Marshall, JJ., concurring in part and dissenting in part).

229 Wolman v. Walter, 433 U.S. 229, 234 (1977) (*overruled* by *Mitchell*, 530 U.S. at 793). It was stipulated that, pursuant to the authorizing state statute, none of the schools receiving state aid discriminated in admissions or hiring on the basis of "race, creed, color, or national origin." Further, despite the Catholic nature of the schools, non-Catholic students were "not required to attend religion classes or to participate in religious exercises or activities." *Wolman*, 433 U.S. at 234–35 & n.3.

identified with the functions of the nonpublic school.' Thus, the services are to be offered under circumstances that reflect their religious neutrality."[230] Even while approving this discrete and limited program, therefore, the Court clearly was concerned about the perception of the relationship between state aid and religious education, specifically the endorsement such assistance suggests. This concern is all the more worrisome today with pervasive state financial aid for parochial school tuition that underwrites the entire educational experience.

With respect to Ohio's program for loaning private schools instructional materials and equipment used in public schools and considered incapable of diversion for religious purposes, Ohio tried to avoid the result in *Meek* by structuring its program actually as a loan to students and not directly to schools. In comparison with more modern arguments relying on supposedly "indirect" aid and private, individual choice, the Court in *Wolman* rejected this structure as a "technical change in legal bailee" that would "exalt form over substance."[231] As in *Meek*, there was no way to separate the secular and religious functions, and this loan component of state aid was impermissible. These instructional materials and equipment thus continued to be treated differently from textbooks, despite several Justices' doubts about *Allen* and the logic of that distinction.[232] Transportation services for field trips also were disallowed because, within a wide range of options, a private school could control their frequencies and destinations. A private school teacher also would contribute greatly to the educational experience of the trip creating "an unacceptable risk of fostering of religion [as] an inevitable byproduct."[233]

To lend some coherence to distinctions the Court was making among the kinds of aid to parochial schools, Justice Marshall offered an approach, which he attributed to Justice Black's dissent in *Allen*. Justice Marshall proposed drawing a line "between general welfare programs that serve children in private parochial schools because the schools happen to be a convenient place to reach the programs' target populations and programs of educational assistance."[234] Because such general welfare programs are divorced from the educational function they do not impermissibly advance the religious mission of a school and so also do not generate political divisiveness along religious lines.[235] Under this approach the loan not only of textbooks, but also of instructional materials and equipment and the provision of transportation for field trips, all would be improper. On

230 *Id.* at 246–47 (internal citation omitted).

231 *Id.* at 250.

232 *See id.* at 251 n.18; *id.* at 256–59 (Marshall, J., concurring in part and dissenting in part).

233 *Id.* at 254 (majority opinion).

234 *Id.* at 259 (Marshall, J., concurring in part and dissenting in part).

235 *Id.* at 259–60 & n.5 ("The distinction is between programs that help the school educate a student and welfare programs that may have the effect of making a student more receptive to being educated").

the other hand, assistance for speech, hearing, and psychological diagnosis and therapy would be just the type of general welfare programs for children that may be provided at parochial schools. But the contemplated guidance and counseling services and programs for special needs children too directly would support the educational functions of parochial schools to be allowed, and the same would hold for standardized testing and scoring services if they served the needs of the private schools rather than those of the state. There is, of course, no perfect algorithm to sort through the myriad forms of state aid to parochial schools and identify just those that the Establishment Clause forbids. But Justice Marshall's approach applied to a specific situation seems a much better approximation than the Court's.[236]

I. Mueller v. Allen

While the Court had struck down the hybrid tax relief system used in *Nyquist* to provide financial assistance to parents who sent their children to parochial schools, it had left open the question of whether an authentic tax deduction could be used to do so. Once Justice O'Connor replaced Justice Potter Stewart, she and Justice Lewis Powell (the author of *Nyquist*) joined the three dissenters from *Nyquist* to answer that question affirmatively in *Mueller v. Allen*. In so doing, they opened the door to proliferating and varied tax expenditure schemes for this purpose. In *Mueller*,

---

236 Adherence to Justice Marshall's general welfare approach, for example, might have avoided at least some troubling incongruities that Justice Rehnquist catalogued at length eight years later in his solitary dissent in *Wallace*, 472 U.S. at 110–11:

> For example, a State may lend to parochial school children geography textbooks that contain maps of the United States, but the State may not lend maps of the United States for use in geography class. A State may lend textbooks on American colonial history, but it may not lend a film on George Washington, or a film projector to show it in history class. A State may lend classroom workbooks, but may not lend workbooks in which the parochial school children write, thus rendering them nonreusable. A State may pay for bus transportation to religious schools but may not pay for bus transportation from the parochial school to the public zoo or natural history museum for a field trip. A State may pay for diagnostic services conducted in the parochial school but therapeutic services must be given in a different building; speech and hearing "services" conducted by the State inside the sectarian school are forbidden, but the State may conduct speech and hearing diagnostic testing inside the sectarian school. Exceptional parochial school students may receive counseling, but it must take place outside of the parochial school, such as in a trailer parked down the street. A State may give cash to a parochial school to pay for the administration of state-written tests and state-ordered reporting services, but it may not provide funds for teacher-prepared tests on secular subjects. Religious instruction may not be given in public school, but the public school may release students during the day for religion classes elsewhere, and may enforce attendance at those classes with its truancy laws. (internal citations and footnotes omitted).

See also Aguillard, 482 U.S. at 639 n.7 (Scalia, J., dissenting) (quoting Jesse H. Choper, *The Religion Clauses of the First Amendment: Reconciling the Conflict*, 41 U. PITT. L. REV. 673, 680–81 (1980)).

Minnesota allowed its taxpayers to claim a deduction from gross income for actual expenses incurred for the "tuition, textbooks and transportation" of their dependents attending elementary or secondary schools, including public and nonprofit private schools.[237] About 95 percent of students in private schools attended sectarian schools. The instructional materials eligible for the deduction were supposed to be suitable for secular, not religious, education, but tuition subsidies in any form cannot be allocated solely to the secular portion of education in a parochial school.

In the Court's analysis, assisting private school education was a legitimate, secular legislative purpose meeting the first *Lemon* guideline. And, unlike the scheme in *Nyquist*, Minnesota's was a genuine tax deduction, one of many tax deductions the state allowed, including a charitable contribution deduction that might benefit many religious organizations.[238] But the Court failed to appreciate or analyze the important, if subtle, differences in this context between a general charitable contribution deduction and the Minnesota targeted tuition-based tax deduction.

As discussed in greater detail in Chapter 3, most private schools, secular or parochial, are organized as nonprofit corporations entitled to tax-exempt status under Internal Revenue Code ("I.R.C.") § 501(c)(3). They qualify for this status and exemption from income taxation under I.R.C. § 501(a) simply as educational institutions regardless of any religious affiliation.[239] Also, under I.R.C. § 170, any taxpayer who makes a donation to such a school may claim a federal income tax deduction. Many states have parallel provisions in their income tax codes. But to qualify for these federal and state deductions, a contribution must be a genuine gift, with the requisite donative intent. In particular, the taxpayer may not receive substantial tangible benefit or value in return for the amount of the claimed deduction.[240]

The Minnesota tax deduction was different as it was based on amounts a taxpayer-parent spent for tuition and other educational expenses. The deduction therefore was tied to sending a child to a qualifying school, and the parent and child did receive tangible value in return for the expenditure.[241] In this way the state program gave parents an incentive to choose a private school education for their children, almost always at a parochial school, by lessening the financial burden of that choice. This pecuniary benefit also easily could redound to the school through increased enrollment or the ability to raise tuition. By contrast, a charitable contribution to a parochial school, even one designated for the school's general scholarship fund,

---

237 *Mueller*, 463 U.S. at 391.

238 *Id.* at 396.

239 Religious, charitable, and educational institutions were the original three types of entities (now expanded to eight categories) that Congress exempted initially from taxation. For further discussion, *see* Chapter 3, nn. 58–59 and accompanying text.

240 *See* Hernandez v. Commissioner, 490 U.S. 680 (1989). *See also* Chapter 3, nn. 15–17 and accompanying text.

241 *See, e.g.*, Sklar v. Commissioner, 549 F.3d 1252 (9th Cir. 2008); Sklar v. Commissioner, 282 F.3d 610 (9th Cir. 2002).

certainly benefits the school but is not related to sending the donor's own child to that school and creates no individual financial incentive to do so.

Rather than focusing on the significant Establishment Clause problem created by this troubling connection between the state tax benefit and the religious education of a specific child, the Court in *Mueller* implicitly inverted this logic by relying heavily on what has become a central tenet of its manufactured rationale in this area. Namely, support for the religious education of students and concomitant assistance to parochial schools provided by the Minnesota deduction were channeled through the private choices of individual parents. The Court asserted that parents' private choices reduced the constitutional objections. But it is by no means clear why this should be so, especially as the Court freely acknowledged that "financial assistance provided to parents ultimately has an economic effect comparable to that of aid given directly to the schools attended by their children." So why do parents as intermediaries for the state financial aid remove the "imprimatur of state approval"?[242] It is, after all, the state that legislates and implements the tax program with the specific intent to facilitate financial aid for private school education, and almost all students who benefit attend parochial schools, which consequently are the ultimate, predominant recipients of the aid. The Court was dismissive of this obvious statistical point, but the four dissenters insisted that the Court only had to look to reality—the actual operation of the program—to see that it had the primary effect of advancing religion.[243] The finances, power, prestige, and endorsement of the state clearly promoted religious education.

Finally, while a deduction for education expenses inures to claimant-parents, it reduces the income tax revenue to the state and places a compensating financial burden on all taxpayers to make up the shortfall through higher rates or other adjustments to the state's tax system. On the other hand, if private schools relieve some of the financial burden of operating public schools for larger numbers of students, some other taxes, such as property taxes used to support local public schools, conceivably might be lower than otherwise necessary. But far more is at stake than a mere financial trade-off, however the monetary balance might come out. Rather, all taxpayers are being forced to support religious education, which directly contradicts a central, historical principle of the Establishment Clause

---

242 *Mueller*, 463 U.S. at 399.

243 *Id.* at 410–11 (Marshall, Brennan, Blackmun, Stevens, JJ., dissenting). There is nothing unusual about this effect. "History and experience likewise instruct us that any generally available financial assistance for elementary and secondary school tuition expenses mainly will further religious education because the majority of the schools which charge tuition are sectarian." *Id.* at 411. This primary effect need not be nefarious to be unconstitutional. Citing *Nyquist*, Marshall also noted that it is "irrelevant whether a reduction in taxes takes the form of a tax 'credit,' a tax 'modification,' or a tax 'deduction.' … What is of controlling significance is not the form but the 'substantive impact' of the financial aid." *Id.* at 408.

as underscored by Madison and Jefferson and as reflected in Justice Black's categorical language in *Everson.*

Of course, one might say that any deduction for a charitable contribution to a religious institution, including a parochial school, has a similar effect. But as argued earlier, coerced taxpayer support specifically targeted for the *religious education of children* through a tuition-based tax deduction or other comparable tax mechanism is of a much different caliber than a long-standing tax concession widely available for contributions to a plethora of secular and religious institutions, educational or not, and requires a far more sensitive analysis. Instead, somewhat incredibly given the persistence of heated controversies in state legislatures and elsewhere over many aspects of religion in the public and political spheres, and especially in schools, the majority in *Mueller* confidently quoted Justice Powell:

> At this point in the 20th century we are quite far removed from the dangers that prompted the Framers to include the Establishment Clause in the Bill of Rights. The risk of significant religious or denominational control over our democratic processes—or even of deep political division along religious lines—is remote, and when viewed against the positive contributions of sectarian schools, any such risk seems entirely tolerable in light of the continuing oversight of this Court.[244]

This optimism is not only greatly misplaced but now, after *Winn*, quite ironic because federal courts are far less available to provide much control over Establishment Clause violations.

J. School District of the City of Grand Rapids v. Ball and Aguilar v. Felton

In two companion cases the Court next dealt with variations on the *Lemon* issue of public payment for teachers in private schools. *School District of the City of Grand Rapids v. Ball* involved two complicated programs in Grand Rapids, Michigan.[245] The Shared Time program offered remedial and enrichment classes in basic secular subjects during the regular school day in private schools, mainly elementary schools. The Shared Time teachers were public school employees, but about ten percent of them were simply assigned to the same nonpublic schools where they previously had been privately employed. The second program was the Community Education initiative. Classes in that program were taught in private schools after the end of the regular school day to students choosing to

244 *Id.* at 400 (majority opinion) (quoting *Wolman*, 433 U.S. at 263 (Powell, J., concurring in part, concurring in judgment in part, and dissenting in part)) (citations omitted). A later manifestation of the considerable, ever-present danger of "deep political division along religious lines" is the raging controversy over the coverage for contraceptive services under the Affordable Care Act. *See supra* note 6 and accompanying text.

245 473 U.S. 373 (1985) (*overruled in part* by Agostini v. Felton, 521 U.S. 203 (1997)).

participate. The teachers in the program were part-time public school teachers, but virtually all also were employed full-time by the same private schools where they taught the Community Education courses. The private school classrooms where the courses in both programs were conducted were leased by the public school system, were cleared of any religious symbols or artifacts, and displayed a sign stating that the room was a public school classroom during that class. But the only students attending courses under either program were those enrolled at the same private school where they were offered, and 40 out of the 41 schools where these programs operated were sectarian. No public school student ever attended one of these classes at a private school. Thus the programs' classes were "segregated by religion as are the schools at which they are offered."[246]

As in its previous school aid cases, the Court in *Ball* applied the *Lemon* guidelines.[247] The Court again acknowledged that these cases are particularly sensitive because "government's activities in this area can have a magnified impact on impressionable young minds, and the occasional rivalry of parallel public and private school systems offers an all-too-ready opportunity for divisive rifts along religious lines in the body politic."[248] Forty of 41 schools were pervasively sectarian in ways substantially different from church-affiliated colleges.[249] The state subsidized these schools by providing teachers for secular subjects. In such an atmosphere, however, even assuming the teachers conscientiously sought to adhere strictly to their secular mission, the programs posed the risk of government-financed or government-sponsored religious indoctrination. Aside from this potential, there was the problem of the "symbolic union of church and state" which was "likely to be perceived by adherents of the controlling denominations as an endorsement, and by the nonadherents as a disapproval."[250] And this symbolism is particularly troublesome when the recipients of this message prominently include impressionable "children in their formative years."[251] For example, "even the student who notices the 'public school' sign temporarily posted would have before him a powerful symbol of

246 *Ball*, 473 U.S. at 375–79.

247 The Court first rejected a challenge to the plaintiffs' standing to bring the action "relying on the numerous cases in which we have adjudicated Establishment Clause challenges by state taxpayers to programs for aiding nonpublic schools." *Id.* at 380 n.5.

248 *Id.* at 383.

249 The Court reaffirmed the importance of these distinctions when it allowed, without dissent, a state's program of vocational rehabilitation to assist an individual blind student at a Christian college even though he was studying the Bible, ethics, speech, and church administration to pursue a career as a pastor, missionary, or church youth director. Witters v. Wash. Dep't of Servs. for the Blind, 474 U.S. 481 (1986). This aid program was "in no way skewed towards religion," depended on the "genuinely independent and private choices of aid recipients," and was "not one of 'the ingenious plans for channeling state aid to sectarian schools that periodically reach this Court.'" *Id.* at 488 (quoting *Nyquist*, 413 U.S. at 785).

250 *Ball*, 473 U.S. at 390.

251 *Id.*

state endorsement and encouragement of the religious beliefs taught in the same class at some other time during the day."[252] The Court thus perfectly identified the very similar and troubling constitutional difficulties that unavoidably arise when political forces are successful in creating ways for government to substantially assist placing students in parochial schools. It is of little consequence to tell such a student with state-subsidized tuition that "you are here only because your parents, not the state, want you to be." The message of state endorsement of religion remains clear, and political discord is fostered.

A New York City program raised very similar problems in *Aguilar v. Felton*. New York City used federal funds appropriated to aid educationally-deprived children from low-income families to pay teachers in parochial schools. The teachers were regular employees of the public schools who volunteered to teach secular subjects in the parochial schools. They were not supposed to be involved with any religious activities, and their classrooms were cleared of any religious materials or symbols. Of the eligible students in private schools (13.2 percent of all pupils eligible to receive funds), 84 percent were enrolled in Catholic schools and 8 percent in Hebrew schools.[253] In addition, New York had a system for monitoring the religious content of the teaching conducted under its auspices in the private schools. But this only compounded the problem of the effects of the program in advancing religion. Under *Lemon*, as then applied in an increasingly controversial way, such instructional supervision in pervasively sectarian elementary and secondary schools created an excessive and impermissible administrative entanglement between church and state.[254] And here, in marked contrast to his earlier genial comments in *Wolman* that the majority opinion in *Mueller* quoted (as noted above[255]), Justice Powell now wrote separately to emphasize that, with the "large and varied sectarian populations" in New York, as well as those who support public schools, there likely would be continuing "competition and strife among them and others to gain, maintain, or increase the financial support of government."[256] The Establishment Clause is designed to avoid or minimize just this type of factional divisiveness.

---

252 *Id.* at 392. Higher education well may be different in this respect, especially regarding free speech. "University students are, of course, young adults. They are less impressionable than younger students and should be able to appreciate that the University's policy is one of neutrality toward religion." Widmar v. Vincent, 454 U.S. 263, 274 n.14 (1981) (university that created an open forum for student use may not exclude a group that engages in religious speech); *see also* Good News Club v. Milford Cent. Sch., 533 U.S. 98, 113–19 (2001); *id.* at 128 (Breyer, J., concurring in part); *id.* at 142–45 (Souter, J., dissenting).

253 *Aguilar*, 473 U.S. at 406–07 (*overruled* by *Agostini*, 521 U.S. at 203).

254 Justice O'Connor, joined by Justice Rehnquist, dissented primarily to question reliance on the entanglement prong of *Lemon*. *Aguilar*, 473 U.S. at 429–30 (O'Connor, Rehnquist JJ., dissenting).

255 *See supra* note 244 and accompanying text.

256 *Aguilar*, 473 U.S. at 416–17 (Powell, J., concurring).

K. Zobrest v. Catalina Foothills School District

The Court's jurisprudence in the school aid cases began to shift dramatically as Justices Scalia (1986), Kennedy (1988), and Thomas (1992) replaced, respectively, Chief Justice Burger,[257] and Justices Powell and Marshall, indicating, for better or worse, the profound effect personal views of the Justices can have on the development of constitutional law. The first pertinent case for this reconstituted Court, *Zobrest v. Catalina Foothills School District*,[258] was relatively straightforward, but it was a significant portent. Pursuant to federal and state statutes providing aid for education for individuals with disabilities, a deaf student asked his public school district to provide him a sign language interpreter at his Catholic high school in Tucson, Arizona, where he enrolled for religious reasons. The public school he previously attended had provided an interpreter. The secular and religious aspects of the student's education at his pervasively sectarian school were inseparable, however, so the publicly provided interpreter unavoidably would convey religious messages and assist his religious education and indoctrination.[259]

As the four dissenters argued, the case well might have been resolved on the basis of federal statutory and regulatory issues. And one of the Court's cardinal principles is to avoid a constitutional ruling when such is not necessary. This is a fundamental rule of judicial restraint stemming from the case or controversy requirement of Article III, the same basis on which some Justices now seek to limit taxpayer plaintiffs' standing to bring challenges under the Establishment Clause. The dissenters therefore would have remanded the matter to lower courts for consideration of the "nonconstitutional" questions. But in its "zeal to address the constitutional question," the majority proceeded to the merits.[260]

The majority first articulated a general proposition: "[G]overnment programs that neutrally provide benefits to a broad class of citizens defined without reference to religion are not readily subject to an Establishment Clause challenge just because sectarian institutions may also receive an attenuated financial benefit."[261] It defended this position by noting the "absurd results" that otherwise would follow, such as religious groups and institutions being denied basic and universal public welfare benefits like police and fire protection.[262] This is a common argument ever since

257 Justice Scalia joined the Court when Chief Justice Burger retired and Justice Rehnquist was elevated to Chief Justice. Additionally, Justice Souter replaced Justice Brennan in 1990.

258 509 U.S. 1 (1993).

259 *Id.* at 4–5.

260 *Id.* at 14–17 (Blackmun, J., dissenting). Sometimes the shoe is on the other foot. *See* United States v. Windsor, 133 S. Ct. 2675, 2698 (2013) (Scalia, J., dissenting, objecting to the Court having standing to rule on a challenge to the Defense of Marriage Act and noting that "[t]he Court is eager—*hungry*—to tell everyone its view of the legal question at the heart of this case").

261 Zobrest v. Catalina Foothills Sch. Dist., 509 U.S. at 8.

262 *Id.*

Everson, but one that is largely inapposite.[263] If a religious organization such as a house of worship paid taxes that supported these government services, there would be no question of its entitlement to the services for which it paid. Certainly nothing disables a religious entity from purchasing something from the government on the same basis as a secular one. Only the fact that religious entities generally are tax-exempt raises any issue. So there is only one Establishment Clause question—the tax exemption for religious organizations—not two. It would be inappropriate double-counting to accept tax-exempt status for religious organizations but then question their entitlement to basic, tax-supported government services. And the tax-exempt status of religious entities, as a matter of legislative discretion rather than constitutional mandate, among a broad class of secular and sectarian tax-exempt nonprofits is well settled.[264]

The Court was on firmer ground in *Zobrest* when it dealt with the particularity of state aid to private, parochial education and essentially applied Justice Marshall's approach in *Wolman* of allowing general and religiously neutral welfare benefits to reach needy students even in parochial schools. In *Zobrest* the parochial school received no direct financial benefit from the state, the student attended parochial school only because of his parents' private, independent choice, and provision of an interpreter created no incentive for this choice. Relying on the parents' private, independent choice made good sense here because apparently the government could have given the parents the money directly to hire an interpreter and, as the student's secular employee not the school district's, this would have avoided any constitutional issue.[265] Still, the program operated in an awkward manner, with a public school employee physically present in the private school and assisting the student's religious education.

Two dissenters understandably were concerned about a public employee who might need to conform to religious strictures (as to dress, for example) on the premises of a parochial school and who might become the "medium for communication of a religious message." This relationship risked creating a symbolic union of church and state, at least in the minds of "impressionable youngsters," with the "imprimatur of governmental approval upon the favored religion" and a message of exclusion to all others.[266] The Court, however, distinguished this human teacher element of state aid that in the past had been problematic because the interpreter, properly performing his or her job of simply

263 *Everson*, 330 U.S at 17–18.

264 *See Walz*, 397 U.S. at 664, discussed in Chapter 3. *See generally* Nina J. Crimm & Laurence H. Winer, Politics, Taxes, and the Pulpit: Provocative First Amendment Conflicts 149 (Oxford Univ. Press 2011). Income tax exemption for religious organizations, which might have limited taxable income anyway, was not based on the First Amendment's Religion Clauses but on these entities' perceived financial and social utility as contributors to public welfare.

265 *Zobrest*, 509 U.S. at 10–11, 13 n.11.

266 *Id.* at 22–23 (Blackmun, J., dissenting).

transmitting accurately the classroom proceedings, could not in any way alter the religious environment. On this assumption there seems little difference between providing a human interpreter, or a physical hearing aid to amplify sound, or, today, a computer program to translate audio into written text. It is not clear how one could distinguish among such alternatives on the basis of their symbolic potential or otherwise.[267]

L. Board of Education of Kiryas Joel Village School District v. Grumet

Viewing the human interpreter as analogous to provision of a hearing aid or a computer program, *Zobrest*, like *Everson*, seems fairly innocuous as an assault on church-state separation through assistance to religious education. But, again like *Everson*, *Zobrest* illustrates the danger of taking even small, factually and conceptually very limited steps toward accommodating sympathetic cases. A few years after issuing its unnecessary constitutional ruling in *Zobrest*, the new majority on the Court greatly extrapolated from that exceedingly modest decision to claim that *Zobrest* effected a "shift ... in our Establishment Clause law."[268] Indeed, the reformation in the Court's Establishment Clause jurisprudence had begun, and the new majority soon overruled *Aguilar*. Along the way, however, six Justices coalesced enough to invalidate a unique form of state support for parochial school education in *Board of Education of Kiryas Joel Village School District v. Grumet*.[269]

By the mid-1970s, pursuant to a religiously neutral, generally applicable New York law, a group of Satmar Hasidim had incorporated their separate Village of Kiryas Joel in Orange County, New York, giving them considerable powers of self-government. The Village fell within the broader Monroe-Woodbury Central School District, but to maintain their strict, insular religious life the Hasidim established private parochial schools for their children. The Village population of about 8,500 included a number of children who required special education services to which they were entitled under state and federal law even when enrolled in private schools. The Satmar parochial schools were unable to provide these expensive services, so Monroe-Woodbury provided them, first at an annex to the girls' parochial school.

The Court's 1985 decisions in *Aguilar* and *Ball* ended this practice, creating a quandary because the special needs children then were forced to attend public schools outside the Village. This exposure to the modern, secular world would not have required any compromise of religious belief or practice, but was traumatic for the distinctive, vulnerable Satmar children. Rather than seeking to minimize their anxiety from the experience and foster diversity and tolerance for differences among both religious and secular students, the New York legislature in 1989 opted for segregation by passing a statute that created a separate school district along the

267 *See Kiryas Joel*, 512 U.S. at 717–18, 731–32, 750 (dissenting opinions).

268 *Agostini*, 521 U.S. at 225.

269 *Kiryas Joel*, 512 U.S. at 687.

Village lines, which Justice Kennedy termed "explicit religious gerrymandering."[270] Most of the Village children stayed in their private parochial schools while the new, public Kiryas Joel Village School District ran only a program for handicapped children. In an arrangement with neighboring public school districts, Kiryas Joel paid tuition to send any of its children wishing a public school education to one of those districts, and special needs Hasidic children from outside Kiryas Joel could attend the Village's public school for such children. So, in contrast to other school aid cases, the Village public school itself was secular in nature, no public money was being spent on religious education, and the statute did not impose any additional burden or cost on taxpayers or others not part of the Satmar community. The problem was not so much any of the Village's schools, public or private, as the Kiryas Joel Village School District itself, which was "exceptional to the point of singularity."[271]

The statute at issue creating this public School District clearly was an attempt to provide an appropriate education for special needs students belonging to a particular religious sect. This "unusual and special legislative Act"[272] delegated the state's political power over public schools to a religious community, and there was no assurance that such power would be delegated or exercised in a religiously neutral manner. The Act was a "fusion of governmental and religious functions."[273] So, with some variation in their rationales, and against a subtext about the continuing strength and validity of the *Lemon* guidelines, six Justices invalidated the New York school district statute. In doing so, however, Justices O'Connor and Kennedy specifically noted that the extent of New York's special accommodation of the Satmar Hasidim would be unnecessary if the Court reconsidered and overruled *Aguilar* and *Ball*, and the three dissenters, Justices Scalia and Thomas and Chief Justice Rehnquist, heartily supported this idea.

M. Agostini v. Felton

Kiryas Joel thus became a pyrrhic victory for a separationist position as it foretold and prompted the unraveling of a number of precedents precluding state aid for religious education. The new five-Justice majority favoring an accommodationist position did not need to wait long. Pursuant to the Court's decision in *Aguilar*, the New York City Board of Education had been enjoined from sending public school teachers into parochial schools to provide secular, remedial educational services for disadvantaged students. The Board then reverted to its prior, more expensive and less convenient approach of providing these services offsite from the parochial schools at public schools or other leased or mobile premises, including vans parked near the private schools. Shortly after the decision in *Kiryas Joel*, however,

---

270 *Id.* at 729 (Kennedy, J., concurring in judgment).

271 *Id.* at 701 (plurality opinion).

272 *Id.* at 699.

273 *Id.* at 702 (quoting *Larkin*, 459 U.S. at 126).

the Board and some parents of eligible children sought relief from the injunction on the grounds that the law underlying *Aguilar* had changed.

The five-Justice majority in *Agostini v. Felton* reevaluated the *Lemon* guidelines and the assumptions that had supported the results in *Aguilar* and *Ball* in light of more recent cases.[274] The Court was no longer willing to assume that the mere presence of public employees in parochial schools necessarily would lead to state-sponsored inculcation of religion or a symbolic union of church and state. Over the dissent's strong objection, the majority inferred this new view, even when applied to teachers with broad responsibilities and significant discretion, had been adopted by allowing in *Zobrest* the perfunctory services of a public interpreter in a religious school. Citing the vocational tuition grant to a blind college student permitted in *Witters v. Washington Department of Services for the Blind*, the Court also rejected the idea that all government aid to a primary or secondary parochial school is invalid, especially when it occurs only because of the independent and private choices of individuals.[275] But *Zobrest* and *Witters* involved aid to individual, physically handicapped students, whereas the New York program challenged in *Agostini* served thousands of private school students, all but a few of whom attended parochial schools despite the formal neutrality of the program.[276] Nonetheless, the Court reasoned that, because the educational services were available to all students regardless of the school attended, there was no incentive to choose a religious education and therefore no government subsidization of religion in that regard. And, dismissing any difference in perceived government endorsement, the Court refused to speculate that the City's on-campus provision of teaching services that the private, parochial school otherwise was itself obligated to provide was of any greater, direct benefit to the parochial school than having those services provided to their students off-campus.

Moreover, the Court found neither excessive entanglement between government and religion nor state endorsement of religion, largely because pervasive monitoring of public school teachers in parochial schools was no longer required. Indeed, the Court abandoned the presumption that such teachers in that setting would inculcate religion despite professional strictures otherwise. This "carefully constrained program," one "containing safeguards," could not be viewed as an endorsement of religion.[277] And the Court simply decreed that neither the necessary administrative cooperation between public authorities and parochial schools, nor the dangers of political divisiveness generated by the program, were sufficient by themselves to amount to excessive entanglement. So neither *stare decisis* nor procedural principles prevented overturning the constitutional rulings in *Aguilar* and the portion of *Ball* addressing the Shared Time program there.

274 *Agostini*, 521 U.S. at 203. In addition to the positions of five Justices in *Kyrias Joel*, the plaintiffs cited *Witters*, *Zobrest*, and *Rosenberger* as establishing a change in the law.

275 *Id.* at 222–27. *See supra* note 249 describing *Witters*.

276 *Id.* at 251 (Souter, J., dissenting).

277 *Id.* at 235 (majority opinion).

Dissenters in *Agostini*, however, addressed a theme that is central to the current debate over school choice in the context of widespread desire for educational alternatives despite encroachments on separation of church and state. Justice Souter's dissent recognized that the New York City program ameliorated circumstances of needy students and did good work. But the fact that it was a worthy program and more expedient than other options did not mean that it necessarily should be considered constitutional. This basic First Amendment principle is well accepted with respect to free speech. There often are good reasons for restricting speech, especially speech that is hateful, harmful, or of little perceptible value. To take just one recent example, why should a fringe religious group be able to exploit the death and private funeral of an American service man or woman killed defending the country just to garner media attention for its anti-gay and anti-American messages? Yet eight members of the Court had little difficulty in deciding that the First Amendment does indeed protect the Westboro Baptist Church's hurtful picketing of soldiers' funerals.[278] We cannot risk chilling debate on matters of public concern even if it means having to tolerate distasteful and repugnant expression. In other words, there are real social costs in adhering to the First Amendment.

Similarly, despite the value of the educational assistance that New York City wanted to provide in a more efficacious manner, three dissenters in *Agostini* recognized the danger in breaching "two central tenets of Establishment Clause jurisprudence. The State is forbidden to subsidize religion directly and is just as surely forbidden to act in any way that could reasonably be viewed as religious endorsement."[279] This is "the hard lesson learned over and over again in the American past and in the experiences of the countries from which we have come, that religions supported by governments are compromised just as surely as the religious freedom of dissenters is burdened when the government supports religion."[280] Constitutional principles, especially those of the Establishment Clause, are meant to guard against the natural temptation to overlook perils in view of perceived benefits and to "stop[] the corrosion before it starts."[281]

N. Mitchell v. Helms

However implausible the majority's assertion was in *Agostini* that prior decisions already had changed the law on which *Aguilar* was based, Justice Thomas' plurality opinion in *Mitchell v. Helms* in 2000 left no doubt as to the Court's dramatic shift in Establishment Clause jurisprudence. *Mitchell* involved "Chapter 2" federal supplementary funds made available for educational assistance, through state and local government agencies, equally in public and

278 Snyder v. Phelps, 131 S. Ct. 1207 (2011).

279 *Agostini*, 521 U.S. at 242 (Souter, Stevens, Ginsburg, JJ., dissenting).

280 *Id.* at 243.

281 *Id.* at 244.

private, nonprofit schools based upon enrollment. Increased funds were available for low-income children and those attending rural schools, and instructional materials and equipment loaned to private schools had to be "secular, neutral, and nonideological."[282] About 30 percent of Chapter 2 assistance in Jefferson Parish, Louisiana, went to private schools, most of which were religiously-affiliated, and these were predominantly Catholic.

The Establishment Clause challenge to the Jefferson Parish program initially was filed in 1985, so the case progressed as the Court's membership and jurisprudence were changing. Now, in 2000, a plurality of the Court focused simply on the primary effect of the law, considered entanglement just one criterion of that inquiry, and, joined by Justices O'Connor and Breyer concurring in the judgment, formed a majority that invoked *Agostini* to uphold the Jefferson Parish program. In doing so, the majority overruled both *Meek* and *Wolman* as "anomalies."[283] The plurality's touchstone for determining whether government subsidizes religion or furthers religious indoctrination became merely formal neutrality in distribution: "[I]f the government, seeking to further some legitimate secular purpose, offers aid on the same terms, without regard to religion, to all who adequately further that purpose, … then it is fair to say that any aid going to a religious recipient only has the effect of furthering that secular purpose."[284] And all that was ruled necessary to assure this required neutrality was that the aid flowed to parochial schools "only as a result of genuinely independent and private choices of individuals" because this makes more difficult government's granting of special favors and "mitigat[es] the preference for pre-existing recipients."[285] The plurality asserted that neutrality and independent private choice also removed any financial incentive here to choose religious education and thus eliminated any attribution of religious indoctrination to the government.

Moreover, the plurality linked private choice to moderating the "directness" of any state aid to private parochial schools in a way that signaled the support to come for school choice voucher systems: "If aid to schools, even 'direct aid,' is neutrally available and, before reaching or benefiting any religious school, first passes through the hands (literally or figuratively) of numerous private citizens who are free to direct the aid elsewhere, the government has not provided any 'support of religion.'"[286] But for this broad, bold, and otherwise unjustified proposition Justice Thomas cited merely the Court's approval in *Witters* of vocational rehabilitation assistance for an individual blind student at a Christian college. That unanimous, yet very narrow, result had the support even of the Justices most hesitant to endorse programs of state aid for parochial elementary and secondary schools, and it is a large and unwarranted leap from assistance to

282 *Mitchell*, 530 U.S. at 802 (plurality opinion).

283 *Id.* at 804, 808; *id.* at 837 (O'Connor, J., concurring in the judgment).

284 *Id.* at 810 (plurality opinion).

285 *Id.*

286 *Id.* at 816 (quoting *Witters*, 417 U.S. at 489).

a single, disabled college student in *Witters* to the plurality's expansive statement in *Mitchell* about primary and secondary school aid generally. Indeed, in one of many criticisms, Justice Souter reiterated the "special concern" and "dangers" associated with government aid to primary and secondary parochial schools.[287] Justice Thomas also seemed to suggest that even direct government payments of money to parochial schools might not be unconstitutional,[288] causing Justice O'Connor, despite concurring in the judgment, to warn of just how radical Justice Thomas' opinion was: "[T]he plurality opinion foreshadows the approval of direct monetary subsidies to religious organizations, even when they use the money to advance their religious objectives."[289]

Most remarkably, perhaps, the plurality extrapolated from the very limited circumstances of the sign language interpreter permitted in *Zobrest*, analogous to a hearing aid, into an unqualified principle: Instructional materials and equipment a state gives to parochial schools, the content of which itself must not be religious in nature, nonetheless may be diverted to, and used for, religious education without raising Establishment Clause problems. In other words, "the *use* of governmental aid to further religious indoctrination [is not] synonymous with religious indoctrination *by* the government."[290] In making this extraordinary move, the plurality ignored the subtle but significant differences between, for example, a computer that the state provides to an individual deaf student to permit translating audio into writing and government-owned computers loaned to a school and then used for explicitly religious lessons. In the first instance, a computer simply allows a single physically handicapped student to participate on a par with his classmates; it compensates for a physical deficit and likely is perceived to do no more. In the second case, the state-provided computers supplant an expense the school otherwise would bear and affirmatively enable religious indoctrination for an entire class of students who could access the material in another manner that would not implicate the state. With respect to the latter situation, there is a much greater danger of a symbolic union of church and state; the state is associated with the religious message it facilitates for the class and inevitably is perceived to endorse that message. Justice O'Connor's concurring opinion recognized just this type of significant difference in public perception regarding government endorsement of religion.[291] There always are difficult line-drawing problems in allowing some level of state aid to sectarian education, but flatly eliminating the "no divertibility" rule opens wide the door for state assisted and sanctioned religious indoctrination.

---

287 *Mitchell*, 530 U.S. at 887, 904–05 (Souter, J., dissenting).

288 *Id.* at 818–20 & n.8 (plurality opinion).

289 *Id.* at 844 (O'Connor, J., concurring in judgment). As the dissent stated: "The plurality position breaks fundamentally with Establishment Clause principle." *Id.* at 869 (Souter, J., dissenting).

290 *Id.* at 820–21 (plurality opinion) (emphasis in original).

291 *Id.* at 842–43 (O'Connor, J., concurring in judgment and joined by Breyer, J.).

Finally, Justice Thomas railed against the characterization of a private school as "pervasively sectarian" as one factor in evaluating the constitutionality of its receiving various forms of state aid. He connected the phrase historically to anti-Catholic sentiment (with some justification) and asserted that such a depiction might reflect "special hostility" and even "bigotry" toward those deeply religious.[292] Yet Justice Souter, dissenting, considered the characterization today "simply … a matter of common sense," an altogether reasonable concern in the necessary Establishment Clause inquiry.[293] Indeed, an Islamic madrassa or Orthodox yeshiva might well be pervasively sectarian in the Court's sense. Simply as a factual matter, in the modern Court's state aid cases most of the private schools receiving assistance were religiously affiliated, and largely were Catholic schools. In these cases the Court appropriately used the sectarian aspect of a private school mainly to assess the degree to which government aid could be confined to assisting secular education rather than promoting religious indoctrination.[294]

Justice O'Connor, joined by Justice Breyer, adhered to the approach in *Agostini*. They concurred only in the judgment to object to the plurality's new "rule of unprecedented breadth for the evaluation of Establishment Clause challenges to government school aid programs" that "does not accurately describe our recent Establishment Clause jurisprudence."[295] In particular, they agreed with Justice Souter's dissent for himself and Justices Stevens and Ruth Bader Ginsburg (thus forming a majority of the Court on this point) in protesting that the plurality inappropriately elevated the important element of neutrality, in the sense of evenhandedness in distribution of aid, to a "single and sufficient" test of constitutionality.[296] While Justices O'Connor and Breyer considered a presumption of religious indoctrination from a neutral school aid program normally inappropriate, they also were clear that "actual diversion of government aid to religious indoctrination" is wholly impermissible.[297] They further agreed with

292 *Id.* at 827–29 (plurality opinion).

293 *See id.* at 885–87, 904–06, 912 (Souter, J., dissenting); *see also Bowen*, 487 U.S. at 610 ("[a]id normally may be thought to have a primary effect of advancing religion when it flows to an institution in which religion is so pervasive that a substantial portion of its functions are subsumed in the religious mission. …") (*quoting Hunt*, 413 U.S. at 743). *But see* Colo. Christian Univ. v. Weaver, 534 F.3d 1245 (10th Cir. 2008) (McConnell, J.).

294 *See Bowen*, 487 U.S. 630–31 (Blackmun, J., dissenting).

295 *Mitchell*, 530 U.S. at 837, 839 (O'Connor, Breyer, JJ., concurring in the judgment).

296 *Id.* at 838; *see also Rosenberger*, 515 U.S. at 882 (Souter, J., dissenting) ("Evenhandedness as one element of a permissibly attenuated benefit is, of course, a far cry from evenhandedness as a sufficient condition of constitutionality for direct financial support of religious proselytization, and our cases have unsurprisingly repudiated any such attempt to cut the Establishment Clause down to a mere prohibition against unequal direct aid.").

297 *Mitchell*, 530 U.S. at 837, 840 (O'Connor, Breyer, JJ., concurring in the judgment). Previously Justice O'Connor had stressed that "*any* use of public funds to

Justice Souter's dissent that the plurality's contrary use of precedent, including *Zobrest* and *Witters*, was wrong in this regard. So, any "religious teaching [must be] done without the instructional aids provided by the government."[298]

Justice Souter began his comprehensive and powerful dissent by recounting the Establishment Clause purposes threatened by government aid to religion, especially funding of parochial schools.

> [The Establishment Clause] is meant to guarantee the right of individual conscience against compulsion, to protect the integrity of religion against the corrosion of secular support, and to preserve the unity of political society against the implied exclusion of the less favored and the antagonism of controversy over public support for religious causes.[299]

Justice Souter then explicated several different ways in which the Court had used the concept of "neutrality" in Establishment Clause cases, and he exposed the inappropriateness of the plurality's simplistic reliance on the "insufficiency of evenhandedness neutrality as a stand-alone criterion of constitutional intent or effect."[300]

> At least three main lines of enquiry addressed particularly to school aid have emerged to complement evenhandedness neutrality. First, we have noted that two types of aid recipients heighten Establishment Clause concern: pervasively religious schools and primary and secondary religious schools. Second, we have identified two important characteristics of the method of distributing aid: directness or indirectness of distribution and distribution by genuinely independent choice. Third, we have found relevance in at least five characteristics of the aid itself: its religious content; its cash form; its divertibility or actually [sic] diversion to religious support; its supplantation of traditional items of religious school expense; and its substantiality.[301]

---

promote religious doctrines violates the Establishment Clause." *Bowen*, 487 U.S. at 623 (O'Connor, J., concurring) (emphasis in original).

298 *Mitchell*, 530 U.S. at 859–60 (O'Connor, Breyer, JJ., concurring in the judgment). Justice O'Connor described safeguards she thought sufficient; evidence they were not complied with was *de minimis*. *Id.* at 861–67. The dissenters sharply disagreed. *Id.* at 902–10 (Souter, Stevens, Ginsburg, JJ., dissenting).

299 *Id.* at 868.

300 *Id.* at 878–84. In contrast to the school aid context, most recently seven Justices agreed that, even though a town that opened its official board meetings with a sectarian prayer acted neutrally among religions because a representative of any faith theoretically could deliver the invocation, the constitutionality of the practice required a "fact-sensitive" analysis of the overall circumstances, including the "course and practice over time." *Town of Greece*, 134 S. Ct. at 1823, 1825, 1838, 1851 (plurality and dissenting opinions).

301 *Mitchell*, 530 U.S. at 885 (Souter, Stevens, Ginsburg, JJ., dissenting).

In his extended dissent, Justice Souter analyzed these traditional factors not only to demonstrate that the Jefferson Parish program clearly violated the Establishment Clause but also to conclude that the plurality's "abandonment of doctrine," if followed by a majority, would mean the "end of the principle of no aid to [private] schools' religious mission."[302]

O. Zelman v. Simmons-Harris

After *Mitchell* it was inevitable that the constitutionality of tax-supported voucher initiatives and related tuition breaks for parents who send their children to private schools would garner majority support on the Court, especially if a sympathetic case led the way. The push for vouchers was fueled by the growing perception and reality of woefully inadequate public schools and the desperate desire of parents for alternatives. Reading the distressing second paragraph of Chief Justice Rehnquist's opinion for the Court in *Zelman,* in which he details how "[f]or more than a generation ... Cleveland's public schools have been among the worst performing public schools in the Nation," one must wonder how this "crisis that is perhaps unprecedented" could occur anywhere in twentieth-century America, let alone in a major city and cultural center.[303] The situation in Cleveland was so dire that in 1995 a federal district court singularly placed the City's school district under state control.

Affluent families can afford private schools, and it is easy to appreciate the plight of those who cannot, especially when they still are taxed to support public schools that so badly fail their children. For many, inculcating religion may be a secondary concern to procuring a safe and effective education for their children. In this regard religion may be considered an incidental aspect of private, parochial schooling as an alternative to public schools, but because the great majority of financially available non-public schools often are sectarian, it remains the primary constitutional concern. As such, it is important to note both the limited nature of the voucher program that the Court approved in *Zelman* and the dismal educational circumstances that prompted it, particularly because *Zelman* is the only such case likely to be adjudicated at the federal level for the foreseeable future now that the Supreme Court in *Winn* has greatly restricted plaintiffs' standing to challenge such tax-supported programs.

To address Cleveland's calamitous educational situation, Ohio created a Pilot Project Scholarship Program for students in kindergarten through third grade (increasing over time to eighth grade) to provide financial assistance to any families in a school district under state control. Under the program, students opting to remain in public school received tutorial help. Alternatively, parents could choose any participating private school and receive a voucher for tuition assistance. Any private, secular or parochial school in the district could participate as long as it

302 *Id.* at 911.

303 *Zelman*, 536 U.S. at 644.

met state educational standards, but, notably, the school could not discriminate in admissions or teach hatred on the basis of race, religion, or ethnicity.[304] Public schools in adjacent districts also could participate and receive a $2,250 tuition grant for each Cleveland student they accepted, in addition to the full amount of regular state funding per enrolled student; none, however, chose to participate. Most of the 75,000 children in the Cleveland City School District were from low-income and minority families, and the amount of programmatic tuition assistance to parents was capped at $2,250, based on financial need. For the lowest income group a participating private school was limited to charging parents a maximum co-payment of $250; otherwise there was no co-payment limit. The choice of a participating private school was entirely up to parents, who received a check from the program and endorsed it to the selected school. Partial grants for tutorial assistance from registered tutors similarly were need-based and capped at $360, and the number of such tutorial grants offered had to equal the number of tuition assistance grants awarded to students attending participating private, or adjacent-district public, schools. In his dissent, Justice Souter summarized the financial effects of the program: "[S]ubstantial amounts of tax money are … systematically underwriting religious practice and indoctrination."[305]

Given the limited financial assistance available to most parents and the cost structure of private, secular versus parochial schools, the resulting statistics were not surprising: 46 of the 56 participating private schools (82 percent) were religiously affiliated, the remaining ten had limited seats available, and the parochial schools enrolled over 96 percent of the 3,700 students in the scholarship program. Ohio also established ten start-up community schools in Cleveland, academically independent and funded by the state at twice the level of support for a participating program school. Community schools, which could not be religiously affiliated, accepted 1,900 students by lottery. Also, 25 new public magnet schools with specialized teaching methods or particularized curricula served 13,000 children and received funding for each pupil greater than the amount provided for a student enrolled in a traditional public school.

Thus Ohio's private school tuition assistance program was one part of a broader initiative with the legitimate secular purpose of serving a discrete group of financially disadvantaged students and their families by providing urgently needed, improved educational opportunities. But most families that chose to use the voucher program for private schools selected a parochial school, and they did so mainly for better and safer educational opportunities, not because of a school's religious affiliation; indeed, about two-thirds opted for schools with a religious

304 Justices Souter and Breyer described inevitable difficulties these provisions could create for some parochial schools, as a price of participating in the program and receiving government money, and for state authorities trying to enforce them. *Id.* at 712–16 (Souter, J., dissenting); *id.* at 724–25 (Breyer, J., dissenting).

305 *Id.* at 711 (Souter, J., dissenting).

affiliation different from their own.[306] Still, almost all students receiving state aid in the private school program attended parochial schools, prompting an Establishment Clause challenge based on the program's effect of advancing religion.

In her separate concurrence, Justice O'Connor acknowledged that the Ohio program was different from other school aid cases because here parochial schools received state aid with no restrictions on its use.[307] Indeed, state funding that subsidized tuition at a participating parochial school helped place a student in that school and partially underwrote the pupil's entire educational experience there. So, as opposed to other forms of state assistance, such as loans of textbooks, with this form of state aid there is little theoretical or realistic ability to segregate and apply it only to neutral, secular materials or nonsectarian components of education. Subsidized school tuition, in particular, supports the salaries of teachers, including religious teachers teaching religious doctrine or leading devotional exercises, as well as the math teacher. But given the shift in the Court over recent years, it was relatively easy for Chief Justice Rehnquist's opinion for a five-Justice majority to ignore this difference and uphold the Cleveland program by characterizing it as a neutral government program providing aid not directly to religious institutions but to a broad class of individuals not defined by religion.[308] Moreover, this government support reached parochial schools only through the "genuine and independent choices of private individuals."[309]

To buttress his constitutional argument, Chief Justice Rehnquist then relied on *Mueller*, *Witters*, and *Zobrest* without confronting, as Justice Souter's dissent noted,[310] the limited applicability of these dissimilar and narrow cases to the far more comprehensive Ohio program of private school tuition subsidies. Instead, the majority stressed its view that given the range of options Ohio made available to parents, including traditional public schools, community schools, magnet schools, and a few private, secular schools, its program was one of true private choice with no financial incentives favoring religious schools.[311] But as Justice

306 *Id.* at 704 & n.12, 712.

307 *Id.* at 663 (O'Connor, J., concurring).

308 Chief Justice Rehnquist ignored several ways tax-supported vouchers also can benefit parochial schools themselves. A parochial school itself benefits if, without the subsidy, some students would attend another school and the parochial school then could not fill its available seats with non-subsidized students. Also, the subsidy may enable a school to charge a somewhat higher tuition. Regardless of any benefit to a parochial school, a government tuition subsidy supports a student's religious education.

309 *Id.* at 649, 652–62 (majority opinion). The Court clarified that its contrary decision in *Nyquist* does not apply to this "neutral" sort of program. *Id.* at 662.

310 *Id.* at 708–09 & n.18 (Souter, J., dissenting).

311 To counter the fact that over 96 percent of families choosing private schools selected sectarian ones, Chief Justice Rehnquist argued that figure should be substantially diluted by considering not just the student population of private schools in the program but that of all schooling choices available to parents—community, magnet, and traditional public schools. *Id.* at 659–60 (majority opinion); *see also id.* at 670–76 (O'Connor, J.,

Souter persuasively argued, both as to neutrality and private choice, the Court should not have focused on the entire range of educational opportunities that parents had, including various types of public schools. Instead, the Court should have concentrated on the much narrower range of private, secular and parochial schools—the only places where the government vouchers could be applied—and asked whether within *that* universe the scheme favored a religious direction. Here the statistics were clear and dramatically refuted the majority's reliance on choice:

> The 96.6% reflects, instead, the fact that too few nonreligious school desks are available and few but religious schools can afford to accept more than a handful of voucher students. … For the overwhelming number of children in the voucher scheme, the only alternative to the public schools is religious. And it is entirely irrelevant that the State did not deliberately design the network of private schools for the sake of channeling money into religious institutions. The criterion is one of genuinely free choice on the part of the private individuals who choose, and a Hobson's choice is not a choice, whatever the reason for being Hobsonian.[312]

Justice Souter's point is well taken. Otherwise, even if all private schools in the program were parochial, their enrollment still would have been dwarfed by that of the various public alternatives, and the majority still could have considered the program of private school tuition subsidies neutral, with parochial school attendance the product of private individual choice.[313] The majority, however, clung to its myth of choice, and neither the fact that most participating private schools were religiously affiliated (mirroring their percentage of all private schools in Ohio), nor that the vast majority (over 96 percent) of student beneficiaries of the Ohio voucher program attended parochial schools, supported an Establishment Clause claim. Rather, the majority focused only on the abstract structure of the voucher initiative, and, despite the constitutional inquiry supposedly focused on

---

concurring). But of the choices available to parents, only the private schools could be religiously affiliated, so that was the appropriate population for comparison. *See id.* at 685 (Stevens, J., dissenting); *id.* at 697–98 (Souter, J., dissenting). Justice O'Connor went much further afield, comparing Cleveland's financial support for religious education with the totality of tax and other benefits religious institutions generally enjoy from state and federal governments. *Id.* at 665–68 (O'Connor, J., concurring). But the enormity of these other existing benefits argues against extending yet additional support to sectarian institutions, especially subsidization of religious indoctrination in primary and secondary schools.

312 *Id.* at 707 (Souter, J., dissenting).

313 "The majority has confused choice in spending scholarships with choice from the entire menu of possible educational placements, most of them open to anyone willing to attend a public school. … If 'choice' is present whenever there is any educational alternative to the religious school to which vouchers can be endorsed, then there will always be a choice and the voucher can always be constitutional, even in a system in which there is not a single private secular school as an alternative to the religious school." *Id.* at 698–700 (Souter, J., dissenting).

the effect of advancing religion, they read the real world effects of the program out of the analysis: "The constitutionality of a neutral educational aid program simply does not turn on whether and why, in a particular area, at a particular time, most private schools are run by religious organizations, or most recipients choose to use the aid at a religious school."[314]

But when it came to evaluating the risk that the Ohio program presented of creating an imprimatur of state support for religion, the Court took the opposite tact. "The incidental advancement of a religious mission, or the perceived endorsement of a religious message, is reasonably attributable to the individual recipient, not to the government, whose role ends with the disbursement of benefits."[315] Yet, this reasonable attribution depended in good measure on the real world context of the Ohio program well known to be a response to a seismic educational crisis, one designed to "assist poor children in failed schools" and not to promote religious education.[316] The Court thus ignored the real world consequences of private, independent choice that resulted in massive public support for religious education; nonetheless, it relied on the real world impetus for the program to avoid government endorsement.

Justice Souter wrote the main dissent, joined by Justices Stevens, Ginsburg, and Breyer, to demonstrate the stages through which the Court's school aid cases had passed in the half-century since *Everson* to now reach "doctrinal bankruptcy."[317] Even before *Winn*, Justice Souter presciently closed with the lament that the current majority has "largely silenced" the Establishment Clause in school aid cases and the hope that the political branches of government, even though beset with the problems of public education, will heed the dangers of further breaching separation of church and state in this area "now that they know a federal court will not save them" from overreaching.[318] The continuing battles over proliferating tax-funded vouchers and tax mechanisms that underwrite religious education and benefit parochial schools indicate this may be a forlorn hope, especially as these programs expand to extend aid beyond financially- or educationally-disadvantaged student populations and perhaps include private schools that follow or facilitate discriminatory policies or practices.[319]

---

314 *Id.* at 658 (majority opinion). Previously, however, both Justices Kennedy and Scalia apparently had accepted the proposition that "a statute which provides for exclusive or disproportionate funding to pervasively sectarian institutions may impermissibly advance religion and as such be invalid on its face." *Bowen*, 487 U.S. at 624 (Kennedy, Scalia, JJ., concurring).

315 *Zelman*, 536 U.S. at 652.

316 *Id.* at 655.

317 *Id.* at 688 (Souter, J., dissenting).

318 *Id.* at 717.

319 *See* Chapter 1, n.90 (discussing Brumfield v. Dodd, 2014 U.S. Dist. LEXIS 106541 (E.D. La. Aug. 4, 2014)) and Introduction chapter, n.22 (regarding Georgia's education tax credit program).

Finally, Justice Breyer, joined by Justices Stevens and Souter, wrote an additional dissent that traced the familiar history of the vastly increased religious diversity of the country, spurred by immigration and growth in previous generations, and the bitter conflicts this engendered over religion in public schools. He expressed the fear that the Court was "turn[ing] back the clock" and "emphasize[d] the risk that publicly financed voucher programs pose in terms of religiously based social conflict."[320] Most importantly, in a single paragraph Justice Breyer strikingly undermined the Court's ubiquitous invocation of "private choice" as a panacea to resolve Establishment Clause problems with government aid to religious schools:

> Parental choice cannot help the taxpayer who does not want to finance the religious education of children. It will not always help the parent who may see little real choice between inadequate nonsectarian public education and adequate education at a school whose religious teachings are contrary to his own. It will not satisfy religious minorities unable to participate because they are too few in number to support the creation of their own private schools. It will not satisfy groups whose religious beliefs preclude them from participating in a government-sponsored program, and who may well feel ignored as government funds primarily support the education of children in the doctrines of the dominant religions. And it does little to ameliorate the entanglement problems or the related problems of social division [described earlier]. Consequently, the fact that the parent may choose which school can cash the government's voucher check does not alleviate the Establishment Clause concerns associated with voucher programs.[321]

V. Conclusion

A strict Madisonian adherent of separation of church and state takes a dim view of the current Supreme Court's allowance of public funds raised through taxation for use in support of religious education. A separationist perceives the Court's reliance on neutrality—in terms merely of abstract evenhandedness in distribution—together with independent private choice as validating proliferating government aid programs to be simply "subterfuges" exalting form over substance

---

320 *Zelman*, 536 U.S. at 715, 717, 728 (Breyer, Stevens, Souter, JJ., dissenting).

321 *Id.* at 728. Subsequent to *Zelman*, however, the Court reiterated its broad and unnuanced position in the context of higher education: "Under our Establishment Clause precedent, the link between government funds and religious training is broken by the independent and private choice of recipients." *Locke*, 540 U.S. at 715, 719 (holding that while the Establishment Clause would not have prevented the State of Washington from allowing a college student to use the State's Promise Scholarship Program to pursue a college degree in devotional theology at a private, Christian college, under its own constitution the State could deny such use of its financial aid without violating the Free Exercise Clause).

to funnel taxpayer money to parochial schools. And such an adherent certainly wants to preserve federal courts as fora for taxpayers to seek constitutional adjudication of specific tax-supported school choice initiatives. On the other hand, one who takes a much more constrained, accommodationist view of the Establishment Clause and, for any of several reasons, wishes to support parochial education as one positive alternative to public schools, is likely to favor various stratagems and legal arguments to maneuver incrementally over time around constitutional barriers. An accommodationist also is inclined to endorse an across-the-board approach to supporting imaginative tax-funded school choice programs by precluding case-by-case federal court review through the denial of taxpayer standing to challenge them. If the latter approach is a fair characterization of a majority of the current Court, then the result in *Winn*, analyzed in Chapter 4, is no surprise.

Indeed, one reasonably may ask whether the Court today would uphold the constitutionality of a slightly modernized version of Patrick Henry's proposed *Virginia Tax Assessment*, assuming citizen or taxpayer standing to challenge it. Without the facial restriction in the eighteenth-century bill exclusively to Christian denominations (and the public, individualized accounting), such assessment could be viewed by a majority of the Court as neutral and evenhanded. Most of the money raised through this refined assessment probably would reach parochial schools, as with most of the modern tax-supported choice programs, but some theoretically could be designated for private, secular schools. This possibility could preserve the assessment's supposed neutrality regarding religion. And taxpayer money would reach its private, secular or sectarian destination only through the genuine, private, independent choices of individual taxpayers. If this thought experiment about the current Court's treatment of a modern version of Henry's *Assessment* is plausible, and Justice Thomas' concurring opinion in *Rosenberger* suggests that it is,[322] it indicates just how far the Court has moved since *Everson* and how very much Madison's *Memorial and Remonstrance*, once a revered canon of American constitutional principle, has faded.

322 *Rosenberger*, 515 U.S. at 852–58 (Thomas, J., concurring). Justice Souter's dissent for four members of the Court, however, soundly refutes Thomas' position. *Id.* at 868–72 & nn.1, 2 (Souter, Stevens, Ginsburg, Breyer, JJ., dissenting), as does Justice Kagan's dissent in *Winn*, 131 S. Ct. at 1461–62 & nn.11, 12 (Kagan, J., dissenting) (noting with respect to the *Memorial and Remonstrance* that "the majority betrays Madison's vision").

Chapter 3
Tax Expenditures and School Financing

> Cash grants and targeted tax breaks are means of accomplishing the same government objective—to provide financial support to select individuals or organizations. Taxpayers who oppose state aid of religion have equal reason to protest whether that aid flows from the one form of subsidy or the other. Either way, the government has financed the religious activity. And so either way, taxpayers should be able to challenge the subsidy.[1]

I. Introduction

Targeted tax breaks of various forms, afforded by Congress or a state legislature pursuant to its taxing and spending powers,[2] are by their very nature government subsidies. Since the 1970s, the Supreme Court repeatedly has recognized this fact. In *Walz v. Tax Commission of the City of New York*, all Justices essentially concurred that tax "exemptions do not differ from subsidies as an economic matter;"[3] even the lone dissenter, Justice William O. Douglas, bluntly commented: "A tax exemption is a subsidy."[4] Almost 20 years later in *Texas Monthly, Inc. v. Bullock*, Justice William J. Brennan, writing for the majority, noted: "Every tax exemption constitutes a subsidy that affects nonqualifying taxpayers, forcing them to become 'indirect and vicarious donors.'"[5] Justice Antonin Scalia, joined by Chief Justice William H. Rehnquist and Justice Anthony Kennedy, agreed in dissent that in some contexts "tax exemptions and subsidies are equivalent."[6] In *Regan v. Taxation with Representation of Washington*, a unanimous court stated more broadly:

> Both tax exemptions and tax-deductibility are a form of subsidy that is administered through the tax system. A tax exemption has much the same effect

---

1 Ariz. Christian Sch. Tuition Org. v. Winn, 131 S. Ct. 1436, 1450 (2011) (Kagan, J., dissenting).

2 Congress exercises its "Power To lay and collect Taxes … and Excises" directly on the people and its spending power to use tax revenues "to pay the Debts and provide for the … general Welfare." This language is from the U.S. Constitution, Art. 1, § 8, conferring taxing and spending powers on Congress. Although the language of state constitutions varies, all confer similar taxing and spending powers on their legislatures.

3 397 U.S. 664, 699 (1970) (Harlan, J., concurring). *See id.* at 674–75 (majority opinion); *id.* at 690–91 (Brennan, J., concurring).

4 *Id.* at 704 (Douglas, J., dissenting).

5 489 U.S. 1, 14 (1989) (quoting Bob Jones Univ. v. United States, 461 U.S. 574, 591 (1983)).

6 *Texas Monthly*, 489 U.S. at 43 (Scalia, J., dissenting) (citation omitted).

> as a [direct] cash grant to the organization of the amount of tax it would have to pay on its income. Deductible [charitable] contributions are similar to cash grants of the amount of a portion of the individual's contributions.[7]

And quite recently in *National Federation of Independent Business v. Sebelius* ("*NFIB*"), regarding the Patient Protection and Affordable Care Act requirement that individuals purchase health insurance, the four dissenting Justices equated tax credits to government subsidies, commenting: "The Act's design is to allocate billions of federal dollars to *subsidize* individuals' purchases on the exchanges. [To achieve this objective,] [i]ndividuals with incomes between 100 and 400 percent of the poverty level receive tax credits to offset the cost of insurance to the individual purchaser."[8]

Each of these cases, except *NFIB*, involved the issue of how the particular tax subsidy comported with either the First Amendment's Establishment Clause or Free Speech Clause. Under the Court's jurisprudence, the simple fact that, as an economic matter, a tax benefit subsidizes religion—in particular, supports the religious education of primary or secondary school students—does not mean it comprises an unconstitutional establishment of religion. Historical considerations as well as the form of the tax benefit and the way it is implemented may make a difference to the Court. Moreover, a stringent application of these factors may determine whether a taxpayer even has standing to raise an Establishment Clause challenge to the tax program in federal court. Indeed, in its most recent pronouncement through Justice Kennedy's five-Justice majority opinion in *Arizona Christian School Tuition Organization v. Winn*, the Court ruled that a state had not "extracted and spent" taxpayer funds sufficiently to create taxpayer standing.[9] This was so even though the Arizona legislature granted a dollar-for-dollar, capped income tax credit to taxpayers for contributions to Arizona's sectarian and nonsectarian Scholarship Tuition Organizations ("STOs"), which in turn used those contributed funds to support children's tuition for private, secular, but mostly parochial, schools. And, in contrast to the position he joined in *Texas Monthly*, Justice Kennedy in *Winn* effectively found the tax credit not equivalent to a government cash grant or direct subsidy. While the standing issue is discussed

7 461 U.S. 540, 544 (1983).

8 132 S. Ct. 2566, 2673 (2012) (joint opinion of Scalia, Kennedy, Thomas, and Alito, JJ.) (emphasis added). Chief Justice John G. Roberts, Jr., writing for a majority in a portion of the opinion, ruled that the shared responsibility payment compelling individuals to pay funds to the Internal Revenue Service if they fail to purchase health insurance is a tax, not a penalty, imposed to influence individuals' conduct. He noted: "That [I.R.C.] §5000A seeks to shape decisions about whether to buy health insurance does not mean that it cannot be a valid exercise of the taxing power." *Id.* at 2596. Logically, this means that the tax credit that government provides to subsidize low-income individuals to induce them to purchase health insurance is a "tax expenditure," a term discussed below in Section IV.

9 *Winn*, 131 S. Ct. at 1446 (internal quotations omitted).

in Chapter 4, this chapter focuses on government expenditures of public funds through legislatively enacted tax concessions that aid religious education and how their form and manner of implementation might affect the significant Establishment Clause issues they raise.

II. Tax Concessions in the Context of School Financing: General Background

Tax accommodations—whether federal, state, or local—are crafted in a variety of forms: exemptions, exclusions, deductions, and credits.[10] Congress or a state legislature enjoys broad constitutional power to tax and spend and must affirmatively enact an income, sales, property, or other type of tax statute to grant the tax concession to individual taxpayers, for-profit businesses, or nonprofit organizations. So, for example, nonprofit organizations that qualify under Internal Revenue Code ("I.R.C.") § 501(c)(3) include charitable entities (such as Arizona's STOs), religious organizations, and private educational institutions (both secular and parochial schools). Each such entity receives numerous tax privileges. On the federal level, they are exempt from income taxation under I.R.C. § 501(a), are exempt from paying the federal unemployment excise tax on employees' wages,[11] and may be entitled to opt out of paying the employer's portion of federal social security taxes and Medicare taxes.[12] They also are eligible to receive contributions that are deductible by their donors under federal estate and gift taxes,[13] as well as donations that qualify for the I.R.C. § 170 income tax deduction available to corporations and the 30 percent of individual taxpayers who itemize income tax deductions rather than claim the standard deduction.[14]

---

10 Tuition vouchers, discussed in Chapter 2 in the context of *Zelman v. Simmons-Harris*, are of course financed by government tax revenues and allow parents to direct state money to private, secular or parochial schools. So they clearly raise Establishment Clause issues. But they are not part of this chapter's discussion because they are not tax mechanisms *per se*. Tax considerations are relevant however. Namely, whether the value of a tuition voucher is excludable from a state taxpayer's gross income depends upon state tax law, but for federal income tax purposes its value likely would be excludable from gross income under I.R.C. § 117 as a scholarship. For further discussion of § 117 in the context of Education Savings Accounts ("ESAs"), *see infra* note 26 and accompanying text.

11 I.R.C. § 3306(c)(8) (West 2012).

12 *Id.* at § 3121(b)(8), (10) (2006 & Supp. II 2008); Treas. Reg. §§ 31.3121(b)(8)-(2); (b)(10)-2 (2013) (applicable to § 501(c)(3) educational organizations and churches and church-controlled, -supported, and -operated elementary and secondary schools).

13 I.R.C. §§ 2055(a)(2), 2522(a)(2) (2006 & Supp. I. 2007).

14 Approximately 70 percent of individual taxpayers—those who tend to have lower incomes—take the standard deduction, which precludes their claiming a separate § 170 contribution deduction currently available only to taxpayers who itemize deductions. The split of about 70 percent non-itemizing individual taxpayers and 30 percent itemizing

Transfers qualify for the § 170 contribution deduction, however, only if the transferor has a donative or altruistic intent—meaning, the transferor cannot expect or receive a substantial measurable benefit in return, namely a *quid pro quo* such as the value of part or all of her child's tuition to a private school.[15] A returned benefit would render the contribution nondeductible, at least as to the benefit's value.[16] The I.R.C. § 170 deduction makes "unrequited payments"[17] to § 501(c)(3) entities less expensive for the donor-taxpayer, a significant inducement for the donor. At the same time, the tax structure of the deduction reduces one source of government revenue and so may cause other taxpayers to pay more, thereby sharing the cost of the gift, without the recipient entity sacrificing a single dollar. As the numerical illustrations below demonstrate, the charitable contribution deduction allows a participating taxpayer a discount on the cost of giving determined by the taxpayer's marginal income tax rate.[18] Because this discount may induce a taxpayer to make a larger contribution, § 501(c)(3) recipient-organizations may reap tangible pecuniary benefits enlarging their revenues.[19] Thus overall Congress uses its taxing and spending powers to impose an income tax on all taxpayers, to grant a special

---

taxpayers has been consistent for more than a decade. For a fuller discussion, *see* Nina J. Crimm & Laurence H. Winer, Politics, Taxes, and the Pulpit: Provocative First Amendment Conflicts 60–61 nn.133–34 (Oxford Univ. Press 2011).

15 Graham v. Commissioner, 822 F.2d 844, 848 (9th Cir. 1987). *See also* Hernandez v. Commissioner, 490 U.S. 680 (1989); Sklar v. Commissioner, 549 F.3d 1252 (9th Cir. 2008); Sklar v. Commissioner, 282 F.3d 610 (9th Cir. 2002).

16 United States v. Am. Bar Ass'n, 477 U.S. 105, 116, 118 (1986) (holding the "*sine qua non* of a charitable contribution is a transfer of money or [tangible or intangible] property without adequate consideration."); Treas. Reg. § 1.170A-1(h); Rev. Rul. 67–246, 1967–2 C.B. 104.

17 *Hernandez*, 490 U.S. at 690.

18 As the Supreme Court in *Regan v. Taxation with Representation of Washington* noted: "Deductible contributions are similar to cash grants [to the donor] of the amount of a portion of the individual's contributions." 461 U.S. at 544. In essence, the § 170 contribution deduction provides the taxpayer the functional equivalent of a matching grant from government, the amount of which depends upon the taxpayer's marginal income tax rate. The deduction therefore is worth more to those in higher income brackets. For a numerical example, *see* illustration #2 in Section III.

19 Numerous studies demonstrate that the federal tax system generally influences the size and distribution of giving. Indeed, for donations to all § 501(c)(3) organizations, the price elasticity for the population of taxpayers is probably greater than one in absolute value, suggesting the efficiency of the § 170 contribution deduction. *See* Crimm & Winer, *supra* note 14, at 62 nn.135–36. This implies that a 10 percent decrease in the price of giving would lead to an increase of more than 10 percent in the amount donated. *See id.* The actual effect of I.R.C. § 170 on revenues of private, secular and parochial K–12 schools collectively, however, is largely indeterminate. A recent study found that the sensitivity of donation amounts to taxes differs for different types of § 501(c)(3) entities. There appears to be significant tax price elasticity for private educational institutions as a whole. Robert J. Yetman & Michelle H. Yetman, *How Does the Incentive Effect of the Charitable*

tax deduction to each qualifying taxpayer for eligible contributions, to exempt the § 501(c)(3) recipient from income taxation on the contribution received, and to spend tax revenues collected from all other taxpayers to subsidize both the § 501(c)(3) entity and each qualifying donor for such transactions.

State income tax privileges for § 501(c)(3) entities and their contributors, again conferred affirmatively by legislative grace, often mirror those under federal income tax laws and provide parallel effects. Therefore this duality can provide the same entities and their contributors twin state and federal benefits of income tax-exemption for the § 501(c)(3) organization and charitable contribution deduction for donors, which enhance the respective potential revenue and giving effects described above. At the same time, a state legislature's taxing and spending powers force all other state taxpayers vicariously to subsidize the donor and donee.

As presented in Chapter 1, states also may provide targeted income tax breaks relevant to educating K–12 students that are not available under federal tax laws. For example, some states provide "plain vanilla" tax deductions or credits, or both, to parents (or guardians) for payments to private education providers for children's qualifying education tuition, instruction, and materials.[20] On a per student basis, it is possible that some tax accommodations might approximate the amount of money the state government raises through some form of taxation—such as property taxes—and spends for comparable education expenses of a child at public school. While these tax dispensations reduce the amount of income taxes

---

Deduction Vary Across Charities?, *available at* http://ssrn.com/abstract=1435150 (last visited Oct. 1, 2013).

20 Illinois and Iowa give tax credits to parents of students for qualified education expenses incurred for tuition, books, and instructional materials. 35 Ill. Comp. Stat. 5/201 (2013); Iowa Code § 422.12 (2013). Louisiana provides a tax deduction to parents for a more extensive array of education expenses whether the parents itemize or alternatively claim the standard deduction for state income tax purposes. The permissible deduction is limited to 50 percent of the actual amount of tuition and fees paid per student or $5,000, whichever is less, and the amount of the deduction cannot exceed the total taxable income of the taxpayer. La. Rev. Stat. §§ 47:293(9)(a)(xiv)–(xvi); 47:297.10–12 (2011). Minnesota allows itemizing and non-itemizing eligible parents either a tax deduction or a tax credit for education expenditures for qualifying students who attend private schools. Both the Minnesota tax deduction and tax credit cover books, tutors, academic after-school programs, and other non-tuition educational expenses, while only the tax deduction includes tuition payments for private schools. Minn. Stat. §§ 290.01(19b); 290.0674 (2013). The Minnesota deduction is available up to a maximum expenditure of $1,625 per K-6 qualifying student and up to $2,500 per grade 7–12 qualifying student. Minn. Dep't of Revenue, K–12 Education Credit and Subtraction, Income Tax Fact Sheet 8, *available at* http://www.revenue.state.mn.us/individuals/individ_income/factsheets/fact_sheets_fs8.pdf (last visited Oct. 1, 2013). For further discussion, *see* Chapter 1, n.177 and accompanying text.

that the parent-taxpayers pay to state governments, the federal income tax laws do not contain corresponding tax deductions or credits for K–12 education expenses.[21]

Some states grant parents and other taxpayers a different tax concession for donations to § 501(c)(3) STOs. This state tax accommodation can take the form of an income tax credit, or alternatively a charitable contribution tax deduction.[22] A tax credit potentially benefits a broader spectrum of individuals because it is available whether or not the taxpayer itemizes deductions. Both state tax breaks have federal tax implications as well. Corporate and itemizing individual contributors for federal income tax purposes are entitled to claim a § 170 charitable contribution deduction for "unrequited payments" to STOs by virtue of these organizations' § 501(c)(3) status.[23] The numerical illustration #5 in Section III below demonstrates the operation of the dual state and federal income tax provisions. These state tax credits and federal and state tax deductions result in governments spending tax revenues collected from all other taxpayers to subsidize the transactions of each claimant taxpayer.

Education savings accounts ("ESAs"), discussed in Chapter 1, are a variation on public funds used to support children's education expenses, including those incurred for tuition at parochial schools, fees for instructional materials from religiously-affiliated cyber-providers, and the like. Arizona and Florida are the only states so far to implement this idea, but others appear interested in the concept. An ESA assumes a hybrid nature—it is essentially a government cash grant to parents but is excluded statutorily from the parents' income for state tax purposes.[24] Specifically, Arizona transfers state taxpayer dollars directly to a

21 The federal government does provide a Hope Credit and a Lifetime Learning Credit, but these are applicable only to eligible students' post-secondary education. I.R.C. § 25A (2006 & Supp. IV. 2010).

22 The § 501(c)(3) tax-exempt status of STOs (discussed in Chapter 1, n.193 and accompanying text) entitles them to accept deductible contributions other than those that qualify for the state tax credit. For example, the Arizona income tax deduction for charitable contributions, like that of other states, mirrors the I.R.C. § 170 requirement that claimant-taxpayers itemize deductions rather than claim the standard deduction on the state income tax return. Arizona reports, however, that "[t]wenty-eight [out of a total of 30] STOs reported that their revenue equaled their donations, meaning that they had no non-tax credit revenue. …" Ariz. Dep't of Revenue, Private School Tuition Organization Income Tax Credits in Arizona: A Summary of Activity FY 2011 2, 23, *available at* http://www.azdor.gov/Portals/0/Reports/2011-Private-School-Tuition-Organization-Individual-and-Corporate-Income-Tax-Credit-Report.pdf (last visited Oct. 1, 2013). And for the subsequent fiscal year this statistic was 19 out of 37 STOs. Ariz. Dep't of Revenue, Private School Tuition Organization Income Tax Credits in Arizona: A Summary of Activity FY2012 1, 23–24, *available at* http://www.azdor.gov/Portals/0/Reports/FY2012%20private%20schl%20tuition%20org%20crdt%20rept.pdf (last visited Oct. 1, 2013). This is unsurprising because tax credits can be worth considerably more financially to contributors than deductions.

23 *See supra* notes 15, 17 and accompanying text.

24 *See, e.g.*, Ariz. Rev. Stat. Ann. § 15–2402(J) (2013).

participating child's dedicated ESA; the amount deposited is based on a stipulated formula tied to the cost of educating the student in a public school.[25] Using debit cards, parents tap the ESA money to pay a dependent child's qualified education expenses. In addition to the state income tax exclusion for the grant recipient, the ESA deposit (like the value of a tuition voucher) may be excludable from federal income taxation as a "qualified scholarship" "paid or allowed to, or for the benefit of, an individual to aid such individual in the pursuit of study …" if the recipient proves the money is spent for tuition or fees to attend a private school, including a parochial school, or for books, fees, and additional related expenses required for instruction at such institutions.[26] Again, all taxpayers are forced vicariously to subsidize the government largesse distributed through the ESA accounts directly to parents and indirectly to private education providers.

It should be clear that these tax mechanisms—that is, exemptions, exclusions, deductions, and credits—provide significant monetary value in the form of tax subsidies to those who take advantage of their availability. They are a powerful alternative means of subsidy in lieu of outright government cash grants, and they can induce particular behaviors to achieve policy goals of governments. Of course, as the five numerical illustrations below demonstrate, some tax mechanisms are more valuable than others to different recipients, a direct result of the manner in which they operate and the wealth of the beneficiaries. Approximately 40 percent of American households—the poorest households—pay no federal income taxes,[27] and may have little or no state income tax liability. Thus, financial benefits resulting from the various tax mechanisms designed to support alternative K–12 educational

---

25 The deposit for each child must be equal to 90 percent of the revenue the state otherwise would have transferred to the child's public school district as "base support" for the child's education. *Id.* at § 15–2402(C).

26 I.R.C. § 117(b) (2006); Prop. Treas. Reg. § 1.117–6(b), (c)(1)-(3), 53 Fed. Reg. 21688, 21690–21691. A primary or secondary school student is considered a "candidate for a degree" entitled to claim the exclusion. Prop. Treas. Reg. § 1.117–6(b)(4)(i), 53 Fed. Reg. 21688, 21692. If the ESA deposit is not eligible for treatment as a "qualified scholarship," an ESA deposit alternatively may be considered the child's "unearned income" and not derived from compensation for the child's personal services, allowing it to elude federal income taxation. A dependent child needs to file a federal income tax return only if the child's income exceeds certain threshold amounts for earned or unearned income; because all of the child's income may be offset by the child's standard deduction, the child may have no taxable income at all. I.R.C. § 6012 (2006 & Supp. IV. 2010). Moreover, the ESA deposit (and gain earned on it, if any) in any year may not be taxable at the dependent child's parents' tax rate. A dependent child's annual unearned income is not treated as essentially shifted to the child's parents and taxed at their tax rate if its amount is below the statutory threshold of I.R.C. § 1(g). A considerably less likely possibility is that the dollars transferred to the ESAs are a "gift," excludable from gross federal income under I.R.C. § 102.

27 Derek Thompson, *How We Pay Taxes*, The Atlantic, Apr. 16, 2012, *available at* http://www.theatlantic.com/business/archive/2012/04/how-we-pay-taxes-11-charts/255954/ (last visited Oct. 1, 2013).

opportunities may not provide tax advantages to the poorest Americans. And children in these families may be those most in need of better school choices.[28] This may be one reason that Arizona's ESAs particularly are hailed by some as a positive, revolutionary school choice creation. Their pecuniary benefits can reach even those who do not pay taxes because money is deposited directly into a child's ESA, which can be used regardless of whether tax-related consequences inure to the family. ESAs thus have extremely broad potential distributional effects and could be said to be the most "progressive" of the mechanisms.

Governments can design and implement tax break structures to achieve specific aims, but always at the expense of non-recipient taxpayers and government treasuries. Tax exemptions (such as the I.R.C. § 501(a) income tax exemption enjoyed by § 501(c)(3) entities) and exclusions (such as Arizona's exclusion for ESA deposits) have similar economic effects. Both are special tax rules that allow sums to be excluded from gross income, which entirely eliminates any income taxation of those amounts. By contrast, income tax deductions (such as the § 170 charitable contribution deduction and state analogues, and state deductions for qualified education expenses) simply offset itemizing taxpayers' gross income, thereby lowering—some say distorting—their taxable income and simultaneously reducing their tax liability and government tax revenues.

Tax credits are distinct; they are a direct charge against, and offset to, a taxpayer's tax liability to the government, thereby reducing that amount dollar-for-dollar up to the limit of the credit and commensurately decreasing government tax revenues. Tax credits can be refundable or nonrefundable.[29] With a refundable tax credit, if in the year claimed a taxpayer's tax liability is less than the available offsetting tax credit, a negative tax liability balance is created. This results in a "refund" from the government; the amount of the claimed tax credit in excess of the taxpayer's tax liability is paid by government from public monies to the taxpayer. By contrast, nonrefundable tax credits reduce a claimant-taxpayer's tax liability, but not below zero. Therefore, nonrefundable tax credits cannot provide a government "refund" when the amount of the claimed tax credit exceeds the claimant-taxpayer's tax liability for the year. Nonetheless, some nonrefundable tax credits provide that the excess amount of the claimed credit over current tax liability is not lost and may be carried forward to a year in which the claimant-taxpayer has sufficient tax liability to offset. At this time, all but one of the relevant state income tax credits—Minnesota's tax credit for qualified education expenses[30]—are nonrefundable, and one—Arizona's STO tax credit program—provides a carry forward provision.

---

28 Children may benefit from scholarship grants under state STO programs, however, regardless of whether their parents contribute to an STO.

29 Federal nonrefundable and refundable tax credits based on earnings include respectively, for example, the Child Tax Credit and the Earned Income Tax Credit. I.R.C. §§ 24, 32 (West 2012).

30 Minn. Stat. § 290.0674 (enacted in 1997).

Several numerical examples may help to clarify this discussion. The following five illustrations highlight the economic effects of the various tax mechanisms that, in the realm of education, subsidize legislatively-privileged taxpayers and that ultimately, as a result of a taxpayer's behavior, can direct government funds to aid religiously-oriented education. One question is how, if at all, the different mechanisms with varying economic effects should impact the analysis of their constitutionality under the Establishment Clause. Each, after all, provides a state subsidy for religious education of far more than Madison's three pence. A related question we address later is whether it is meaningful to balance competing interests by considering a continuum of encroachment upon separation of church and state depending on the breadth of the class of beneficiaries and the degree of financial assistance received. How far beyond the most economically- and educationally-disadvantaged students should states strive to support private education alternatives especially when most of that aid goes to parochial schools and other religiously-affiliated education providers and threatens to undermine public schools?

III. Relevant Tax Concessions: Numerical Illustrations

Illustration #1: "Plain Vanilla" State Income Tax Deduction for Education Expenses

Suppose a state permits an income tax deduction for expenditures up to $500 by parents for children's primary and secondary education expenses, such as private school tuition and books. Assume an eligible parent-taxpayer expends the full amount for a dependent child's tuition for a private, parochial primary or secondary school and claims the state income tax deduction on her state income tax return. Because there is no federal income tax education expense deduction analogue, the taxpayer cannot make a corresponding claim on her federal tax return. The taxpayer is in the 6 percent state income tax bracket. The claimed deduction reduces her taxable income and lowers her state income tax liability by $30 ($500 x 6%), so she receives that amount alone as a direct tax benefit.[31] The parochial school receives $500, and by virtue of its income tax-exempt status, that tuition amount is not taxed as income at the state or federal levels.

The ramifications of this program targeted for the support of educational options can be viewed in alternative ways. First, the individual parent has paid the full $500 to the school. The state government, and thus other state taxpayers (including parents who do not send their children to private school, the elderly

31 Because an itemizing taxpayer's reduced state income tax liability and payment should be reflected on her federal income tax return (Schedule A), ultimately the combined state and federal tax treatments will result in a slightly lower overall tax benefit. For simplicity's sake, however, we use the $30 figure. All numerical illustrations also ignore any potential effects from the federal alternative minimum tax.

without school-age children, and others), merely "reimburse" the parent for $30 of the $500 qualifying education expenses. In this conception, the state arguably is insulated from any direct subsidy to the parochial school, thereby preserving an illusion of separation of church and state. Alternatively, only $470 comes from the parent's personal pocketbook; the remaining $30 received by the school effectively is paid from the state government's coffers using other state taxpayers' dollars. Either way, the economic consequences are the same: the parent's after-tax benefit is $30, which is made possible by shifting non-claimant taxpayers' funds to her. Therefore, government compels the non-claimant taxpayers to be at least vicarious donors to the parochial school.

Illustration #2: Federal and State Income Tax Charitable Contribution Deduction

Suppose an individual who itemizes deductions altruistically donates $500 to a § 501(c)(3) private, parochial school without receiving anything of value in return. This individual taxpayer is in the 6 percent state income tax bracket and the 28 percent federal income tax bracket. She claims a § 170 charitable contribution deduction and a deduction under the state analogue. Therefore each deduction reduces her taxable income, but separately for federal and state purposes. Claiming the state deduction lowers her state income tax liability by $30 ($500 × 6%); claiming the federal § 170 deduction reduces her federal income tax liability by $140 ($500 × 28%). Thus in that tax year she receives a direct pecuniary benefit totaling $170.[32] The value of the dual tax benefits is $140 greater for the same amount of money ($500) expended by the taxpayer than in illustration #1 limited to a state deduction for expenses. The parochial school receives the full $500 donation for its treasury, and the school is not taxed by the state or federal government on the receipt of this gift (under I.R.C. § 501(a) by virtue of the entity's § 501(c)(3) status or because it comprises a gift under I.R.C. § 102 and state analogues).

As with illustration #1, the transaction can be perceived in alternate ways. First, the donor-taxpayer gives the school $500 at her own initiative and the state and federal governments "reimburse" her for $30 and $140, respectively, totaling $170 of her $500 contribution. Alternatively, the donor-taxpayer gives the school only $330 ($500 – $30 – $140) of her own money and elects to have the state and federal governments partially "match" her contribution to the parochial school with $30 and $140 respectively of their taxpayers' funds.

This situation, however, involving simply § 501(c)(3) tax-exempt status, the § 170 contribution deduction, and state analogues is least problematic from an

32 The precise monetary benefit to any taxpayer from the § 170 federal income tax charitable contribution deduction and the state analogue is determined by a taxpayer's contribution amount and marginal income tax rate, which the write-off itself may lower thereby reducing the dollar value of the deduction to the taxpayer. A combined state and federal slightly lower tax benefit similar to that in the previous footnote also might apply.

Establishment Clause perspective, although not without difficulties, for several reasons. As discussed in Chapter 1 and below in Section V, § 501(c)(3) status applies to eight wide categories of nonprofit entities, both secular and religious, not considered to be within a "natural" income tax base because of their nonprofit nature. Educational and religious organizations are two of the three original categories established in the late nineteenth century, with religious organizations included because of their perceived contributions to social welfare and not because of their religious nature *per se*. A private, parochial school qualifies simply as an educational institution regardless of its religious nature. The $170 in state and federal government funds goes to the parochial school only as one charitable recipient chosen from an extremely large universe of secular and sectarian § 501(c)(3) organizations. Inclusion of religious entities in this very broad class dates back more than a century, is well-accepted, and is entrenched in the law.

Moreover, as we shall see, for good reasons the Supreme Court has long distinguished the § 501(a) income tax exemption for § 501(c)(3) entities from other government subsidies for purposes of Establishment Clause analysis. This distinction, however, is not even necessary for situations such as that contemplated in this illustration because, like any other recipient, under I.R.C. § 102 a parochial school, regardless of its tax-exempt status, can exclude from its gross income the value of a gift received. Furthermore, the benefits from the state and federal deductions available for contributions to all § 501(c)(3) organizations are limited, because a distinct minority of individual taxpayers itemize deductions, and thus are eligible to claim them, and because the amount of the deduction depends on the taxpayer's marginal tax rate, a current maximum federal rate of 39.6 percent. So, in particular, as in illustration #1, with most state tax rates in single digits, the absolute value of any deduction is fairly small. The donor bears the financial brunt of her contribution; the available deduction is only a relatively modest inducement to give.[33] Finally, a transferor can restrict her contribution to support a specific secular feature of a particular school—its athletic facilities, for example; unlike other forms of state aid, it need not directly underwrite the religious education of a certain student. Such earmarking for a specified secular purpose, while freeing other non-restricted funds of the school to support religious objectives, still can be seen as minimizing Establishment Clause problems.

Illustration #3: Education Savings Accounts

Suppose that the state deposits $500 into a child's ESA for use for qualified education expenses, including private, parochial school tuition or religiously-affiliated education provider fees. The child's parent uses a debit card to draw on this account and make a parochial school tuition payment. For state income tax purposes, the entire $500 is excluded from the parent's gross income, totally

33 The status of the § 170 contribution deduction as a tax expenditure is discussed below in Section V.

eluding state income taxation. Regardless of the parent's state marginal income tax rate or whether the parent pays state income taxes, the parent enjoys the full tax-free state benefit of $500.[34] Additionally, the $500 ESA deposit might escape federal income taxation as a "qualified scholarship."[35] The result is that the parent-taxpayer has saved $500 on the child's private, parochial school tuition, but other taxpayers have paid that amount vicariously. And, of course, as with illustration #2, the parochial school is not taxed on the $500 received.[36]

ESAs may provide the greatest potential affront to the Establishment Clause when used to support religious education. Their tax-free nature makes them highly desirable for parents, and they are nothing but a subsidy from the state to a private, parochial school or other religiously-affiliated education provider. They could be structured to be widely available to any parents who choose qualified alternative schooling for their children regardless of the parents' socio-economic status or the quality of educational opportunities otherwise available to their children. Their amount is whatever the legislature sets, and the state could divert most of its per student expenditures for K–12 education from public schools to private, mainly parochial, schools. The only constitutional defense for ESAs would seem to be that the state subsidy is somehow laundered through parents' hands, thereby triggering the artificial notion that parental choice should salve the constitutional injury. But as discussed in Chapter 2, independent parental choice is hardly a universal solvent dissolving all Establishment Clause objections to ever more inventive state methods of funneling government money to parochial schools. The Supreme Court has never endorsed so broad a concept, though *Winn* may limit the judicial fora available to raise the issue for the foreseeable future.

Illustration #4: "Plain Vanilla" State Income Tax Credit for Education Expenses

Now suppose that in contrast to the deduction in illustration #1 a state legislature structures the tax privilege for tuition (or other qualified educational expenses) as an income tax credit. The tax credit may be a dollar-for-dollar (100 percent) credit so

---

34 *See supra* Section II (discussing ESAs).

35 ESAs are too new for there to have been a test case to determine if the $500 benefit constitutes a "qualified scholarship" for federal income tax purposes. *See* I.R.C. § 117 (2006). If the benefit does not qualify, then, as discussed in footnote 26, the $500 is below the threshold required for unearned income to be treated as taxable to either the child or the child's parent. But even if it were taxable to the parent at the federal level—and actual ESAs may be sufficiently large to trigger such tax—for simplicity and comparison sake, a parent-taxpayer in the 28 percent marginal tax bracket would pay $140 ($500 × 28 percent) in federal income tax on it. In that event, her after-tax benefit is $360.

36 If the qualified expense payments were made to another education service provider, organized as a for-profit enterprise, it would include the $500 in gross income but receive a business expense deduction for costs associated with providing the education services. Thus, the for-profit business would reduce its taxable income and tax liability according to its marginal tax rate.

that for every dollar expended for the qualified expense up to the limit of the credit the taxpayer is granted a one-dollar credit against her state income tax. Or the tax credit may be a lesser percent, say 90 percent, so that for every dollar expended the taxpayer receives a 90-cent tax credit. The following analysis applies regardless of the percentage, although of course the numbers would be different. This illustration is based on a state tax credit available to a parent-taxpayer of a student for tuition paid for her child to attend a private, parochial, primary or secondary school.

First assume that state law provides a 100 percent nonrefundable income tax credit for every dollar of tuition paid up to $500 and that the parent-taxpayer pays at least that maximum amount in tuition to a child's parochial school. The parent receives a $500 state tax credit if her income tax liability is $500 or more. The tax credit is far more widely available and considerably more valuable than a tax deduction because any parent-taxpayer paying her child's tuition may claim it, regardless of whether she itemizes or claims a standard deduction for state income tax purposes, and can utilize the full tax credit amount, assuming sufficient tax liability, regardless of her marginal state income tax rate.[37] Also, unlike a tax deduction that must be triggered by a voluntary contribution, a parent claiming a tax credit does not have the option of leaving the $500 in her own pocketbook; if her state tax liability is at least $500 her only choice is either to pay that amount to the state or use it for the school tuition. And not using the $500 in partial payment of her child's tuition and claiming the tax credit would be financially imprudent for the taxpayer. The tax credit effectively reimburses her from state revenues collected from other taxpayers for this portion of her child's tuition. The $500 tax subsidy to the parent gives her a strong incentive to avail herself of this state support for religious education. The subsidy also may accrue to the parochial school's benefit in several ways as discussed above.

If the parent's state tax liability is only $400, but she pays parochial school tuition of $500 or more, she is entitled to reduce her income tax liability only to zero for the year, leaving a $100 tax credit balance. Because the tax credit is nonrefundable, she cannot take advantage of that $100 tax credit balance (at least not in that tax year). The subsidy from other taxpayers would be limited to $400, unless a carry forward provision permits the parent to offset her tax liability in a future year with the remaining $100 tax credit balance.

If state tax law provides that the tax credit is refundable, however, the parent still reduces her $400 tax liability to zero for the year, but now receives a "refund" of $100 from the government.[38] That is, the parent is again fully subsidized by other taxpayers for her child's $500 portion of tuition to parochial school. Both a carry forward provision and a refundable tax credit particularly favor lower income taxpayers likely to have a lower tax liability.

---

37 The state tax credit, however, might have ramifications for the parent's federal income tax; ultimately the combined state and federal tax treatments for an itemizing taypayer may result in a slightly lower tax benefit.

38 Again, there may be federal tax repercussions for a taxpayer. *See supra* n.37.

Illustration #5: Complex Tax Credit Structured Contributions to STOs

Arizona is a pioneer in developing an STO program that other states increasingly are interested in emulating. So consider an individual taxpayer residing in Arizona, which now permits any individual taxpayer, regardless of marginal tax rate or whether the individual itemizes deductions or is a parent paying private school tuition, to donate a maximum of approximately $500 to state-approved STOs and claim a dollar-for-dollar nonrefundable income tax credit.[39] Claiming this credit, however, precludes taking a state tax deduction. So a single, childless taxpayer, for example, with a $500 state tax liability has the choice of writing a check to the state for that amount or contributing it to an approved STO—likely one that is religiously affiliated and grants scholarships only at parochial schools—and claiming the state nonrefundable income tax credit. Because of her state tax liability the taxpayer cannot keep the $500; in this sense it is not her money. The tax credit then operates as in illustration #4, although here the financial effect, and therefore the incentive, on the taxpayer is neutral, unlike the parent-taxpayer in that illustration who can take a tax credit against the tuition she must pay for her child's schooling. (An Arizona parent who contributes to an STO cannot earmark those funds for her own child's tuition but may benefit from encouraging others also to donate to the same STO, creating a pool of scholarship money from which her child may benefit.) Even if the taxpayer's tax liability is $400 in the year of the $500 STO contribution—that is, $100 less than the contribution amount—under Arizona's carry forward provision the $100 unused tax credit can be used to offset her tax liability for up to five subsequent years. Thus, over time, the taxpayer likely will be made whole for the full amount of her $500 contribution.

The Arizona legislature structured this income tax credit scheme to ostensibly minimize the state's involvement in sending government money to parochial schools, thereby trying to avoid Establishment Clause problems. The state refrains from actually collecting any taxes from the taxpayer and then refunding the same amount, so the money does not flow through government hands. Instead, the taxpayer writes a $500 check not to the state but to an STO, which in turn uses the money to distribute scholarships to students who must apply it to pay tuition at one of the two or more schools participating in the program with the STO. Many of the STOs are religiously-affiliated and grant scholarships for use only at parochial schools of like religious affiliation. As tax-exempt nonprofit entities, both the STO and the school receive the $500 tax-free. But the supposed

39 Ariz. Rev. Stat. Ann. §§ 43–1089, 43–1089.01 (2012); *see also School Tax Credits for Individuals*, Ariz. Dep't of Revenue, http://www.azdor.gov/TaxCredits/SchoolTaxCreditsforIndividuals.aspx (last visited Oct. 1, 2013). The latest amount is $514, but we use $500 for consistency with the other illustrations. Although the tax credit is nonrefundable, the Arizona statute permits an individual taxpayer whose tax liability is less than the contribution to the STO to carry forward for up to five years the excess contribution for use to offset those future years' tax liability. Ariz. Rev. Stat. Ann. § 43–1089(D) (2012).

lack of government involvement is illusory; the "never touched by government hands" approach should not affect the substantial constitutional problem.[40] The $500, owed to the state, that supports religious education is government money, which the state-created and -managed program simply allows a taxpayer to divert to a sectarian STO and then to a private, parochial school. Thus, in reality, the contributing taxpayer provides zero money of her own to the sectarian STO or parochial school.[41]

Summary of the Numerical Illustrations

At this juncture, it is worth making several observations. First, in each illustration #1 through #5 the same $500 dollar amount is transferred to a parochial school by a taxpayer having the same marginal tax rates (6 percent and 28 percent for state and federal income tax purposes, respectively). The pecuniary value of the overall after-tax benefit to the taxpayer depends on the particular tax mechanisms and whether dual levels of government provide a tax advantage. The $30 dollar after-tax value to the parent-taxpayer in illustration #1, where there is only a state level income tax deduction for education expenses, provides the lowest amount. The $170 dollar after-tax value to the general taxpayer for the dual state and federal income tax charitable deductions in illustration #2 is higher. But an even greater sum is realized in illustration #3 where there is a $500 dollar after-tax value to a parent from the dual state and federal income tax exclusions for the ESA deposit.[42] In illustration #4, assuming sufficient tax liability or a carry forward feature, $500 is provided a parent by

40 For Establishment Clause purposes, as Justice David Souter argued regarding vouchers, one should consider whether a state STO-tax credit scheme favors religion based on the limited universe of choices practically available to parents. *Zelman*, 536 U.S. at 697–707 (Souter, J., dissenting).

41 Arizona's fiscal year 2012 report shows that individual contributions to the STO-tax credit program, costs to the government, and hence costs to non-claimant taxpayers, have escalated significantly since 1998. Ariz. Dep't of Revenue, *supra* note 22, at 2.

An itemizing federal taxpayer's benefit from also claiming a § 170 contribution deduction for donating to a § 501(c)(3) STO would be neutralized by a lower deduction for state tax paid due to the claimed tax credit.

42 ESAs are similar to direct mandatory or discretionary government entitlements, like the Supplemental Nutrition Assistance Program ("SNAP," formerly the federal Food Stamp Program). But SNAP entitlements are means-tested and thus are targeted to benefit low-income individuals and families. Center on Budget and Policy Priorities, Introduction to SNAP 1 (Mar. 28, 2013), http://www.cbpp.org/files/policybasics-foodstamps.pdf. Arizona's ESAs, however, are not so limited; before school year 2012–2013, they were available only to children with special needs, but their availability expanded in the 2013–2014 school year to include children in foster care, of active military members, and in certain low-performing or failing public schools and school districts. *See* Chapter 1, nn.202–11 and accompanying text (discussing Arizona's ESAs). Legislatures conceivably could provide

the "plain vanilla," single nonrefundable or refundable state income tax credit for parochial school tuition. In contrast, the complex STO-tax credit structure of illustration #5 is financially neutral to the individual contributor who bears no expense. However, because participation is open to all taxpayers, an STO-tax credit program can divert huge sums of government money to private, secular and parochial schools. Nonetheless, in the future even more state funds may be diverted by ESAs because, at least as structured in Arizona, deposits can approach the state's per student public school spending level.

Second, in each illustration #1 through #5, states automatically lose or spend income tax revenues they otherwise could devote to public schools. These government expenditures through tax mechanisms are not fiscally costless; the financial burden is lifted from any claimant-taxpayer and shifted to non-claimant taxpayers, who thereby are subsidizing claimant-taxpayers and the private, often parochial, schools that benefit from the programs. Even if states may save some money from educating fewer students in public schools, the fact remains that many students receive a state-subsidized religious education, and their parochial schools benefit both financially and intangibly.[43] To fully appreciate the constitutional implications of these programs and their treatment by legislatures and courts we need to consider these legislatively designed tax mechanisms as "tax expenditures."

IV. What is a Tax Expenditure?

Budgeting and accounting for taxpayer dollars spent by federal, state, and local governments are critical tasks. Governments periodically, if not annually, approve direct spending and grant provisions; they easily can, and do, track and publicly account for the tax funds used. For example, government might make direct grants—subsidies—to private universities, colleges, and schools for specific projects, such as to assist with construction financing for new science laboratories or to expand arts and music programs. These taxpayer-funded subsidies may be motivated by governmental concern for the welfare of the institutions and the students they serve or the government's interest in promoting the institutions' activities otherwise deemed to produce valued, positive externalities deserving of support.[44] But where direct government monetary assistance is given, or property is transferred without adequate consideration, to religiously-affiliated entities, including parochial schools and sectarian-related cyber-providers, the Supreme

ESAs expansively to middle-class or affluent children and eliminate the low-performing or failing public school or school district requirement.

43 *See* Chapter 1, Section V (discussing the various benefits to students and parochial schools).

44 *See* Edward A. Zelinsky, *Are Tax "Benefits" Equivalent to Direct Expenditures?*, 112 Harv. L. Rev. 379, 411 & n.160 (1998).

Court long has recognized special constitutional dangers.[45] Such aid hazards "direct and substantial advancement of the sectarian enterprise" in violation of the Establishment Clause.[46] This issue has been debated repeatedly in a variety of contexts—for example, where the federal government contemplates providing disaster relief aid to eligible victims, including houses of worship and other religiously-affiliated organizations, of natural and man-made disasters such as Hurricane Sandy in 2012, a 2002 Seattle earthquake, and the 1995 Oklahoma City bombing.[47] Recently, capital construction grants proposed by New Jersey Governor Chris Christie for two religious schools of higher education, Beth Medrash Gavoha, a Haredi yeshiva, and the Presbyterian Princeton Theological Seminary, prompted a lawsuit alleging such direct grants would violate the Establishment Clause.[48]

So in recent years, in an effort to avoid Establishment Clause difficulties, rather than directly subsidizing sectarian institutions and religiously-affiliated entities, governments increasingly and deliberately have channeled public money more indirectly using various tax mechanisms—exemptions, exclusions, deductions, and credits—such as in the illustrations in Section III. As this chapter's introduction demonstrates, the Supreme Court (as well as a large body of academic literature) repeatedly has recognized over a 40-year period that these

45 *See, e.g.*, Bowen v. Kendrick, 487 U.S. 589 (1988); Valley Forge Christian Coll. v. Ams. United for Separation of Church and State, Inc., 454 U.S. 464 (1982); Roemer v. Bd. of Pub. Works, 426 U.S. 736 (1976); Hunt v. McNair, 413 U.S. 734 (1973); Tilton v. Richardson, 403 U.S. 672 (1971); Bd. of Educ. v. Allen, 392 U.S. 236 (1968); Bradfield v. Roberts, 175 U.S. 291 (1899).

46 Wolman v. Walter, 433 U.S. 229, 250 (1977) (overruled by Mitchell v. Helms, 530 U.S. 793 (2000)).

47 *See* Pete Kasperowicz, *House Approves Bill Forcing FEMA to Allow Churches to Apply for Aid*, The Hill (Feb. 13, 2013, 2:38 PM), http://thehill.com/blogs/floor-action/house/282879-house-votes-to-let-federal-disaster-aid-flow-to-churches-mosques-other-houses-of-worship; Margot Alder, *Federal Aid for Religious Institutions in Murky Waters after Sandy*, NPR (Feb. 8, 2013, 3:29 AM), http://www.npr.org/2013/02/08/171415610/federal-aid-for-religious-institutions-in-murky-waters-after-sandy; Avi Schick, *Separation of Church and State, Disaster Edition*, Wall St. J., Jan. 25, 2013, at A11, *available at* http://online.wsj.com/article/SB10001424127887324039504578261581899619590.html. On February 13, 2013, the U.S. House of Representatives passed a bill that would amend the Stafford Disaster Relief and Emergency Assistance Act to include houses of worship in the list of nonprofit groups eligible for federal disaster aid for repair, restoration and replacement of damaged facilities regardless of religious character including, for example, a steeple or pediment with a religious symbol. Federal Disaster Assistance Nonprofit Fairness Act of 2013, H.R. 592, 113th Cong. (2013). Such a bill, if enacted, would allow Congress to use its taxing and spending powers problematically to appropriate taxpayer money directly for religious institutions.

48 *See* Anthony Campisi, *Civil Liberties Groups Sue to Stop N.J. from Awarding $11M in Grants to Two Religious Schools*, NorthJersey.com (June 26, 2013, 6:44 PM), http://www.northjersey.com/news/state/Groups_sue_NJ_for_funding_religious_schools.html.

tax concessions economically are functionally equivalent to outright entitlement spending or grant provisions. The government easily can structure tax mechanisms to provide the same economic benefits to recipients as outright monetary grants.[49] And like government's direct entitlement spending (such as food stamps or low-income housing assistance), or outright grants (such as federal Pell Grants or state grants for higher education), the tax mechanisms are devised to reward, stimulate, incentivize, and achieve certain economic, fiscal, social, and public policy goals. The varying approaches reflect differences in design, but all "meet objectives that the government considers to require financial assistance."[50] Importantly, both outright monetary grants and tax dispensations reduce a government's immediate net revenues although they ultimately may produce savings by shifting particular government obligations into private hands. But because tax concessions enshrined in the tax code generally are more permanent and less often publicly debated than outright grants, their "more hidden nature of financial assistance … masks where benefits are directed and thereby limits discussion of the[ir] impact …."[51]

Unlike direct government spending or outright grants, these less visible tax allowances, which also result in revenue losses to governments, had been difficult to account for in a budget process before Stanley S. Surrey, Assistant Secretary

49 One example is provided by the Supreme Court: "'[A] government with a general income tax, wanting to add $7,000 to the spendable income of a preacher whose top tax rate is 30%, has two ways of subsidizing him. The government can send the preacher a check for $10,000 and tax him on all of his income, or it can authorize him [as the federal government has done by providing the I.R.C. § 107 income tax exclusion for a rental allowance] to reduce his taxable income by $23,333.33 [resulting in a tax savings of $ 7,000]. If the direct payment were itself taxable and did not alter his tax bracket, the preacher would receive the same benefit from the tax deduction as he would from the direct payment.'" Rosenberger v. Rector & Visitors of the Univ. of Va., 515 U.S. 819, 859 n.5 (1995) (first bracketed phrase added) (internal citation omitted).

50 Stanley S. Surrey & Paul R. McDaniel, Tax Expenditures 116 (1985).

51 Donna D. Adler, *The Internal Revenue Code, the Constitution, and the Courts: The Use of Tax Expenditure Analysis in Judicial Decision Making*, 28 Wake Forest L. Rev. 855, 856 (1993); *see* Edward D. Kleinbard, *The Congress Within the Congress: How Tax Expenditures Distort Our Budget and Our Political Processes*, 36 Ohio N.U. L. Rev. 1, 28 (2010) ("the irresistible political attraction of tax expenditures lies in their invisibility to normal inspection of the budget. …"). Unless saddled with sunset provisions, tax laws may have more permanence than direct government entitlement spending or grants that need annual reauthorization. *See* Bernard Wolfman, *Tax Expenditures: From Idea to Ideology*, 99 Harv. L. Rev. 491, 493 (1985) (stating "tax expenditures, much more than direct subsidies, often enjoy a long, seemingly perpetual, life of their own" in a review of Surrey & McDaniel, Tax Expenditures, *supra* note 50). Yet other scholars suggest that this distinguishing feature may be benign or immaterial for analyzing the two governmental funding methods for constitutional law purposes. *See, e.g.*, Zelinsky, *Are Tax "Benefits" Equivalent to Direct Expenditures?*, *supra* note 44, at 400–03 (arguing a hard and fast dichotomy between the two types of government expenditures should be avoided and urging government expenditures be evaluated for asserted constitutional violations using a case-by-case approach).

of Treasury in the 1960s, formulated a "tax expenditure" approach. He developed this method specifically as a tax policy tool to enable the federal government to account for the "vast *subsidy* apparatus that uses the mechanics of the income tax as the method of paying the *subsidies*"[52] that operate apart from, and as an alternative to, outright government grants and entitlement spending programs.[53] Congress adopted this income tax expenditure system of discretionary spending in 1974 as a budgetary tool,[54] and state and local governments also began utilizing it to account for income tax expenditures that result in tax revenue reductions.

The special state "plain vanilla" tax deductions and credits, complex STO-tax credit structures, and income tax exclusions for ESA deposits precisely fit the conventional definition of income tax expenditures. They are an array of economic subsidies that legislatures, under their taxing and spending powers, affirmatively enact within their state income tax systems to specially confer benefits on select groups of income taxpayers. And the states recognize that indeed they are income tax expenditures, reporting them as such for budgetary purposes. For example, Arizona reports its STO-tax credit as an income tax expenditure,[55] and Minnesota

---

52 Staff of Joint Committee on Taxation, A Reconsideration of Tax Expenditure Analysis 2 (2008), *available at* http://www.jct.gov/x-37–08.pdf (quoting Stanley S. Surrey's speech before the Boston Economic Club on May 15, 1968 (emphasis added)).

53 Surrey & McDaniel, *supra* note 50, at 99, 115–16, 116 n.21 (describing how Congress faced choices in 1962 for structuring aid to college and graduate students alternatively as direct loans to students or as a tax expenditure in the form of federal tuition tax credits and, again, in 1978 for extending aid to lower school students; explaining how political forces caused Congress to effect the assistance through non-tax legislation; and suggesting that, like direct student grants and loans that require Congress' public periodic review, the less publicly visible proposed tax credit design of the 1978 program largely was driven by consideration that students would choose to attend religiously-affiliated schools, thus potentially triggering an Establishment Clause challenge). This demonstrates congressional concern that tax expenditures are the same as outright monetary grants for Establishment Clause purposes.

The congressional Joint Committee on Taxation, recognizing criticisms of Professor Surrey's formulation of tax expenditures, stated that "many tax expenditures have vaguely similar distributional effects to those achieved through spending programs, but the two delivery systems are so different that in many cases each is a highly imperfect economic substitute for the other." Staff of Joint Committee on Taxation, *supra* note 52, at 4.

54 Congressional Budget and Impoundment Control Act of 1974, Pub. L. No. 93–344, § 3(a)(3), 88 Stat. 297, 299 (codified at 2 U.S.C. § 622(3) (2006)) (requiring the President's annual budget submission to list tax expenditures and defining tax expenditures as "revenue losses attributable to provisions of the Federal tax laws which allow a special exclusion, exemption, or deduction from gross income or which provide a special credit, a preferential rate of tax, or a deferral of tax liability").

55 *See* Ariz. Dep't of Revenue, Revenue Impact of Arizona's Tax Expenditures FY 2012 1, 54–55 (July 15, 2013) (revised preliminary), *available at* http://www.azdor.gov/LinkClick.aspx?fileticket=NJj4xZlN_54%3d&tabid=108&mid=492 ("Tax expenditures are provisions within the law (exemptions, exclusions, deductions and credits) designed to encourage certain kinds of activity or to aid taxpayers in certain categories. Such provisions

accounts for both its tax deduction and tax credit for educational expenses as budgeted income tax expenditures.[56] Similarly, the federal income tax deduction of I.R.C. § 170 for all charitable contributions and the I.R.C. § 102 exemption of the value of gifts received by any recipient squarely are income tax expenditures. The federal budget annually reflects them as such. The state and federal income tax exemptions for § 501(c)(3) organizations, however, are not tax expenditures. This difference has important consequences for Establishment Clause purposes. In this regard, the income tax exemption for the broad § 501(c)(3) categories of religious, educational, charitable, and other organizations must be distinguished from the various state funding programs that rely on deductions, credits, and ESAs targeted at private schools and alternative education providers, especially when a major portion of such government money supports religious education.

V. Distinguishing Tax Exemptions for § 501(c)(3) Organizations from Tax Expenditures

A. The Historical Context

The distinction is grounded in the historical approach which became a fixture in federal income tax laws. In 1894, and again in 1909, as Congress debated and then enacted both the Wilson-Gorman Tariff Act and the Payne-Aldrich Tariff Act, it conceived a divide between those types of enterprises that had "net profits" or "net income" for taxation purposes, and those that did not.[57] Congress determined that charitable, religious, and educational organizations comprised a category of enterprises without "net profits" or "net income" and thus lacked the ability to pay taxes. It deemed them worthy of an exemption from taxation under the tariff acts, partly relying on financial and social utility rationales. Charitable and religious

---

result in a loss of tax revenues, thereby reducing the amount of revenues available for state (as well as local) programs. In effect, the fiscal impact of implementing a tax expenditure would be similar to a direct expenditure of state funds."). The lost state tax revenue from individual taxpayer tax credits for scholarship tuition organization contributions for fiscal year 2012 was $43.15 million dollars, compared with $50.88 million dollars for fiscal year 2011 and $55.26 million dollars for fiscal year 2009/10. *See id.*; ARIZ. DEP'T OF REVENUE, REVENUE IMPACT OF ARIZONA'S TAX EXPENDITURES FY 2011 54 (Jan. 27, 2013) (revised preliminary), *available at* http://www.azdor.gov/LinkClick.aspx?fileticket=WQJo4tyBtcU%3d&tabid=108&mid=492; ARIZ. DEP'T OF REVENUE, REVENUE IMPACT OF ARIZONA'S TAX EXPENDITURES FY 2009/10 48 (Nov. 15, 2010) (preliminary), *available at* http://www.azdor.gov/LinkClick.aspx?fileticket=JL-F9b7MZ-M%3D&tabid=108&mid=492.

56 2010 Minn. Laws, ch. 389, art. 10, sec. 5; MINN. STAT. § 270C.11 (2005).

57 Wilson-Gorman Tariff Act, Revenue Act of 1894, §§ 27–37, 23 Stat. 556 (1894) ("An Act to reduce taxation [during an economic depression], to provide revenue for the government, and for other purposes."); 1909 Payne-Aldrich Tariff Act, ch. 6, § 38, 36 Stat. 11, 113 (1909).

organizations, such as houses of worship, were thought to expend all of their revenues to serve social welfare needs of the public for which the responsibility and burdens otherwise would fall on the government. Non-profitable private educational organizations provided beneficial educations that otherwise public, common schools would be obligated to provide. Congress thought it more expedient to foster all of these entities as providers of social goods and services.

When Congress enacted the 1913 federal income tax, it expanded the familiar tariff tax-exempt categories to add scientific organizations. It did not revisit the determination it previously had made for the triumvirate; it merely incorporated their exemption into the new income tax laws. Congress thereafter had multiple opportunities to revisit the income tax exemption for charitable, religious, and educational organizations, but it largely abstained despite enacting complementary income tax provisions and subsequently codifying and re-codifying the Internal Revenue Code.[58] In particular as to the category of religious organizations, at no time did Congress base their exemption on grounds rooted in the First Amendment Religion Clauses. So as to religiously-affiliated entities now within current I.R.C. § 501(c)(3), Congress never has justified their income tax exemption on the basis of their specific religious roles, activities, or functions, nor has it considered how their exemption comports with the Establishment Clause.[59] Today, while it is doubtful the Constitution requires an income tax exemption for religious organizations, even houses of worship, their inclusion in the eight broad categories of secular and sectarian entities covered by current § 501(c)(3) also is not considered constitutionally problematic.[60] Moreover, it is particularly important to note for purposes of this book—so bears repeating—that private, parochial schools are entitled to § 501(c)(3) tax-exempt status simply on the basis of their educational function quite aside from their religious character.

B. Section 501(c)(3) As a "Normative" Tax Provision Contrasted with Other Tax Mechanisms Considered "Tax Expenditures"

The federal income tax exemption regime for the three original categories of § 501(c)(3) organizations, designed from practical considerations, is the backdrop for

---

58 For a discussion of the impetus for the 1917 enactment of the charitable contribution deduction, its subsequent history, and that of the tax-exemption for § 501(c)(3) entities, especially as to how the tax exemption applies to houses of worship, *see* CRIMM & WINER, *supra* note 14, at 100–04, 145, 367.

59 Some legal scholars look to Congress' debates with respect to the 1917 legislation creating the charitable contribution deduction and emphasize a subsidy theory for the federal income tax exemption benefiting numerous categories of nonprofit organizations. Basically they suggest that such tax relief should be provided on the basis of specific roles, activities, and functions of the benefited entities because of the social good they contribute to the welfare of the people. For further discussion, *see id.* at 100–04.

60 *See id.* at 71–110, 149–77.

understanding how the tax expenditure concept was derived. In the words of tax expert Professor Boris I. Bittker, government cannot "tax everything; a legislative body, no matter how avid for revenue, can do no more than pick out from the universe of people, entities, and events … those that, in its view, are appropriate objects of taxation."[61] In essence Congress perceived charitable, religious, and educational nonprofit organizations inappropriate objects of taxation, partly because they were unable to pay taxes, and Congress took this into account in constructing the country's income tax regime. Section § 501(c)(3) is thus referred to as a "normative" or baseline tax provision around which the comprehensive income tax system absolutely must be structured and implemented; it divides the "natural base" of "appropriate" taxpayers able to pay taxes from those considered unable. By contrast, statutory departures from these "normative" provisions in the form of other tax exemptions, exclusions, deductions, and credits are considered "tax expenditures." But Congress never clearly identified these essential "normative" provisions, leaving academicians and policymakers plenty of room to engage in "seemingly endless debates about what should and should not be included in the [tax expenditure analysis]."[62]

For our purposes perhaps the most important facet of this debate is the argument that the

> main focus [of tax expenditure analysis] is on transparency and accountability concerning governmental programs delivered through the tax system. … [It] is meant to have a much needed restraining effect on the strong impulse by [legislatures] to enact governmental programs in the form of tax incentives and subsidies that would not pass muster under a cost/benefit analysis as direct spending programs. … [T]he central purpose of TEA [tax expenditure analysis] is to serve as a triggering mechanism for a rigorous cost/benefit analysis of governmental programs ….[63]

Tax incentives and subsidies, of course, should have to pass muster not only under economic cost/benefit analysis but even more crucially under fundamental

61 Boris I. Bittker, *Churches, Taxes, and the Constitution*, 78 Yale L.J. 1285, 1288 (1969).

62 J. Clifton Fleming, Jr. & Robert J. Peroni, *Can Tax Expenditure Analysis Be Divorced from a Normative Tax Base?: A Critique of the "New Paradigm" and Its Denouement*, 30 Va. Tax Rev. 135, 136 (2010). Early on, Professor Bittker entered that debate criticizing the concept of a "normal" tax base and the value of the tax expenditure system based on its imprecision. Boris I. Bittker, *The Tax Expenditure Budget: A Reply to Professors Surrey & Hellmuth*, 22 Nat'l Tax J. 538 (1969); Boris I. Bittker, *Accounting for Federal "Tax Subsidies" in the National Budget*, 22 Nat'l Tax J. 244 (1969). Thereafter, Professors Michael J. Graetz and Deborah H. Schenk suggested that the analysis relies on the absurdity of government's entitlement to all money of taxpayers. Michael J. Graetz & Deborah H. Schenk, Federal Income Taxation: Principles and Policies 57 (3rd ed. 1995). *But see* Julie Roin, *Truth in Government: Beyond the Tax Expenditure Budget*, 54 Hastings L.J. 603, 640 (2003).

63 Fleming & Peroni, *supra* note 62, at 179.

constitutional analysis as well, particularly when individual liberties are at stake. Otherwise, the danger stems from "the unexamined premise that the tax laws should be uniquely 'privileged,' through not being burdened by the political compromises and policy agendas reflected in appropriations legislation."[64]

State governments incorporated into their own income tax regimes the federal "normative" provision that excludes from income taxation religious, educational, and charitable nonprofit organizations. So, as under the federal income tax laws, private, parochial and secular elementary and secondary schools, for example, are exempt from state income taxation as a baseline to states' own comprehensive systems. State and local governments also generally assimilated the exemption for charitable, educational, and religious nonprofits into their property tax and sales and use tax law regimes, but perhaps for different reasons.[65] The effect of the various

---

64 Staff of the Joint Committee on Taxation, *supra* note 52, at 7, describing aspects of the debate over tax expenditure analysis.

65 Prior to the Revolutionary War, under both common law and equity principles, colonies presumptively taxed houses of worship on their properties. But colonial legislative acts exempted from taxation property of the established church dedicated to "religious uses." And under equity principles, church properties devoted to qualified "charitable uses" also were exempt from taxation—a standard reliant on England's Statute of Charitable Uses of 1601 and one easily met by the established churches (as state instrumentalities) but not by "dissenting" churches. After the Revolutionary War, with the Statute of Charitable Uses no longer applicable and the disestablishment of churches, debates arose as states ratified their constitutions over whether church properties should be subject to taxation. Critics argued that state constitutional provisions providing for fair, "equal and uniform" tax treatment "throughout the State," regardless of the nature of the property owner, dictated that exemptions should be granted only for "good and compelling reasons," among which would be the advancement of "public welfare," a charitable purpose rather than a purely religious purpose. Expending revenues for the public welfare perhaps left organizations without the fiscal means to pay taxes without financial ruin, even if taxes were levied only sporadically for emergency purposes. Thus, charity was central to the tax exemption policy adopted by states; strictly religious features did not provide valid reasons for exemption from taxation, even of houses of worship. This continued to be the justification in the mid-1800s once state property taxation became an annual obligation. Usually states enacted property tax exemptions for the land of the triumvirate of entities, but not for income produced from the property and from endowments. During the post-Civil War era, as parochial schools below the college level appeared, the public debate was generally about the efficiency and effectiveness of property tax exemptions versus direct subsidies for these institutions, not about the inappropriateness of some form of financial benefit for religious, educational, and charitable organizations. And as more parochial schools developed during the early twentieth century, despite suggestions by tax experts that states take a more fiscally calibrated approach to property tax exemptions based on a true financial cost/benefit equivalency analysis, at least for the three categories of entities the status quo was already entrenched and there was no public appetite for a change. *See* Crimm & Winer, *supra* note 14, at 72–79, 121–22, 124–25, 135–39 and references therein.

Arguably state property tax exemptions for charitable, educational, and religious organizations should not be considered "normative" provisions, separating the three from the federal, state, and local tax exemptions for these categories of entities, of course, is that governments forego significant tax revenues from them and so must look to those non-exempted taxpayers—individuals and for-profit businesses—to make up for those reduced revenues. Thus, all individuals and entities not exempt under the "normative" provisions of the particular tax regime subsidize those entities that are tax-exempt—including for our purpose private, secular and sectarian schools.

"natural base" of appropriate taxpayers. These entities hold real property of value, critical to the structure of a property tax, and that property value can be taxed. Rather, it is logical to include the triumvirate in the real property taxpayer base because, for example, like owners of homes used for personal purposes, these entities can obtain mortgages, secured by the real property, based on the fair market value of that property. Over time there has been no direct denial that these institutions are within the potential group of taxpayer-owners of real property having a "market value" (despite perhaps not producing income). *See*, *e.g.*, MINN. DEP'T OF REVENUE, TAX EXPENDITURE REVIEW REPORT: BRINGING TAX EXPENDITURES INTO THE BUDGET PROCESS 13 (Feb. 2011), *available at* http://www.revenue.state.mn.us/research_stats/Documents/TE_Review_Report_02_15_11.pdf. The Supreme Court in *Walz*, rejecting an Establishment Clause challenge to a property tax exemption for houses of worship, considered the exemption equivalent to an economic subsidy, but the Court did not address whether property tax exemptions are "normative" provisions or tax expenditures.

Today, some states statutorily specify that property is exempt from taxation based upon its use. *See*, *e.g.*, N.Y. REAL PROP. TAX LAW § 420-a (2013) (providing "[r]eal property owned by a corporation or association organized or conducted exclusively for religious, charitable, hospital, educational, … and used exclusively for carrying out thereupon one or more of such purposes … shall be exempt from taxation …"). While these categories of entities may not pay property taxes, they may receive public services, such as fire and police protection. In recent years, some states squeezed by financial setbacks have started to rethink the status quo approach for at least some of these entities as to the taxation of their real property wealth. This perhaps applies particularly to institutions of higher education. *See*, *e.g.*, MINN. DEP'T OF REVENUE, TAX EXPENDITURE REVIEW REPORT: BRINGING TAX EXPENDITURES INTO THE BUDGET PROCESS, *supra* at 26; Pamela Leland, *PILOTs: The Large City Experience*, *in* PROPERTY TAX-EXEMPTION FOR CHARITIES 193 (Evelyn Brody ed. 2002).

Less clear is the reason these categories of entities, as consumers, are exempt from state sales taxes. It is unclear whether legislatures consider the exemption a "normative" or baseline provision; that is, whether they deem it absolutely necessary for the implementation of their states' comprehensive sales tax system. If so, such organizations would not be part of the "natural" sales tax taxpayer base, even though they have the capacity and power to consume taxable objects and services. As for individuals and for-profit enterprises, their consumption ability stems from their income capability. As a practical matter, most states exempt private, secular and parochial schools from real property taxation, and some exempt these schools from sales and use taxes. *See* U.S. DEP'T OF EDUCATION, STATE REGULATION OF PRIVATE SCHOOLS (2009). The Supreme Court in *Texas Monthly*, 489 U.S. at 1, compared the sales tax exemption to a government subsidy in the context of First Amendment analysis, but again it did not address in this context whether the sales tax exemption for a religious organization was a "normative" provision or a tax expenditure.

C. Tax Expenditure Provisions Now Associated with School Choice Legislation: Differences for Establishment Clause Purposes?

The "normative" provision of tax exemption under I.R.C. § 501(c)(3) thus fundamentally differs from the income tax deductions, credits, and exclusions currently associated with school choice legislation, as presented in the five numerical illustrations above. Both types of provisions afford subsidies and result in government losses of revenues from the income tax regime. (And these too are common characteristics of the separate state property tax and sales tax systems.) The government justifications underlying their inclusion in the comprehensive income tax system, however, are quite different. While the "normative" provision is considered absolutely necessary to the structure and implementation of the income tax regime, the various tax expenditure provisions are enacted through legislative discretion to provide rewards, stimuli, and incentives to select groups of taxpayers in order to achieve targeted goals. Outright government monetary grants also reduce government revenues and are economic subsidies that reward, stimulate, and incentivize recipients' behavior. Direct government grants to parochial schools conflict with core Establishment Clause principles. So the natural question is whether, as a substitute, the tax expenditures at issue—tax deductions, credits, and exclusions—designed to funnel government money into private education alternatives must be treated equivalently, especially when a major portion of the funds so generated supports religiously-imbued education in parochial schools.

The § 170 charitable contribution deduction available to donors who give money to parochial schools certainly is a tax expenditure. But it differs in significant ways in this context from the other tax expenditures, which arguably justify its more lenient constitutional treatment.[66] First, a parochial school qualifies for this indirect tax benefit by virtue of its § 501(c)(3) status and therefore, in turn, simply by virtue of its educational function regardless of any religious affiliation or component to its mission. The contribution which justifies the deduction may not directly support the religious mission of the school or be tied, as is a tuition subsidy, to the religious education of a student. Indeed, as pointed out in illustration #2, such contributions can be earmarked for a particular secular purpose, although admittedly with the effect of freeing other non-restricted funds of the school to support religious objectives. Moreover, the effect of the § 170 deduction itself in supporting private schools is measured. The deduction is available for contributions to a vast array of secular and sectarian entities; it is not targeted at supporting private, let alone parochial, schools.[67] Only 30 percent of

66 *But see* E.C. Lashbrooke, Jr., *An Economic and Constitutional Case for Repeal of the I.R.C. Section 170 Deduction for Charitable Contributions to Religious Organizations*, 27 Duq. L. Rev. 695, 717 (1989).

67 In fact, contributors can claim a § 170 deduction for donations that support programs at public elementary and secondary schools by contributing to them directly or to a § 501(c)(3) local school foundation created to channel donations, largely from parents, to

individual taxpayers itemize deductions on their federal income tax returns, and schools must compete for their contributions with many other worthy causes and organizations. Finally, the effect is further minimized because, unlike other tax expenditures discussed above, for purposes of federal income taxation the donor is out of pocket the full contributed amount and has her § 170 deduction limited by her marginal tax rate.[68]

VI. Are Tax Expenditures Equivalent to Outright Government Grants for Constitutional Purposes?

Tax experts in academia and government have warned that the "tax expenditure" inquiry is an imperfect tax policy analytical tool. So it is natural to question the usefulness of a fallible tax policy analytical tool for constitutional purposes—namely, for our purposes, to consider how tax expenditures, which economically are equivalent to direct government grants, should be treated under the Establishment Clause in the specific context of state aid to religiously-affiliated education providers, including private, parochial schools. The more general issue of the appropriate constitutional evaluation of tax expenditures has been of enduring debate among legal academicians, tax experts, and the judiciary—perhaps due in part to the prominence of the law and economics movement in recent decades—with some disparaging the reasoning that "economic equivalents must be legal equivalents."[69]

Professor Edward A. Zelinsky repeatedly has been outspoken. He argues that "tax expenditure analysis has little to contribute" to constitutional examination because the tax expenditure analytical system fails to develop a uniform, definitive means to distinguish between "normative" tax provisions absolutely necessary to structure and implement the tax regime and the "special" tax expenditure provisions.[70] This flaw has led federal courts to use inconsistent standards to evaluate the treatment of tax expenditures (on the one hand) and direct subsidies (on the other hand) for constitutional purposes despite tax expenditure analysis

---

particular public schools. I.R.C. § 170(c)(1). *See also* Bob Reich, Op.-ed, *Not Very Giving*, N.Y. Times, Sept. 5, 2013, at A25 (criticizing § 501(c)(3) local school foundations as bad tax policy for perpetuating and deepening inequalities between public schools for children of affluent and poor families).

68 Obviously, state income tax deductions for qualified educational expenses, as well as those that qualify for a state charitable contribution deduction, are subject to a taxpayer's state marginal income tax rate.

69 Linda Sugin, *The Great and Mighty Tax Law: How the Roberts Court Has Reduced Constitutional Scrutiny of Taxes and Tax Expenditures*, 78 Brook. L. Rev. 777, 792 (2013).

70 Edward A. Zelinsky, Winn *and the Inadvisability of Constitutionalizing Tax Expenditure Analysis*, 121 Yale L.J. Online 25, 27–28 (2011).

"'posit[ing] that, regardless of where the program or policy appears, all subsidy, incentive, and relief programs should be evaluated by the same standards.'"[71]

The confusion posed by tax expenditure analysis in the context of government aid to religiously-affiliated entities is evident from the sparring of Supreme Court justices over the years.[72] Notably, in *Walz*, a taxpayer-owner of property in New York City asserted that the state statute permitting a property tax exemption for a house of worship violated the Establishment Clause. The Court's analysis did not depend on whether the statute exempting the house of worship was a "normative" provision or a tax expenditure; rather, all Justices agreed the property tax exemption was economically equivalent to a cash subsidy. Nonetheless, the Justices' Establishment Clause analyses then seized upon relevant distinguishing characteristics of a property tax exemption and the symbolism it involves in struggling with whether the statutory tax accommodation was constitutional.

Chief Justice Warren Burger, writing the five-Justice majority opinion holding the property tax exemption statute constitutional, wrote of the latent dangers of government involvement in religion. He compared "a direct money subsidy [which] would be a relationship pregnant with involvement," to "[t]he grant of a tax exemption ... [that] creates only a minimal and remote involvement between

71 Zelinsky, *Are Tax "Benefits" Equivalent to Direct Expenditures?*, *supra* note 44, at 380–81 ((considering constitutional questions under the Commerce, Equal Protection, and Establishment Clauses) (quoting Adler, *supra* note 51, at 860–61, evaluating various cases involving the Free Speech, Equal Protection, and Establishment Clauses)); Zelinsky, Winn *and the Inadvisability of Constitutionalizing Tax Expenditure Analysis*, *supra* note 70, at 27.

72 The confusion can be found even where the Establishment Clause issue actually involves direct government spending. In *Rosenberger*, 515 U.S. at 819, Justice Clarence Thomas, writing a concurring opinion, and Justice Souter, writing for the four dissenters, were at odds on what tax expenditure analysis offered for determining whether the state university violated the Establishment Clause (or the Free Speech Clause) by refusing to authorize payment from student activity funds, generated from a mandatory student assessment, for the printing of a student organization's publication, "Wide Awake: A Christian Perspective at the University of Virginia." Justice Thomas, asserting that tax expenditures and direct government spending are economic equivalents, turned Establishment Clause jurisprudence on its head by seeming to suggest that even direct government spending for religion should be constitutionally permissible. *Id.* at 859–62. Justice Souter countered: "If Justice Thomas's assertion of equivalence should prevail then the *Walz* Court necessarily was wrong about a distinction critical to its holding. Justice Thomas can hardly use *Walz* coherently for support after removing the basis on which it relies." *Id.* at 881 n.7 (Souter, J., dissenting) (Justice Souter invoked, and Justice Thomas spurned, Professor Bittker's suggestion in *Churches, Taxes and the Constitution*, *supra* note 61, that it can be tricky or elusive to distinguish between tax expenditures and direct grants because they can have common features). For further comments on this dialogue, *see* Linda Sugin, *Tax Expenditure Analysis and Constitutional Decisions*, 50 Hastings L.J. 407, 463 (1999) (stating that Justice Thomas turned tax expenditure reasoning "upside-down," and that "his radical position [was] shared by no other member of the court").

church and state and far less than taxation of churches."[73] Justice Brennan, concurring, similarly noted that "[t]ax exemptions … constitute mere passive state involvement with religion and not the affirmative involvement characteristic of outright governmental subsidy."[74] And Justice John Marshall Harlan's concurrence expressed like thoughts: "[Direct] [s]ubsidies, unlike exemptions, must be passed on periodically and thus invite more political controversy than exemptions. Moreover, [direct] subsidies or direct aid, as a general rule, are granted on the basis of enumerated and more complicated qualifications and frequently involve the state in administration to a higher degree …."[75] These considerations, however, that may apply to a property tax exemption do not characterize affirmative state aid to "qualified" parochial schools and students through a tax expenditure program requiring considerable state administration and oversight. And Justice Harlan failed to appreciate the beneficial effects of political accountability that may be lost when state aid programs are implemented through an opaque tax system.

Elsewhere in his concurring opinion Justice Brennan was more persuasive in distinguishing the property tax exemption at issue from a direct subsidy for purposes of the Establishment Clause. First, "'the symbolism of tax exemption is significant as a manifestation that organized religion is not expected to support the state; by the same token the state is not expected to support the church.'"[76] He then highlighted characteristics that have particular relevance for the constitutional problem of tax expenditures that channel state funds to private, parochial schools and other religiously-affiliated education providers: "A [direct] subsidy involves the direct transfer [diversion] of public monies to the subsidized enterprise and uses resources exacted from taxpayers as a whole. An exemption, on the other hand, involves no such transfer."[77] And then, hinting of the history that engendered the Establishment Clause, Justice Brennan quoted approvingly from a law review article: "'[I]n the case of direct subsidy, the state forcibly diverts the income of both believers and nonbelievers to churches'"—and houses of worship can use the subsidy for religious purposes—while "'[i]n the case of an exemption, the state merely refrains from diverting to its own uses income independently generated by the churches through voluntary contributions'"—and houses of worship receive

73 *Walz*, 397 U.S. at 675. *See* Surrey & McDaniel, *supra* note 50, at 132–33 (labeling Chief Justice Warren's opinion "naive[]," "inadequate," and one that "will not withstand economic analysis."); Lashbrooke, *supra* note 66, at 717 ("The majority in *Walz* completely misunderstood or deliberately misconstrued the tax expenditure concept when it drew a distinction between a direct money subsidy and a tax exemption.").

74 *Walz*, 397 U.S. at 691 (Brennan, J., concurring).

75 *Id.* at 699 (Harlan, J., concurring).

76 *Id.* at 691 (Brennan, J., concurring) (quoting Paul A. Freund, *Public Aid to Parochial Schools*, 82 Harv. L. Rev. 1680, 1687 n.16 (1969)).

77 *Walz*, 397 U.S. at 690 (Brennan, J., concurring).

no public funds for expenditure on religious activities.[78] Finally, Justice Brennan further explained:

> If the only state assistance received by a religious organization is a real property tax exemption, the church must raise privately every cent that it spends. If, on the other hand, the only state aid to a church is a general subsidy, the church is relieved of the need to support itself to the extent that its subsidy payments from the State exceed its tax payments to the State. Thus, to take the extreme case, a lightly taxed religious organization that received a large, general subsidy could purchase property, construct buildings and maintain its program wholly at public expense. Such dependence on state support is impossible when the only aid provided is a real property tax exemption.[79]

Whether Justice Brennan's support for the property tax exemption in *Walz* was correct, his reasoning as applied to tax expenditures that subsidize private, parochial schools and other religiously-affiliated education providers—which already benefit from income and property tax exemptions—clearly demonstrates the constitutional difficulties as the government unquestionably extracts money from all taxpayers, diverts it to those providers, and thereby supports their religious instruction and indoctrination.

In his dissent in *Everson v. Board of Education* objecting to state reimbursement of parents for bus fares for transporting their children to parochial schools Justice Wiley B. Rutledge, joined by three other Justices, more directly invoked history: "No provision of the Constitution is more closely tied to or given content by its generating history than the religious clause of the First Amendment."[80] The reimbursements in *Everson* came from tax revenues, but they were achieved directly and not through tax expenditures. Still, Justice Rutledge's summary of James Madison's position in 1784–1785, the years leading up to drafting the U.S. Constitution and the First Amendment, is directly relevant to the constitutional status of tax expenditures:

> In no phase was he more unrelentingly absolute than in opposing state support or aid by taxation. Not even "three pence" contribution was thus to be exacted from any citizen for such a purpose. Tithes had been the lifeblood of establishment

78 *Id.* at 691 (Brennan, J., concurring) (quoting Donald A. Giannella, *Religious Liberty, Nonestablishment, and Doctrinal Development Part II. The Nonestablishment Principle*, 81 HARV. L. REV. 513, 553 (1968)).

79 *Walz*, 397 U.S. at 690 n.9 (Brennan, J., concurring). *But see id.* at 704 (Douglas, J., dissenting) (perhaps appreciating Justice Brennan's reasoning but not his conclusion: "A tax exemption is a subsidy. Is my Brother Brennan correct in saying that we would hold that state or federal grants to churches, say, to construct the edifice itself would be unconstitutional? What is the difference between that kind of subsidy and the present subsidy?").

80 330 U.S. 1, 33 (1947) (Rutledge, Frankfurter, Jackson, Burton, JJ., dissenting).

> before and after other compulsions disappeared. Madison and his coworkers made no exceptions or abridgments to the complete separation [between church and state] they created. Their objection was not to small tithes. It was to any tithes whatsoever. "If it were lawful to impose a small tax for religion the admission would pave the way for oppressive levies." Not the amount, but "the *principle of the assessment was wrong.*"[81]

Justice Brennan recounted this passage in his dissent in *Valley Forge Christian College v. Americans United for Separation of Church and State, Inc.*, and went on to say: "It is clear, in the light of this history, that one of the primary purposes of the Establishment Clause was to prevent the use of tax moneys for religious purposes. *The taxpayer was the direct and intended beneficiary of the prohibition on financial aid to religion.*"[82] The plain purpose of that prohibition is to safeguard freedom of conscience by ensuring that government is neither aligned with one religion nor with religion generally. This basic tenet needs little elucidation, but as Justice David Souter expounded in *Mitchell v. Helms*, "compelling an individual to support religion violates the fundamental principle of freedom of conscience. Madison's and Jefferson's now familiar words establish clearly that liberty of personal conviction requires freedom from coercion to support religion, and this means that the government can compel *no* aid to fund it."[83]

The elevation of the form of government funding—whether achieved by outright government grants or tax expenditures—over substance (economic equivalency), despite their potential "qualitative"[84] differences, obfuscates relevant history and diminishes a fundamental purpose of the Establishment Clause. Justice Lewis Powell expressed the view of six members of the Court in this regard in *Committee for Public Education & Religious Liberty v. Nyquist*.[85] There, as discussed in Chapter 2, the Court ruled against the constitutionality of two New York statutes that granted government financial assistance—one by direct tuition reimbursement and the other by a hybrid income tax adjustment that the state labeled a tax deduction but plaintiffs labeled a tax credit—to tuition-paying parents of students who attended private, secular and parochial elementary and secondary schools. Commenting that substance must prevail over form, Justice Powell remarked as to the tax adjustment:

---

81 *Id.* at 40–41 (citation omitted) (emphasis added).

82 454 U.S. 464, 504 (1982) (Brennan, J., dissenting) (emphasis in original).

83 *Mitchell*, 530 U.S. at 870 (Souter, J., dissenting) (emphasis added).

84 Justice Brennan's own subsequent assessment of the views that he expressed in his concurring opinion in *Walz* when contrasting the property tax exemption there with a direct government subsidy for Establishment Clause analysis was that "the position of a taxpayer with respect to a Government grant of a tax exemption to a religious institution is qualitatively different from the position of a taxpayer objecting to a subsidy." *Valley Forge*, 454 U.S. at 504 n.15 (1982) (Brennan, J., dissenting).

85 413 U.S. 756 (1973).

> ... the constitutionality of this hybrid benefit does not turn in any event on the label we accord it. As Mr. Chief Justice Burger's opinion for the Court in *Lemon v. Kurtzman* ... notes, constitutional analysis is not a "legalistic minuet in which precise rules and forms must govern." Instead we must "examine the form of the relationship for the light that it casts on the substance."[86]

Even Chief Justice Burger, although dissenting in part, called attention to a basic reason for a careful, substantive evaluation, one that is perhaps particularly salient in this era of legislatures enacting innovative tax schemes that enable taxpayer funds to be funneled to parochial schools and other religiously-affiliated education providers: "[G]overnment aid to individuals generally stands on an entirely different footing from direct aid to religious institutions. I say 'generally' because it is obviously possible to conjure hypothetical statutes that constitute either a *subterfuge for direct aid to religious institutions* or a discriminatory enactment favoring religious over nonreligious activities."[87] With the evolution of the Court's jurisprudence, described in Chapter 2, culminating in *Winn*, discussed in the next chapter, the legalistic minuet warned against in constitutional analysis of state aid to private schools gradually seems to have become more akin to a "Gangnam Style" romp.

Ten years after *Nyquist*, Justice Thurgood Marshall and three other Justices, dissenting in *Mueller v. Allen*, voiced a similar concern that a legislative subterfuge was at work and insisted that the Court inappropriately was elevating form over substance.[88] There, as explained in Chapter 2, the Minnesota legislature used its taxing and spending powers to enact a "genuine" income tax deduction that granted assistance to parents for payments for tuition, transportation, and nonreligious instructional materials at public and private, primary and secondary schools, both secular and parochial. The Supreme Court upheld the tax deduction as constitutional under the Establishment Clause. But the dissenters maintained:

86 *Id.* at 789–90 (citation omitted). No Justice in *Nyquist* waded into a constitutional analysis of a genuine tax deduction because the "hybrid" tax allowance at issue "does not have the elements of a genuine tax deduction, such as for charitable contributions, [and so] we do not have before us, and do not decide, whether that form of tax benefit is constitutionally acceptable under the 'neutrality' test in *Walz*." *Id.* at 790 n.49. Justice Powell saw little to distinguish constitutionally the direct tuition grant (reimbursement to parents) from the tax adjustment before the Court. "The only difference is that one parent receives an actual cash payment while the other is allowed to reduce by an arbitrary amount the sum he would otherwise be obliged to pay over to the State. ... '[I]n both instances the money involved represents a charge made upon the state for the purpose of religious education.'" *Id.* at 791 (citation omitted).

87 *Id.* at 801 (Burger, C. J., dissenting in part) (emphasis added).

88 463 U.S. 388, 411–13, 411–13 n.5 (1983) (Marshall, Brennan, Blackmun, Stevens JJ., dissenting).

> [T]he effect of the aid is unmistakably to provide desired financial support for nonpublic, sectarian institutions. … That parents receive a reduction of their tax liability, rather than a direct reimbursement, is of no greater significance here than it was in *Nyquist*. … It is equally irrelevant whether a reduction in taxes takes the form of a tax "credit," a tax "modification," or a tax "deduction." What is of controlling significance is not the form but the "substantive impact" of the financial aid. … The statute is little more than a subsidy of tuition *masquerading* as a subsidy of general educational expenses.[89]

The masquerade recently culminated in *Winn* where the Supreme Court provided state legislatures "a roadmap—more truly, just a one-step instruction"[90] by which, using their taxing and spending powers, they can design a tax law that diverts taxpayer funds to support private education provided by private, parochial schools and other religiously-affiliated sources. And masquerade is an appropriate metaphor because, as explained in the next chapter, the ruling in *Winn* denying taxpayer standing to bring an Establishment Clause challenge effectively blindfolds federal courts from even considering the substantive constitutionality of such tax entitlement programs.

Justice Kennedy, writing for the five-Justice majority in *Winn*, sparred with Justice Kagan, writing for the four dissenting Justices, over whether the Arizona tax credit for contributions to STOs provided a basis for non-contributing, objecting taxpayers to assert the state program violates the Establishment Clause. Justice Kennedy, professing to "see that tax credits and governmental expenditures can have similar economic consequences,"[91] nonetheless twisted the Arizona tax credit and the tax liability it relieved into an amount not "owed to the State."[92] The tax credit was nothing more than "government [merely] declin[ing] to impose a tax" on eligible taxpayers.[93] It therefore, according to Justice Kennedy, did not reduce net revenues of the state, a basic and elemental outcome of a "proper" tax expenditure. Moreover, he asserted, contributors to the STOs "spend their own money" for the STO contributions, so the money cannot be public money aiding religious entities, even though much of it flows directly to sectarian STOs and then to parochial schools.[94] Thus, the majority construed the tax credit program in a highly artificial

89 *Id.* at 407–09 (citations omitted and emphasis added).

90 *Winn*, 131 S. Ct. at 1462 (Kagan, J., dissenting).

91 *Id.* at 1447 (majority opinion).

92 *Id.* at 1448.

93 *Id.* at 1447. Justice Kennedy claimed that the "Madisonian prohibition" on coercing taxpayers to support religion through a tax assessment was not violated, in part because the legislature had not used its taxing power in a manner "tantamount to a religious tax or to a tithe." *Id.* at 1446–47. As discussed in the text above and elucidated below, while one could consider a tax exemption as the legislature refraining from imposing a tax, the STO-tax credit simply gives a taxpayer the opportunity to divert his payment owed to the state to a § 501(c)(3) organization.

94 *Id.* at 1447.

and literal sense to not "extract and spend" plaintiffs' taxes sufficiently to give them standing to object. To the majority's exceedingly obtuse perspective, Justice Kagan vigorously retorted that the majority's "novel distinction" is "one in search of a difference."[95] "[T]argeted tax breaks … are just [government] spending under a different name."[96] This tax credit is a tax expenditure that "deplete[s] funds in the government's coffers by transferring money to select recipients,"[97] as would a direct government grant.

Justice Kagan got it right, and Justice Kennedy was plainly wrong. The Arizona income tax credit is a tax expenditure in every sense. First, the legislature exercised its taxing and spending power to grant tax relief to claimant-taxpayers and spend the money of non-claimant taxpayers by subsidizing the claimants through the tax credit afforded them. This was state, not private, money because but for the tax credit contributors owed it to the state as a tax liability they already otherwise had incurred. Second, the tax credit reduced the government's net *income* tax revenues, a classic feature of a tax expenditure. Although the majority in *Winn* suggested the STO-tax credit *may* "on net save the State money" by reducing the costs of educating in the public school system those children who instead attend private secular or parochial schools because of the program,[98] this is a palpable distraction. Arizona's public schools are supported almost exclusively by property taxes,[99] so any possible savings would come principally from not fully expending property tax revenues; the STO-tax credit certainly reduces the government's net

95 *Id.* at 1450, 1455 (Kagan, J., dissenting).

96 *Id.* at 1456. Such special tax adjustments have been treated by both the U.S. Department of Treasury and the Staff of the Joint Committee on Taxation as constituting tax expenditures. *See* Staff of Joint Committee on Taxation, *supra* note 52, at 25–26, 37, 39. The Supreme Court also has referred to tax credits as tax expenditures. *See* DaimlerChrysler Corp. v. Cuno, 547 U.S. 332, 344 (2006).

97 *Winn*, 131 S. Ct. at 1456, 1458 (Kagan, J., dissenting) (particularly noting that, from 1998 to 2008, the Arizona Department of Revenue reported, as required by Arizona law, the tax credit "cost Arizona almost $350 million in redirected tax revenue").

98 *Id.* at 1444. *See* Stephen D. Sugarman, *Tax Credit School Scholarship Plans*, 43 J.L. & Educ. 1, *43–*47 (2014). Early in the Arizona program, in 2001, the conservative think tank, the Cato Institute, released a policy analysis in which it concluded: "Although the state forgoes revenue as people exercise the credit, taxpayers save money when students who would have been educated at public expense use the scholarships to transfer to nonpublic schools. Therefore, although Arizona lost $13.7 million in 1999, we find that, once savings are taken into account, the credit was revenue neutral." Carrie Lips & Jennifer Jacoby, The Arizona Scholarship Tax Credit: Giving Parents Choices, Saving Taxpayers Money 1, Cato Institute Policy Analysis, *available at* http://object.cato.org/sites/cato.org/files/pubs/pdf/pa414.pdf. But this conclusion depends heavily on the dated study's somewhat dubious estimate of the percent of students receiving STO scholarships who would attend public schools but for the scholarships, *see id.* at 8, and this in turn may depend on whether the scholarships primarily serve the neediest of students.

99 *See Q and A on Public School Finance and Equalization: Part I: Traditional Public Schools*, Arizona Education Network, *available at* http://www.arizonaeducationnetwork.

income tax revenues.[100] More importantly, the use of government funds to spur and support religious education is what raises the Establishment Clause problem. It is immaterial whether the ultimate net financial effect on the overall public fisc is positive, negative, or neutral.

The third indicium of a tax expenditure is that for policy (and perhaps practical) reasons the state legislature affirmatively acted to give taxpayers a financial incentive to make contributions to STOs with the full knowledge and expectation that a substantial portion of the scholarship funds so raised would support students at parochial schools. Indeed, the STO-tax credit is a tax expenditure *par excellence*. Taxpayers who donate to an STO do not spend even "three pence" of their own money. Other taxpayers who do not participate in the program vicariously subsidize in full the contributing taxpayers' transactions.

Compelling taxpayers to provide such subsidies that support religion, especially one not their own, and particularly when those subsidies are used for the religious education and indoctrination of children, violates freedom of conscience and is intrinsically inconsistent with the Establishment Clause. In no other context does the metaphorical notion of separation of church and state have more concrete constitutional meaning and urgency. Justice Rutledge recognized this in *Everson*:

> [Apart] from efforts to inject religious training or exercises and sectarian issues into the public schools, the only serious surviving threat to maintaining that complete and permanent separation … is through [the] use of the taxing power to support religion, religious establishments, or establishments having a religious foundation whatever their form or special religious function. … [Money] taken by taxation from one is not to be used or given to support another's religious training or belief, or indeed one's own.[101]

Now, the grave danger of which Justice Rutledge warned appears all the more disconcerting. As Chapter 4 explains, *Winn* unnecessarily and inappropriately virtually immunizes tax statutes that state legislatures intentionally design as very real tax expenditures—whether or not they are subterfuges for direct government spending and outright grants—from Establishment Clause challenges by taxpayers *qua* taxpayers in the federal courts. By precluding those who object to the proliferating and expanding programs from even having their constitutional day in federal court, *Winn* may well prove to fuel the very widespread religious divisiveness that the Establishment Clause is intended to avoid.

---

com/2010/06/traditional-public-school-finance-and-equalized-funding-your-questions-answered/ (last visited Oct. 1, 2013).

100 *See supra* note 55 (discussing the Arizona Department of Revenue reports on income tax revenues lost from the STO-tax credit for individuals).

101 *Everson*, 330 U.S. at 44 (Rutledge, J., dissenting).

VII. Conclusion

Webster's Third New International Dictionary defines "equivalent" as "equal in force or amount," "like in signification or import," "equal in value," and "equal in might or authority."[102] Congress, state legislatures, and courts, including the Supreme Court, have recognized for several decades that tax expenditures are the economic equivalents of direct government spending and cash grants. So in economic impact, tax expenditures, on the one hand, and direct government spending and cash grants, on the other, are "equal in force or amount," "like in signification or import," "equal in value," and "equal in might or authority." Over the past 40 years, however, several Supreme Court Justices sporadically questioned whether they should treat tax expenditures as the equivalent of direct government spending and cash grants for Establishment Clause purposes. As the next chapter explains, the Roberts Court ruling in *Winn* answered that question, at least for purposes of standing, in the tax credit context of that case: tax expenditures and direct government spending may not be constitutional equivalents even if they are economic equivalents and equivalents in the common sense meaning of Webster's. In so ruling, the Roberts Court provided a blueprint to enable legislatures to funnel public funds to aid religion—specifically private, parochial schools and religiously-affiliated education providers—and to do so in a relatively indiscernible and politically unaccountable way through the tax system. This disturbing development may make it easier for states to fulfill their constitutionally mandated educational responsibilities as fewer students demand public education and more students are publicly assisted in paying for private, largely religiously-oriented education alternatives. But the ultimate civic, political, and spiritual costs to all citizens may be quite profound.

102 Webster's Third New International Dictionary of the English Language, Unabridged 769 (1966).

Chapter 4
Establishment Clause Standing and Challenges to School Aid

> [T]here is an impulse [at the Supreme Court] to decide difficult questions of substantive law obliquely in the course of opinions purporting to do nothing more than determine what the Court labels "standing" .... [Such opinions] tend merely to obfuscate, rather than inform, our understanding of the meaning of rights under the law. The serious by-product of that practice is that the Court disregards its constitutional responsibility. ...[1]

I. Introduction

As an integral part of the basic structure of separation of powers among the legislative, executive, and judicial branches of government, Article III of the U.S. Constitution limits the jurisdiction of federal courts to "Cases" or "Controversies." The Constitution, however, does not define these terms, leaving it to the Supreme Court over time to interpret the appropriate limits of federal judicial power.[2] As early as President George Washington's administration, the Court declined Secretary of State Thomas Jefferson's request for its advice on matters regarding the country's neutrality in the war between England and France.[3] Thus, unlike some state high courts, federal courts do not issue advisory opinions in the absence of a true case or controversy. Another of the Court's nonjusticiability principles is the political question doctrine through which the Court declines to adjudicate a matter it believes is textually or prudentially left to another branch of government to resolve—matters involving foreign relations, for example. Similarly, issues of ripeness and mootness fall within these principles of judicial restraint.[4] But the question of standing—which parties are entitled to litigate the merits of a substantive or procedural challenge to laws, constitutional provisions, or executive, legislative, or administrative actions—is the most significant way in which the Court may avoid ruling on the merits of a claim. This

---

1 Valley Forge Christian Coll. v. Ams. United for Separation of Church & State, Inc., 454 U.S. 464, 490 (1982) (Brennan, J., dissenting).

2 "[T]hose two words have an iceberg quality, containing beneath their surface simplicity submerged complexities which go to the very heart of our constitutional form of government." Flast v. Cohen, 392 U.S. 83, 94 (1968).

3 *See* Richard H. Fallon, Jr., et al., Hart and Wechsler's The Federal Courts and the Federal System 50–52 (6th ed. 2009).

4 *See* Massachusetts v. E.P.A., 549 U.S. 497, 516 (2007).

is because standing is the right to commence litigation, to take the initial step that frames legal issues for ultimate adjudication on the merits of the issues raised. So standing is a "'threshold question' to be resolved before turning attention to more 'substantive' issues."[5] Indeed, if the litigants lack standing the Court has no jurisdiction to reach the merits. But standing also is "one of 'the most amorphous [concepts] in the entire domain of public law.'"[6]

As one noted scholar wrote in the early 1960s, "[t]he question of standing of citizen or taxpayer is one of great difficulty and of great importance, particularly of great importance in the immediate future."[7] This statement proved especially prescient as the Court began grappling with Establishment Clause claims. It is especially true now, more than 50 years later, in light of the 2011 Supreme Court ruling in *Arizona Christian School Tuition Organization v. Winn*.[8] There, in a sharp 5–4 split, the majority held that state taxpayers lacked standing to challenge the constitutionality under the Establishment Clause of an Arizona statute providing significant tax benefits reaching private, mainly parochial, schools. The Court essentially put the federal courts off-limit as venues for such challenges.

In this chapter we first describe the doctrine of standing and its evolution generally. We then focus on its troubling application to Establishment Clause claims, particularly those involving taxpayer standing that prior to *Winn* had been most relevant to school aid cases. This background, along with an appreciation of the Supreme Court Justices' confusion about the role of tax expenditure analysis for Establishment Clause purposes (presented in Chapter 3), demonstrates just how intellectually indefensible the majority's opinion in *Winn* is and what that decision likely means for the future.

II. Historical Background of the Standing Doctrine

The Court's standing doctrine derives from what Justice Antonin Scalia expressed in his 1992 opinion for the Court in *Lujan v. Defenders of Wildlife*[9] as "the Constitution's central mechanism of separation of powers [which] depends largely upon common understanding of what activities are appropriate to legislatures,

5 *Valley Forge*, 454 U.S. at 490 (Brennan, J., dissenting). Questions of standing may be raised by parties at any stage of the judicial process or by a court itself.

6 *Flast*, 392 U.S. at 99 (quoting *Hearing on S. 2097 Before the Subcomm. on Constitutional Rights of the S. Judiciary Comm.*, 89th Cong. 498 (1966) (statement of Professor Paul A. Freund)).

7 Louis L. Jaffe, *Standing to Secure Judicial Review: Public Actions*, 74 Harv. L. Rev. 1265, 1266 (1961). *See* William P. Marshall & Gene R. Nichol, *Not a Winn-Win: Misconstruing Standing and the Establishment Clause*, 2011 Sup. Ct. Rev. 215, 251 (2011) (standing is a "difficult," "frustrating" area of constitutional law and one that can be "extraordinarily amorphous and malleable").

8 131 S. Ct. 1436 (2011).

9 504 U.S. 555 (1992).

to executives, and to courts."[10] As Justice Scalia described the doctrine, it is deceptively easy to encapsulate:

> Over the years, our cases have established that the irreducible constitutional minimum of standing contains three elements. First, the plaintiff must have suffered an "injury in fact"—an invasion of a legally protected interest which is (a) concrete and particularized and (b) "actual or imminent, not 'conjectural' or 'hypothetical.'" Second, there must be a causal connection between the injury and the conduct complained of—the injury has to be "fairly … trace[able] to the challenged action of the defendant, and not … th[e] result [of] the independent action of some third party not before the court." Third, it must be "likely," as opposed to merely "speculative," that the injury will be "redressed by a favorable decision."[11]

The Court adheres to requiring a party seeking to invoke federal jurisdiction to prove the three elements of "personal and individual" injury in fact with the party's "direct stake in the outcome" of the case and the "causation" components of traceability and redressability.[12] A "sharp and acrimonious" disagreement by itself is not sufficient for standing.[13]

In addition to these three elements that the Court deems irreducible, minimal constitutional requirements, there are some "merely prudential considerations that are part of judicial self-government."[14] These more flexible rules embody "'judicially self-imposed limits on the exercise of federal jurisdiction,'" which the Court is freer to adjust as a case may require.[15]

Although the Court purports to keep separate the constitutional and prudential strands of its standing doctrine,[16] the distinctions are not always clear. In 1984, the Court described its discretionary, prudential limits as including a "general prohibition on a litigant's raising another person's legal rights, the rule barring adjudication of generalized grievances more appropriately addressed in the

---

10 *Id.* at 559. *See also* Allen v. Wright, 468 U.S. 737, 752 (1984) ("[T]he law of Art. III standing is built on a single basic idea—the idea of separation of powers.").

11 *Lujan*, 504 U.S. at 560–61 (citations omitted). *See also id.* at 577 (emphasizing the "separation-of-powers significance" of the concrete injury requirement).

12 Hollingsworth v. Perry, 133 S. Ct. 2652, 2662 (2013) (quoting *Lujan*, 504 U.S. at 560 n.1 and Arizonans for Official English v. Arizona, 520 U.S. 43, 64 (1997)).

13 *Hollingsworth*, at 2661 (internal citation omitted).

14 *Lujan*, 504 U.S. at 560.

15 United States v. Windsor, 133 S. Ct. 2675, 2685 (2013) (quoting Elk Grove Unified Sch. Dist. v. Newdow, 542 U.S. 1, 11–12 (2004)).

16 *Windsor*, 133 S. Ct. at 2685. One important difference is that Congress can overcome a non-constitutional, prudential restraint by statutorily bestowing standing on certain parties to assert claims under particular legislation but cannot legislate around what the Court deems to be constitutional requirements of standing. *See* Warth v. Seldin, 422 U.S. 490, 501, 509, 514 (1975); *Massachusetts*, 549 U.S. at 516.

representative branches, and the requirement that a plaintiff's complaint fall within the zone of interests protected by the law invoked."[17] At the same time, however, the Court noted that all cases or controversies doctrines involve an "idea, which is more than an intuition but less than a rigorous and explicit theory, about the constitutional and prudential limits to the powers of an unelected, unrepresentative judiciary in our kind of government."[18] Thus both the prudential and constitutional components of standing "incorporate[] concepts concededly not susceptible of precise definition."[19] Twenty years later the Court still frankly acknowledged the ambiguity in this area.[20]

In one example highly relevant to the school aid issue, the Court most recently asserted:

> We have repeatedly held that … a "generalized grievance," no matter how sincere, is insufficient to confer standing. A litigant "raising only a generally available grievance about government—claiming only harm to his and every citizen's interest in proper application of the Constitution and laws, and seeking relief that no more directly and tangibly benefits him than it does the public at large—does not state an Article III case or controversy."[21]

But the generalized grievance disqualification appears among the Court's prudential, not constitutional, elements of standing,[22] and stems in its very articulation from the rationale that such matters are "more appropriately addressed in the representative branches."[23] How this discretionary disqualification relates to an Establishment Clause claim raising fundamental issues of individual liberty therefore requires careful and thoughtful analysis. Moreover, as a dissent by

17 *Wright*, 468 U.S. at 751; *see also Elk Grove*, 542 U.S. at 12.

18 *Id.* at 11 (quoting *Wright*, 468 U.S. at 750 (internal citation and quotation marks omitted)).

19 *Wright*, 468 U.S. at 751.

20 *Elk Grove*, 542 U.S. at 11–12.

21 *Hollingsworth*, 133 S. Ct. at 2662 (quoting *Lujan*, 504 U.S. at 573–74).

22 *Elk Grove*, 542 U.S. at 12 (quoting *Wright*, 468 U.S. at 751); *see Warth*, 422 U.S. at 499. *See also Valley Forge*, 454 U.S. at 471 ("The term 'standing' subsumes a blend of constitutional requirements and prudential considerations …, and it has not always been clear in the opinions of this Court whether particular features of the 'standing' requirement have been required by Art. III *ex proprio vigore*, or whether they are requirements that the Court itself has erected and which were not compelled by the language of the Constitution.") (citation omitted). The Court then listed only the three elements of injury, traceability, and redressability as the Article III requirements and later placed its reluctance to adjudicate generalized grievances among its prudential principles of self-restraint. *Id.* at 474–75; F.E.C. v. Akins, 524 U.S. 11, 23 (1998). *Cf.* Hein v. Freedom from Religion Found., Inc., 551 U.S. 587, 634 n.5 (2007) (Scalia, J., concurring) (attempting *ipse dixit* to place generalized grievances among the constitutional disqualifications).

23 *Wright*, 468 U.S. at 751.

Justice David Souter for four Justices once noted regarding injury that is deemed "generalized" and "shared with the public at large," "those properties on their own do not strip a would-be plaintiff of standing."[24] Indeed, "where a harm is concrete, though widely shared, the Court has found 'injury in fact.'"[25] What the Court acknowledged 30 years ago remains true today:

> We need not mince words when we say that the concept of "Art. III standing" has not been defined with complete consistency in all of the various cases decided by this Court which have discussed it, nor when we say that this very fact is probably proof that the concept cannot be reduced to a one-sentence or one-paragraph definition.[26]

Especially in evaluating how a bare majority of the Court has applied its amorphous, judicially created doctrine of standing to constrict fundamental First Amendment rights, it therefore is essential to keep well in mind the research of a leading academic commentator. Writing shortly after the Court decided *Lujan*, Professor Cass Sunstein noted that not only does Article III contain no explicit requirement of standing or personal injury in fact, but the Court's standing doctrine is a very modern creation. The Court's "insistence that Article III requires injury in fact, causation, and redressability [are] requirements unknown to our law until the 1970s.... [T]he injury-in-fact test played no role in administrative and constitutional law until the past quarter century."[27] The historical practice in England, which might inform what the Framers meant by "Cases" or "Controversies," indicates that "'the argument for a constitutional bar to strangers as complainants against unconstitutional action' is 'without foundation.'"[28] In the U.S., "[c]ertainly there

24 *Hein*, 551 U.S. at 642 n.3 (Souter, Stevens, Ginsburg, Breyer JJ., dissenting).

25 *Id.* (quoting *Akins*, 524 U.S. at 24); *Massachusetts*, 549 U.S. at 522 (quoting *Akins*, 524 U.S. at 24).

26 *Valley Forge*, 454 U.S. at 475.

27 Cass R. Sunstein, *What's Standing After* Lujan*? Of Constitutional Citizen Suits, "Injuries," and Article III*, 91 Mich. L. Rev. 163, 168–70 (1992). Professor Sunstein's article focuses on Congress' ability to create standing, but much of his scholarship is more broadly applicable.

There is little guidance from the constitutional drafting process. *See* 2 The Records of the Federal Convention of 1787 430 (Max Farrand, ed., Yale Univ. Press rev. ed. 1966) (James Madison's notes relating to Article III indicate "it being generally supposed that jurisdiction given was constructively limited to cases of a Judiciary Nature"). *See also* William R. Casto, *An Orthodox View of the Two-Tier Analysis of Congressional Control over Federal Jurisdiction*, 7 Const. Comment. 89, 90 (1990) ("There is no extant comprehensive record of the Committee of Detail's internal drafting process [pertaining to Article III]").

28 Sunstein, *supra* note 27, at 172 (quoting Raoul Berger, *Standing to Sue in Public Actions: Is It a Constitutional Requirement?*, 78 Yale L.J. 816, 827 (1969)). Prerogative writs gave the English courts the ability "'to prevent disorder from a failure of justice,'" and were used mainly to exercise control over actions and failures to act by local governmental

is no direct evidence that injury in fact or concrete interest was intended to be a constitutional prerequisite under Article III."[29] So Professor Sunstein concludes that, historically, "[t]here is no affirmative evidence of a requirement of a 'personal stake' or an 'injury in fact'—beyond the genuine requirement that some source of law confer a cause of action."[30] The question then is under what circumstances the Establishment Clause's guarantee of fundamental rights should confer a cause of action for their violation by government.[31]

III. Modern Establishment Clause Standing

In some cases it is readily apparent that a plaintiff should have standing to bring a claim based upon the Establishment Clause. It is clear, for example, that a student (and the student's parents) subjected to prayer or similar religious exercises at an official public school event should have standing to challenge that government action.[32] These plaintiffs are directly confronted and affected by the religious practice, and a court can remedy their harm. On the other hand, to avoid having to rule on the constitutionality of a public school district's mandate for daily, teacher-led recitation of the Pledge of Allegiance including the words "under God," the

---

authorities, especially "'where the law has established no specific remedy, and where in justice and government, there *ought* to be one.'" Jaffe, *supra* note 7, at 1269 (internal citation omitted) (emphasis in original)). Citizens' actions within the court system thus arose "no less in matters that concern them as a body than in those which affect them individually." *Id.* at 1270. Indeed, these occasionally included "ratepayers ... secur[ing] review by certiorari when [a governmental] order involved the expenditure of funds," even where the litigants were not considered to have a specially affected interest. *Id.* at 1274–75. *See generally* FALLON, JR., ET AL., *supra* note 3, at 146–48 (summarizing various views on the historical background).

29 Sunstein, *supra* note 27, at 173. Early practice in the state courts supports this view of Article III. *See* Jaffe, *supra* note 7, at 1276. While some state courts were reluctant to permit taxpayers' lawsuits for injunctions "in the form of a bill in equity to enjoin illegal expenditure by public officers" because the taxpayers were not specially affected, others were considerably less hesitant, perhaps particularly allowing taxpayers to pursue injunctive relief. *Id.* at 1277.

30 Sunstein, *supra* note 27, at 178.

31 Here Professor Sunstein himself seems a bit ambivalent, apparently agreeing with *Flast* but finding Justice William J. Brennan's dissent in *Valley Forge* unpersuasive. *Id.* at 210 & n.218.

32 *See* Sch. Dist. of Abington Twp. v. Schempp, 374 U.S. 203, 224 n.9, and *id.* at 266 n.30 (1963) (Brennan, J., concurring); Lee v. Weisman, 505 U.S. 577, 584 (1992) (finding school graduation prayer unconstitutional). In one early case challenging school bible reading, the Court denied standing to either the parent of a student who had graduated by the time of the appeal or to a taxpayer raising only a "feigned issue of taxation." Doremus v. Bd. of Educ., 342 U.S. 429, 435 (1952).

malleability of the Court's standing doctrine allowed a majority to deny standing to a noncustodial parent.[33]

The religious display cases are somewhat more problematic with regard to standing but also reflect an appropriate permissive approach to judicial review of government action that may improperly promote or endorse religion. Indeed, because we later argue that these cases provide a constructive contrast to *Winn*, they are worth considering in some detail. The Court's two most recent such cases were decided the same day, and each involved public displays of monuments of the Ten Commandments on government property. In one, plaintiff Van Orden, a lawyer and resident of Austin, Texas, asserted that he frequently encountered the monument over six years on his visits to the Texas State Capitol grounds where he used the law library. Although the monument was one of a number of other similar items and had stood for 40 years, as a non-believer Van Orden was sufficiently offended by what he took to be state policy favoring Judeo-Christian religions that he sued under a federal civil rights statute claiming an Establishment Clause violation. In the accompanying Supreme Court case, when two Kentucky counties placed versions of the Ten Commandments on the walls of their courthouses, the American Civil Liberties Union and several individuals brought civil rights actions against the counties. In each instance, federal district courts found that the plaintiffs' unwelcome contact with the monuments were sufficient to establish standing.[34] With Justice Stephen Breyer providing the swing vote, in 5–4 decisions the Supreme Court allowed the Texas display but not those in the Kentucky courthouses.[35] Nonetheless, in neither case did the Court find it necessary to even discuss standing to bring the action.[36] And in two earlier display cases, one involving a city's inclusion of a crèche in its annual Christmas display, and the other concerning a crèche in a county courthouse as well as a Christmas tree

33 *Elk Grove*, 542 U.S. at 17–18. The concurrence termed the majority's approach a "'novel' prudential standing principle." *Id.* at 18 (Rehnquist, C.J., concurring in judgment).

34 Van Orden v. Perry, No. A-01-CA-833-H, 2002 U.S. Dist. LEXIS 26709, *6–*8 (W.D. Tex. Oct. 2, 2002); A.C.L.U. v. Pulaski Cnty., 96 F. Supp. 2d 691, 694 (E.D. Ky. 2000); A.C.L.U. v. McCreary Cnty., Ky., 96 F. Supp. 2d 679, 682–83 (E.D. Ky. 2000).

35 The Court's opinion in *McCreary*, the Kentucky case, was based on its finding of a predominantly religious purpose for the displays at issue. McCreary Cnty., Ky. v. A.C.L.U., 545 U.S. 844, 881 (2005). Justice Breyer's controlling opinion concurring in the judgment in *Van Orden v. Perry*, 545 U.S. 677, 700 (2005), the Texas case, rejected any mechanical formula for resolving "difficult borderline cases" regarding the Establishment Clause. "I see no test-related substitute for the exercise of legal judgment … [that] must take account of context and consequences measured in light of" the purposes of the Clause.

36 *See generally id.*; *McCreary Cnty.*, 545 U.S. at 844. An organization such as the A.C.L.U. has "standing to bring suit on behalf of its members when its members would otherwise have standing to sue in their own right, the interests at stake are germane to the organization's purpose, and neither the claim asserted nor the relief requested requires the participation of individual members in the lawsuit." Friends of the Earth, Inc. v. Laidlaw Envtl. Servs. (TOC), Inc., 528 U.S. 167, 181 (2000).

together with a menorah outside a government office building, the Court similarly did not feel the need to address the question of standing that either was not raised or had been resolved in plaintiffs' favor in the lower court.[37]

Several other lower federal courts have addressed the issue in more detail, often allowing plaintiffs who are affronted by religious displays on government property to prosecute challenges under the Establishment Clause. Even though such a complaint could be considered a generalized grievance many others might share, the individual plaintiff himself or herself experiences a personal, adverse effect. Prior to the Supreme Court's two Ten Commandments cases, for example, a distinguished panel of the Fourth Circuit considered a citizen's challenge to a courtroom display of the Decalogue brought by a "contentious character" who was involved in various judicial proceedings and other public meetings in that venue. As an atheist he expressed his revulsion and distress at the display. His two-part injury was "caused by unwelcome direct contact with a religious display that appears to be endorsed by the state." Mere abstract objection to unconstitutional government action is not actionable, but "direct contact with an unwelcome religious exercise or display works a personal injury distinct from and in addition to each citizen's general grievance against unconstitutional government conduct."[38] The court also agreed with the majority of other federal circuit courts that had addressed the question of whether standing requires a plaintiff to have changed his behavior in response to the display, to avoid contact with it for example. These circuit courts answered in the negative; all that is required for standing is a plaintiff's direct contact with the religious display.[39]

Another Ten Commandments monument donated by a civic organization to the City of Fargo, North Dakota, sat on public land for over 40 years before being challenged. The plaintiff organization asserted that its members who lived in and around Fargo had experienced unwanted contact with the monument and "suffered feelings of exclusion, discomfort, and anger," but they did not alter their behavior in any way to avoid the contact or resulting reactions. In accord with what the circuit court termed "[b]y far the prevailing view," this was sufficient for standing to assert the Establishment Clause claim. Such a suit "'is not the mere vindication of a public grievance, but an allegation of government establishment of religion to which [the plaintiff's members], personally and directly, [have] been

37 Cnty. of Allegheny v. A.C.L.U., 492 U.S. 573 (1989); Lynch v. Donnelly, 465 US 668 (1984); Donnelly v. Lynch, 691 F.2d 1029, 1030–32 (1st Cir. 1982) (municipal taxpayer standing).

38 Suhre v. Haywood Cnty., 131 F.3d 1083, 1085–86 (4th Cir. 1997). The court elaborated: "Plaintiffs who 'are part of the [community where challenged religious symbolism is located] and are directly affronted by the presence of [this symbolism]' certainly 'have more than an abstract interest in seeing that [the government] observes the Constitution.'" *Id.* at 1087 (alterations in original) (internal citation omitted).

39 *Id.* at 1087–89 (describing other circuit court opinions).

subjected.'"[40] Moreover, "[t]o the extent that emotional harms differ from other, more readily quantifiable harms, that difference lacks expression in Article III's case-or-controversy requirement."[41]

A nice distinction drawn in a third, recent "display" case further illustrates an approach to Establishment Clause standing that arguably should be relevant to the school aid cases. As one of a number of lawsuits he has brought in recent years, Michael A. Newdow, a committed atheist, challenged the federal statute that establishes "In God We Trust" as the national motto and the statutes that require its inscription on coins and currency. Mr. Newdow lacked standing to dispute the motto itself despite his claim that it stigmatizes atheists like him and renders them "political outsiders." Such an injury was too abstract to confer standing.[42] But he did have standing to challenge the statutes requiring the inscription on coins and currency because this "forces him repeatedly to encounter a religious belief he finds offensive."[43] And "'spiritual harm resulting from unwelcome direct contact with an allegedly offensive religious (or anti-religious) symbol is a legally cognizable injury and suffices to confer Article III standing.'"[44] Because Mr. Newdow asserted a "concrete, particularized, and personal injury," the fact that this was widely shared, indeed common to all Americans, did not destroy his standing.[45]

We later suggest that, as the Supreme Court unfortunately has largely eviscerated taxpayer standing in the school aid cases, arguments analogous to those in these display cases might provide alternative ways of creating standing for certain plaintiffs to challenge the constitutionality of some methods of channeling public money to parochial schools when the plaintiffs are aware of the public source of the financial support and directly observe the religious nature of its consequences and effects in education. This comparison highlights how inappropriate it is to deny traditional taxpayer standing in these cases. Indeed, why should one need to resort to legal machinations to invoke judicial control over majoritarian legislative excesses impinging on fundamental First Amendment rights? But first we review what, prior to *Winn*, was the common and often unexceptional way in which school aid cases had been brought through taxpayer standing. This series of cases demonstrates the Court's radical about-face on taxpayer standing in *Winn*, parallel to and reinforcing the antagonistic approach a majority already had been taking on the substance of Establishment Clause objections to state aid to religious education.

---

40 Red River Freethinkers v. Fargo, 679 F.3d 1015, 1024 (8th Cir. 2012) (internal citation omitted).

41 *Id.*

42 Newdow v. Lefevre, 598 F.3d 638, 643 (9th Cir. 2010).

43 *Id.* at 642.

44 *Id.* (internal citation omitted).

45 *Id.* (citing *Akins*, 524 U.S. at 24).

IV. Taxpayer Standing Cases Leading to *Arizona Christian School Tuition Organization v. Winn*

Paying taxes is bad enough; but suppose the executive or legislative branch of government is using tax dollars in an illegal or unconstitutional manner. May a taxpayer challenge such use in federal court seeking a declaratory judgment that such use is improper and an injunction to stop it? As taxing and spending are basic to virtually all government action, there obviously have to be significant Article III constraints on such judicial actions. Otherwise, courts would be empowered to generally superintend the other branches contrary to the basic separation of powers structure of the Constitution. A classic example would be a claim that the President as Commander in Chief is conducting military operations that amount to an undeclared, illegal war, and Congress is abetting this action by continuing to fund these activities. Allowing a taxpayer to sue in federal court to protest and end such expenditure of his tax dollars would convert a quintessential political issue between Congress and the Executive, and one ultimately for the electorate, into a judicial question that courts are not equipped nor constitutionally authorized to answer. "Vindicating the *public* interest (including the public interest in Government observance of the Constitution and laws) is the function of Congress and the Chief Executive."[46] Other taxpayer suits, however, might be quite appropriate for judicial resolution.

A. Bradfield v. Roberts

An early case, *Bradfield v. Roberts*,[47] perhaps inadvertently created a strange distinction that persists today. Mr. Bradfield, a federal taxpayer and resident of the District of Columbia, which was under the exclusive control of Congress, alleged irreparable harm to himself "and all other citizens and taxpayers of the United States" if a District official distributed a congressional appropriation to an alleged sectarian nonprofit corporation for the construction of hospital buildings. The taxpayer sought an injunction to prevent the disbursement of the funds. The Supreme Court allowed the taxpayer standing to present the Establishment Clause challenge.[48]

B. Frothingham v. Mellon

But nearly 25 years later, in *Frothingham v. Mellon*, the Supreme Court denied standing to a federal taxpayer. The taxpayer did not contest her particular tax liability. Rather, she challenged the constitutionality of the Federal Maternity

46 *Lujan*, 504 U.S. at 576.

47 175 U.S. 291 (1899).

48 *Id.* at 295. Ruling against the taxpayer on the merits, the Court found that he failed to show that the formal legal character of the corporate entity was sectarian.

Act of 1921, which appropriated federal funding for states' use to reduce infant and maternal mortality.[49] The taxpayer alleged that the federal statute violated the Tenth Amendment by intruding on areas traditionally those of states. She also asserted that the federal expenditures would increase her future tax burden in violation of her property interests under the Due Process Clause of the Fifth Amendment. Attempting to distinguish *Bradfield*—and perhaps mislabeling or misunderstanding the actual jurisdictional status of the federal taxpayer there who resided in a federal municipality—Justice George Sutherland, writing for the Court, treated Mr. Bradfield as a "municipal" taxpayer,[50] and then held that the Article III case or controversy requirement for standing was not satisfied in *Frothingham*. First, in the Court's view, a municipal taxpayer has a "direct and immediate" interest in the use of his local tax dollars, making an injunction against their improper use appropriate. The corresponding interest of a federal taxpayer, such as Ms. Frothingham, however, is diluted within a sea of "millions of others ... [and is] comparatively minute and indeterminable."[51] The future effect on an individual taxpayer of a court order regarding the constitutional propriety of any federal tax would be "so remote, fluctuating and uncertain" as to render judicial intervention unsuitable.[52]

It is certainly true that a Court's invalidation of a particular tax, and the tax authority's possible response, would have an indeterminate effect on any future taxpayer. But an individual or corporate taxpayer might take issue with the Court's undervaluing his or its proportional, monetary interest in protesting and removing a specific unconstitutional tax. So the Court in *Frothingham* turned to a more significant issue. If a federal taxpayer's due process grievance against a government expenditure (one shared by myriad discontent taxpayers) were deemed to satisfy the case or controversy mandate of Article III, untold numbers of such lawsuits would be unleashed, straining not only the federal court system but also the due administration of government. To this pragmatic concern Justice Sutherland then added the principle of judicial restraint arising from separation of powers and concluded:

> The party who invokes the [judicial] power must be able to show not only that the statute is invalid but that he has sustained or is immediately in danger of sustaining some direct injury as the result of its enforcement, and not merely that he suffers in some indefinite way in common with people generally.[53]

---

49 262 U.S. 447 (1923).

50 This mislabeling acquired a life of its own, allowing the Court to carve out a special standing exception under Article III for municipal taxpayers. *See infra* note 59 and accompanying text.

51 *Frothingham*, 262 U.S. at 487.

52 *Id.*

53 *Id.* at 488.

Fifty years later, Justice William Brennan sharply criticized Justice Sutherland's "obscure" reasoning with its direct injury requirement for justiciability, a critique some scholars have reiterated after *Winn*.[54]

C. Doremus v. Board of Education

Nearly three decades after *Frothingham*, the Supreme Court in *Doremus v. Board of Education* somewhat incongruously extended its restrictive view of taxpayer standing to state taxpayers, this time in the context of an Establishment Clause claim.[55] "Citizens" and "taxpayers" of New Jersey challenged a state statute requiring "the reading, without comment, of five verses of the Old Testament at the opening of each public-school day."[56] Plaintiffs sued in state court claiming a violation of the First Amendment. Although the New Jersey Supreme Court expressed doubts about the taxpayers' standing, it reached the merits of the case, upholding the statute. On appeal to the U.S. Supreme Court, Justice Robert Jackson, writing for the majority, quoted with approval *Frothingham*'s stringent direct injury standard and held that the complainant "citizens" and "taxpayers" were raising essentially a religious dispute and did not have the "direct and particular financial interest" necessary for standing to adjudicate the matter in federal court.[57] Dissenting, Justice William O. Douglas wrote that the majority's requirement of a "good faith pocketbook action" should not be necessary for standing. Standing should have been granted because, if the state taxpayers "were right in their [Establishment Clause] contentions on the merits, they would establish that their public schools were being deflected from the educational program for which the

---

54 *Valley Forge*, 454 U.S. at 496–97 (Brennan, J., dissenting). *See* Matthew A. Melone, *A Leg to Stand On: Is There a Legal and Prudential Solution to the Problem of Taxpayer Standing in the Federal Tax Context?*, 9 Pitt. Tax Rev. 97, 140 (2012) (suggesting the magnitude of a taxpayer's dollars at stake is irrelevant to a conferral of standing to adjudicate in federal court the merits of a potential, legitimate, particularized grievous injury caused by government's spending power, and quoting Richard A. Epstein, *Standing or Spending: The Role of Legal and Equitable Principles*, 4 Chap. L. Rev. 1, 10 (2001): "It is not correct to say that 'no particular person is injured' .... Rather, it is that a great many individuals are all injured by some small but perceptible amount. The task of courts of equity was to develop rules that allowed the amalgamation of small interests."). For further discussion in the context of *Arizona Christian School Tuition Organization v. Winn*, see *infra* notes 141–42 and accompanying text.

55 342 U.S. 429 (1952).

56 *Id.* at 430–31. One plaintiff also was a parent of a student, but did not claim any offense at the bible reading from which the student could have been excused. The child had graduated by the time of the appeal, so the parent's status as such was irrelevant.

57 *Id.* at 434–35. The Court adheres to treating state taxpayers the same as federal taxpayers for purposes of standing. DaimlerChrysler Corp. v. Cuno, 547 U.S. 332, 345 (2006).

taxes were raised."[58] Justice Douglas's comment nicely captures the essence of future disputes.

The Court's very sparse opinion in *Doremus* is curious in at least two regards. First, treating, without analysis, state taxpayers' interest on par with the minimal level of federal taxpayers for purposes of federal standing, and not at the sufficient level of municipal taxpayers, created a strange anomaly. Taxpayers of New York City apparently can challenge in federal court an allegedly unconstitutional city tax, but taxpayers of Wyoming cannot similarly challenge a state tax, although the population of New York City is many times that of Wyoming. Second, the Court in *Doremus* reviewed a state court's upholding of a state statute challenged on federal constitutional grounds. Unlike review of a congressional enactment, this federal judicial examination of a state statute would not implicate the national separation of powers doctrine enshrined in Article III, which the Court repeatedly notes is the basis and rationale for the Court's limitation of federal standing to cases or controversies and, especially, for its restrictive interpretation of those concepts.[59]

The Court very recently reaffirmed "the clear dictate of the separation-of-powers principle that 'when an Act of Congress is alleged to conflict with the Constitution, "[i]t is emphatically the province and duty of the judicial department to say what the law is."'"[60] The same is true of allegedly unconstitutional state laws. Such federal judicial review does raise issues of federalism, but the supremacy of federal law and the power of federal courts both to review judgments from state high courts and to invalidate state law that violates the federal constitution was settled in the early days of the Nation. Federal courts do both all the time with First Amendment free speech cases. The real issue for state taxpayers challenging state aid for religion is one of the incorporation of the Establishment Clause and how it should be applied to the states in various contexts. This hugely important

58 *Id.* at 435 (Douglas, J., dissenting). In a modern context, *Doremus* belongs with the school prayer cases in which standing appears to turn on whether "a plaintiff's status has led to being *personally* exposed to her government's religious expression, the message being one with which she disagrees, or she had to assume a burden to avoid such exposure." Carl Esbeck, *Unwanted Exposure to Religious Expression by Government: Standing and the Establishment Clause*, 7 Charleston L. Rev. 607, 633 (2013) (emphasis added).

59 As the Court has noted, "[t]he constitutional and prudential considerations canvassed at length in *Warth v. Seldin* … respond to concerns that are peculiarly federal in nature." Village of Arlington Heights v. Metro. Hous. Dev. Corp., 429 U.S. 252, 262 n.8 (1977). On the anomalous distinction of municipal taxpayers, *see* Nancy C. Staudt, *Taxpayers in Court: A Systematic Study of a (Misunderstood) Standing Doctrine*, 52 Emory L.J. 771, 841 (2003); Edward A. Zelinsky, *Putting State Courts in the Constitutional Driver's Seat: State Taxpayer Standing after* Cuno *and* Winn, 40 Hastings Const. L.Q. 1, 52–54 (2012).

60 *Windsor*, 133 S. Ct. at 2688 (internal citations omitted). Justice Scalia termed this invocation of the Court's power to review a section of the Defense of Marriage Act "jaw-dropping." *Id.* at 2698 (Scalia, J., dissenting).

substantive question should be decided on the merits of individual cases, not insulated from federal judicial review by invoking a misplaced concept of standing.

D. Flast v. Cohen

In effect that is the sensible approach the Court eventually took, though not in such explicit terms. The *Frothingham* direct injury standard remained a significant impediment to federal (and, per *Doremus*, state) taxpayer standing for another 16 years. Then, in 1968, at the same time the Court allowed the New York school textbook loan program in *Board of Education v. Allen*, in *Flast v. Cohen* it considered "whether the *Frothingham* barrier should be lowered when a [federal] taxpayer attacks a federal statute on the ground that it violates the Establishment and Free Exercise Clauses of the First Amendment."[61] From a three-judge district court panel, which held that the federal taxpayers did not have standing, seven federal taxpayers, acting exclusively in that capacity, appealed directly to the Supreme Court.

At issue in *Flast* was financial assistance, provided through local government agencies under Title I of the federal Elementary and Secondary Education Act of 1965 ("ESEA"), for educational services for low-income, educationally-deprived students in private elementary and secondary schools.[62] The federal taxpayers sought declaratory and injunctive relief, specifically alleging that they were compelled to pay federal taxes that had "been used and will continue to be used to finance 'instruction in reading, arithmetic and other subjects and for guidance in religious and sectarian schools' and 'the purchase of textbooks and instructional and library materials for use in religious and sectarian schools.'"[63] Notably, in passing Title I, members of Congress anticipated Establishment Clause challenges to the law once enacted. After a robust debate on whether to include a provision to expressly confer standing on federal taxpayers to raise such claims, Congress rejected doing so.[64] Several members of Congress thought that a specific provision was unnecessary as it was clear there would be federal judicial review, including by the Supreme Court, of any church-state issues arising from the legislation.[65] There was no concern about infringement upon separation of powers. Thus the issue of standing to challenge Title I was left to the Supreme Court.

Chief Justice Earl Warren wrote for eight Justices in holding the federal taxpayers had standing. He first noted that the ruling of the Court in *Frothingham*,

---

61 *Flast*, 392 U.S. at 85. In *Board of Education v. Allen*, 392 U.S. 236, 241 n.5 (1968), the appellants, members of the Board, were concerned their official duties might conflict with their constitutional obligations. This gave them standing in the Supreme Court.

62 79 Stat. 27, 20 U. S. C. §§ 241a et seq., 821 et seq. (1964 ed., Supp. II).

63 *Flast*, 392 U.S. at 87 (internal citations omitted).

64 111 Cong. Rec. 5973 (1965) (remarks of Rep. Puchinski); *id.* at 6131–32 (remarks of Rep. Celler); 111 Cong. Rec. 7317 (1965) (remarks of Sen. Cooper).

65 111 Cong. Rec. 5973, 6131–32 (March 25–26, 1965); 111 Cong. Rec. 7317 (Apr. 7, 1965).

the "source of some confusion and the object of considerable criticism," "rest[ed] on something less than a constitutional foundation;" indeed the statements there of Justice Sutherland "suggest[] pure policy considerations."[66] Thus *Frothingham* was ambiguous as to whether it "establishe[d] a constitutional bar to taxpayer suits or whether the Court was simply imposing a rule of self-restraint which was not constitutionally compelled."[67] The Court therefore undertook a re-examination of the standing question and the "uncertain historical antecedents of the case-and-controversy doctrine."[68]

After discussing the more general concept of Article III justiciability, Chief Justice Warren turned to the specific problem of standing that shares the "complexities and vagaries" of the broader doctrine as well as "'many subtle pressures' which cause policy considerations to blend into the constitutional limitations of Article III."[69] Standing depends upon whether a particular person is a proper litigant, and this focus on the party by itself does not implicate separation of powers; only the substantive issue at stake can do that. The Court's concern was that the party seeking relief should have a sufficient personal stake in the matter so that "the dispute … will be presented in an adversary context and in a form historically viewed as capable of judicial resolution."[70] Thus there is "no absolute bar in Article III to suits by federal taxpayers challenging allegedly unconstitutional federal taxing and spending programs."[71]

The question then becomes under what circumstances federal taxpayers can bring such actions. The Court created a two-part test "to determine whether there is a logical nexus between the status asserted and the claim sought to be adjudicated."[72] In academic terms, the taxpayer cannot be a "non-Hohfeldian" or purely ideological, public interest plaintiff without a sufficient personal interest and stake.[73] Rather, first "the taxpayer must establish a logical link between that status and the type of legislative enactment attacked. Thus, a taxpayer will be a proper party to allege the unconstitutionality only of exercises of congressional

66 *Flast*, 392 U.S. at 92–93.

67 *Id.* at 92.

68 *Id.* at 96.

69 *Id.* at 97–98 (footnote and citation omitted).

70 *Id.* at 101. *See also Hollingsworth*, 133 S. Ct. at 2659; Sprint Communs. Co. v. APCC Servs., Inc. 554 U.S. 269, 274 (2008) ("We have always taken [the case-or-controversy requirement] to mean cases and controversies of the sort *traditionally* amenable to, and resolved by, the judicial process.") (alteration and emphasis in original) (internal citation omitted).

71 *Flast*, 392 U.S. at 101.

72 *Id.* at 102.

73 *See* Louis L. Jaffe, *The Citizen As Litigant in Public Actions: The Non-Hohfeldian or Ideological Plaintiff*, 116 U. Pa. L. Rev. 1033, 1034–35 (1968); *see also* Richard H. Fallon, Jr., *Of Justiciability, Remedies, and Public Law Litigation: Notes on the Jurisprudence of* Lyons, 59 N.Y.U. L. Rev. 1, 3–4 & n.12 (1984).

power under the taxing and spending clause" of the Constitution.[74] This condition naturally ties taxpayer status to the relevant legislative power, and it was satisfied by the plaintiffs in *Flast* who objected to a specific federal expenditure. The second part of the nexus requirement is that "the taxpayer must establish a nexus between that status and the precise nature of the constitutional infringement alleged," namely a "specific constitutional limitation[]" on the taxing and spending power.[75] But what are these "specific constitutional limitations?" Appealing to history and the architect of the First Amendment, the Court cited James Madison's *Memorial and Remonstrance Against Religious Assessments* and found that one of the "specific evils" which the Establishment Clause was designed to protect against was taxation and spending in support of religion.[76] Indeed, all nine Justices in *Everson v. Board of Education* had agreed that the Establishment Clause imposes specific restrictions on government's power to tax.[77] In this way the Court distinguished the general due process claim made in *Frothingham* and carved out an exception to its standing requirements, at least for taxpayers pressing Establishment Clause violations. Such assertions of First Amendment rights are certainly both adversarial and the types of cases courts historically and traditionally have adjudicated.

The central holding of Chief Justice Warren's opinion in *Flast* was nearly unanimous. Justice Douglas, concerned that "[t]he mounting federal aid to sectarian schools is notorious and the subterfuges numerous,"[78] would have overruled *Frothingham* and been more liberal in granting standing because of "the importance of the role that the federal judiciary was designed to play in guarding basic rights against majoritarian control."[79] Justices Potter Stewart and Abe Fortas each specified that the holding should be limited to Establishment Clause claims as that Clause specifically prohibits taxing and spending in aid of religion and, as Justice Fortas remarked about separation of church and state: "In terms of the structure and basic philosophy of our constitutional government, it would be difficult to point to any issue that has a more intimate, pervasive, and fundamental impact upon the life of the taxpayer—and upon the life of all citizens."[80] Only Justice John Marshall Harlan dissented, taking issue with the majority's position distinguishing between the specificity of limitations imposed by the First

---

74 *Flast*, 392 U.S. at 102.

75 *Id.* at 102–03.

76 *Id.* at 103.

77 *See Valley Forge*, 454 U.S. at 500–01 & n.12 (Brennan, J., dissenting) (citing Everson v. Bd. of Educ., 330 U.S. 1, 15, 22, 33 (1947)). For a discussion of *Everson, see* Chapter 2, notes 175–87 and accompanying text.

78 *Flast*, 392 U.S. at 113 (Douglas, J., concurring) (footnote omitted). For Justice Douglas' prescient, full elaboration on the subterfuge possibilities, *see* Introduction chapter, n.6 and accompanying text.

79 *Id.* at 110.

80 *Id.* at 115 (Fortas, J., concurring).

Amendment's Establishment Clause as opposed to the Fifth Amendment's Due Process Clause.

> [O]nly in some Pickwickian sense are any of the provisions with which the Court is concerned "specific[ally]" limitations upon spending for they contain nothing that is expressly directed at the expenditure of public funds. The specificity to which the Court repeatedly refers must therefore arise, not from the provisions' language, but from something implicit in their purposes.[81]

And for Justice Harlan, there was nothing special about the Establishment Clause. The question examined later in this chapter is whether the eight-Justice majority in *Flast* has the better position as compared to the retrenchment from *Flast* of a five-Justice majority of the current Roberts Court.

E. Valley Forge Christian College v. Americans United for Separation of Church and State, Inc.

After *Flast*, the Supreme Court maintained its Establishment Clause exceptionalism for federal taxpayer standing even in the face of passionate attempts to obtain federal court rulings prompted by opposition to the war in Vietnam.[82] In 1982, the Court

---

81 *Id.* at 127 (Harlan, J., dissenting). Justice Harlan also strangely distinguished a tax for the support of religion, such as Patrick Henry's proposed *Virginia Tax Assessment*, which he would allow taxpayers to challenge in federal court, and an expenditure of government funds as to which any taxpayer only has interests in common with those of the general public. *Id.* at 128–29. Justice Harlan, however, did not believe that public actions by non-Hohfeldian plaintiffs were constitutionally barred by Article III. *Id.* at 130, 132 n.21.

82 For example, in 1974, the Supreme Court simultaneously denied taxpayer standing in *United States v. Richardson*, 418 U.S. 166 (1974), and *Schlesinger v. Reservists Committee to Stop the War*, 418 U.S. 208 (1974). In *Richardson*, the federal taxpayer claimed that the secrecy of the Central Intelligence Agency's budget violated the Statement and Account provision of Article I, § 9, cl. 7 of the Constitution. The Court found that the taxpayer "falls short of the standing criteria of *Flast*," and "neatly … falls within the *Frothingham* holding left undisturbed" by *Flast*, as the alleged harm was not personal but "plainly undifferentiated and common to all members of the public." 418 U.S. at 174–75, 177 (internal quotation marks omitted). In *Schlesinger*, suing as citizens and federal taxpayers, plaintiffs claimed that under the Incompatibility Clause of Article I, § 6, cl. 2 of the Constitution members of Congress, while holding that position, were ineligible for a commission in the Armed Forces Reserve. The Court found that there was no federal taxpayer standing under *Flast* because the plaintiffs "did not challenge an enactment under Article I, § 8, but rather the action of the Executive Branch in permitting Members of Congress to maintain their Reserve status." 418 U.S. at 228. *But see* Tilton v. Richardson, 403 U.S. 672 (1971), in which the Court granted federal taxpayers standing under the *Flast* exception to challenge on Establishment Clause grounds federal construction grants made under the Higher Education Facilities Act, pursuant to the Article I, § 8 Spending Clause, for church-related colleges and universities.

confronted in *Valley Forge Christian College v. Americans United for Separation of Church and State, Inc.*, the issue of whether the Constitution's Property Clause in Article IV, section 3, clause 2 is sufficiently similar to Congress' taxing and spending power of Article I, section 8, so as to allow standing to a nonprofit organization on behalf of federal taxpayers claiming that a free transfer of surplus U.S. real property to a religious college violated the Establishment Clause.[83] In a 5–4 split, the Court denied standing, distinguishing the circumstances from those in *Flast*.

Writing for the majority, Justice William Rehnquist found that the plaintiffs failed the first of *Flast*'s two-prong nexus test for federal taxpayer standing because "the source of their complaint [was] not a congressional action, but a decision by [the Secretary of] HEW [Health, Education and Welfare] to transfer a parcel of federal property. … [And], the property transfer … was not an exercise of authority conferred by the Taxing and Spending Clause of Art. I, § 8," as was at issue in *Flast*.[84] The Court thereby reinforced the "rigor with which [it would apply] the *Flast* exception to the *Frothingham* principle."[85]

Beyond denying taxpayer standing not comporting with *Flast*, the Court also more broadly rejected Establishment Clause exceptionalism for standing. The plaintiffs were not actually concerned about their status as taxpayers or any financial effect upon them from the property transfer. Rather, the gravamen of their action, on the basis of which the court of appeals had granted standing, was an "'injury in fact' to their shared individuated right to a government that 'shall make no law respecting the establishment of religion.'"[86] But this abstract injury was not enough for the Supreme Court even though it resulted from a violation of the Establishment Clause and not some other constitutional provision. Here the Court was unwilling to "create a hierarchy of constitutional values or a complementary 'sliding scale' of standing …."[87]

Justice Rehnquist added dicta that nonetheless may be relevant to standing in school aid cases. He reaffirmed that the Court was not "retreat[ing] from [its] earlier holdings that standing may be predicated on noneconomic injury," but there still must be a sufficient injury of some kind. "[T]he intensity of the litigant's interest or the fervor of his advocacy" alone is not adequate.[88] The problem in *Valley Forge* was that

---

83 454 U.S. 464 (1982). The court of appeals unanimously had denied taxpayer standing, but that court's majority had allowed plaintiffs standing merely as citizens seeking to protect their shared rights under the Establishment Clause, an "unusually broad and novel view" of standing. *Id.* at 470.

84 *Id.* at 479–80.

85 *Id.* at 481.

86 *Id.* at 482 (internal citation omitted).

87 *Id.* at 484.

88 *Id.* at 486.

> … [a]lthough respondents claim[ed] that the Constitution ha[d] been violated, they claim[ed] nothing else. They fail[ed] to identify any personal injury suffered by them as a *consequence* of the alleged constitutional error, other than the psychological consequence presumably produced by observation of conduct with which one disagrees. That is not an injury sufficient to confer standing under Art. III even though the disagreement is phrased in constitutional terms.[89]

But as Justice Rehnquist noted, the plaintiffs had no connection whatsoever with the property, the transfer of which they protested. The property was located in Pennsylvania; the named plaintiffs resided in Maryland and Virginia; their organizational headquarters were in Washington, D.C.; and, rather than directly observing anything, they simply learned of the transfer through a news release. The Court was not about to countenance a "special license" under the Establishment Clause for citizens to "roam the country in search of governmental wrongdoing and to reveal their discoveries in federal court."[90]

Justice John Paul Stevens dissented stressing the singular importance of the Establishment Clause as recognized in *Flast*.[91] The major, powerful dissent, however, was by Justice Brennan, joined by Justices Thurgood Marshall and Harry Blackmun. Justice Brennan also emphasized the special significance of the Establishment Clause, particularly with respect to its prohibition on taxation in support of religion, which the case or controversy limitation in Article III cannot trump. Invoking Madison, Justice Brennan asserted that "Article III was designed to provide a hospitable forum in which persons enjoying rights under the Constitution could assert those rights."[92] But because the Court was "[b]lind to history," the majority refused to recognize that "[*t*]*he taxpayer was the direct and intended beneficiary of the prohibition on financial aid to religion*."[93] These facts formed the "constitutional imperative" for the ruling in *Flast*.[94] Justice Brennan therefore considered the majority's distinctions between congressional versus executive action or among the forms of government largesse (cash grants versus transfers in kind) as meaningless in light of the power and scope of the

89 *Id.* at 485–86 (emphasis in original).

90 *Id.* at 487.

91 *Id.* at 515 (Stevens, J., dissenting).

92 *Id.* at 493–94 (Brennan, Marshall, Blackmun, JJ., dissenting). Madison had argued for the importance of a bill of rights by asserting that "independent tribunals of justice will consider themselves in a peculiar manner the guardians of those rights; they will be an impenetrable bulwark against every assumption of power in the Legislative or Executive; they will be naturally led to resist every encroachment upon rights expressly stipulated for in the Constitution by the declaration of rights." *Id.* at 494, n.6 (quoting James Madison, 1 Annals of Cong. 439 (1789)).

93 *Valley Forge*, 454 U.S. at 504, 510 (Brennan, Marshall, Blackmun, JJ., dissenting) (emphasis in original).

94 *Id.* at 507.

Establishment Clause prohibition. Justice Brennan closed his dissent with a prescient, rhetorical flourish:

> Plainly hostile to the Framers' understanding of the Establishment Clause, and *Flast*'s enforcement of that understanding, the Court vents that hostility under the guise of standing, "to slam the courthouse door against plaintiffs who [as the Framers intended] are entitled to full consideration of their [Establishment Clause] claims on the merits."[95]

F. Hein v. Freedom from Religion Foundation, Inc.

Indeed, as the composition of the Court changed over the years, the Justices perpetuated "tortuous distinctions [that] … are specious, at best: at worst, they are pernicious to our constitutional heritage."[96] These developments paralleled and complemented the majority's increasingly narrow view of the Establishment Clause in the context of state aid for parochial education, as described in Chapter 2. The Court's 2007 decision in *Hein v. Freedom from Religion Foundation, Inc.*[97] proved to be a particularly significant portent for the majority's approach in *Winn.*

In *Hein*, federal taxpayers charged that expenditures for certain conferences by the White House Office of Faith-Based and Community Initiatives violated the Establishment Clause because President George W. Bush and a former Secretary of Education gave speeches at these meetings that used "religious imagery" and praised the efficacy of faith-based programs in delivering social services. The expenditures at issue were not specifically authorized by Congress but were paid from general appropriations for the Executive Branch. This allowed a plurality of the Court to distinguish *Flast* and deny plaintiffs standing based on their status as federal taxpayers.

Justice Samuel Alito's plurality opinion first recounted the usual arguments about Article III standing, separation of powers, and taxpayers' generalized grievances. He then acknowledged the narrow exception from *Flast* for taxpayer standing to raise Establishment Clause claims. But "[t]he expenditures challenged in *Flast* … were funded by a specific congressional appropriation and were disbursed … pursuant to a direct and unambiguous congressional mandate."[98] This made all the difference to the plurality because *Flast* involved claims of improper exercise of

---

95 *Id.* at 513 (quoting Barlow v. Collins, 397 U.S. 159, 178 (1970) (Brennan, J., concurring in result and dissenting)) (alterations in original).

96 *Valley Forge*, 454 U.S. at 510 (Brennan, Marshall, Blackmun, JJ., dissenting).

97 551 U.S. 587 (2007). Previously, in *Bowen v. Kendrick*, 487 U.S. 589, 618–20 (1988), all Justices agreed that, because the Court "consistently adhered" to *Flast*, federal taxpayers had standing to bring facial and as-applied challenges to a federal law, the Adolescent Family Life Act, and its administration by the Secretary of H.E.W. as a violation of the Establishment Clause. *Valley Forge* did not preclude standing.

98 *Hein*, 551 U.S. at 604 (plurality opinion).

Congress' power under the Tax and Spending Clause of Article I. The Court had never applied the relaxed rule of taxpayer standing in any other circumstances, and it refused to do so in *Hein*. The Court relied on a hyper-technical distinction between Executive Branch expenditures made from congressional general appropriations and congressional specific appropriations of taxpayer revenues. But the Court never adequately explained why this difference should matter; after all, the Executive is as bound by the Establishment Clause as Congress, and executive violation is as harmful to the liberty of conscience as a congressional one. Justice Alito merely argued that "extending" *Flast* to discretionary Executive Branch expenditures would involve the Court in overseeing a vast amount of federal government action when challenged by any taxpayer and, as such, would compound *Flast*'s incursion on separation of powers.[99] Justice Anthony Kennedy echoed these concerns, although he reaffirmed *Flast* itself because "separation-of-powers principles ..., in some cases, must accommodate the First Amendment's Establishment Clause," which "expresses the Constitution's special concern that freedom of conscience not be compromised by government taxing and spending in support of religion."[100]

Justice Souter's dissent for four Justices attacked the plurality's distinction as without "basis ... in logic or precedent." And he refuted the plurality's concerns about multiple taxpayer lawsuits challenging government action, noting that such meritorious cases deserve to be adjudicated and frivolous ones can be dismissed on that basis without resorting to overbroad, preclusive notions of standing.[101] But the true significance of *Hein* lies with Justice Scalia's philippic, joined by Justice Clarence Thomas, concurring in the judgment. Justice Scalia's immediate objective was to argue for overruling *Flast*, but the true object of his scorn likely was "the disreputable disarray of our Establishment Clause standing jurisprudence."[102]

Justice Scalia focused on the standing requirement of a concrete and particularized injury in fact and distinguished between what he termed "Wallet Injury" and "Psychic Injury." A taxpayer lawsuit, he reasoned, should depend on "Wallet Injury," a higher tax liability caused by the challenged government action. But a plaintiff making such a claim would have difficulty showing causation, namely both that his higher tax payments are actually traceable to the allegedly unconstitutional government expenditure—what his taxes otherwise would be—and that a favorable court ruling would redress the injury by requiring the government to lower his taxes. These problems would be eliminated by a taxpayer plaintiff focusing instead on "Psychic Injury," "*mental displeasure* that money

99 *Id.* at 610–12.

100 *Id.* at 615–16 (Kennedy, J., concurring).

101 *Id.* at 637, 640 n.1 (Souter, Stevens, Ginsburg, Breyer, JJ., dissenting).

102 *Id.* at 629 (Scalia, J., concurring in judgment). Justice Scalia continues to rail against the "notorious" "power-grabbing" decision in *Flast* that has created "chaos." *Windsor*, 133 S. Ct. at 2702 (Scalia, J., dissenting).

extracted from him is being spent in an unlawful manner."[103] This sort of injury easily can flow from how the government uses the taxpayer's money and is curable by a court order forbidding such use. Justice Scalia's characterization of two types of injury thus creates a useful analytical distinction.

But what Justice Scalia cannot abide is that through its two-part nexus test in *Flast* the Court developed a specific, limited exception to its normal standing approach for taxing and spending claimed to violate the Establishment Clause. And it unabashedly did so to protect against "one of the specific evils feared by" the proponents and supporters of the First Amendment. This is why Justice Scalia's insistence that *Flast* is inconsistent with such other cases as *Frothingham*, *Doremus*, and *Valley Forge* is so misplaced. An exception, after all, is just that, an exception, even if one can argue about its proper application with respect to any particular circumstances. Whether the exception is justified is the gravamen of Justice Scalia's attack. He correctly agrees with the dissent in criticizing the plurality's illogic in limiting *Flast* to cases involving a specific congressional appropriation rather than a discretionary executive expenditure.[104] His main charge, however, is that the "Psychic Injury rationale," the real basis for *Flast*, is inconsistent with Article III. This actually means, however, that he is arguing that "Psychic Injury" is inconsistent, not with some straightforward, self-executing constitutional provision, but with the standing doctrine the Court has developed over the years in interpreting and applying the cases or controversies concept. Framed this way, Justice Scalia merely is voicing his opinion that as a policy matter the Court should not take judicial cognizance of "Psychic Injury" flowing from government actions that violate the Establishment Clause. And this in turn is another way for him to assert and implement a very crabbed view of the meaning and application of that fundamental constitutional guarantee.

The very point of Madison's *Memorial and Remonstrance Against Religious Assessments* is an appeal to the liberty of religious conscience as "unalienable" because otherwise "the majority may trespass on the rights of the minority."[105] And Madison did not protest just a significant amount of taxation in aid of religion; he famously objected to "three pence only." This is because government taxation in support of religion is not truly just a pocketbook issue; it is indeed a form of Psychic Injury, but more than that it is an affront to religious conscience and

103 *Hein*, 551 U.S. at 619 (Scalia, J., concurring in judgment) (emphasis in original).

104 *Id.* at 630 (describing "absurd results" flowing from the plurality's unwarranted distinctions).

105 James Madison, *Memorial and Remonstrance Against Religious Assessments* (1785), *reprinted in* 5 The Founders' Constitution 82 (Philip B. Kurland & Ralph Lerner eds., Univ. Chicago Press 1987). As discussed below, in *Winn*, 131 S. Ct. at 1446, Justice Kennedy recognized that Madison's objection "does not depend on the amount of property conscripted for sectarian ends. Any such taking, even one amounting to 'three pence only' violates conscience." Nonetheless, Justice Kennedy managed to assert that the "specific evils" against which Madison fought were lacking in *Winn*.

sensibility that sows discord, divisiveness, and "mischiefs." Justice Scalia noted that Madison does not assert that federal courts should have cognizance of such "generalized grievances," but this of course would be an anachronism. And despite Justice Scalia's attempt to place generalized grievances under the constitutional limitations of Article III, it often has been merely a prudential consideration that, at any rate, is part of the *Flast* exception.[106] Or, as Justice Souter reminded the Court in *Hein*, in his concurring opinion in *Flast* Justice Stewart said that "'every taxpayer can claim a personal constitutional right not to be taxed for the support of a religious institution,'" and Justice Stewart "thus distinguished the case from one in which a taxpayer sought only to air a generalized grievance in federal court."[107] So, "where a harm is concrete, though widely shared, the Court has found 'injury in fact.'"[108]

The *Flast* exception explicitly survives *Hein*. Perhaps goaded by Justice Scalia's criticisms, both Justices Alito and Kennedy reaffirmed their support for *Flast* although they were unwilling to "extend" it.[109] Thus Justice Souter in dissent was able to say accurately that "*Flast* speaks for this Court's recognition (shared by a majority of the Court today) that when the Government spends money for religious purposes a taxpayer's injury is serious and concrete enough to be 'judicially cognizable.'"[110]

The obtuse approach to the Establishment Clause by five Justices in *Hein* provoked Ronald Dworkin's cogent criticism:

> The establishment clause is different: when government violates that clause by spending money in support of religion, the expenditure is not just a means to some further harm. The expenditure is itself the harm. It is part of people's right to freedom of conscience that their government, acting on their behalf and in their name, not support any religion or religious institution. Scalia misunderstood that: he said that the [standing] principle supposed a right to be free from "psychic" injury, as if the damage to citizens when government discriminates in favor of religion is only psychological. In fact the damage is to every citizen's religious independence.[111]

In other words, religion is different, as even the five Justices who denied standing in *Hein* sometimes realize. In a different context, involving an accommodation for religion, the Court unanimously extended a First Amendment "ministerial

---

106 *See supra*, notes 14–26 and accompanying text; *Richardson*, 418 U.S. 166 (1974).

107 *Hein*, 551 U.S. at 639 (Souter, J., dissenting) (quoting *Flast*, 392 U.S. at 114 (Stewart, J., concurring)).

108 *Hein*, 551 U.S. at 642 n.3 (Souter, J., dissenting) (quoting *Akins*, 524 U.S. at 24).

109 *Hein*, 551 U.S. at 615 (plurality opinion); *id.* at 616 (Kennedy, J., concurring).

110 *Id.* at 643 (Souter, J., dissenting) (quoting *Wright*, 468 U.S. at 752).

111 Ronald Dworkin, *The Supreme Court: The Court's New Right-Wing Bloc*, N.Y. Rev. of Books, Sept. 27, 2007, at 66.

exception" to a church-run school to shield it from a lawsuit by the Equal Employment Opportunity Commission ("E.E.O.C.") on behalf of a teacher who claimed discrimination and retaliation prohibited by the Americans With Disabilities Act.[112] The E.E.O.C. and the teacher argued that the law should apply the same whether the employer was a secular organization or a church. The Court forcefully rejected this "remarkable view" that the Religion Clauses of the First Amendment do not afford "special solicitude to the rights of religious organizations."[113] The ministerial exception therefore constitutes an affirmative defense to the merits of such a claim; religious interests are constitutionally unique. But then special solicitude for the religious sensibilities of individuals also should extend to affording taxpayers the simple procedural right of standing to contest government expenditures in support of religion.

As discussed in Chapter 2, Justice Scalia also denigrates "Psychic Injury" as a basis for relief in the school prayer cases, where it is especially palpable. In one respect his attitude in Establishment Clause cases is puzzling because, in his opinion for the Court in *Lujan*, he explicitly acknowledged that harm to "purely esthetic" interests "is undeniably a cognizable interest for purpose of standing."[114] *Lujan* was a suit by environmentalists claiming that a government regulation pursuant to the Endangered Species Act would adversely affect their future ability to observe various animal species in their natural habitat. Injury to the specific plaintiffs in *Lujan* was too uncertain for a majority of the Court to allow them to proceed. But if this type of esthetic, emotional, "Psychic Injury" can be sufficient for standing by environmentalists, why isn't a taxpayer's claimed violation of constitutional rights under the Establishment Clause also sufficient? Government affront to one's liberty of conscience must be at least as great a personal injury as frustration of esthetic interests. The psychological effect on the plaintiffs in *Valley Forge* from the transfer of surplus, remotely situated government property to a religious college was not a sufficient injury to confer standing. But even if one discounts Justice Brennan's persuasive dissent in *Valley Forge*, that case involved neither legislative action nor the taxing and spending power. Moreover, in sharp contrast to taxpayers protesting state use of their taxes to aid local parochial schools, the plaintiffs in *Valley Forge* were geographically distant from, and had no contact or relationship with, the property in issue.

The danger from Justice Scalia's dismissal of "Psychic Injury" as a basis for taxpayer standing is readily apparent and instructive. In a passive display case the plaintiff has some direct and immediate contact with the objectionable religious display, but the injury is essentially psychological or emotional. The content of the religious display itself is not offensive and does not produce the injury. A nativity display on private church grounds generally is not offensive to most. A non-

112 Hosanna-Tabor Evangelical Lutheran Church & Sch. v. E.E.O.C., 132 S. Ct. 694 (2012).

113 *Id.* at 706, 712–13.

114 *Lujan*, 504 U.S. at 562–63. *See also Laidlaw*, 528 U.S. at 183.

believer might be bemused by it, but certainly has no recourse except to look away. The display is protected free speech.[115] But once the religious symbolism is on government property, it carries the government's imprimatur with the appearance of government support or endorsement. No disclaimer adequately counteracts the message of official inclusion and exclusion based on religious identity. Now, looking away or avoiding the display is not adequate redress because the injury lies in the fact and the knowledge that the government is inappropriately supporting religion. And these factors allow for standing to bring an Establishment Clause claim, as we will argue it should under analogous circumstances for a taxpayer in a school aid case. Justice Scalia's approach, however, undermines the basis for standing in a passive display case, and this may be his intent. Indeed, such possible further erosion of Establishment Clause limits on government action demonstrates the wisdom and importance in maintaining a vigorous *Flast* exception.

A final difficulty with Justice Scalia's desired decimation of *Flast* would be to reinforce what already is a considerable problem after *Winn*. The Court once stated: "To deny standing to persons who are in fact injured simply because many others are also injured, would mean that the most injurious and widespread Government actions could be questioned by nobody. We cannot accept that conclusion."[116] It certainly should not be the case that there can be many instances in which the government may be violating the Establishment Clause and no plaintiff has standing to obtain judicial review on the merits. The Court, however, now seems to persistently maintain the opposite, namely that "'[t]he assumption that if [opponents to such government action] have no standing to sue, no one would have standing, is not a reason to find standing.'"[117] Not surprisingly, Justice Scalia recently relied on this proposition to justify his dissent to the Court's adjudication of a challenge to a section of the Defense of Marriage Act.[118]

But the cases provoked by the Vietnam War that Justice Scalia and the Court have relied on for the general maxim about standing that some controversies should be resolved through the political, not judicial, process belie suitable application to an Establishment Clause case. *Schlesinger v. Reservists Committee to Stop the War* claimed that under the Constitution's Incompatibility Clause members of Congress could not hold a commission in the Armed Forces Reserve, and *United States v. Richardson* challenged the secrecy of the Central Intelligence Agency's

115 *See* Erznoznik v. City of Jacksonville, 422 U.S. 205 (1975) (ordinance prohibiting drive-in movie theater from showing nudity visible from the street is invalid; unwilling viewers can avert their eyes).

116 United States v. Students Challenging Regulatory Agency Procedures, 412 U.S. 669, 688 (1973).

117 Clapper v. Amnesty Int'l USA, 133 S. Ct. 1138, 1154 (2013) (quoting *Valley Forge*, 454 U.S. at 489 (quoting *Schlesinger*, 418 U.S. at 227)).

118 *Windsor*, 133 S. Ct. at 2699 (Scalia, J., dissenting) ("some questions of law will *never* be presented to this Court, because there will never be anyone with standing to bring a lawsuit") (emphasis in original).

budget.[119] These are quintessential matters for majoritarian resolution by the other branches of government or through the political process; *Richardson* explicitly acknowledged this.[120] Those challenges did not involve First Amendment individual rights, which decidedly are not subject to majoritarian political power. As Justice O'Connor has stated, "we do not count heads before enforcing the First Amendment."[121] Prior to ascending to the Supreme Court, Justice Scalia himself articulated this crucial distinction. In a 1983 law review article explicating his view of the doctrine of standing, then Judge Scalia wrote: "[T]he law of standing roughly restricts courts to their traditional undemocratic role of protecting individuals and minorities against impositions of the majority, and excludes them from the even more undemocratic role of prescribing how the other two branches should function in order to serve the interest *of the majority itself*."[122] Yet, in *Hein*, Justice Scalia said that "generalized grievances affecting the public at large have their remedy in the political process."[123] These two positions are wholly incompatible when the grievance involves individual rights under the First Amendment that may affect many, albeit a minority, of the people. Especially in an era when numerous state legislatures may be dominated by one political faction and face considerable public pressure to do something about the discouraging state of public education, it is fanciful to rely on the political process to protect individuals from legislative overreach that funnels state aid to mainstream (or even less conventional) parochial schools and other private, religiously-affiliated education providers and thereby encroaches on freedom of religious conscience.

---

119 *See supra* note 82.

120 *Richardson*, 418 U.S. at 179. *See also Wright*, 468 U.S. at 751 (the "[s]tanding doctrine embraces several judicially self-imposed limits on the exercise of federal jurisdiction, such as … the rule barring adjudication of generalized grievances more appropriately addressed in the representative branches").

121 *McCreary*, 545 U.S. at 884 (O'Connor, J., concurring). *See also* Justice Robert Jackson's encomium, quoted in Chapter 2, n.152, to the anti-majoritarian virtues of the Bill of Rights in *West Virginia State Board of Education v. Barnette*, 319 U.S. 624, 638 (1943) (*overruling* Minersville Sch. Dist. v. Gobitis, 310 U.S. 586 (1940)). If First Amendment freedoms were subject to majority control we likely would have a very different legal regime. *See* First Amendment Center, State of the First Amendment: 2013 (2013), *available at* http://www.firstamendmentcenter.org/madison/wp-content/uploads/2013/07/SOFA-2013-final-report.pdf.

122 Antonin Scalia, *The Doctrine of Standing as an Essential Element of the Separation of Powers*, 17 Suffolk U. L. Rev. 881, 894 (1983) (emphasis in original). Even then Justice Scalia was critical of *Flast*. Justice Scalia's next sentence described an appropriate plaintiff as one who is the "very *object* of a law's requirement or prohibition," but this just restates the relevant question regarding taxpayer standing in the Establishment Clause context. *Id.* (emphasis in original).

123 *Hein*, 551 U.S. at 636 (Scalia, J., concurring in judgment).

Majoritarian dysfunction that imperils fundamental individual rights presents the classic case for judicial intervention.[124]

On the free speech and press side of the First Amendment, the Court has recognized that it must relax some of its barriers to litigation to give full meaning and effect to those fundamental rights that affect the public at large. In some important cases, for example, the Court has circumvented the statute that gives it appellate jurisdiction over a state case only if the highest state court which could rule on the matter has rendered a final judgment. One such case involved a state statute that granted a political candidate a right to reply to a newspaper's criticism of him. The state supreme court upheld the constitutionality of the statute at an early procedural stage and remanded the matter for trial. The Supreme Court then took the case despite the lack of a final state court judgment and reversed the state supreme court, simply commenting in a footnote that it would be "intolerable" to leave the question of the constitutionality of such a statute so intrusive on freedom of press temporarily unresolved.[125] There the Court was concerned with simply a delay in adjudication of a vital First Amendment question because of the effect on the operation of a free press in the interim. Denying plaintiffs standing to challenge an Establishment Clause violation is far more draconian if it forever precludes testing the constitutionality of an alleged infringement of religious liberty. And as for standing itself, the Court has long applied its overbreadth doctrine in free speech cases as an exception to its traditional bar on a plaintiff's relying on the rights of others through third party standing. In other words, a litigant whose own speech might not be constitutionally protected still might be able to facially challenge a restriction on speech that operates too broadly and therefore improperly chills the expression of others who would be entitled to First Amendment protection.[126] In both contexts, the Court's special solicitude for speech arises from its transcendent societal value.

These analogies to the Court's treatment of some important free speech claims are imperfect, of course. But the same transcendent importance of religious liberty embodied in the Establishment Clause fully justifies a vigorous *Flast* exception for taxpayer standing unencumbered by the artificial distinctions in *Hein*.[127]

---

124 *See* United States v. Carolene Products Co., 304 U.S. 144, 152 n.4 (1938). As described in Chapter 5, Section II, the many states that adopt a permissive approach to taxpayer standing consistent with their own separation of powers principles apparently do not perceive any threat to their basic democratic structure or nature.

125 Miami Herald Publ'g Co. v. Tornillo, 418 U.S. 241, 247 n.6 (1974). *See generally* Fallon, Jr., et al., *supra* note 3, at 527–29.

126 *See, e.g.*, United States v. Stevens, 559 U.S. 460 (2010); Bd. of Airport Comm'rs v. Jews for Jesus, Inc., 482 U.S. 569 (1987).

127 For a variety of views, *see* Micah Schwartzman, *Conscience, Speech, and Money*, 97 Va. L. Rev. 317, 338 (2011); Richard W. Garnett, *Standing, Spending, and Separation: How the No-Establishment Rule Does (and Does Not) Protect Conscience*, 54 Vill. L. Rev. 655, 661 (2009); Ira C. Lupu & Robert Tuttle, *Ball on a Needle:* Hein v. Freedom from Religion Foundation, Inc. *and the Future of Establishment Clause Adjudication*, 2008 BYU L. Rev. 115, 122 (2008). *See also* Marshall & Nichol, *supra* note 7, at 232–33; Patrick

V. The Dénouement to Taxpayer Standing in Federal Courts: *Arizona Christian School Tuition Organization v. Winn*

Considering the reluctance of some members of the Supreme Court to accord much substance to the Establishment Clause, combined with the apparent interest of Chief Justice John G. Roberts, Jr. and others in maintaining "a tight lid on standing" generally, the outcome in *Winn* is perhaps no surprise.[128] Arizona, a leader in inventive ways to support alternatives to public education, first established a system of significant tax benefits involving School Tuition Organizations ("STOs") in 1997. The program was immediately controversial and led to protracted state and federal lawsuits. Over the years the Arizona legislature amended the program to address some criticisms. When the Supreme Court finally ruled in 2011 denying the challengers taxpayer standing, the essential elements of the program were the following.

An STO is a nonprofit, tax-exempt entity under Internal Revenue Code ("I.R.C.") § 501(c)(3) that uses contributions to provide scholarships to students to attend private, mostly parochial, "qualified" schools.[129] Qualified schools cannot discriminate in their student admissions policies on the basis of race, color, handicap, familial status, or national origin, but they may be pervasively sectarian,

---

T. Gillen, *A* Winn *for Originalism Puts Establishment Clause Reform Within Reach*, 21 Wm. & Mary Bill Rts. J. 1107, 1112 (2013).

128 *See* Erwin Chemerinsky, *Closing the Courthouse Doors*, 90 Denv. U. L. Rev. 317 (2012) (explaining how the Supreme Court under Chief Justice Roberts has denied standing repeatedly to those suing the government, to criminal defendants, and to plaintiffs in general); Linda Greenhouse, *Standing and Delivering*, N.Y. Times (Dec. 12, 2012, 9:00 PM), http://opinionator.blogs.nytimes.com/2012/12/12/standing-and-delivering/?_r=0 (using the phrase "a tight lid on standing" to describe the possible Court position in denying petitioners standing to challenge the constitutionality of California's Proposition 8 prohibiting same-sex marriage as before the Court in *Hollingsworth*, 133 S. Ct. at 2652, and in the constitutional challenge to the Defense of Marriage Act in *Windsor*, 133 S. Ct. at 2675). Chief Justice Roberts' majority opinion in *Hollingsworth* did indeed deny petitioners standing to appeal.

129 A Scholarship Tuition Organization ("STO") cannot extend scholarships for students at only a single school. *See Winn*, 131 S. Ct. at 1440; Ariz. Rev. Stat. Ann. § 43–1089(G)(3) (2005) (current version at Ariz. Rev. Stat. Ann. § 43–1603(B)(2) (2013)). But the largest STOs restricted their scholarships to sectarian schools, leading to the contention that students who might have wanted "to attend non-religious private schools are disadvantaged in terms of the STO-provided scholarships available to them." Winn v. Ariz. Christian Sch. Tuition Org., 562 F.3d 1002, 1006 (9th Cir. 2009). An STO must allocate at least 90 percent of its annual revenues from contributions made for the statutory educational scholarships to grants to students attending qualifying schools and in doing so is supposed to "consider the financial needs of applicants." Ariz. Rev. Stat. Ann. § 43–1603(B)(1), (D)(2) (2013); *Winn*, 131 S. Ct. at 1440. But STO awards need not be granted exclusively to educationally-disadvantaged students from lower socio-economic backgrounds; nothing prevents STOs from supporting wealthy students attending expensive private schools. *See* Chapters 1 and 3 for further discussion of STOs.

discriminating in admissions on the basis of religion and offering religious instruction.[130] A donor to an STO may recommend, but not specifically designate, an individual student beneficiary to receive a scholarship from his contribution, but the student cannot be the donor's dependent. Nor may donors seek to evade this restriction by reciprocal agreements regarding their contributions.[131]

In 1998, the first full year of the tax credit program, at least 94 percent of the contributions to STOs went to organizations that restricted their scholarship grants to students attending parochial schools; 85 percent of that year's donations went to just three sectarian STOs.[132] The heart of the school choice plan is that Arizona permits a dollar-for-dollar state tax credit for contributions (up to approximately $500) to an STO.[133] The effectiveness of using such a tax credit—or its perniciousness if one believes it is constitutionally improper—is that, unlike a tax deduction, all taxpayers can take advantage of it (assuming sufficient tax liability) and not just the minority of taxpayers who itemize deductions.[134] A state tax credit also is worth substantially more to a contributor than a tax deduction, which is limited by a state's relatively low marginal income tax rates. With a tax credit, the contribution becomes costless to the individual donor, stimulating willingness to participate; the cost from considerably lower state tax revenues is spread among all state taxpayers. By the time of the Court's *Winn* decision, the estimated annual value of Arizona's STO-tax credit was over $50 million, and the total in diverted state tax revenues since inception of the program was $350 million (mostly directed to sectarian STOs)![135]

---

130 *See* Ariz. Rev. Stat. Ann. § 43–1089(G)(2) (1997) (current version at Ariz. Rev. Stat. Ann. § 43–1601(3) (2013)); *Winn*, 131 S. Ct. at 1440–41. Charter schools cannot be qualified schools. Ariz. Rev. Stat. Ann. § 43–1601 (2013). But Arizona allows a different, smaller tax credit for contributions to public schools, including charter schools, to support extracurricular activities or "character education programs." Ariz. Rev. Stat. Ann. § 43–1089.01 (2013).

131 *Id.* at §§ 43–1089(F), -1089.03(F), -1603(B)(3)–(4).

132 Winn v. Killian, 307 F.3d 1011, 1014, 1014 n.2 (9th Cir. 2002), *aff'd sub nom.* Hibbs v. Winn, 542 U.S. 88 (2004) (the three STOs then-receiving the largest amount of donations included the Catholic Tuition Organization of the Diocese of Phoenix, Arizona Christian School Tuition Organization, and Brophy Community Foundation. (Brophy College Preparatory School is an all-boys Catholic high school in Phoenix; Xavier College Preparatory School is its sister school.)).

133 Ariz. Rev. Stat. Ann. § 43–1089 (1997). When the Supreme Court decided *Winn*, the tax credit was limited to $500 per individual and $1,000 per married couple, with a five-year carry forward provision for any tax credit claimed in excess of the tax liability. The amount of the tax credit now may be adjusted upwards based on the consumer price index. Ariz. Rev. Stat. Ann. §§ 43–1089(C), -1089.03(C) (2013). For further discussion, *see* Chapter 3, illustration #5.

134 The assumption is that approximately the same percentage of taxpayers itemize for state income tax purposes as for federal income taxation, about 30 percent.

135 *Winn*, 131 S. Ct. at 1444.

After unsuccessful constitutional challenges in state court,[136] Kathleen M. Winn and other Arizona residents challenged the STO program in federal court in their capacity as state taxpayers. The plaintiffs first survived opposition to their lawsuit on the grounds it was jurisdictionally barred by the Tax Injunction Act. Indeed, the Supreme Court itself resolved this issue in the plaintiffs' favor without raising any question of standing.[137] When the merits, however, of their Establishment Clause complaint that Arizona was using tax revenues to pay students' tuition at parochial schools, some of which discriminated in admissions on the basis of religion, later reached the Court, five Justices decided that in fact the plaintiffs lacked standing to bring the action in the first place.

The case involved an unusual and complex mix of Article III taxpayer standing, a tax expenditure, and the Establishment Clause, and all Justices struggled analytically with the role that tax expenditure analysis (discussed in Chapter 3) should play in the Article III determination. Previously the Court had integrated a type of tax expenditure analysis, an economic-based tax policy tool, into constitutional analysis only in deciding cases on the merits.[138] Nearly 30 years earlier Justice Brennan warned of the Court's "impulse to decide difficult questions of substantive law obliquely in the course of opinions purporting to do nothing more than determine what the Court labels 'standing.'"[139] And this is precisely what the sharply divided Court did in *Winn*. The Court's majority used an excruciatingly strained and narrow interpretation of *Flast* and a novel, flawed tax expenditure analysis to deny standing to the state taxpayers and avoid deciding the merits of their thorny, but substantial, Establishment Clause claim.[140]

The Arizona legislature deliberately had constructed a circuitous route by which taxpayer monies, clearly owed to the state, first are transferred instead to STOs and then, via students, ultimately to private schools. Justice Kennedy, writing

---

136 *See* Kotterman v. Killian, 972 P.2d 606 (Ariz. 1999), *cert. denied*, 528 U.S. 921 (1999).

137 *Hibbs*, 542 U.S. at 88. On remand the Arizona Christian School Tuition Organization and other parties intervened as defendants. Now the district court dismissed the case for the taxpayers' failure to state a claim. But the Ninth Circuit reversed, holding that not only did the state taxpayers have standing under *Flast*, but that, on the merits, the Arizona tax credit statute violated the First Amendment's Establishment Clause. *Winn*, 562 F.3d at 1002, *reh'g en banc denied*, 586 F.3d 649 (9th Cir. Ariz. 2009).

138 *See* Chapter 3, nn.3–7 and accompanying text.

139 *Valley Forge*, 454 U.S. at 490 (Brennan, J., dissenting).

140 Given the preclusive effect of the majority's decision on the ability now to mount federal court challenges to state aid to parochial schools, one legal scholar commented that "plaintiffs' decision to challenge Arizona's scholarship tax credit program may well be one of the great tactical blunders in constitutional litigation history." Nicole Steele Garnett, *A* Winn *for Educational Pluralism*, 121 Yale L. J. Online 31, 33 (2011), http://www.yalelawjournal.org/images/pdfs/995.pdf. While descriptively accurate after the fact, this criticism is unfair considering, as Justice Elena Kagan's dissent makes clear, that based on ample precedent there was no reason initially to anticipate plaintiffs would be denied standing.

for the five-Justice majority, primarily focused not on the parochial school or the student seeking a religious education as the pecuniary beneficiaries but instead on the STO conduit entities, which themselves largely were sectarian. The first part of his opinion discusses the red herring under general standing principles of plaintiffs' "unjustifiable economic and political speculation." The STO program's net financial impact on the Arizona public fisc is uncertain, Justice Kennedy asserted, and so too would be the Arizona legislature's response to an injunction against the STO-tax credit and the ultimate effect on plaintiffs' tax liability.[141] But the essence of plaintiffs' complaint was the Establishment Clause violation from the state financing religious education, whether in an amount of three pence or $50 million annually. Speculation as to the amount of any eventual financial impact on the state's treasury or taxpayers is immaterial. Indeed, the Court in *Winn* acknowledged that the amount of money "conscripted for sectarian ends" is irrelevant to the violation of conscience that was the gravamen of plaintiffs' protest.[142] And, an injunction against the STO program certainly would have cured the constitutional violation.

Justice Kennedy then addressed *Flast*'s "narrow exception" to the no-taxpayer-standing rule based on "unique features of Establishment Clause violations" and the "specific evils" addressed in Madison's *Memorial and Remonstrance*.[143] He cited *Flast* for the proposition that "individuals suffer a particular injury for standing purposes when, in violation of the Establishment Clause and by means of 'the taxing and spending power,' their property is transferred through the Government's Treasury to a sectarian entity."[144] But in a highly literal and formalistic way, Justice Kennedy shifted ground, went beyond this straightforward principle, and focused on the particular wording of *Flast* that the "'taxpayer's … tax money is being *extracted and spent* in violation of specific constitutional protections against such abuses of legislative power.'"[145] Although he had to agree that "tax credits and governmental expenditures can have similar economic consequences," he claimed

141 *Winn*, 131 S. Ct. at 1443–44, 1447.

142 *Id.* at 1446–47.

143 *Id.* at 1445–46. Nonetheless, Justice Kennedy dismissed the Establishment Clause danger that contributing taxpayers vicariously would "force a [non-contributing] citizen to contribute three pence only of his property, to a sectarian organization …. On the contrary … taxpayers remain free to pay their own tax bills without contributing to an STO." *Id.* at 1447 (citations omitted). He inexplicably disregarded the huge diversion of state tax revenues to support religious education.

144 *Id.* (quoting *Flast*, 392 U.S. at 105–06).

145 *Winn*, 131 S. Ct. at 1446 (emphasis added) (quoting *Flast*, 392 U.S. at 106). As Justice Kagan demonstrated, however, the evil the *Flast* exception addresses has nothing to do with any individual's out-of-pocket loss or, even assuming it makes sense to trace from their origin the specific dollars government uses to subsidize religion, whether the funds come from those who object to the program. Her tax return check-the-box hypothetical and Madison's opposition to Patrick Henry's proposed *Virginia Tax Assessment* conclusively illustrate the irrelevance of the source of the funds the government diverts in support of

that a tax credit is not a governmental expenditure for purposes of *Flast*.[146] Yet "[a] tax credit, of course, is one variety of 'let the government pay.'"[147] Incredibly, Justice Kennedy three times defied reason and reality. He tenaciously maintained that "[w]hen Arizona taxpayers choose to contribute to STOs, they spend their *own* money, not money the State has collected from respondents or from other taxpayers;" he claimed "contributions result from the decisions of private taxpayers regarding their *own* funds;" and he asserted that "contributions yielding STO tax credits are not owed to the State."[148]

But this financial conception is palpably and demonstrably false; there is no other way to say it. The proof is straightforward. Consider an Arizona taxpayer with at least a $500 state tax liability and $500 in his pocket. If the $500 in his pocket were the taxpayer's own money, it could stay in his pocket. But it cannot. On April 15, the $500 belongs to the state as a direct and immediate result of the taxpayer's tax liability. If the taxpayer tried to retain the $500 beyond April 15, the state could obtain it through legal process. As Justice Elena Kagan pointed out in her powerful dissent, the only choice this taxpayer has is whether to write a check to the Arizona Department of Revenue or to an STO, most of which grant scholarships only to students attending parochial schools. Assume the taxpayer writes a $500 check to an STO. The state then effectively reimburses him for the full amount by a tax credit, just as surely as if the state required the taxpayer first to pay the full amount of the tax he owed and then sent the taxpayer a $500 "refund." Under Justice Kennedy's illogic, as far as standing or constitutional issues are concerned, Arizona's legislature could have designed the program to allow a contributor to an STO to claim *both* a state tax credit *and* a state charitable contribution deduction. In that event, an Arizona taxpayer with a marginal state income tax rate of 4.5 percent could contribute $500 to an STO and reduce his Arizona income tax liability by the $500 tax credit plus $22.50 ($500 × 4.5%) for the charitable contribution deduction, for a total of $522.50. Then Justice Kennedy's reasoning would lead to the absurd result that the taxpayer's profit of $22.50 on the transaction somehow also was the taxpayer's own money even though it, like the $500 credit itself, came from the state.

So, by the state legislature's decision to design, enact, and implement the STO-tax credit initiative, Arizona certainly "extracts" $500 from every donor-taxpayer whose tax liability is at least that amount. This extraction is in stark contrast to a wholly voluntary contribution a taxpayer might make to a § 501(c)(3) religious or educational organization, including a parochial school, for which the itemizing taxpayer may claim a deduction. The Court was oblivious to this basic,

---

religion or the private choice of taxpayers who consent to the diversion. *See Winn*, 131 S. Ct. at 1459–61 (Kagan, J., dissenting).

146 *Id.* at 1447 (majority opinion).

147 Burwell v. Hobby Lobby Stores, Inc., 134 S. Ct. 2751, 2803 (2014) (Ginsburg, J., dissenting).

148 *Winn*, 131 S. Ct. at 1447–48 (majority opinion) (emphasis added).

crucial distinction between a discretionary contribution *cum* tax deduction and an obligatory tax liability offset by a tax credit.[149] Through the tax credit Arizona then "spends" $500 of state tax revenue for every taxpayer who chooses to divert this portion of his obligatory tax liability to an STO instead of sending it to the state treasury. But what possible difference should it make, either to the merits of an Establishment Clause challenge to the STO program or to plaintiffs' standing to bring the challenge, whether the $500 flows first into the state's treasury and then by grant to a parochial school (perhaps at the designation of the taxpayer on his tax return), or first to an STO chosen by the taxpayer and then to one or more students for tuition payments to a parochial school? The Court's "untouched by government hands" theory is wholly incoherent. Either way the money—the *state's* money—reaches students and parochial schools through operation of state programs designed for that specific purpose, and the economic and constitutional consequences of government aid to religious education are identical.

Predictably, Justice Scalia, joined by Justice Thomas, continued to fulminate against *Flast*—"an anomaly in our jurisprudence, irreconcilable with the Article III restrictions on federal judicial power"[150]—and the majority's failure to overrule it, while still joining the Court's opinion. Justice Elena Kagan's vehement dissent (her first as a member of the Court), joined by Justices Breyer, Ruth Bader Ginsburg, and Sonia Sotomayor, exposed the many irreconcilable flaws in the majority's opinion. She first noted the dramatic change the majority effected reflecting new, constrained attitudes toward the Establishment Clause:

> Until today, this Court has never so much as hinted that litigants in the same shoes as the Plaintiffs lack standing under *Flast*. To the contrary: We have faced the identical situation five times—including in a prior incarnation of this very case!—and we have five times resolved the suit without questioning the plaintiffs' standing.[151]

Justice Kennedy merely dismissed this compelling precedent as not binding on the Court because the previous cases had assumed standing without addressing the matter.[152] But Justice Kagan responded that, as standing is a jurisdictional matter, a federal court has an obligation to consider it even if no party objects. Moreover, she demonstrated that the Court had proceeded to the merits of those previous cases not because it was unmindful of the taxpayer standing issue but because it

---

149 *See id.* at 1448. Justice Kennedy also ignored the not insubstantial direct costs to the state of implementing and administering the STO program. This drain on state tax revenues alone should have been enough for taxpayer standing. *Id.* at 1458 n.9 (Kagan, J., dissenting).

150 *Id.* at 1450 (Scalia, J. concurring) (adding "I would repudiate that misguided decision").

151 *Id.* at 1452–53 (Kagan, J., dissenting).

152 *Id.* at 1448–49 (majority opinion).

was well aware of it and believed standing existed. The precedent does not lack force simply because it did not discuss the obvious.[153]

On the central substantive issue, Justice Kagan excoriated the majority for irrationally distinguishing a direct government appropriation from a tax expenditure such as a tax credit, a "distinction ... in search of a difference."[154] She cited many cases in which the Court in fact had recognized their equivalence, including statements by Justices Thomas and Scalia. Government tax breaks are "just spending under a different name,"[155] and when in aid of religion they inflict the same injury on taxpayers for purposes of standing.[156] That is why, as Justice Kagan emphatically noted: "In the decades since *Flast*, no court—not one—has differentiated between appropriations and tax expenditures in deciding whether litigants have standing."[157]

One of Justice Kagan's examples, ignored by Justice Kennedy, thoroughly demolished his reasoning. She hypothesized that a state decides to subsidize individuals who wish to own a crucifix. The state "could purchase the religious symbols in bulk and distribute them to all takers. Or it could mail a reimbursement check to any individual who buys her own and submits a receipt for the purchase. Or it could authorize that person to claim a tax credit equal to the price she paid."[158] Could anyone possibly maintain that the manner of state subsidization, including the tax credit, should make the slightest difference as to taxpayers' standing to challenge the practice under the Establishment Clause? Can the tax credit approach rationally avoid taxpayer standing because it does not literally "extract and spend" an objecting plaintiff's tax monies or because the money spent somehow is conceived to belong to the willing participant rather than the state? And the hypothetical would have equal force if the state more "neutrally" offered to subsidize symbols of many different religions, as well as some purely secular icons, depending on the private, independent choice of the recipient.

That the majority in *Winn* denied standing to challenge the tax credit approach shows just how harmful its opinion is. These different forms of subsidization are essentially interchangeable, so, as Justice Kagan noted, the government merely must subsidize parochial and other private schools through a tax expenditure to

---

153 *Id.* at 1454–55 (Kagan, J., dissenting).

154 *Id.* at 1455.

155 *Id.* at 1456.

156 *Id.* at 1455–57. Professor Dworkin characterized as "silly" the distinction between government itself appropriating funds for religion and government legislating a tax credit that enables taxpayers to do so via a contribution, commenting: "In fact, there is no difference in motive, consequence, or principle between a direct expenditure to a religious school from the state treasury and a full tax credit for those who contribute to a religious school themselves." Ronald Dworkin, *The Court's Embarrassingly Bad Decisions*, N.Y. Rev. of Books, May 26, 2011.

157 *Winn*, 131 S. Ct. at 1452 (Kagan, J., dissenting).

158 *Id.* at 1457.

preclude plaintiffs' standing and thereby insulate its program from judicial review.[159] Indeed, she pointedly observed that the majority "offer[ed] a roadmap—more truly just a one-step instruction" to accomplish this outcome.[160] *Flast* essentially was eviscerated, and the Establishment Clause devalued.[161] The only reasonable conclusion about *Winn* is the prophetic one Justice Brennan reached at the close of his dissent in *Valley Forge*, as quoted above.[162]

VI. Establishment Clause Standing after *Winn*

In *Winn*, Justice Kennedy noted that "standing in Establishment Clause cases can be shown in various ways," in particular "[i]f an establishment of religion is alleged to cause real injury to particular individuals."[163] He likely added this comment to implausibly assuage the actual draconian effect of his opinion precluding taxpayer standing to challenge government financial aid to religious education. He never indicated how anybody could bring an Establishment Clause claim against the Arizona tax credit, other than to say that if it could be shown to "disadvantage[] a particular religious group or a particular nonreligious group" plaintiffs would not need to rely on *Flast* for standing.[164] But it is far from clear that this forlorn suggestion has any real-world application. Only slightly more hopeful, Justice Kagan asserted that "based on individualized injury, separate and apart from taxpayer status ... some parents or children likely have standing to challenge the Arizona tax credit on such grounds."[165] But again, one must wonder how this might work in practice. The more fundamental point is that, as the Court in *Flast* said, a "taxpayer's access to federal courts should not be barred because there might be at large in society a hypothetical plaintiff who might possibly bring such a suit."[166]

But if we accept Justice Kennedy's assurance that potential government violations of the Establishment Clause in the school aid context will not be entirely beyond the reach of federal courts to address, we can analogize from the passive display cases. Imagine a neighbor of a large, private, parochial school in Arizona

159 "However blatantly the government may violate the Establishment Clause, taxpayers cannot gain access to the federal courts." *Id.* at 1462. *See also* Linda Sugin, *The Great and Mighty Tax Law: How the Roberts Court Has Reduced Constitutional Scrutiny of Taxes and Tax Expenditures*, 78 Brook. L. Rev. 777, 792 (2013) (the "opaque reduction in the tax liability of some people ... eludes legal analysis; it ignores the existence of the public policy that a targeted tax reduction reflects. Such a nebulous 'tax cut' cannot be reviewed, whether it is structured as state aid to religion or anything else.").

160 *Winn*, 131 S. Ct. at 1462 (Kagan, J., dissenting).

161 *Id.*

162 *See supra* note 95 and accompanying text.

163 *Winn*, 131 S. Ct. at 1449; *see also id.* at 1440.

164 *Id.* at 1449.

165 *Id.* at 1457 n.7 (Kagan, J., dissenting).

166 *Flast*, 392 U.S. at 98 n.17.

who knows full well that through the state's STO program a substantial amount of state money is subsidizing the tuition of some, if not many, students at parochial schools throughout the state.[167] Every school day the neighbor watches students exit the school bus and enter the school. The school clearly is pervasively sectarian as is apparent from its name, particular religious affiliation, and perhaps its advertising materials and mission statement. Maybe from off-campus the neighbor even can see religious symbols or signs or hear religious exercises being conducted. Given the size of the school and its student body, it is statistically certain that some of the $50 million dollars contributed annually to STOs through the tax credit initiative support at least some of those students. This might be confirmed by promotional literature of the school or of an STO that funnels money to the school, or certainly by the annual report an STO must file with the state, presumably a public record.[168] The neighbor might not know the identity of any particular student receiving a set amount of STO funds, but why should this be necessary? If it were, we could posit that the neighbor is personally acquainted with the family of a student at the school and therefore knows that student receives a scholarship from a specific STO. For an even more direct connection, the "neighbor" might be a parent of a child attending the school who supports religious education, especially for his child, but has a principled view of strong separation of church and state. This parent refuses any STO scholarship money for his own child because he thinks the STO-tax credit program is unconstitutional. But he knows specifically of other students in the school—friends of his child—who do receive tax-supported STO scholarships, and he might be inclined to complain anonymously.[169]

Just as Van Orden had standing to challenge the Ten Commandments monument on the grounds of the Texas State Capitol, either the neighbor or the "neighbor-parent" should have standing, quite aside from *Flast*, to challenge the STO program under the Establishment Clause. On a daily basis these potential plaintiffs observe various indicia of state money being used to support the religious indoctrination of impressionable schoolchildren and experience a resulting "Psychic Injury" that likely is a considerably greater affront to religious conscience than Van Orden's occasional encounters with a stone monument. The hyper-technical objection might be that these plaintiffs in fact are not "observing" the improper use of state money. They are observing students receiving religious education, and they know that

167 The *Winn* Court's fiction that the tax credits were not state money was asserted to avoid the *Flast* language of "extract and spend." Outside the taxpayer standing context of *Flast*, it cannot be maintained plausibly that a tax expenditure such as the tax credit is not state money, a state subsidy.

168 *See* Ariz. Rev. Stat. § 43–1604 (2013). *See also Winn*, 131 S. Ct. at 1458 n.9 (Kagan, J., dissenting).

169 Establishment Clause claims are often brought by courageous litigants willing to risk harassment and ostracism. *See, e.g.*, Douglas Laycock, *Edward Schempp and His Family*, 38 J. Sup. Ct. Hist. 63 (2013) (recounting the story of the school prayer case *Schempp*); Stephen D. Solomon, Ellery' s Protest (Univ. Mich. Press 2007) (same).

state money is being used for that purpose. But this observation coupled with this knowledge must constitute sufficient injury for purposes of standing. Indeed, the essence of Van Orden's injury is his knowledge that the religious monument is being maintained on state grounds even when he does not observe it there. If Van Orden suddenly were struck blind (an act of divine retribution?) would he lose his standing because he no longer can observe the monument? Could a blind plaintiff informed of the monument not bring the claim initially? Merely the knowledge of government funds being expended in aid of religion perhaps should be sufficient for standing. But the direct, immediate, and particularized injury of the neighbor or "neighbor-parent" surely should suffice. And the much larger point is that such machinations should not be necessary. The majority in *Winn* was egregiously and indefensibly wrong; the plaintiffs clearly qualified for taxpayer standing under *Flast*.

Alternatively, another shoe might drop. Those Justices who deride the "Psychic Injury" many Establishment Clause violations create, together with those who maintain a crabbed view of the nature and scope of the Clause generally, might perform a *volte-face* comparable to *Winn* and now restrict standing in display cases as well.[170] If this should happen, another of Justice Brennan's warnings will materialize: "[T]he opinion, which tosses out of court almost every conceivable kind of plaintiff who could be injured by the activity claimed to be unconstitutional, can be explained only by an indefensible hostility to the claim on the merits."[171]

VII. School Aid Litigation after *Winn*

Winn richly deserves to be overruled so that federal courts can return to their fundamental role in overseeing government expenditures in aid of religious education that imperil basic individual freedoms that the Establishment Clause was meant to protect. *Winn* is a badly reasoned 5–4 decision by a deeply divided Court, and it is inconsistent with a long line of precedent, including the very case itself when it was first before the Court on the Tax Injunction Act issue. It has upset reliance by taxpayer citizens on federal courts as an avenue to air grievances that, if denied federal judicial review, will only foster increased religious and political divisiveness. The doctrine of *stare decisis*, which is simply "'a principle of policy'"

170 Justice Scalia, for example, has made clear he would render the Establishment Clause largely superfluous and nugatory. When asked in a recent public forum, "What is the greatest miscarriage of constitutional justice during your tenure?," he reportedly replied: "The most disreputable area of our law is the Establishment Clause. … A violation of the Establishment Clause that does not affect someone's free exercise—there is no reason why you should have standing." Cindy George, *At Houston Lecture, Scalia Explores Christian Virtues and Economic Systems*, Hous. Chron., September 7, 2013, http://www.houstonchronicle.com/news/houston-texas/houston/article/At-Houston-lecture-Scalia-explores-Christian-4794443.php?t=1c711cf5704c5e314b.

171 *Warth*, 422 U.S. at 520 (Brennan, J., dissenting).

and not "an inexorable command" or "'a mechanical formula of adherence to the latest decision,'"[172] should not preclude overturning *Winn* and returning to the proper application of *Flast*. Because the Court realizes that it has the last word on constitutional issues such as standing, while a legislature can change a law in response to a court's statutory interpretation with which it disagrees, the Court has never applied *stare decisis* "as rigidly in constitutional as in nonconstitutional cases."[173] This is especially true as to the First Amendment, even when a recent precedent is involved. Indeed, Justice Scalia so argued (citing ample authority) in urging the Court, with prompt success, to overrule a central holding restricting political speech imposed through campaign finance regulation.[174] Contrary to Justice Scalia in *Winn*, that case, not *Flast*, should be overruled.

Until that happens, however, the question becomes what taxpayers or citizens generally can do to seek judicial review of state government tax-supported programs that aid parochial schools and their students. Perhaps, as suggested above, an inventive approach to standing with appropriate plaintiffs could succeed in federal court. If not, plaintiffs as taxpayers or otherwise would be relegated by *Winn* to challenging their state's initiatives in state court. State courts are fully competent to adjudicate claims based on the First Amendment's Establishment Clause, cognate provisions in state constitutions, or other state anti-funding provisions that more specifically address government aid for religious entities. And in entertaining such lawsuits, states are not bound by the standing requirements of Article III of the U.S. Constitution or its "Cases" or "Controversies" limitation. Rather, states may follow their own rules regarding standing, even when applying federal law.[175] But unlike the federal judiciary with lifetime tenure, state courts may be subject to political pressures similar to those that fostered the challenged state legislative program of aid for religious education.

In adjudicating a challenge to a state's tax-supported school choice initiative on any of the various possible theories, a state court could rule simply on the basis of "adequate and independent" state law grounds, an anti-funding provision in the state constitution for example. In that case, regardless of any issue regarding federal standing, a state's highest court's ruling most likely would be unreviewable in the U.S. Supreme Court for lack of a federal question.[176] Alternatively, in various

172 Payne v. Tennessee, 501 U.S. 808, 828 (1991) (internal citation omitted).

173 Glidden Co. v. Zdanok, 370 U.S. 530, 543 (1962); see also *Payne*, 501 U.S. at 828 (commenting that adherence to precedent is less appropriate in constitutional cases because in such cases "'correction through legislative action is practically impossible'") (internal citation omitted).

174 F.E.C. v. Wisconsin Right to Life, Inc., 551 U.S. 449, 500–03 (2007) (Scalia, J., concurring in part and in the judgment) (urging the overruling of a part of McConnell v. F.E.C., 540 U.S. 93 (2003), soon accomplished in Citizens United v. F.E.C., 558 U.S. 310 (2010)).

175 *See* ASARCO Inc. v. Kadish, 490 U.S. 605, 617, 620 (1989).

176 *See id.* at 624.

ways a state court's opinion might depend on its interpretation and application of federal law, in which case Supreme Court review would raise the standing issue.[177]

A state court, for instance, might directly and unambiguously construe the First Amendment's Establishment Clause. Or, a state court could purport to apply its state constitution's religion clauses but consider that they accord at least as much protection as their cognate federal provisions. In this perhaps more subtle and indirect manner, the state court ruling, ostensibly based only on state law, in fact could be infused with sufficient federal law issues to allow for possible Supreme Court review. In either case, the state court could look to the Supreme Court's school aid cases decided prior to *Winn* to the extent they were apposite to the case at issue. Even though the Court in *Winn* indicated that the plaintiffs in many of those prior cases should not have had standing, this does not retroactively invalidate the substantive rulings in those cases. Indeed, the effect of *Winn* is essentially to lock in those rulings on the merits about the validity of certain forms of aid to parochial schools under the Establishment Clause. And here it is important to note that the most recent of those prior cases, *Zelman v. Simmons-Harris*, involved an extremely limited school voucher program designed to help only low-income, educationally-disadvantaged students stuck in a city system with "among the worst performing public schools in the Nation."[178] The students received modest financial assistance, based on need, and participating private schools could not discriminate in admissions based on race, religion, or ethnicity. *Zelman*, therefore, may have merely narrow, supportive application in a state court adjudication of a far more extensive and unrestricted state aid program.

At any rate, assume a state's highest court issues a ruling that does sufficiently implicate federal law to provide a basis for Supreme Court review. If the taxpayer-plaintiffs lost in state court, *Winn* likely would make futile their petition for *certiorari*. If, however, the taxpayer-plaintiffs were successful in state court on their claim grounded on the Establishment Clause, the aggrieved defendant presumably would be the state or some other governmental agency or party. And that defendant likely would have standing on its petition for Supreme Court review. Standing must exist at all stages of the litigation, on appeal as well as when the complaint is filed. The taxpayer-plaintiffs would not have had standing in federal district court, but that is not the question for federal appellate review. The party who first seeks to invoke federal judicial power is the one who must demonstrate standing, and that party would be the state-defendant who lost in the state's highest court.[179] So even though the taxpayer-plaintiffs would not have had

177 For explication of the many complexities involved in the doctrine regarding adequate and independent state law grounds for decisions, *see* FALLON, JR., ET AL., *supra* note 3, at 458–80.

178 536 U.S. 639, 644 (2002). *See* the discussion and analysis of *Zelman* in Chapter 2, notes 303–21 and accompanying text.

179 *ASARCO*, 490 U.S. at 618; *see also Hollingsworth*, 133 S. Ct. at 2661; *Arizonans for Official English*, 520 U.S. at 64, 67.

federal standing to initiate their complaint, at the Supreme Court level standing would depend on the petitioners to that Court—that is, the state-defendant—and not on the plaintiffs-respondents.[180] In other words, the state-defendant would be aggrieved by the state court's adverse ruling on its school aid program, and this should be sufficient, particularized injury, which could be redressed by Supreme Court reversal. So the state court's adjudication frustrating the state-defendant's legitimate interest in the "continued enforceability" of its laws should give that defendant standing on *certiorari* to the Supreme Court.[181] The Supreme Court might even be particularly solicitous of a state's standing to vindicate its "quasi-sovereign interests."[182] And the Supreme Court might have a special incentive to accept such a case for review in order "to assure that the binding application of federal law is uniform and ultimately subject to control by this Court."[183] This concern would be at a zenith with respect to a First Amendment issue regarding the Establishment Clause.

Thus *Winn* enacts a triple play against taxpayers seeking to raise a constitutional challenge to any program of state financial aid for education that substantially benefits religious education. Plaintiffs cannot sue initially in federal court. If they sue in state court and lose, they cannot seek Supreme Court review. And even if they sue in state court and win, they likely still must survive Supreme Court review, initiated by the state, by a Court that currently is unreceptive to the merits of such claims. All this was accomplished in a 5–4 decision dealing "merely" with the technical, jurisdictional issue of standing.

VIII. Conclusion

The Supreme Court's decision in *Winn* not only is not required by Article III but is inconsistent with precedent and irreconcilable with the Court's basic duty to assure that the majestic freedoms guaranteed by the First Amendment are enjoyed by all Americans and not undermined by political exigencies of the moment. As long as taxpayer standing is governed by *Winn*, the focus must shift to state legislatures, governors, and courts, each with their own obligations under both federal and state constitutions. Our final Chapter therefore discusses recent developments at the state level and offers some compromise suggestions for reasonable and

180 *See ASARCO*, 490 U.S. at 623–24.

181 *See Hollingsworth*, 133 S. Ct. at 2664 (citing Maine v. Taylor, 477 U.S. 131, 137 (1986)).

182 *Massachusetts*, 549 U.S. at 518, 520.

183 *ASARCO*, 490 U.S. at 622. Of course, to the extent state courts now have the last word on Establishment Clause challenges to state aid to parochial schools by unsuccessful plaintiffs, national uniformity on this crucial issue will be undermined. A state's governor and legislature will be limited only by what their own state's highest court and local political processes allow.

responsible ways by which states can address the understandable public demand for better primary and secondary educational opportunities, including alternatives to traditional public schools, while remaining sensitive to matters of religious conscience and religious pluralism that are so central to our country's history and ethos.

Chapter 5
Where States Are and Proposals for Reform

> When the judiciary is no longer "a great rock" in the storm, … when the courts are niggardly in the use of their power and reach great issues only timidly and reluctantly, the force of the Constitution in the life of the Nation is greatly weakened.[1]

I. Introduction

With the Supreme Court's ruling in *Arizona Christian Scholarship Tuition Organization v. Winn*, "[h]owever blatantly the government may violate the Establishment Clause, taxpayers cannot gain access to the federal courts."[2] As disturbing as this lament by the dissent, the implications are clear. Those taxpayers and citizens who object to increasing amounts of state funds being directed to aid religious education in a variety of inventive ways and are troubled by the consequent erosion of basic principles of separation of church and state must now look primarily to state courts and legislatures for relief. In an earlier context Justice William J. Brennan called for a larger role for state judiciaries in safeguarding constitutional liberties:

> [T]he very premise of … cases that foreclose federal remedies constitutes a clear call to state courts to step into the breach. With the federal locus of our double protections weakened, our liberties cannot survive if the states betray the trust the [U.S. Supreme] Court has put in them. … With federal scrutiny diminished, state courts must respond by increasing their own.[3]

Unconstrained by Article III of the U.S. Constitution and the Supreme Court's restrictive application of it, state courts readily can accord standing to taxpayers or other citizens to challenge the constitutionality of government aid directly or indirectly reaching religious organizations, such as sectarian Scholarship Tuition Organizations ("STOs"), parochial schools, private religiously-affiliated education providers, and religiously-oriented charter schools. State courts can do so whether the plaintiffs' "generalized grievances" are based on asserted violations of the First Amendment's Establishment Clause, state anti-establishment analogues,

---

1 Flast v. Cohen, 392 U.S. 83, 112 (1968) (Douglas, J., concurring) (footnotes omitted).

2 Ariz. Christian Sch. Tuition Org. v. Winn, 131 S. Ct. 1436, 1462 (2011) (Kagan, J., dissenting).

3 William J. Brennan, Jr., *State Constitutions and the Protection of Individual Rights*, 90 Harv. L. Rev. 489, 502 (1977).

state constitution anti-funding provisions invocable to proscribe the use of government funds to support sectarian schools and religious education,[4] or other state constitutional provisions.[5] It is essential that state courts take a permissive pro-standing position because "these constitutional provisions are never mere technicalities, but are part of the basic, fundamental provisions in our system of laws"[6] and must be aggressively enforced.

There also is a crucial, preliminary role for state legislatures in the aftermath of *Winn*. As Justice David Souter implored in his dissent in *Zelman v. Harris-Simmons*, political branches of government unconstrained by federal courts must recognize the danger in further eroding separation of church and state even as they address the contentious issues of public education.[7] Those legislatures so inclined create and design tax funding mechanisms to avoid constitutional issues as best they can. The resulting legislation is, to be sure, a consequence of the political process and its attendant influences from many quarters. What many deem a necessary and beneficial movement for "school choice," in accord with parents' valued liberty to direct their children's upbringing and education, others suggest is little more than a pretext for channeling public funds to religion-imbued education. Legislatures thus must realize the extreme sensitivity of measures that, for some, threaten to trench upon cherished religious freedoms and can generate harmful divisiveness in an increasingly pluralistic society. Mindful, therefore, of their own constitutional obligations in exercising their broad taxing and spending powers, and respectful of the fundamental democratic principle of checks and balances while acknowledging their own potential fallibility in

---

4 Forty-two states have anti-funding provisions in their state constitutions; only eight do not. In some states, such as Alaska and Arizona, courts explicitly have cited concerns for the integrity of the public school system as underlying their anti-funding provisions. *See, e.g.*, Sheldon Jackson Coll. v. State, 599 P.2d 127, 129 n.6 (Alaska 1979) (citing 2 Proceedings of the Alaska Constitutional Convention 1520); Cain v. Horne, 202 P.3d 1178, 1183 (Ariz. 2009) (citing Records of the Arizona Constitutional Convention of 1910 at 523–38, 660, 894, 940 (John S. Goff ed., 1991)).

Anti-funding provisions vary in their wording and breadth. One version generally prohibits the use of public funds for any sectarian purpose. *See, e.g.*, Ill. Const. Art. 10, § 3. Sponsorship of religious education is typically listed among, or merely subsumed within, the forbidden sectarian purposes. Another formulation is a stand-alone provision that specifically addresses the issue of public support for sectarian schools. *See, e.g.*, Alaska Const. Art. 7, § 1. Other versions are incorporated within a general constitutional provision pertaining to public education. *See, e.g.*, Haw. Const. Art. 10, § 1.

5 Two scholars categorize some additional, non-religion-based state constitutional strictures relevant to school choice programs: uniformity, local control, and public-purpose provisions. Preston C. Green, III & Peter L. Moran, *The State Constitutionality of Voucher Programs: Religion Is Not the Sole Determination*, 2010 BYU Educ. & L.J. 275 (2010). This book does not address such provisions.

6 La. Fed'n of Teachers v. State, 118 So.3d 1033, 1037 (La. 2013).

7 536 U.S. 639, 716–17 (2002) (Souter, J. dissenting).

responding to political pressures, state legislatures should enact statutes that specifically confer standing on taxpayers, or citizens more generally, to contest in state courts the constitutionality of government aid that directly or indirectly supports religious education. Although state courts themselves generally may grant such standing liberally, statutes mandating standing would remove any doubts or potential obstacles.

This final chapter begins with an exploration of the theories on which state taxpayers may be able to secure state court review by anchoring claims relating to government use of state tax revenues in support of school choice alternatives to one or more state constitutional provisions, particularly anti-funding provisions which school choice supporters perceive as a potentially significant impediment to their objective. These claims can supplement anti-establishment arguments based on federal or analogous state prohibitions. We then review several state court adjudications of the merits of such claims, the outcomes of which in some instances seem to reflect decidedly *ad hoc* rationales difficult to reconcile with a state constitution's language. The discussion thereafter turns to the advantages of state legislatures enacting statutes that explicitly confer standing to contest in state courts the constitutionality of government aid directly or indirectly reaching religiously-affiliated educational organizations. We next suggest various approaches state legislatures should consider and some constraints they should incorporate, through a balancing-of-interests approach, into their systems for funding school choice options with taxpayer money. These include sunset and means-testing provisions, limiting the financial incentives and the amounts involved in diverting state funds to private schools, targeting state aid as much as possible toward secular components of formal education (in or outside the home), and imposing religious non-discrimination student admissions requirements on beneficiary parochial schools. We also propose an alternative means of raising money for private schools through a dedicated lottery system, which might alleviate some of the current problems in the use of general state tax revenues for religious education. And with the growing popularity of charter schools we urge that states clarify that these hybrid public schools, directly financed by state and local governments, are in fact public schools for all constitutional purposes, including complying with the guarantees of the First Amendment.

As history amply demonstrates, there can be no purity at the intersection of the First Amendment's Religion Clauses, especially the Establishment Clause, with primary and secondary education. With an appreciation for the conflicting interests at stake, we hope our suggestions will be sufficiently politically moderate and socially palatable to appeal to a broad spectrum, as well as reasonably, if not perfectly, compatible with fundamental constitutional principles as currently understood. At a minimum, they may stimulate helpful debate on vital issues.

II. State Courts: Taxpayer Standing to Challenge the Use of Government Funds for Religious Education

As a general proposition, state taxpayers often may obtain state court review of claims relating to use of state tax revenues to support sectarian organizations, including parochial schools, religiously-allied charter schools, or private education providers, by invoking one or more state constitutional provisions. A majority of states have anti-funding provisions, and five states—California, Colorado, Missouri, New Mexico, and Wyoming—have not only an anti-funding provision targeted at sectarian schools but one or more additional interlacing provisions intended to prevent the use of public funds to support religion more generally.[8] The most common state constitutional structure is one that contains free exercise and anti-establishment guarantees combined with multiple provisions explicitly barring the use of public funds for sectarian purposes. Moreover, all 50 state constitutions contain an education clause setting forth the state's responsibility, financial and otherwise, to maintain its public education system,[9] and these provisions may impact what a state is able to do in aiding private education.

State courts naturally have a strong duty to interpret and apply their state constitutions, and they often confer standing in constitutional challenges relatively freely. They do so unconstrained by Article III of the U.S. Constitution and often despite any principle of separation of powers at the state level. In particular, a majority of state courts look more favorably upon taxpayer standing than do federal courts.[10] Some state courts have a well-developed jurisprudence expressly permitting taxpayer standing based on constitutional provisions, inferences from

---

8 *See* Cal. Const. Art. 9, §§ 8, 9(f); Art. 16, § 5; Colo. Const. Art. 5, § 34; Art. 9, §§ 7, 8; Mo. Const. Art. 1, §§ 6, 7; N.M. Const. Art. 12, §§ 3, 9; Art. 21, § 4; Wyo. Const. Art. 1, § 19; Art. 3, § 36; Art. 7, §§ 8, 12. The courts in these five states generally interpret their patchwork of constitutional provisions as indicative of the intention of the delegates to the states' constitutional conventions to send a clear message about the impropriety of aiding sectarian causes in all instances and as calling for a more exacting standard for upholding the constitutionality of government expenditures than would be applied under the Religion Clauses of the First Amendment. *See, e.g.*, St. Louis Univ. v. Masonic Temple Ass'n of St. Louis, 220 S.W.3d 721, 729 (Mo. 2007).

9 *See* Chapter 1, notes 8–10 and accompanying text.

10 Edward A. Zelinsky, *Putting State Courts in the Constitutional Driver's Seat: State Taxpayer Standing after* Cuno *and* Winn, 40 Hastings Const. L.Q. 1, 36 (2012); Joshua G. Urquhart, *Disfavored Constitution, Passive Virtues? Linking State Constitutional Fiscal Limitations and Permissive Taxpayer Standing Doctrines*, 81 Fordham L. Rev. 1263, 1263 (2012). Mr. Urquhart counts 36 states as permitting taxpayer standing, eight states as restricting taxpayer standing, and six states as being unclear as to taxpayer standing. Of the eight states that restrict taxpayer standing, three reject it outright; the other five have doctrines that operate in lieu of taxpayer standing statutes under which courts can confer taxpayer standing based on the "public importance" or "public interest" of lawsuits. *Id.* at 1277–78.

statutory or procedural rules,[11] or other judicial doctrine.[12] Other state courts considering the merits of taxpayers' constitutional challenges to government use of public funds have assumed taxpayer standing *sub silentio*.[13]

Where state courts specifically have addressed taxpayer standing, the threshold applied often has been a relatively expansive and relaxed alternative to the traditional three-prong standing doctrine requirements of personal injury,

11 At least nine states expressly permit taxpayer standing to challenge state aid to religion. *See, e.g.*, Conrad v. City & Cnty. of Denver, 656 P.2d 662 (Colo. 1982) (evaluating and authorizing taxpayer standing to challenge expenditure of public funds for the display of a nativity scene, and finding that plaintiff-taxpayers had suffered an injury in fact as required under state law); Dep't of Admin. v. Horne, 269 So. 2d 659, 663 (Fla. 1972) ("[W]here there is an attack *upon* constitutional grounds based directly upon the Legislature's *taxing and spending* power, there is standing to sue without the [] requirement of special injury" that normally is a prerequisite for standing.) (emphasis in original); Meredith v. Pence, 984 N.E.2d 1213 (Ind. 2013) (ruling that taxpayers have standing under the state's public standing doctrine to challenge as unconstitutional a state voucher program, and holding that the initiative did not violate the state constitution's education clause or anti-funding provisions); Mitchell v. Consol. Sch. Dist. No. 201, 135 P.2d 79 (Wash. 1943) (holding that a taxpayer had standing to challenge the constitutionality of a statute authorizing the use of public funds for transportation of students to parochial schools); Tooley v. O'Connell, 253 N.W.2d 335, 342 (Wis. 1977) (using the relatively low threshold of inferring the taxpayer had suffered or would suffer pecuniary loss as a result of an unconstitutional statute, and finding taxpayer standing to challenge use of public funds for school financing); Washakie Cnty. Sch. Dist. No. 1 v. Herschler, 606 P.2d 310 (Wyo. 1980) (applying Wyoming statutes that allow relaxed standing rules to permit a taxpayer suit to challenge educational appropriations).

12 Professor Edward Zelinsky describes several categories in which taxpayer standing is conferred in states: (1) cases of particular or great public importance, (2) cases not depending on the significance of the issues presented, and (3) cases involving particular state statutes. Zelinsky, *supra* note 10, at 36–46. Mr. Urquhart provides a more detailed rendition of state taxpayer standing, which demonstrates some striking contrasts from U.S. Supreme Court doctrine. Urquhart, *supra* note 10, at 128–83.

13 *See, e.g.*, State *ex rel.* Johnson v. Boyd, 23 N.E.2d 256 (Ind. 1940) (reaching the merits in a suit brought by taxpayers to contest the use of a school treasurer's bonds for sectarian purposes as violating the state anti-funding provision); Fiscal Court of Jefferson Cnty. v. Brady, 885 S.W.2d 681, 682, 686 (Ky. 1994) (allowing taxpayers to challenge direct county payments to private schools that were designated as transportation subsidies, and noting Kentucky's anti-establishment clause and anti-funding provision "appear to restrict direct aid from state or local government to sectarian schools much more specifically and significantly than the only counterpart provision in the Federal Constitution, which is the 'establishment of religion' clause in the First Amendment"); Seegers v. Parker, 241 So. 2d 213, 215 (La. 1970) (adjudicating taxpayers' constitutional claims regarding a Louisiana statute that would have benefited private school teachers); Rhoades v. Sch. Dist. of Abington Twp., 226 A.2d 53 (Pa. 1967) (reaching the merits of a taxpayer suit challenging transportation of children to private, sectarian schools).

causation, and redressibility.[14] Indeed, in contrast to the U.S. Supreme Court's restrictive approach, some states' highest courts explicitly have authorized taxpayer standing primarily on one, or a combination, of several bases: (1) taxpayers are an appropriate party to represent a public interest;[15] (2) taxpayers are in a unique position to vindicate the common public interest in the proper use of tax funds when the inherent injury a taxpayer suffers is a violation of a state constitutional provision;[16] or (3) reminiscent of a concern expressed by Justice Elena Kagan's dissent in *Winn*, if standing were denied no one may be able to challenge the government's use of public funds to aid religion.[17] These

---

14 *See* Zelinsky, *supra* note 10, at 36–46 ("A minority of states emulates the federal approach and thus always denies standing to taxpayers absent individualized harm."); Urquhart, *supra* note 10, at 1274–77. *See also supra* note 11 (citing several cases where the court used a liberal taxpayer standing standard).

15 *See, e.g.*, Gregory v. Shurtleff, 299 P.3d 1098, 1104, 1110 (Utah 2013) (clarifying that taxpayer standing is a subset of its public interest standing doctrine and that conferral of standing on taxpayers depends upon their being not necessarily the "*most* appropriate party" but rather "*an* appropriate party" possessing simply "the interest necessary to effectively assist the court in developing and reviewing all relevant legal and factual questions;" noting as long as "'the issues are of a sufficient weight … [and] not more appropriately addressed by another branch of government pursuant to the political process,'" standing is not reserved for other, hypothetical plaintiffs when "'the issues are unlikely to be raised at all if the party is denied [public interest] standing'") (all citations omitted) (emphasis in original). *See also* Berghorn v. Reorganized Sch. Dist. No. 8, 260 S.W.2d 573, 581–82 (Mo. 1953) (commenting that taxpayers could vindicate the public interest when there is an inherent injury).

Some states' highest courts explicitly or implicitly have rejected such a liberal "public interest" alternative standing doctrine. *See, e.g.*, *In re* Sandy Pappas Senate Comm., 488 N.W.2d 795, 797 (Minn. 1992); City of Chattanooga v. Davis, 54 S.W.3d 248, 280 (Tenn. 2001). Michigan's highest court, on the other hand, recently reaffirmed the appropriateness of such an approach. *See* Lansing Sch. Educ. Ass'n. v. Lansing Bd. of Educ., 792 N.W.2d 686, 689, 693 (Mich. 2010) (restoring a public-interest alternative standing standard, explaining "[t]here is no support in either the text of the Michigan Constitution or in Michigan jurisprudence … for recognizing standing as a constitutional requirement or for adopting the federal standing doctrine.").

16 *See, e.g.*, Cunningham v. Exon, 276 N.W.2d 213, 216 (Neb. 1979) (authorizing taxpayer standing to challenge the procedural validity and linguistic accuracy of an amendment to the state constitution regarding use of public funds for sectarian purposes partly because "[i]t is also obvious that if [Neb. Const. Art. 7, § 11] cannot be challenged by a citizen and taxpayer unless and until he has a special pecuniary interest or injury different from that of the public generally, it is entirely possible that no one may have standing to challenge it.").

17 *See, e.g.*, *id.* at 213; Saratoga Cnty. Chamber of Commerce, Inc. v. Pataki, 798 N.E.2d 1047, 1054 (N.Y. 2003) (denying standing would mean an important constitutional issue would be insulated from judicial review because no one would have standing to sue); Colella v. Bd. of Assessors of the Cnty. of Nassau, 741 N.E.2d 113, 117 (N.Y. 2000) (common law standing allows "taxpayers to challenge important government actions, despite such parties being otherwise insufficiently interested for standing purposes, when

state courts appreciate that the historic tradition of permitting local (municipal) taxpayer lawsuits at the state level, the express aim of fiscal limitation provisions in state constitutions to protect taxpayers against state government wrongfully or imprudently using public funds, and prudent public policy all support liberally according standing to state taxpayers who seek to challenge the constitutionality of government expenditures as a check on two of the most fundamental and far-reaching powers of governments, those of taxing and spending.[18] The permissive approach of these state courts also demonstrates, contrary to intimations by some Justices of the U.S. Supreme Court, that such judicial review can enhance rather than compromise the respective roles of the legislative and judicial branches in our democratic society.

New Mexico, on the other hand, exemplifies the danger of taxpayer preclusion. Since 1926, the New Mexico Supreme Court has not found "any legal or logical principle to support a taxpayer's suit to enjoin the expenditure of state funds, [so] we are constrained to hold that he has no such right in this state."[19] Thus, now after *Winn*, New Mexico's taxpayers apparently have no possibility of standing in *any* court to challenge the constitutionality of state tax expenditures for religiously-affiliated organizations, unless they somehow fit within all four narrow corners of the *Flast v. Cohen* exception discussed in Chapter 4.

Two possible trends in state taxpayer standing are discernible. On the one hand, it is conceivable that some state courts will retrench on permissible taxpayer standing in controversies involving challenges to tax expenditures under the First Amendment's Establishment Clause or state counterparts, particularly in the context of aid to religious education. A variety of forces might lead state courts to tighten standards for taxpayer standing: a popular and expanding school choice movement whose initiatives often may conflict with such constitutional provisions; reaction against an increased litigiousness over church-state issues; the lack of taxpayer access to federal courts that compels resort to state fora, resulting in unwelcome burgeoning case loads; and even the contentious politics of these potentially divisive matters from which state judiciaries are not immune. Despite important differences at the state and federal levels, "[s]tate courts tend to be influenced by federal standing principles …."[20] So for purposes of a state's own minimum constitutional standing requirements, a state's highest court might adopt Justice Anthony Kennedy's constricted logic in *Winn* by which he found the state

'the failure to accord such standing would be in effect to erect an impenetrable barrier to any judicial scrutiny of legislative action.'" [citation omitted]).

18 *See* Urquhart, *supra* note 10, at 1284–85, 1294–95, 1304–08.

19 Asplund v. Hannett, 249 P. 1074, 1083 (N.M. 1926). The New Mexico Supreme Court persistently has adhered to this rule against taxpayer standing. *See* Kuhn v. Burroughs, 342 P.2d 1086 (N.M. 1959); Miller v. Cooper, 244 P.2d 520 (N.M. 1952); Shipley v. Smith, 107 P.2d 1050 (N.M. 1940).

20 John C. Reitz, *Standing to Raise Constitutional Issues*, 50 AM. J. COMP. L. 437, 439 (2002).

taxpayer's injury and the causation and redressibility elements too speculative, attenuated, or inapplicable to warrant standing. Adoption of such a constraining tact by state courts would be most regrettable and troubling.

On the other hand, courts in those states that have provisions restricting state funding of religious institutions, in addition to a state anti-establishment clause, may be more amenable to granting taxpayer standing. This notion is supported by a recent empirical study which suggests that state constitutional fiscal limitations specifically constraining government taxing, spending, and borrowing powers are "a major impetus for the creation and development of permissive taxpayer standing doctrines ...."[21] The study theorizes that because such fiscal restrictions are intended to protect the broad class of state taxpayers as a whole, state courts are more permissive in granting taxpayer standing than in cases alleging violation of other constitutional provisions, such as general anti-establishment provisions.

Indeed, accompanying states' escalating implementation of primary and secondary school voucher, tax deduction, tax credit, and education savings programs, several state courts have granted taxpayers standing to contest those programs as violating state anti-establishment clauses or anti-funding provisions.[22] Arizona, a state for years at the forefront of the school choice movement, provides

---

21 Urquhart, *supra* note 10, at 1268. Mr. Urquhart's study does not focus specifically on Blaine Amendment types of provisions; rather it addresses the broad grouping of various constitutional fiscal restrictions on government taxing, spending, and borrowing powers. His theory is based on, and ties together, prior work by Professors Richard Briffault and Helen Hershkoff. *See* Richard Briffault, *Foreword: The Disfavored Constitution: State Fiscal Limits and State Constitutional Law*, 34 RUTGERS L.J. 907 (2003); Helen Hershkoff, *State Courts and the "Passive Virtues": Rethinking the Judicial Function*, 114 HARV. L. REV. 1833 (2001).

The authors of this book compiled and compared a list of states with anti-funding provisions to Mr. Urquhart's catalog of states with permissive taxpayer standing theoretically resulting from state constitutional fiscal limitations. The comparison reveals that seven of those permissive taxpayer standing states do not have constitutional anti-funding provisions, but more than 25 do. However, of the 14 states that Mr. Urquhart categorizes as either rejecting taxpayer standing or having an unclear taxpayer standing doctrine, 13 have some version of an anti-funding provision and only one does not.

22 *See, e.g.*, Toney v. Bower, 744 N.E.2d 351 (Ill. App. Ct. 2001) (allowing taxpayers to mount a constitutional challenge to the use of a tuition tax credit to fund sectarian schools, and concluding that this credit did not violate ILL. CONST. Art. 1, § 3 or Art. 10, § 3); Simmons-Harris v. Goff, 711 N.E.2d 203 (Ohio 1999) (permitting taxpayers to contest a Cleveland voucher scholarship program under Ohio's and the First Amendment's Establishment Clauses, but finding the program invalid because of a technical violation of the Ohio Constitution's one-subject rule that prohibits the creation of a substantive program in a general appropriation).

One noteworthy trend underlying states' treatment of taxpayer challenges under anti-funding provisions is the tendency of courts not to address the issue of taxpayer standing directly. Eleven states that have an anti-funding provision have not produced judicial determinations directly considering the availability of taxpayer standing. A number of these a prime example. In 1999, in *Kotterman v. Killian*, state taxpayers attacked the predecessor STO-tax credit statute to that in *Winn* but before the tax credit's effective date and prior to any contributions to STOs. Plaintiffs unsuccessfully argued the tax credit violated Arizona's Aid Clause (anti-funding provision) and Religion Clause (anti-establishment clause), as well as the First Amendment's Establishment Clause. The Arizona Supreme Court heard the case on its merits, assuming *sub silentio* the taxpayers' standing.[23] Ten years later, in *Cain v. Horne*, the Arizona Supreme Court expressly recognized taxpayers' standing to challenge under the state constitution statutory school voucher programs.[24] And most recently, in *Niehaus v. Huppenthal*, state taxpayers asserted that the "Arizona Empowerment Scholarship Accounts" program, establishing Education Savings Accounts ("ESAs"), violated the state Aid Clause and sought to enjoin the state Department of Education from disbursing government funds to pay tuition and fees of disabled students at secular and parochial schools.[25] Even after *Winn*, the court assumed taxpayer standing without discussion. Neither prudential concerns about judicial economy—rooted in dangers about opening litigation floodgates or rendering advisory opinions regarding constitutional matters—nor the state's separation of powers doctrine appears to have been a significant barrier to taxpayer standing in Arizona in any of the three cases.[26]

In the aftermath of *Winn* other state courts have been more inclined to explicitly address the issue of taxpayer standing in constitutional challenges to public funding mechanisms implementing school choice initiatives. For example, a school choice program implemented through a voucher system in Douglas County, Colorado, was opposed as a violation of that state's constitutional provisions, including

---

states (including Delaware, Massachusetts, and Michigan), however, typically have lenient rules regarding standing and even authorize the issuance of advisory opinions.

23 Kotterman v. Killian, 972 P.2d 606 (Ariz. 1999), *cert. denied*, 528 U.S. 921 (1999). For further discussion of *Kotterman*, see *infra* notes 30–41 and accompanying text. Similarly, *see, e.g.*, *Toney*, 744 N.E.2d at 351 (holding a state income tax credit used for qualified education expenses at sectarian schools was not the equivalent of a governmental "appropriation" or the use of "public money" under the plain meanings of these terms, and therefore such tax credit did not violate the anti-funding provision of Ill. Const. Art. 3, § 1 (1970)).

24 202 P.3d 1178, 1185 (Ariz. 2009).

25 310 P.3d 983 (Ariz. Ct. App. 2013), *review denied*, 2014 Ariz. LEXIS 59 (Ariz. Mar. 21, 2014). The court of appeals denied a request to block the Arizona program and then ruled against plaintiffs on the merits. *See infra* notes 45–46, and accompanying text.

26 Arizona's Constitution Article III provides: "[t]he powers of the government [shall] be divided into three separate departments, the legislative, the executive, and the judicial; … and no one of such departments shall exercise the powers properly belonging to either of the others." Arizona courts even have awarded attorneys' fees to taxpayer-litigants who have brought anti-funding provision actions "on behalf of the state." *See, e.g.*, *Cain*, 202 P.3d at 1185 (relying on Ariz. Rev. Stat. Ann. § 35–313 (2000), finding that the voucher program violated Arizona's Aid Clause, and holding that the plaintiffs must be reimbursed attorneys' fees in accordance with the statute).

anti-funding provisions. A Colorado appellate court in 2013 denied taxpayers standing, but the case is on appeal to the state's Supreme Court.[27] And in August 2014, the New Hampshire Supreme Court ruled that taxpayers lacked standing to challenge an STO-tax credit program under that state's anti-funding provision.[28] Also in 2013, Indiana taxpayers challenged a state school voucher program under three provisions of the state constitution—an education clause, a combination anti-establishment clause and anti-funding provision, and a second anti-funding provision. The Indiana Supreme Court conferred standing "under Indiana's public standing doctrine, an exception to the general [traditional three-prong standing] requirement."[29]

III. State Courts: Merits of Taxpayers' Challenges to the Use of Government Funds to Aid Religious Education

So through several decades of judicial review of various state-structured tax expenditures and tax-supported scholarships aiding parochial schools and other sectarian organizations, state courts often have been willing to rather liberally allow taxpayer standing to contest allegedly unconstitutional government assistance to religion. Of course, even if taxpayers succeed in securing standing, this does not mean that taxpayers should or will win on the merits of their claims. Arizona again provides a representative and particularly instructive case study of the possible approaches state courts may take in reviewing the merits of constitutional challenges to school aid plans.

In *Kotterman*, over a strong dissent the Arizona Supreme Court held that the early STO-tax credit program did not violate either the state constitution's Religion Clause, which mandates that "[n]o public money … shall be appropriated for or applied to any religious … instruction, or to the support of any religious establishment," or the state Aid Clause, which provides that "[n]o tax shall be laid or appropriation of public money made in aid of any church, or private or sectarian school, or any public service corporation."[30] Despite the specificity of these provisions that clearly seemed to preclude the STO-tax credit, the majority

---

27 Taxpayers for Pub. Educ. v. Douglas Cnty. Sch. Distr., 203 COA 20 (Colo. 2013), *cert. granted* 2014 Colo. LEXIS 176 (Mar. 17, 2014).

28 Duncan v. State, 2014 N.H. LEXIS 101 (holding that the pertinent state statute conferring standing violated the state constitution because it failed to require taxpayers to demonstrate their "personal rights were impaired or prejudiced" and allowed the court "to render advisory opinions to private individuals"). *Id.* at *22, *12.

29 *Meredith*, 984 N.E.2d at 1217 n.4 (citation omitted). *See infra* notes 47–53 and accompanying text.

30 Ariz. Const. Art. II, § 12 (Religion Clause), Art. IX, § 10 (Aid Clause). The court also ruled that the initiative did not violate Arizona Constitution, Art. IX, § 7, which directs the state to not "give or loan its credit in the aid of, or make any donation or grant, by subsidy or otherwise, to any individual, association, or corporation …." *Kotterman*, 972 P.2d at 606.

opinion seems to be the prequel to Justice Kennedy's opinion in *Winn* and its "untouched by government hands" approach. Although the "framers [of the Arizona provisions] opposed *direct* public funding of religion, including sectarian schools, we see no evidence of a similar concern for *indirect* benefits."[31] Taxpayers never actually "deposited [the funds] in the state treasury or other accounts under the management or possession of governmental agencies or public officials,"[32] so government could not make a direct payment to advance religion. Rather, similar to the reasoning a majority of the U.S. Supreme Court soon would utilize in *Zelman*,[33] the contributions to sectarian STOs were viewed as made, not by the state, but solely through the private, independent choices of taxpayers who then claimed the tax credit.

As for the Arizona legislature's use of its taxing power, the majority in *Kotterman* obtusely stated that, despite taking affirmative legislative action to impose an income tax on all taxpayers and then conferring the offsetting tax credit,

> … no tax has been laid here. To the contrary, this measure reduces the tax liability of those choosing to donate to STOs. We cannot say that the legislature has somehow imposed a tax by declining to collect potential revenue from its citizens. Nor does this credit amount to the laying of a tax by causing an increase in the tax liability of those not taking advantage of it. Such a construction tortures the plain meaning of the constitutional text.[34]

With regard to the legislature's spending power, the Arizona court exemplified the difficulty courts have in properly construing a tax expenditure. The majority maintained that, notwithstanding Arizona's annual budget reflecting the STO-tax credit as a tax expenditure,[35] "reducing a taxpayer's liability is [not] the equivalent of spending a certain sum of money. … [It is not an] appropriation [that] earmarks funds from 'the general revenue of the state' for an identified purpose or destination."[36] In other words, the STO-tax credit program was not an exercise of the Arizona legislature's taxing or spending powers for purposes of the state constitution's restrictions. The money attributable to the tax credit entirely

31 *Id.* at 619 (emphasis added).

32 *Id.* at 618. The court, however, acknowledged that its opinion did not comport with the tax expenditure concept relied upon by the legislature for budgetary purposes.

33 536 U.S. at 639. For a discussion of *Zelman*, *see* Chapter 2, Section IV. O.

34 *Kotterman*, 972 P.2d at 621.

35 *See, e.g.*, Ariz. Dep't of Revenue, Revenue Impact of Arizona's Tax Expenditures, Fiscal Year 2012, 54–55 (rev. prelim. 2013) *available at* http://www.azdor.gov/LinkClick.aspx?fileticket=NJj4xZIN_54%3d&tabid=108&mid=492 (the most recent tax expenditure budgetary information).

36 *Kotterman*, 972 P.2d at 620 (internal citation omitted). Other state courts have held similarly. *See, e.g.*, *Toney*, 744 N.E. 2d at 351.

circumvented the treasury, and thus no one was taxed and no public funds were spent by the government at all.[37]

Perhaps because the majority realized its reasoning was so counterintuitive, the court resorted to some more general principles it deemed relevant. The majority considered "'[t]he state constitutional provisions ... in light of contemporaneous assumptions concerning the appropriate sphere of action for each institution [church and state].'"[38] And in so doing, it concluded that "[t]here is no evidence ... that the framers intended to divorce completely any hint of religion from all conceivably state-related functions, nor would such a goal be realistically attainable in today's world."[39] Rather, because the framers of Arizona's Constitution took children's education "seriously," their intent not only should be respected but accorded decisive weight in interpreting Arizona's constitutional provisions in light of the modern school choice movement.[40] Moreover, with respect to the Aid Clause specifically, the majority briefly professed an inability "to divorce the amendment's language from the insidious [anti-Catholic] discriminatory intent that prompted it."[41] So the court essentially upended—one might say "tortured"—the plain language of the state constitution's Religion Clause and Aid Clause, seemingly crafting a means to obtain desired ends.

A decade later, however, with a substantially changed membership, the Arizona Supreme Court distinguished *Kotterman* in ruling on the merits of a taxpayers' lawsuit attacking Arizona's school voucher initiative under the state's Religion Clause and Aid Clause. Now, in *Cain*, the majority stated that "[u]nlike the funds in *Kotterman*, the funds at issue here are withdrawn from the public treasury and earmarked for an identified purpose," namely, reimbursing parochial schools for children's education expenses.[42] The court discerned a different and broader purpose for the Aid Clause than for the state's Religion Clause—that is, "to protect the public fisc and the public schools" by "prohibiting appropriation of funds from the public treasury to private schools."[43] And here the court was not distracted by the indirectness of the funding mechanism or the involvement of parents:

> For all intents and purposes, the voucher programs do precisely what the Aid Clause prohibits. These programs transfer state funds directly from the state

37 *Kotterman*, 972 P.2d at 618 (looking to the dictionary for the plain meaning of "tax credit").

38 *Id.* at 622 (internal citation omitted).

39 *Id.* at 623.

40 *Id.*

41 *Id.* at 624. The majority apparently was attempting to undercut the dissent's intense focus on "Arizona's Blaine Amendment clauses [as] contain[ing] a stringent proscription on educational aid, forbidding state aid to all private schools, sectarian or secular." *Id.* at 633 (Feldman, J., dissenting).

42 *Cain*, 202 P.3d at 1183.

43 *Id.* at 1182, 1183.

> treasury to private schools. That the checks or warrants first pass through the hands of parents [to be endorsed] is immaterial; once a pupil has been accepted into a qualified school under either program, the parents or guardians have no choice; they must endorse the check or warrant to the qualified school. Thus, given the composition of these voucher programs, applying the true [child] beneficiary theory exception would nullify the Aid Clause's clear prohibition against the use of public funds to aid private or sectarian education.[44]

Most recently, in *Niehaus*, Arizona taxpayers alleged that the "Arizona Empowerment Scholarship Accounts" program violates the state Religion Clause and Aid Clause. In October, 2013, the Arizona court of appeals applied a standard of review that requires "[t]he party challenging the validity of the statute … [to prove] beyond a reasonable doubt that the legislation is unconstitutional"[45]—a demanding standard not applied by the Arizona Supreme Court in *Cain*. The appellate court found that the state funds were appropriated by the state, not ineluctably for parochial schools, but instead for the beneficiary families, who were the "specified objects" of the appropriations, which they could choose to use for parochial school tuition or various other educational-related services.[46] So here the appellate court essentially applied "the true beneficiary exception" to avoid the scope of the state's Aid Clause, and the Arizona Supreme Court declined to review the case.

Arizona is not the only jurisdiction producing essentially *ad hoc* decisions that are difficult to reconcile with language of a state constitution that is often far more specific and preclusive of state aid to parochial education than the sparse words of the First Amendment's Establishment Clause. In the recent case of *Meredith v. Pence*,[47] Indiana taxpayers challenged a state school voucher program under multiple constitutional provisions—a uniform education clause, a combination anti-establishment clause and anti-funding provision, and a second anti-funding provision.[48] The Indiana Supreme Court ruled that the voucher program did not violate any of the three despite the program's lack of constraints on participating

---

44 *Id.* at 1184 (citations omitted). *See supra* note 4 (regarding the concerns of the Arizona constitution's framers in maintaining the integrity of the public schools).

45 *Niehaus*, 310 P.3d at 985, *review denied*, 2014 Ariz. LEXIS 59 (Ariz. Mar. 21, 2014).

46 *Id.* at 987 (internal citation omitted).

47 984 N.E.2d 1213 (Ind. 2013).

48 The Indiana Constitution clauses provide:

[Article 8,] Section 1 [Uniformity Clause]. … [I]t shall be the duty of the General Assembly … to provide, by law, for a general and uniform system of Common Schools, wherein tuition shall be without charge, and equally open to all.

[Article 1,] Section 4 [Combined anti-establishment clause and anti-funding provision]. No preference shall be given, by law, to any creed, religious society, …; and no person shall be compelled to … support, any place of worship, or to maintain any ministry, against his consent.

private schools' pedagogy or the absence of any requirements for use of subsidized tuition funds for purely secular components of their operations. In other words, participating parochial schools could teach all curricular subjects through a religious perspective and use the state tuition money for purely religious elements of their operations.

The court noted that the voucher program ostensibly leaves the makeup and availability of public, traditional and charter schools intact, so the state satisfied its constitutional "duty to provide for a general and uniform system of open common schools without tuition."[49] Moreover, the framers of the state constitution intended the combined anti-establishment clause and anti-funding provision to be a restraint only on "government compulsion of individuals to engage in religious practices [worship, not schooling] absent their consent;" it was "neither intended nor understood to limit government expenditures, which is addressed by [the separate anti-funding provision]."[50] And the separate prohibition against funds being "drawn from the treasury, for the benefit of any religious or theological institution," applies only to government expenditures that *directly* benefit such institutions.[51] Here, once again, a court used reasoning analogous to that of the Supreme Court in *Zelman*—that is, the direct beneficiaries were the lower-income "families of eligible students. ... The voucher program does not directly fund religious activities because *no* funds may be dispersed *to any* program-eligible school without the *private, independent selection by the parents of a program-eligible student.*"[52] The court concluded that,

---

[Article 1,] Section 6 [Anti-funding provision]. No money shall be drawn from the treasury, for the benefit of any religious or theological institution.

49 *Meredith*, 984 N.E.2d at 1221. The court commented that "a significant number of students [up to 60 percent] *may* be eligible for the voucher program," but not all, so even with maximum participation "[t]he school voucher program does not replace the public school system, which remains in place and available to all Indiana schoolchildren ...." *Id.* at 1222–23 (emphasis in original). Additionally, invoking separation of powers the court interpreted the additional Article 8, § 1 obligation of the legislature to "encourage" knowledge and learning by "all suitable means ..." as a separate aspirational provision as to which the legislature had exclusive power and discretion. *Id.* at 1222.

50 *Id.* at 1226.

51 *Id.* at 1227 (referring to Ind. Const. Art. 1, § 6).

52 *Id.* at 1229–30 (emphasis in original). "The voucher program helps alleviate [an economic] barrier by providing lower-income Indiana families with the educational options generally available primarily to higher-income Indiana families." *Id.* at 1229. The court, however, overlooked the economic criteria for student eligibility, which could include some more middle-class children. That the vouchers can be used at some program-eligible schools that discriminate in admissions based on religion appeared irrelevant to the court's entire analysis. *Id.* at 1213. Yet, as discussed in Chapter 2, the voucher program in *Zelman* was quite narrow, but the *Meredith* court took no heed of this.

> in light of the prevailing social, cultural, and legal circumstances when Indiana's Constitution was enacted [in 1851], we understand [the separate anti-funding provision] as not intended to prohibit government support of primary and secondary education which at the time included a substantial religious component. This interpretation is consistent with the presumption of constitutionality which we apply when reviewing a claim of statutory unconstitutionality.[53]

In contrast to Arizona and Indiana, a Florida appeals court found that Florida's constitution, which provides that "[n]o revenue of the state or any political subdivision or agency thereof shall be taken from the public treasury directly or indirectly in aid of any church, sect, or religious denomination or in aid of any sectarian institution," means that "[a]n indirect or secondary benefit to sectarian institutions from the use of state funds would be sufficient to violate the provision."[54] The child benefit theory therefore did not save the challenged school tuition voucher program under this Florida anti-funding provision. Rather, the court interpreted the broad constitutional language as prohibiting money from the state treasury from being used for, and ultimately paid to, sectarian schools despite the state voucher program giving "parents and guardians a choice as to which school to apply a tuition voucher [sic]" and providing the "parents must restrictively endorse the voucher to the school …."[55] Upon review the Florida Supreme Court declined to reach the issue of the voucher program's constitutionality under the anti-funding provision. Instead, the higher court found that the voucher program violated the state constitution's "uniformity provision," which requires Florida to provide an adequate system of free public schools to all children. This requirement was violated because the voucher program diverted public funds to private schools, thereby reducing funding and making education non-uniform across all publicly supported schools.[56]

Thus, not surprisingly, state high courts take divergent approaches in interpreting their state constitutions' anti-establishment clauses and anti-funding provisions. Some use questionable reasoning when reaching the substance of taxpayers' claims where government financial support "indirectly" reaches parochial schools and other religiously-oriented education providers. The trend may be for these courts to assume a permissive approach to their states' more specific anti-establishment and anti-funding provisions even though the U.S. Supreme Court has approved on the merits under the Establishment Clause only relatively narrow and limited school aid programs.

Ordinarily, experimentation among the states might be welcomed on social policies such as school reform; indeed Justice Louis Brandeis once famously

---

53 *Id.* at 1230.

54 Bush v. Holmes, 886 So.2d 340, 352 (Fla. Dist. Ct. App. 2004), *aff'd. on other grounds by* 919 So.2d 392 (Fla. 2006) (interpreting Fla. Const. Art. I, § 3).

55 *Bush*, 886 So.2d at 352.

56 *Bush*, 919 So.2d at 392.

lauded the availability of a state to serve as a "laboratory" for experiment on social and economic policies.[57] When the experiment, however, threatens to compromise fundamental constitutional rights, especially liberty of conscience protected by anti-establishment and anti-funding provisions, the scope of permissible experiment should be far more constrained.[58] Americans would not favor a system of freedom of expression in which states were free to experiment with different levels of censorship of political speech; rather, all depend on U.S. Supreme Court review to restrain any state suppressing free speech. This unifying force is now largely missing with new programs of state aid to private, religious education. After *Winn*, state courts can provide individualized roadmaps for their legislatures easily to structure constitutionally "acceptable" programs that fund religiously-affiliated schools. In doing so they effectively may reduce the force, may narrow the meanings, and may constrict the spirit of state anti-funding and state anti-establishment provisions. Challengers to such programs may find success on the merits elusive, but they at least should be heard fully on fundamental matters of liberty of conscience. We therefore urge that state legislatures, at a minimum, should remove an uncertain and unnecessary impediment by statutorily mandating taxpayer, or more generally citizen, standing in this area.

IV. Legislating Taxpayer Standing

Although a majority of states permit taxpayer standing, it would be an overstatement that nearly all assure taxpayers may sue in that capacity in state court to challenge allegedly unconstitutional state taxing and spending that result in financial aid reaching religiously-affiliated organizations.[59] And of those states that have permitted taxpayer standing to bring such lawsuits, this often occurs only by virtue of judicial discretion. Very few states have explicit statutes governing taxpayer standing, although state legislatures generally are free to provide for it. Of those states with express statutes, most provide specific qualifiers. Massachusetts, for example, requires a minimum number of taxpayer-plaintiffs from several different counties.[60] Several states permit taxpayers to bring "derivative" lawsuits pursuant to which taxpayers essentially stand in the shoes of the attorney general. For instance, Arizona provides that any state taxpayer may request the attorney general to institute a lawsuit "in the name of the state to enjoin the illegal payment of public monies, … or if the monies have been paid, to recover such monies …,"

---

57 New State Ice Co. v. Liebmann, 285 U.S. 262, 311 (U.S. 1932) (Brandeis, J., dissenting).

58 *Compare* Boy Scouts of Am. v. Dale, 530 U.S. 640, 660–61 (2000) (majority opinion) *with id.* at 664 (Stevens, J., dissenting) (debating the applicability of Justice Brandeis' advocacy of state experimentation to First Amendment issues).

59 *See* Urquhart, *supra* note 10, at 1277.

60 Mass. Gen. Laws ch. 29, § 63 (2012).

and, if the attorney general does not do so within 60 days of the request, the taxpayer "may institute the action in his own name ... with the same effect as if brought by the attorney general."[61]

So, state legislatures can and should devise explicit taxpayer standing statutes with appropriate qualifiers. They could formulate statutes with the specific purpose and intent to confer taxpayer standing to contest purported violations of state constitutional provisions, importantly including a state's anti-establishment clause and its anti-funding provisions. In particular, these affirmative assurances of standing should include government's use of its taxing and spending power for school choice initiatives that result in taxpayer money flowing directly or indirectly to, or for the benefit of, sectarian institutions providing scholarships, parochial schools, religiously-affiliated private education providers, charter schools with religious traits, or the like. Without unduly opening the courthouse doors to all sorts of taxpayer lawsuits, such a targeted statute, like the *Flast* exception in its initial formulation, would provide numerous benefits.

First, it could ensure taxpayers who incur "merely" a "generalized injury," even mainly "Psychic Injury," an opportunity to adjudicate the merits of their constitutional grievances against government aid to religiously-affiliated organizations or religious interests. It also would eliminate the need for courts to interpret their state standing doctrine liberally on a case-by-case basis, as some do now, if they determine a plaintiff is an appropriate party to vindicate a common public interest in the proper use of tax funds, or if no one else may have standing to contest the government's use of public funds that reach religiously-imbued organizations. Moreover, a specific taxpayer standing statute would eliminate uncertainty, promote judicial efficiency, and assure the availability of an important check on legislative excess. As an additional benefit, courts, unlike legislatures, must explain publicly their decisions and advance plausible rationales. Full judicial consideration of the constitutionality of legislative initiatives enhances the integrity of those provisions that survive such scrutiny, even among unsuccessful opponents who at least will have been able to fully air their objections in a politically more neutral forum. The increased transparency and accountability from judicial review thus may promote greater public acceptance. Therefore, we recommend that state legislatures, aware of the political pressures that influence their work and of their own fallibility, assure taxpayer standing.

V. Legislating Sunset Provisions

As discussed in Chapter 3, statutory tax concessions are often permanent and not repeatedly publicly debated. In contrast to overt legislative appropriations, tax provisions too easily mask the nature and extent of the financial assistance they provide, the identities of direct and indirect beneficiaries, and the magnitude

61 Ariz. Rev. Stat. Ann. §§ 35–212(A), 35–213(A) (2012).

of subsidization they offer. Moreover, once extended it is often difficult to affirmatively retract a tax benefit to which various interest groups have become accustomed and on which they purport to rely. To avoid these more hidden and entrenched effects of tax measures, statutes providing tax support for school choice options should contain automatic sunset provisions. Legislatures and the public should measure the effects over time of any program—how much money actually is diverted from public schools, with what effects on public and private education, and how much state money in both absolute and percentage terms actually is used to support religious education. Public perceptions of, and attitudes toward, both public and private, parochial and secular education may change over time and so too the need for, and desirability of, government aid reaching private schools and other nonpublic education providers. In recently upholding, over vigorous dissents, the practice of a town board opening its official meetings with a sectarian prayer, the Supreme Court's "fact-sensitive" analysis specifically allows federal courts to "remain free to review the pattern of prayers over time to determine whether they comport" with applicable constitutional principles.[62] Yet, after *Winn*, federal courts no longer may perform the analogous function in taxpayer suits over school aid, making it all the more imperative that state legislatures do so.

Sunset provisions inherently would foster greater visibility and legislative accountability. Requiring legislatures periodically to consider positive renewal of the tax accommodations likely would raise public awareness and discussion of these tax subsidies and their financial and related consequences. Moreover, sunset provisions could restrain legislative impulses to succumb quietly to interest groups' pressures. In short, such provisions could induce government officials and the public they represent to engage in ongoing cost/benefit analyses—in terms of financial, social, and constitutional interests—that might not be undertaken without these statutory mandates. Legislatures would need to act prospectively enough so that any changes could be phased in over time without disrupting legitimate reliance interests. But with this caveat, we urge that any tax concessions designed to support private, primary and secondary education be accompanied by appropriate sunset provisions.

VI. Means-Testing and Limiting Financial Incentives: A Balancing Approach

Much First Amendment jurisprudence consists of a balancing approach, albeit with considerable deference afforded the fundamental interests protected. Any content-based government restriction on pure, protected speech, for example, is presumptively unconstitutional and must survive strict judicial scrutiny. The government must demonstrate that its regulation is narrowly tailored to promote a

62 Town of Greece v. Galloway, 134 S. Ct. 1811, 1825, 1826–27, 1838, 1851 (2014) (plurality and dissenting opinions).

compelling interest that could not be met by a less speech restrictive alternative.[63] A regulation of expressive or symbolic conduct such as nude dancing, however, can survive under intermediate scrutiny if it furthers an important government interest unrelated to the suppression of expression, with restrictions that are no greater than essential to achieve that end.[64] And when, in 1990, the Supreme Court shifted away from strict scrutiny of government regulations that impinge on an individual's free exercise of religion, Congress forcefully restored (to the extent of its constitutional power to do so) that demanding standard in the Religious Freedom Restoration Act of 1993 ("RFRA").[65] All of these methods of analysis are weighted balancing approaches.

In contrast, "Establishment Clause violations ... are usually flatly forbidden without reference to the strength of governmental purposes."[66] The Supreme Court, of course, has developed tests—the controversial *Lemon* test and its modifications, for example—for considering what action constitutes a government establishment of religion. Applying some of the *Lemon* test components implicitly may involve elements of balancing. But a law that has the purpose or effect of promoting religion generally will be considered invalid without explicit consideration of the strength of the government's interest purportedly being advanced, the nature or degree of intrusion upon separation of church and state, or the available alternatives.

However difficult it might be for a court to engage in overt balancing in evaluating an Establishment Clause claim, a legislature is well situated to do so. Indeed, legislating is all about balancing competing interests and claims. We propose that legislatures do exactly this when fashioning schemes that aid religious education and that they do not simply capitulate to a popular school choice movement or other special interest. For example, as suggested in Chapter 2 in discussing the *McCollum v. Board of Education* and *Zorach v. Clauson* cases involving release time from public school for religious education, the rationale advanced for using the power and prestige of state machinery to assist parents in compelling their children to attend religious schools, or making it more convenient, seems extraordinarily weak. Parents must take responsibility for their children's educations, secular and religious; if religious instruction is sufficiently important

63 *See, e.g.*, United States v. Playboy Entm't Group, 529 U.S. 803 (2000).

64 *See, e.g.*, City of Erie v. Pap's A.M., 529 U.S. 277 (2000).

65 134 S.Ct. 2751, 2792 (2014) (codified as 42 U.S.C. §§ 2000bb-2000bb-4), reacting to Employment Div., Dep't of Human Resources v. Smith, 494 U.S. 872 (1990). As for balancing in free exercise matters generally, *see* Douglas Laycock, *The Religious Exemption Debate*, 11 Rutgers J. Law & Relig. 139 (2009). The Roberts Court currently is split on whether Congress intended RFRA "only to restore, not to scrap or alter, the balancing text as this Court had applied it pre-*Smith*." Burwell v. Hobby Lobby Stores, Inc., 134 S. Ct. 2751, 2792 (2014) (Ginsburg, J., dissenting).

66 Colo. Christian Univ. v. Weaver, 534 F.3d 1245, 1266 (10th Cir. 2008) (opinion of Judge Michael W. McConnell). *See also* Frederick Mar Gedicks, *Incorporation of the Establishment Clause Against the States: A Logical, Textual, and Historical Account*, 88 Ind. L.J. 669 (2013).

to them they should see to it that their children receive that education without relying on the state. In comparing and balancing parents' interests in religious instruction for their children against state-supported release time programs with the inevitable, adverse effects of stigma, pressure, and symbolic union of church and state, it should be fairly easy for a legislature to resist the impetus to establish such a program. The New York legislature similarly should have resisted the political pressure to engage in "religious gerrymandering," creating the problem in *Board of Education of Kiryas Joel Village School District v. Grumet*,[67] simply to shield children within an insular religious community from secular contact that would have required no compromise of religious beliefs or practices.

By contrast, providing quality primary and secondary education for children obviously is a government interest of a significantly greater magnitude. Nonetheless, we suggest that in at least two complementary respects legislatures should carefully weigh competing interests in devising tax mechanisms that divert public funds to private schools, especially parochial schools, and religiously-affiliated education providers. The purpose of aiding these alternative education programs should be simply to advance the interest in quality education and address real inadequacies in current public school systems. Legislatures should not imperil constitutional principle and weaken public schools by promoting school choice simply for the sake of some abstract idea of choice, however popular, and divorced from the actual needs of children. And in meeting these imperative needs, legislatures should act in a way that is least intrusive upon fundamental Establishment Clause values.

First, therefore, government aid for alternative educational opportunities should be means-tested—that is, targeted to benefit low-income, educationally-disadvantaged children. It should not subsidize children from more affluent families, many of whom otherwise could afford to pay private school tuition, fees of private education providers, and other education expenses without government financial assistance. Original tuition voucher plans, such as the Ohio plan in *Zelman*, were restricted appropriately to the first category of children, and these are the only such plans the Supreme Court actually has sustained. But with time, boldness, and innovations some legislatures have extended several school choice initiatives to cover even the second group. States tend to begin with modest, narrow plans, gain approval for the concept, and then expand. For example, as noted in Chapter 1, wealthier children now are eligible for the Douglas County, Colorado, voucher program. And Arizona's legislature has enlarged its ESA program's reach and appears to have great latitude to continue to do so after *Niehaus*.[68] Such broadly available assistance easily could impact adversely the welfare of public school systems and the ability to develop and maintain pluralistic student bodies at public schools. Perhaps to avoid some criticism, Arizona's STO-tax credit program now statutorily provides the vague guideline that STOs "[s]hall consider

67 512 U.S. 687, 729 (1994) (Kennedy, J. concurring in judgment).

68 *See supra* nn.25 & 46–47; Chapter 1, nn.210–12;.

the financial need of applicants" in evaluating and awarding scholarships.[69] But this is merely hortatory; there is no statutory minimum percentage or aggregate dollar amount of scholarships that a STO must award to low-income students. The public, especially contributors, well understand that STOs are free to grant scholarships not exclusively to needy students.[70]

Tax-supported school choice programs also should limit the financial benefits potentially realizable by participating taxpayers. As discussed in Chapter 3, legislatures can create generous financial incentives by the types and characteristics of the tax mechanisms they make available to support these initiatives. For example, tax credits can provide greater monetary benefits than tax deductions; refundable tax credits can result in financial gains unavailable with non-refundable tax credits. And some programs allow dual tax advantages, such as the state and federal income tax exclusions likely available for Arizona's ESA initiative. Moreover, the magnitude of a tax deduction, tax credit, or other tax mechanism can impact greatly the extent of a taxpayer's financial incentive.[71] For example, Arizona's, Georgia's, and Florida's STO-tax credit programs provide claimant taxpayers a 100 percent tax credit—for every dollar contributed (up to a maximum amount), a dollar tax credit is available. Other states provide more modest tax credits for such donations, worth between 50 percent and 95 percent of the amount contributed.

As discussed in Chapters 2 and 3, the greater the financial incentive for a taxpayer to direct tuition voucher funds or other government aid to private, secular or parochial schools (or other religiously-affiliated entities), the inherent, realistic nature of the program—under which statistically religious institutions are the predominant beneficiaries—makes it more likely that government is inappropriately subsidizing religion.[72] It is one thing if a state designs its initiative

---

69 Ariz. Rev. Stat. Ann. § 43–1603(D)(2) (2013). Each STO must annually report to the state Department of Revenue the total dollar amount of scholarships and grants awarded to low-income children and those above the established low-income level. But the statutory authority of the Department to ensure ongoing certification of an STO does not require the Department take into account whether an STO has considered the financial need of applicant students. *Id.* at §§ 43–1604; 43–1602.

70 For contributors to qualify for the tax credit, their contributions cannot be earmarked for specific student applicants. *Id.* at §§ 43–1089(F); 43–1089.03(F). Nonetheless, because 90 percent of the annual contributions it receives must be disbursed as scholarships, if an STO is well-endowed a student applicant has an increased probability of receiving scholarship money regardless of financial need. *Id.* at § 43–1603(B)(1).

71 A tax deduction can be available with or without an offsetting "floor." For example, some deductions are available only after an individual itemizing taxpayer's relevant expenditures exceed 2 percent of adjusted gross income, while others are available with respect to all pertinent expenditures without offset.

72 *See Zelman*, 536 U.S. at 653 (upholding a program of tuition vouchers but distinguishing a tuition subsidy program that could create an inappropriate financial incentive); Witters v. Wash. Dep't of Servs. for the Blind, 474 U.S. 481, 487–88 (1986)

just to take some of the financial "edge" off parents of educationally-disadvantaged children who want to send them to private school while still paying taxes to support public schools. It is far more constitutionally serious for a state to relieve a significant portion of the financial sacrifice such a parent should bear to substitute private, religiously-oriented schooling for available public education, especially if the latter is perfectly adequate and even high quality.

State legislatures therefore should structure school choice initiatives—be it for contributions to STOs or another type of program—with tax mechanisms formulated in a nuanced manner to allow only a calibrated, appropriate level of financial benefit to those most in need. And legislatures should be specifically mindful that wealthier taxpayers may be unwarrantedly advantaged by participating in some of these tax-structured programs, thus accentuating their seeming inappropriateness.

VII. A Basic Religious Non-Discrimination Principle

In *Mitchell v. Helms*, discussed in Chapter 2, a plurality of the Supreme Court sought to minimize the constitutional problems of government support for religion where state aid reaches or benefits private, parochial schools "even [if it is] 'direct aid,' [as long as it] is neutrally available, and … first passes through the hands (literally or figuratively) of numerous private citizens who are free to direct the aid …."[73] Justice Sandra Day O'Connor's controlling opinion, concurring in the judgment, refused to go so far. She reiterated the long-standing concern of the Court that state aid, even when determined on a per student basis and thus flowing because of student choices to attend certain schools, should not be available for teaching or promoting religious views, for "religious indoctrination," for "advanc[ing] the religious missions of the recipient schools," or for "financ[ing] [their] religious activities."[74] One central problem with tax mechanisms and vouchers that subsidize tuition is that they enable students to attend the school itself; thus, such funds help expose those students to all aspects of the school's educational program, including any religious instruction, indoctrination, or mission.

Still, *Mitchell* opened the door for the Court in *Zelman* to hold constitutional a program of tax-supported funds paid by Ohio to parochial schools as a result of parents' independent choices to use state-issued tuition vouchers to enroll

(financial incentives can skew a government program so that it is not neutral toward religion); Comm. for Pub. Educ. & Religious Liberty v. Nyquist, 413 U.S. 756, 783, 790 (1973) (state aid for education was not neutral toward religion because the statute allowed tax benefits to parents of students in parochial schools "unrelated to the amount of money actually expended by any parent on tuition" and "unmistakably … provide[d] desired financial support for nonpublic, sectarian institutions").

73 530 U.S. 793, 816 (2000) (plurality opinion).

74 *Id.* at 840–41 (O'Connor, J., concurring in judgment).

their children in such schools.[75] In *Zelman*, however, little noticed by some, state law mandated that the government assistance could not reach any private, secular or parochial school unless the school adopted a broad and encompassing nondiscrimination admissions provision, including nondiscrimination based on religion.[76]

Our proposal builds upon this aspect of *Zelman* and is grounded in both the First Amendment's Religion Clauses and the Fourteenth Amendment's Equal Protection Clause. For compelling reasons, we offer what perhaps is our most contentious recommendation, one on which we would expect much discussion and debate by legislators, education providers, and the public.[77] In order to qualify to participate in any school choice program for which the government subsidizes student tuition, private, secular and parochial schools should be required to adopt, and adhere to, student admissions policies and practices that do not discriminate on the basis of religion.

State and federal laws require public schools, including culture-oriented charter schools with a religious character, such as those discussed in Chapter 1, to admit students regardless of religion. On the other hand, as a general matter private, secular and parochial schools are not subject to such nondiscrimination strictures for student admissions. Strong public policy, however, argues in favor of state laws mandating a religion-based nondiscrimination student admissions condition on private, secular and parochial schools in order for them to participate in tax-supported school choice programs.

Overt discrimination by private schools, whether based on race, ethnicity, sexual orientation, or religion, is harmful to students and to a robust civil society. Such discrimination in schooling simply accentuates the problems of discrimination in the broader society. This principle is well recognized and not just with respect to racial discrimination. Although "a private school—even one that discriminates—fulfills an important educational function … [that] legitimate educational function cannot be isolated from discriminatory practices … [D]iscriminatory treatment exerts a pervasive influence on the entire educational process."[78] Whether at the primary, secondary, or post-secondary school level, the "process of learning occurs both formally in a classroom setting and informally outside of it. … Students may be

75 *Zelman*, 536 U.S. at 639.

76 *See infra* note 87 and accompanying text.

77 Indeed, such debate is precisely what U.S. Senator Lamar Alexander, a former U.S. Secretary of Education, may engender from submitting a bill to provide federal funding to supplement educational opportunities for low-income children at eligible public or private, secular and parochial schools if such education providers "agree not to discriminate against program participants or applicants on the basis of race, color … religion or sex." S. 1968, 113th Cong., 2d Sess. § 3(f)(1) (2014).

78 Norwood v. Harrison, 413 U.S. 455, 468–69 (1973) (invalidating state loans of textbooks to children attending private schools with racially discriminatory admissions policies).

shaped as profoundly by their peers as by their teachers. … [The education process] facilitate[s] interactions between students, enabling them to explore new points of view, to develop interests and talents, and to nurture a growing sense of self."[79] "[A] great deal of learning occurs informally … through interactions among students of … different races, religions, and backgrounds … who are able, directly or indirectly, to learn from their differences and to stimulate one another to reexamine even their most deeply held assumptions about themselves and their world."[80] And "[a] vibrant [pluralistic] dialogue is not possible if students [are] wall[ed] … off from opposing points of view."[81] In short, discrimination policies and practices in student admissions by educational institutions do not "encourage[] tolerance, cooperation, and learning among students."[82] On the other hand, nondiscrimination policies do promote and foster tolerance, cooperation, civility, and learning by students individually and collectively.

It is not sufficient that private schools participating in a state school choice initiative are diverse in the aggregate; singularly each private school that insulates its student body through discriminatory admission policies is at odds with students learning values long considered crucial to a strong democracy and healthy civil society. To permit participating private parochial (or secular) schools to discriminate in student admissions would exact a considerable cost even long after a child's primary and secondary education is completed. As a result of a less diverse and enlightened educational experience, individuals may approach others in society and the world with intolerance and disdain; they may be set in their beliefs of one version of the "truth" and not accepting of diverse viewpoints; they may be limited by insular thinking in daily life, closing themselves off from opportunities and opening themselves to harsh opposition; and they may find themselves contributing less productively to civil society than if they had been exposed to broader perspectives early in life. Whatever debate there might be on these matters, a state may and should promote pluralism and diversity in the children's private educations it substantially subsidizes through targeted programs.

In the twenty-first century one easily accepts a broad principle and social policy of nondiscrimination in education on most bases. Some, however, may maintain that surely religion must be treated differently, even when directed tax benefits underwrite children's religious education. A central component of the entire *raison d'être* of a parochial school, after all, is its religious mission—to instruct, foster, indoctrinate, and promote its religious views and values along intellectual, moral

79 Christian Legal Soc'y Chapter of the Univ. of Cal. v. Martinez, 130 S. Ct. 2971, 2999 (2010) (Kennedy, J., concurring) (citations omitted) (regarding religious discrimination in membership of student organization).

80 Regents of Univ. of Cal. v. Bakke, 438 U.S. 265, 312 n.48 (1978) (quoting President Bowen of Princeton University, *Admissions and the Relevance of Race*, Princeton Alumni Weekly 7, 9 (Sept. 26, 1977)).

81 *Martinez*, 130 S. Ct. at 3000 (Kennedy, J., concurring).

82 *Id.* at 2990 (majority opinion).

and spiritual planes of its young students' lives. Thus it seems incongruous to maintain that the state can tell a religious organization, especially a school, that it cannot discriminate on the basis of religion. This certainly is true along numerous dimensions. Government certainly cannot insist that a house of worship not discriminate in its membership on the basis of religion. But the proposition is too general to apply to a parochial school that wants to benefit from targeted state aid that significantly subsidizes the tuition it charges which therefore is responsible for many students attending the school.[83]

To be very clear, in proposing a condition of religious nondiscrimination in student admissions we are not suggesting that a participating parochial school should not be able to maintain its essential religious character and identity and promote its religious mission. That would be wrong and self-defeating. The Supreme Court, for example, has long recognized that parochial schools are "an integral part of the religious mission of the Catholic Church ... [and] a powerful vehicle for transmitting the Catholic faith to the next generation. ... [T]his process of inculcating religious doctrine is, of course, enhanced by the impressionable age of the pupils, in primary schools particularly."[84] But even a pervasively sectarian parochial school—be it a Catholic academy, an Orthodox yeshiva, or an Islamic madrassa—can admit some students of other faiths without compromising its essential religious character while gaining the benefits of diversity and pluralism; there is unlikely to be a "significant" adverse effect.[85] Any parochial school that is so insular to believe it would be truly threatened by opening itself to some non-adherents can simply opt out of participating in the state subsidy program.

A parochial school with an announced sectarian mission will be attractive mainly to parents and students of its faith regardless of its admissions policy. Most will choose the school because of its denominational affiliation; others will be indifferent and will accept the religious component of the school because of the

---

83 In *Martinez*, 130 S. Ct. at 2971, the Court upheld a public law school's "accept-all-comers" policy regarding membership in student organizations that precluded a chapter of the Christian Legal Society from excluding students who do not share the Society's core religious beliefs. In his concurrence, Justice John Paul Stevens characterized the dissent's view of the university policy as: "by proscribing unlawful discrimination on the basis of religion, the policy discriminates unlawfully on the basis of religion." He immediately added: "There are numerous reasons why this counterintuitive theory is unsound." *Id.* at 2996 (Stevens, J., concurring).

84 Lemon v. Kurtzman, 403 U.S. 602, 616 (1971) (footnote omitted). *See also* Meek v. Pittenger, 421 U.S. 349, 366 (1975) (*overruled by Mitchell*, 530 U.S. at 793) (commenting that parochial schools' secular and religious instruction is "devoted to the inculcation of religious values and belief"); Bd. of Educ. v. Allen, 392 U.S. 236, 245 (1968) ("[R]eligious schools pursue two goals, religious instruction and secular education.").

85 *See Dale*, 530 U.S. at 648; *see also* Runyon v. McCrary, 427 U.S. 160, 176 (1976) (quoting McCrary v. Runyon, 515 F.2d 1082, 1087 (4th Cir. 1975), where the court minimized the effects on a racially segregated private school's teaching of "ideas or dogma" from it being required to admit racial minorities).

many benefits provided by its secular education. The overwhelming number of students seeking admission to a parochial school therefore is highly likely to be quite willing to conform to its religious tradition and practices. There may be some students, of course, who are attracted to a particular parochial school because of the unique quality of its overall educational milieu but who adhere to a different faith, or no faith at all, and would prefer to avoid the more sectarian aspects of its environment. The prospect that a parochial school will be inundated by so many such applicants as to threaten its core religious identity, however, is quite doubtful. As the Supreme Court said in *Christian Legal Society Chapter of the University of California v. Martinez*, addressing a Hastings College of Law nondiscrimination policy requiring a student religious group to follow the school's open "all-comers" membership policy, the concern is more "hypothetical than real" and not a basis for invalidating the policy.[86] For over a decade, the parochial schools participating in the Ohio voucher program upheld in *Zelman* have been required to not "discriminate on the basis of race, religion, or ethnic background" and not "teach hatred of any person or group on the basis of race, ethnicity, national origin, or religion."[87] This condition does not appear to significantly inhibit or preclude parochial school participation; indeed a strong majority of the participating Cleveland schools are Catholic.[88]

In order to assure that a parochial school is not in fact discriminating in admissions on the basis of religion by discouraging potential applicants outside the faith, despite a stated policy otherwise, the school would need to offer some minor, reasonable accommodations to those who wish to attend but distance themselves from the school's most highly religious aspects. By making appropriate accommodations for such enrolled students, who would have to accept their obvious minority status as partial "outsiders," the school would demonstrate respect for others' religious beliefs. Such accommodation would be readily achievable, and state legislatures should not assume otherwise. For example, a parochial school might offer students the ability, with parental consent, to opt out of worship, bible studies, or other explicit religious exercises and perhaps provide concurrent opportunities for silent reflection, a study hall, or another suitable alternative for them.

Only those limited activities that require affirmation of faith would necessitate such adjustments. The schools receiving state aid in *Wolman v. Walter*, for example, could not discriminate in admissions on the basis of religion, and the many Catholic schools apparently were able to accommodate non-Catholic

---

86 130 S. Ct. at 2992.

87 Ohio Rev. Code Ann. § 3313.976(A)(4)(6) (2013). By contrast, the sectarian schools participating in the financial aid programs invalidated in *Committee for Public Education & Religious Liberty v. Nyquist* could discriminate on the basis of religion in admissions and require students to participate fully in their religious missions. 413 U.S. 756, 767–68 (1973).

88 *See* Ohio.gov, Program Selection, Cleveland Scholarship (Cleveland), https://scholarship.ode.state.oh.us/Provider (last visited Nov. 30, 2013).

students in this manner without difficulty.[89] Monitoring compliance would entail little additional state involvement with the educational experience. Parochial schools certainly could maintain religious symbols throughout their premises, celebrate religious holidays, promote religiously based values and behavior, instruct about religion, teach even secular subjects with a religious orientation, and honor their religious tradition in myriad other ways. The intent of requiring religious nondiscrimination in student admissions is not to destroy the essential religious nature of any parochial school, but to establish for the sake of all students and civil society a reasonable and enlightened policy that fosters tolerance and diversity within a school specially subsidized by the state.[90] The symbolism of the state not significantly subsidizing an educational program that permits religious discrimination is extremely important. Moreover, the common experience is that most tax-funded tuition subsidies are used at parochial schools. So, requiring a participating school not to discriminate on the basis of religion in admissions of students somewhat counteracts the natural perception that a goal of the subsidy program is not just the legitimate one of providing alternatives for quality education but also specifically and inappropriately to support religious education. To some extent this may ameliorate an already highly sensitive and divisive issue under the Establishment Clause and state analogues.

After much turmoil, this country now generally subscribes to the principle that discrimination, especially in education, is contrary to "fundamental national public policy."[91] Like racial discrimination, with respect to which "[f]ew social or political issues in our history have been more vigorously debated and more extensively ventilated …,"[92] religious discrimination and bias have endured in this country, generating vociferous discourse and heated exchanges. The country's founders scrupulously protected against government favoritism toward certain Christian denominations and their adherents. They safeguarded minority religions and denominations, and non-believers, by the fundamental guarantees of the First Amendment's Religion Clauses. So imposing a condition on all private schools, including parochial ones, that they not discriminate based on religion in student admissions in order to participate in government programs that considerably underwrite their tuitions necessarily stretches beyond a public policy issue to one with constitutional implications. There is ample authority supporting such a requirement.

---

89 433 U.S. 229, 234–35 & n.3 (1977) (*overruled by Mitchell*, 530 U.S. at 793).

90 This approach is in accord with *Martinez*, 130 S. Ct. at 2993, in which the Court considered the "all-comers" membership policy of Hastings College of Law a reasonable means of imposing its nondiscrimination condition for funding student organizations, including those religiously-affiliated, without distorting or destroying their core missions.

91 Bob Jones Univ. v. United States, 461 U.S. 574, 593 (1983) (ruling that racial discrimination in education, even at a private school, violates fundamental national public policy).

92 *Id.* at 595.

From one perspective, a religion-based nondiscrimination condition for state funding amounts to government forcing inclusion of unwanted persons[93] and impermissibly intruding on schools' internal, religious affairs.[94] As the Supreme Court has noted, the "[f]reedom of association ... plainly presupposes a freedom not to associate."[95] Private, parochial and secular schools incontestably are associations engaged in expressive activity accorded First Amendment protections, and their freedom of association rights complement their freedoms of speech and of religious exercise. But, this "is not to say that an expressive association can erect a shield against antidiscrimination laws simply by asserting that mere acceptance of a member from a particular group would impair its message,"[96] despite some "neolibertarian" scholars' position to that effect.[97] Not only has the Supreme Court observed that "freedom of expressive association, like many freedoms, is not absolute,"[98] but some Justices have indicated that there is a basic question as to whether a nondiscrimination policy "regulate[s] expression or belief at all."[99]

Addressing this issue in his concurring opinion in *Martinez*, Justice John Paul Stevens noted that a policy of nondiscrimination based on religion "'is directed at the organization's activities rather than its philosophy.' Those who hold religious beliefs are not 'singled out;' those who engage in discriminatory *conduct* based

93 *See Dale*, 530 U.S. at 640; Hurley v. Irish-American Gay, Lesbian and Bisexual Group of Boston, 515 U.S. 557, 573 (1995).

94 Roberts v. U.S. Jaycees, 468 U.S. 609, 623 (1984) ("There can be no clearer example of an intrusion into the internal structure or affairs of an association than a regulation that forces the group to accept members it does not desire. Such a regulation may impair the ability of the original members to express only those views that brought them together."). *See also Martinez*, 130 S. Ct. at 2985 ("Insisting that an organization embrace unwelcome members, we have therefore concluded, 'directly and immediately affects associational rights.'" (citing *Dale*, 530 U.S. at 659)).

95 *Roberts*, 468 U.S. at 623.

96 *Dale*, 530 U.S. at 653.

97 *See* Andrew Koppelman & Tobias Barrington Wolff, A Right to Discriminate? How the Case of *Boy Scouts of America v. James Dale* Warped the Law of Free Association 63, 63–80 (Yale Univ. Press 2009) (refuting the approach of "neolibertarians," "a group of scholars who argue, based on various rationales, that noncommercial private associations should have an absolute right to discriminate ... [and whose] approach promises 'to draw a line [between freedom of association and antidiscrimination law] that will preserve a large realm for group expression and organization while allowing the state to promote its equality objectives in the most compelling contexts.'" (internal citation omitted)).

98 *Dale*, 530 U.S. at 648. For example, Justice Samuel Alito noted in *Martinez* that "the right of expressive association permits a group to exclude an applicant for membership only if the admission of that person would 'affec[t] in a significant way the group's ability to advocate public or private viewpoints,'" but then suggested that a religious group might differ in this regard. *Martinez*, 130 S. Ct. at 3012 (Alito, J., dissenting) (quoting *Dale*, 530 U.S. at 648).

99 *Martinez*, 130 U.S. at 2996 (Stevens, J., concurring).

on someone else's religious status and belief are singled out."[100] He further noted that even Justice Samuel Alito in his dissent "appears to accept that Hastings [law school, as a state actor,] may prohibit discrimination on the basis of religious *status* …."[101] So, as the Court proclaimed when considering state aid to private, racially discriminatory schools, although "[i]nvidious private discrimination may be characterized as a form of exercising freedom of association protected by the First Amendment, … it has never been accorded affirmative constitutional protections."[102] Indeed, "the Constitution … places no value on discrimination …."[103] What is true of racial discrimination may apply in some contexts to religious discrimination as well, especially when that discrimination would be significantly supported financially by the government.

For the symbolic and policy reasons noted above, taxpayer money should not directly or through an intermediary subsidize tuition at those private schools that maintain religiously discriminatory student admissions policies and practices. The harms from allowing state support for religious discrimination in higher education, such as at Hastings College of Law, are only greatly accentuated at the primary and secondary school levels. Strict Madisonian separationists take the specific position that there should be absolutely no tax support for religious education, and they find it especially troubling if taxpayer subsidies fund religious discrimination at parochial schools. Money is fungible, and if government subsidizes tuition at parochial schools that discriminate on the basis of children's religious status or beliefs, those taxpayer funds, however unintentionally, support

---

100 *Id.* (citations omitted) (emphasis in original).

101 *Id.* at 2996 n.1 (emphasis in original) (acknowledging, however, that Justice Alito rejected the notion that the University may prohibit discrimination for religious belief). The distinctions among status, conduct, and belief are not unfamiliar in the law. *See* Christian Legal Soc'y v. Walker, 453 F.3d 853, 860 (7th Cir. 2006) ("CLS's membership policies are … based on belief and behavior rather than status."); Eugene Volokh, *Freedom of Expressive Association and Government Subsidies*, 58 Stan. L. Rev. 1919, 1938 (2006) ("*Freedom of Expressive Association*") ("[A] religious group (say, a Catholic group) that condemns homosexuality might demand that its members share those views. Such a demand would be neither religious discrimination nor sexual orientation discrimination, but only discrimination based on holding a certain viewpoint that secular people could hold as well as religious ones. But such a group rule wouldn't just exclude practicing homosexuals, or at least those practicing homosexuals who believe that homosexuality is proper—it would also exclude heterosexual Catholics who disagree with church teachings on this issue."); John D. Inazu, *Justice Ginsburg and Religious Liberty*, 63 Hastings L.J. 1213, 1235 (2012).

102 *Norwood*, 413 U.S. at 470.

103 *Id.* at 469.

that discrimination.[104] Certainly, First Amendment protections cannot mean that government financially *must* aid such discrimination.[105]

Supreme Court jurisprudence readily suggests that state legislatures may (and indeed, should) impose a religion-based nondiscrimination student admissions policy as a condition for all private schools to qualify for tax-supported school choice initiatives. In 1973, in *Norwood v. Harrison,* which involved state loans of textbooks to children attending private schools with racially discriminatory policies, the Court advised that government is permitted to attach nondiscrimination strings to its educational aid.[106] "That the Constitution may compel toleration of private discrimination in some circumstances does not mean that it requires state support for such discrimination."[107] The Court then went further, ruling unequivocally that

> … the Constitution does *not permit* the State to aid discrimination even when there is no precise causal relationship between state financial aid to a private school and the continued well-being of that school. A State may not grant … financial aid … if that aid has a significant tendency to facilitate, reinforce, and support private discrimination.[108]

That the financial benefit directly aided "parents and children, not … schools" was irrelevant to the Court in *Norwood*; "[t]he leeway for indirect aid to sectarian schools has no place in defining the permissible scope of state aid to private racially discriminatory schools."[109] What is true for racial discrimination should apply as well to religious discrimination in student admissions when government aid in the form of targeted tax subsidies is helping to determine the very composition of the student body. Despite the Supreme Court's evolved,

---

104 Justice William J. Brennan, dissenting in part in *Grove City College v. Bell*, 465 U.S. 555, 581 (1984), made this point. He maintained that the majority was incorrect in interpreting the sexual nondiscrimination condition of the Title IX statute and regulations at issue there to apply only to each recipient's education program or activity that receives or benefits from the funding—there the college's financial aid program—rather than institution-wide. He suggested "that the entire undergraduate institution operated by Grove City College is subject to the antidiscrimination provisions included in Title IX." *Id.* at 599. *See also* Volokh, *Freedom of Expressive Association, supra* note 101, at 1925 ("[E]ven if the government chooses to subsidize private schooling, it may limit the subsidy to schools that do not discriminate [on the basis of religion], so that the subsidy does not inadvertently support a school's discrimination." (footnote omitted)).

105 *See id.* ("Private schools may likewise have an expressive association right to engage in religious discrimination (though likely not race discrimination) in choosing students or teachers. Yet the government need not subsidize the constitutional right to send one's children to private school or the schools' constitutional right to discriminate." (footnote omitted)).

106 413 U.S. 455, 463 (1973).

107 *Id.*

108 *Id.* at 465–66 (emphasis added).

109 *Id.* at 464, n.7.

permissive approach to Establishment Clause issues regarding state aid to parochial schools, when it decided *Zelman* in 2002 the Court implicitly permitted states to condition government aid for education on schools' adopting, and adhering to, nondiscrimination policies and practices. The funding condition in *Zelman* explicitly prohibited discrimination based on religion despite the obvious and direct impact on schools' First Amendment freedoms of expressive association, speech, and religious exercise.[110]

In between *Norwood* and *Zelman*, in *Bob Jones University v. United States* (consolidated with *Goldsboro Christian Schools, Inc. v. United States*) the Court explicitly rejected the proposition that government must provide aid in the form of a federal income tax exemption to a university or private, parochial school that maintains racially discriminatory admissions policies "on the basis of sincerely held religious beliefs."[111] Concomitantly, the Court implicitly denied the federal income tax charitable contribution deduction to the entities' donors.[112] These cases, whether addressing racial or religious discrimination, speak forcefully with respect to contemporary tax-supported school choice programs, regardless of their form. If taxpayer funds are allowed to help children of impressionable ages attend private, secular or parochial schools that adhere to student admissions policies that discriminate on the basis of religion, constitutional difficulties with these programs are compounded with harmful repercussions for students and society. States may and should condition taxpayer financial support on requiring private schools to adopt and adhere to broad nondiscrimination student admissions policies.

---

110 In other instances not involving discrimination, the Supreme Court has ruled that government may condition tax benefits to organizations upon their refraining from content-based political speech despite an organization's First Amendment Free Speech rights. *See, e.g.*, Regan v. Taxation with Representation of Washington ("TRW"), 461 U.S. 540, 549 (1983) (upholding the I.R.C. § 501(c)(3) statutory constraint on lobbying imposed as a qualification for an organization's tax-exempt status and commenting that "[a] legislature's decision not to subsidize the exercise of a fundamental [speech] right does not infringe that right ..."). Houses of worship that wish to maintain their § 501(c)(3) tax-exempt status must curtail both their free speech and free exercise rights and totally abstain from endorsements of political candidates even when clergy feel theologically compelled to speak to their congregants and the public on vital moral issues implicated by candidates' announced positions. *See generally* Nina J. Crimm & Laurence H. Winer, Politics, Taxes, and the Pulpit: Provocative First Amendment Conflicts (Oxford Univ. Press 2011).

111 *Bob Jones Univ.*, 461 U.S. at 602. The Court ruled: "The governmental interest at stake here is compelling. ... [T]he Government has a fundamental, overriding interest in eradicating racial discrimination in education. ... That governmental interest substantially outweighs whatever burden denial of tax benefits places on petitioners' exercise of their religious beliefs. The interests asserted by petitioners cannot be accommodated with that compelling governmental interest ...." *Id.* at 604 (footnote and citations omitted).

112 For taxpayers to claim the charitable contribution deduction of I.R.C. § 170, the recipient private, nonprofit entity must qualify as a tax-exempt § 501(c)(3) organization.

Additional cases on the post-secondary education level buttress this conclusion. For instance, the Court in *Grove City College v. Bell* required a Christian private college to affirm its compliance with Title IX's prohibition of sex discrimination as a condition for its eligibility to participate in, and receive, federal funding. The funding benefitted enrolled students and the college's student financial aid program, and the condition did not infringe upon the First Amendment rights of the recipient students or those of the private college.[113] And in *Martinez*, the Court found it reasonable and constitutional for the educational institution to impose its religiously-neutral, "all-comers" membership policy as a condition for any secular or religiously-affiliated student organizations to receive the benefit of University facilities, amenities, and funding.[114] So one principle appears constant in the educational context: Regardless of whether government aid is perceived as direct or indirect in reaching private, secular or religiously-affiliated schools (or school groups), and regardless of the form of government assistance—a monetary grant, tangible property, or tax-supported benefits—government even-handedly may condition its largesse on a beneficiary's adopting and adhering to a student admissions or membership policy and practice of nondiscrimination, including nondiscrimination based on religion. There is no constitutional right to state support of such discrimination.

Some might argue, however, that such a condition on funding is an impermissible unconstitutional condition—that is, an intolerable "bribe" by government that coerces private, secular and parochial schools to relinquish their First Amendment rights in return for government assistance. The judicially developed unconstitutional conditions doctrine has a long pedigree, is a confused and "troubled area of our jurisprudence" according to Justice Harry Blackmun,

113 465 U.S. 555 (1984). The Basic Educational Opportunity Grants ("BEOG") program at issue "was structured to ensure that it effectively supplements the College's own financial aid program." *Id.* at 565. Importantly for application to tax-funded tuition subsidies, the Court remarked: "Student financial aid programs, we believe, are *sui generis*. In neither purpose nor effect can BEOGs be fairly characterized as unrestricted grants that institutions may use for whatever purpose they desire. The BEOG program was designed, not merely to increase the total resources available to educational institutions, but to enable them to offer their services to students who had previously been unable to afford higher education." *Id.* at 573.

114 *See Martinez*, 130 S. Ct. at 2971. The funding came from fees collected from all students for distribution to University-authorized student organizations. The student chapter of the Christian Legal Society asserted that the "all-comers" membership policy impaired, and forced the relinquishment of, its First Amendment rights to expressive association, freedom of speech, and freedom of religious exercise because the policy forced the group to accept members who did not share its faith and beliefs about sexual orientation. The Court found that the group could organize and meet off-campus. It had no constitutional right to state subvention of its membership selectivity.

and is in intractable disarray.[115] Yet, one principle on which the Supreme Court has been consistent is that

> … [t]here is a basic difference between direct state interference with a protected activity and state encouragement of an alternative activity [by providing a benefit] consonant with legislative policy. Constitutional concerns are greatest when the State attempts to impose its will by force of law; the State's power to encourage actions deemed to be in the public interest is necessarily far broader.[116]

The Court recently tried to clarify its distinction between a constitutional funding condition and one that is unconstitutional:

> [T]he relevant distinction that has emerged from our cases is between [constitutional] conditions that define the limits of the government spending program—those that specify the activities Congress wants to subsidize—and [unconstitutional] conditions that seek to leverage funding to regulate [constitutionally protected] speech [and religious exercise] outside the contours of the program itself. The line is hardly clear.[117]

---

115 Rust v. Sullivan, 500 U.S. 173, 205 (1991) (Blackmun, J., dissenting). The Supreme Court's recent discussion of the unconstitutional conditions doctrine reveals just how indeterminate it is: "In some cases, a funding condition can result in an unconstitutional burden on First Amendment rights. The dissent thinks that can only be true when the condition is not relevant to the objectives of the program (although it has its doubts about that), or when the condition is actually coercive, in the sense of an offer that cannot be refused. Our precedents, however, are not so limited." Agency for Int'l Dev. v. Alliance for Open Soc'y Int'l, Inc., 133 S. Ct. 2321, 2328 (2013) (citations omitted).

The unconstitutional conditions doctrine is evident in Supreme Court opinions as early as 1926. Frost & Frost Trucking Co. v. R.R. Comm'n of Cal., 271 U.S. 583, 593–94 (1926) (commenting that in granting a privilege or benefit, government "may not impose conditions which require the relinquishment of constitutional rights" because "[i]t is inconceivable that guaranties embedded in the Constitution of the United States may thus be manipulated out of existence"). For a discussion of the unconstitutional conditions doctrine and its perplexing indeterminate nature, *see* Crimm & Winer, *supra* note 110, at 266–82.

116 Maher v. Roe, 432 U.S. 464, 475–76 (1977).

117 *Alliance for Open Soc'y Int'l, Inc.*, 133 S. Ct. at 2328 (regarding protected speech). To distinguish between a constitutional funding condition and an unconstitutional one, the Court contrasted *TRW*, 461 U.S. at 540, with *F.C.C. v. League of Women Voters of Cal.*, 468 U.S. 364 (1984). In *TRW*, the Court ruled that a grant of § 501(c)(3) tax-exempt status, which would provide tax benefits to the organization (an income tax exemption) and to its donors (a charitable contribution deduction), based on the condition that TRW not engage in substantial lobbying activity, was not an unconstitutional condition. The condition did not prohibit TRW from lobbying altogether; TRW had an alternative means of doing so by forming a tax-exempt § 501(c)(4) organization, which would permit that organization to use its funds to lobby. But because donors to the § 501(c)(4) entity would not be entitled to the § 170 charitable contribution deduction, those funds would not be tax subsidized. The tax

Nonetheless, a government funding condition "'designed to ensure that the limits of the … program are observed' and 'that public funds [are] spent for the purposes for which they were authorized'" is permissible.[118] One commentator distilled part of the doctrine's essence to: "While the government may generally place conditions on the use of benefits that it provides, it generally may not control the use of the recipient's other assets as a condition of providing the benefit."[119]

By requiring a private, secular or parochial school participating in a school choice aid program not to discriminate in admissions of students on the basis of religion, a state would not be leveraging its funding to regulate protected First Amendment rights outside the contours of the aid initiative. Nor would it be exerting any control over a school's use of its own assets. Rather, state tuition subsidies are designed to, and do, directly affect which students are able to attend certain private schools. The subsidies are responsible for placing some students in their seats. The "contours of the program itself" involve the student composition of a school's classrooms. A state therefore is free to specify the composition it wishes to subsidize—namely, one that does not exclude students based on religion. And the condition also does not coerce a school to take the money and relinquish First Amendment rights. As discussed above, a parochial school admitting a small minority of students of other faiths easily can maintain fully its own religious character, activities, and mission. A student body that is religiously diverse, even if modestly so, can only enhance the educational experience for all students. A school that is convinced otherwise can opt out of the subsidy program. But the nondiscrimination funding condition would not be an obstacle to private schools' or students' expressive association, nor would it obstruct free speech or religious exercise. It is unlikely to be deemed an unconstitutional condition.

Still, some might challenge the condition under special state laws or state constitutional provisions intended to protect religious liberty against government infringement, which often are similar to the federal RFRA that is inapplicable to the

---

subsidy "condition did not deny the organization a government benefit 'on account of its intention to lobby.'" *Alliance for Open Soc'y Int'l, Inc.*, 133 S. Ct. at 2329 (quoting *TRW*, 461 U.S. at 545). By comparison, the condition imposed on federal financial assistance in *League of Women Voters* prohibited all editorializing by a public broadcast television or radio station that accepts federal funding, including such speech financed solely with the organization's private funds. There was no alternative means for a station "to make known its views on matters of public importance." *League of Women Voters*, 468 U.S. at 400. "The prohibition thus went beyond ensuring that federal funds not be used to subsidize 'public broadcasting station editorials,' and instead leveraged the federal funding to regulate the stations' speech outside the scope of the program." *Alliance for Open Soc'y Int'l, Inc.*, 133 S. Ct. at 2329 (quoting *League of Women Voters*, 468 U.S. at 399).

118 *Alliance for Open Soc'y Int'l, Inc.*, 133 S. Ct. at 2329–30 (quoting *Rust*, 500 U.S. at 193, 196).

119 Volokh, *Freedom of Expressive Association*, *supra* note 101, at 1945.

states.[120] By mid-2013, 15 states had enacted their own RFRA-type statutes;[121] one state, Alabama, has a RFRA-type provision in its constitution;[122] and approximately 11 other states' constitutions contain similar religiously-protective provisions.[123] These various measures commonly require that even neutral, generally applicable laws be the least restrictive means of furthering a compelling government interest if they impose a substantial burden on religious exercise.[124]

It is quite uncertain, however, whether imposing a religious nondiscrimination student admissions policy as a condition for participating in a state's school choice initiative that subsidizes private school tuition even would be considered a substantial burden on a parochial school's religious exercise. Several years ago, Professor Eugene Volokh suggested first that "[a] substantial burden clearly exists if a group's religious beliefs obligate it to discriminate. … The matter is more uncertain if a group merely feels religiously motivated, not compelled, to discriminate …."[125] Then he conjectured that, despite *Bob Jones University* where "the Court did downplay in some measure the magnitude of the burden,"[126] "when the government simply denies the group a benefit, which is to say the government refuses to fund the group's religiously compelled behavior … the answer is usually yes," it is a substantial burden on religious exercise.[127] But there is a wide gulf between discrimination that is religiously "compelled," religiously "motivated," or merely religiously desirous, with only the first clearly constituting a substantial burden. There can be no definitive answer; much necessarily would depend on the particular school and the effect on it of not being able to discriminate in admissions on the basis of religion.

Emphasizing the financial aspect, Professor Thomas C. Berg has posited that statutorily denying government subsidies to some religious organizations may constitute a substantial burden on their religious exercise by virtue of the resulting broad pecuniary repercussions to them. Forfeiture of benefits can

---

120 *See supra* n.65 and accompanying text. The Supreme Court held RFRA inapplicable to states and local governments in *City of Boerne v. Flores*, 521 U.S. 507 (1997).

121 A compilation of state statutes is on file with the authors of this book.

122 Ala. Const. art. I, § 3.01. Other state legislatures, such as Wisconsin's, have proposed RFRA-type constitutional amendments.

123 *See* Eugene Volokh, The First Amendment and Related Statutes: Problems, Cases, and Policy Arguments 982–83 (5th ed. 2014).

124 In three states protection is triggered whenever government simply "burdens" a person's "freedom of religion" or "exercise of religion." Ala. Const. art. I, § 3.01; Mo. Ann. Stat. §§ 1.302–1.307 (West 2013); N.M. Stat. Ann. §§ 28–22–1 to 28–22–5 (West 2013). Kentucky specifically provides that a "'burden' shall include indirect burdens such as withholding benefits, assessing penalties, or an exclusion from programs or access to facilities." 2013 Ky. Acts 554.

125 Volokh, *Freedom of Expressive Association*, *supra* note 101, at 1951–52.

126 *Id.* at 1955.

127 *Id.* at 1954.

harm "a school … not just [in] that it has to curtail its operations, serving fewer students … [but] [f]requently this also means transferring resources from activities where its religiously inspired mission would have put them. … [T]he threat of lost benefits can put 'unmistakable pressure' on an organization's choices concerning its religious character and practices."[128] But again the financial impact on any particular parochial school from being religiously compelled to opt out of a tuition subsidy program rather than conform to a nondiscrimination mandate is highly uncertain and presumably quite variable among schools. Many private, secular and parochial schools have proved quite successful without the tuition subsidies and would not be financially threatened by having to reject them. The extent to which a parochial school actually is dependent upon government subsidies for its financial health, let alone for its very existence, only accentuates the constitutional problems with government supporting it. Moreover, only a parochial school with directors who consider the school theologically compelled to discriminate in student admissions based on religion and who consequently exclude the school from the state's program potentially incurs some financial loss. Schools that remain in the program suffer no financial hardship and, as discussed above, face no meaningful, let alone substantial, burden on their First Amendment rights from the modest accommodations they might need to make for a small minority of students.

Even if the nondiscrimination condition does substantially burden a particular parochial school's religious rights, whether the government is permitted to impose that condition, under most RFRA-type provisions, still depends on whether the requirement is the least restrictive means of furthering a compelling government interest. The Supreme Court, applying this strict scrutiny standard in *Bob Jones University*, ruled that government has a compelling interest in preventing taxpayer funds from supporting racial discrimination at the primary, secondary, and post-secondary school levels even when religious belief mandates such discrimination.[129] By contrast, Justice Alito in *Martinez* asserted in his dissenting opinion that "no legitimate state interest could override the powerful effect that an accept-all-comers law would have on the ability of religious groups to express their views."[130] Given the divergent views, it is not surprising that, writing several years prior to *Martinez*, Professor Volokh found it

> … hard to draw much precedential help from [Supreme Court] … decisions in cases where the refusal to subsidize stems not from a desire not to subsidize religious practice, but from a desire that "public funds, to which all taxpayers

128 Thomas C. Berg, *Religious Organizational Freedom and Conditions on Government Benefits*, 7 Geo. J.L. & Pub. Pol'y 165, 181 (2009) (quoting Sherbert v. Verner, 374 U.S. 398, 404 (1963)).

129 *Bob Jones Univ.*, 461 U.S. at 574.

130 *Martinez*, 130 S. Ct. at 3014 (Alito, J., dissenting).

> of all [identity groups] contribute, not be spent in any fashion which … subsidizes … [identity-group-based] discrimination ….”[131]

Because in many settings he discerns little harmful or preclusive effect, Professor Volokh opines that, while “[t]here is surely a rational basis for the government to exclude discriminating organizations from a broad subsidy program, … I don’t think there’s a compelling interest.”[132]

In our context, we disagree. *Martinez* upheld an “all-comers” membership policy at the university level. In the very special and sensitive setting of primary and secondary education we believe that, in the unlikely event of a substantial burden on a parochial school, there clearly would be a compelling interest in the state not appearing to endorse religious exclusivity. Moreover, there often may not be a large universe of parochial schools of various denominations desirous of participating in a school choice initiative. Most of the participating private schools, both historically and currently, in Ohio’s voucher program adjudicated in *Zelman* are “mainstream” parochial schools,[133] as are most schools participating in Arizona’s STO-tax credit initiative.[134] If parochial schools are permitted to accept only students of their faiths, a student relegated to finding a school of his own, perhaps less common, denomination might have little actual choice in a program intended to expand choice in education. At any rate, the state should stand for a principle of diversity and pluralism in education, not insularity. Lastly, avoiding an Establishment Clause violation is always a compelling government interest.[135] To force taxpayers vicariously to support parochial schools at all, let alone those that discriminate on the basis of religion, is objectionable from both a Madisonian separationist view and a “fundamental national public policy” perspective.

As a final argument, we note that excluding parochial schools from government school choice funding if they discriminate in student admissions on the basis of religion may implicate private individuals’ First Amendment interests. Families may want to educate their children at parochial schools of their own faiths that do not admit youths of other faiths or denominations so that their children associate only with like-minded students and are exposed only to, and indoctrinated by, a particular religious viewpoint through pervasively religious educational approaches, teachings, and messages. Parents may not want the intensity of their children’s secular and religious training diluted by the presence of outsiders for

---

131 Volokh, *Freedom of Expressive Association, supra* note 101, at 1964–65 (quoting with modifications President John F. Kennedy’s justification for Title VI of the Civil Rights Act in his Special Message to the Congress on Civil Rights and Job Opportunities, 1 Pub. Papers 483, 492 (June 19, 1963)).

132 Volokh, *Freedom of Expressive Association, supra* note 101, at 1965.

133 *See supra* note 88; Chapter 2, nn.306–07 and accompanying text.

134 *See* Chapters 1, n.197 and 4, n.132 and their accompanying text.

135 Good News Club v. Milford Cent. Sch., 533 U.S. 98, 112–13 (2001); Capitol Square Review & Advisory Bd. v. Pinette, 515 U.S. 753, 761–62 (1995).

whom even very modest, personal accommodations must be made. Those parents may even fear their children's exposure to other ways of thinking and other ways of life. Such parents may have the right to inflexibly control the upbringing and education of their children at their own expense, but not with the assistance of public funds provided by tax-supported school choice programs from which both students and their schools benefit. In the context of racial segregation the Court has been clear that even if the First Amendment protects the right of parents to send their children to private schools that promote racial segregation, "it does not follow that the practice of excluding racial minorities from such institutions is also protected by the same principle."[136]

About ten years ago, the Supreme Court in *Locke v. Davey* confronted the constitutionality of Washington State forbidding a college student, Joshua Davey, to apply a taxpayer funded state scholarship to support targeted religious instruction—courses leading to a theology degree. Davey could apply state scholarship funding to courses for the study of religion, just not those in pursuit of a devotional theology degree. As with school vouchers, the First Amendment's Establishment Clause would have permitted, but did not require, the state to aid such religious education through its scholarship program.[137] But Chief Justice William Rehnquist's opinion for the Court found that the government has greater latitude to condition tax funding of initiatives that might "disfavor" religion than it does if it imposes a direct regulation of religion. Because the Washington scholarship initiative fell within the former category, the "State's disfavor of religion (if it can be called that) is of a far milder kind. It imposes neither criminal nor civil sanctions on any type of religious service or rite."[138] The scholarship program did not exclude all religiously-affiliated organizations and their students from eligibility and participation and did "not require students to choose between their religious beliefs and receiving a government benefit."[139] On the other hand, by precluding the use of taxpayer funds to prepare a student for the ministry, Washington's funding restriction protected the freedom of religious conscience of the broad community of state taxpayers. Overall, nothing about the conditional scholarship program "suggests animus towards religion," and "the historic and substantial state interest at issue" in avoiding a possible establishment of religion favored the state's decision to impose the funding restriction.[140]

Locke supports the proposition that a state has the constitutional latitude to incorporate in any school choice initiative a requirement that participating schools

---

136 *Runyon*, 427 U.S. at 176.

137 Locke v. Davey, 540 U.S. 712, 719 (2004) (based on a long line of cases, there is "no doubt that the State could, consistent with the Federal Constitution, permit [scholarship students to exercise their independent, private choice] to pursue a degree in devotional theology," but it is not required to do so).

138 *Id.* at 720.

139 *Id.* at 720–21.

140 *Id.* at 725.

not discriminate on the basis of religion in student admissions. Absent any unlikely animus toward religion, such a legislative condition would not impermissibly impact the rights of parents or students any more than Washington's scholarship restriction unconstitutionally affected a college student. Washington "merely chose[] not to fund a distinct category of instruction."[141] Similarly, a state could simply choose not to subsidize a particular type of primary or secondary education, namely, one at a religiously discriminatory school.[142]

In sum, as long as applied neutrally and even-handedly to all eligible individuals and all participating private, secular and parochial schools, as part of their school choice initiatives state legislatures may and should condition their taxpayer-funded subsidies on the requirement that participating schools adopt and implement a policy of not discriminating in student admissions on the basis of religion.[143] If schools do discriminate on the basis of religion, states have latitude to refuse to subsidize all who benefit from the program—parents and children whose private choices result in the children's attendance at the discriminatory schools, and such schools themselves (or intermediaries like STOs that support them). As Justice Stevens has written, "[a] free society must tolerate such [individuals and] groups. It need not subsidize them ...."[144]

VIII. Education Specific Lotteries: A Less Problematic Way to Fund School Choice Initiatives

School choice initiatives underwritten solely by non-taxpayer funds could eliminate many of the problems associated with government aid discussed in this book. One possibility is to reinvigorate and expand an old idea of legislatively created state lotteries dedicated to supporting private education alternatives, both secular and sectarian, at the primary and secondary levels. The funds raised could be distributed to students and schools in a variety of neutral and evenhanded ways. Those playing the lotteries and thereby contributing to the program would

141 *Id.* at 721.

142 *But see, e.g.*, Berg, *supra* note128, at 181 (excluding certain religious institutions from aid programs may intrude on the religion-based choices of individuals); Douglas Laycock, *Theology Scholarships, the Pledge of Allegiance, and Religious Liberty: Avoiding the Extremes but Missing the Liberty*, 118 Harv. L. Rev. 155, 180–81 (2004) (expressing concern that *Locke* permits government's refusal to fund an individual's choice, grounded in that person's freedom of religious exercise, to swallow up and penalize that right). *See also* Judge Michael W. McConnell's opinion in *Weaver*, 534 F.3d at 1254, in which he questioned the "precise bounds" of *Locke*, but was "disinclined to think that *Locke* is confined to its facts."

143 *See* Volokh, *Freedom of Expressive Association*, *supra* note 101, at 1922–23 ("Such conditions are religion-neutral, viewpoint-neutral, and generally even content-neutral, at least if they're applied evenhandedly to all participating groups.").

144 *Martinez*, 130 S. Ct. at 2998 (Stevens, J., concurring).

understand their money would be used for only these purposes. There would be no direct drain on tax revenues and no dollars diverted away from public schools. State lotteries have proliferated lately, become quite popular and successful, and are an important source of government revenue. The success of the dedicated lottery, fueled by the prospect of winning a jackpot, would be an excellent marketplace measure of actual public support for school choice and private education alternatives, including parochial schools. Most importantly, all people playing would consent to the use of their money to support religious education, thereby eliminating the most significant Establishment Clause issues.

Not relying on taxpayer money, such a dedicated lottery would be self-supporting, and careful legislative planning of its structure, administration, and oversight also could avoid difficulties under state anti-establishment and anti-funding provisions. In particular, although created by a state, like a casino a lottery could be privately owned and operated and, except for necessary oversight of that business, not administered by state agencies. Revenues need not be collected by the state or deposited into state treasuries at all, thereby truly reducing even further entanglement and endorsement issues and other potential constitutional problems.[145] Finally, those with personal objections to lotteries as a form of gambling, on a religious basis or otherwise, either might not participate or might allay their concerns by pledging to donate any possible winnings back to the worthy cause of funding private school choice. Still, some moral objections or concerns about the regressive nature of a lottery may persist.

Funding private schooling, including religiously-affiliated schools, through lotteries is by no means a new concept. As early as 1801, New York law provided that $12,500 in lottery money "shall" be distributed to private "academies" in the state in "proportions" and "manner" judged "most beneficial" and "most advantageous to literature," with residual lottery funds allotted by the legislature to "the encouragement of common schools," then run by private religious groups.[146] Today, numerous states have lotteries that benefit K–12 education and post-secondary education, among other causes; sometimes, but not always, the proceeds are dedicated explicitly to public education.[147] Several states, such as Arkansas, Georgia, and Tennessee, dedicate lottery proceeds to fund higher education scholarships and grants, whether used by students at public or private,

145 In her concurring opinion in *Rosenberger v. Rector & Visitors of the University of Virginia*, 515 U.S. 819, 851–52 (1995) (O'Connor, J., concurring), Justice O'Connor suggested ways of distinguishing the proceeds of the student fees at issue there "from proceeds of the general assessments in support of religion that lie at the core of the prohibition against religious funding."

146 1801 N.Y. Laws 299–300.

147 For example, Missouri's lottery proceeds are earmarked solely for public education and comprise approximately 4.25 percent of the state's funding for education. *Where the Money Goes*, Mo. Lottery, http://www.molottery.com/where_the_money_goes/where_the_money_goes.shtm (last visited Oct. 7, 2013).

nonprofit institutions.[148] The District of Columbia and several states, including New Jersey, provide that lottery proceeds be directed to the states' general funds to benefit public education, non-public education tuition, higher education, capital projects for education facilities, or some combination.[149]

There are, of course, downside risks of reliance on lotteries to support education. Lotteries can produce erratic returns, often depending upon broad economic conditions and fiscal environments. Moreover, absent sufficient statutory restrictions on disbursements from lottery funds—such as those capping financial aid per student, establishing suitable student and school qualification criteria, and limiting the numbers of students eligible—demand readily can exceed the available money supply.[150] But, as with other school aid programs, a dedicated lottery would be meant only to supplement nonpublic funding for private, secular and parochial education, not replace support from families and other independent funders who are the primary and most appropriate sources. So, where tax-supported school choice programs exist or state legislatures intend to create or expand these initiatives, privately-funded lotteries dedicated to education should be considered an especially palatable alternative from a constitutional perspective and otherwise.

IX. Legislation Regarding Charter Schools and Home Schooling

As more religiously-based, culture-oriented charter schools appear and raise establishment concerns, Congress and state legislatures should legislate on several fronts to ameliorate potential problems. First, as noted in Chapter 1, some academicians assert that, despite the direct government funding of charter schools, as a result of their hybrid nature such schools might not be considered "state

148 *See Arkansas Lottery Commission*, Ark. Scholarship Lottery, http://myarkansaslottery.com/about/arkansas-lottery-commission (last visited Oct. 7, 2013); *Proceeds to Education*, Ga. Lottery, http://www.galottery.com/education (last visited Oct. 7, 2013); *Where the Money Goes*, Tn. Lottery, http://www.tnlottery.com/wheremoneygoes/where_benefits.aspx (last visited Oct. 7, 2013).

149 *See, e.g.*, http://dclottery.com/default.aspx; http://www.state.nj.us/lottery/home.shtml; N.J.S.A. 5:9–1; 18A: 46A-1; 18A: 58–37.2 (2012); http://www.state.nj.us/lottery/where/annual_reports/annual_report_fy2011.pdf.

A recent exposé reported that over the past 30 years sales revenues from Arizona's lottery have totaled over $9.8 billion. The state has marketed and advertised the lottery as benefitting education, among other causes. Ironically, however, considering that Arizona has been in the forefront of the school choice movement with innovative ways of diverting tax revenues from public schools to private education alternatives, "[n]o Lottery money has ever been given directly to K–12 education, according to state budget documents." Alia Beard Rau, *Arizona Lottery Revenue Has Grown, but Tracking How Funds Are Used Proves Difficult*, Ariz. Rep., Dec. 1, 2013, at A1.

150 *See* Kim Severson, *Recession Threatens Scholarships in Georgia*, N.Y. Times, Jan. 7, 2011, at A13.

actors" but rather "private actors." If so, they might be largely unconstrained by the First Amendment's Establishment Clause, state anti-establishment analogues, or state anti-funding provisions.[151] This issue can be easily resolved by states enacting legislation that expressly provides that all charter schools shall be deemed "state actors," if not for every purpose then at least for these constitutional ones. Congress also could adopt regulatory measures that prohibit the federal government from aiding a charter school unless the state in which the school is chartered has adopted such a "state actor" law. Such legislation would preserve an appropriate level of constitutional accountability over schools educating children primarily with public funds.

Second, the "hybrid," private entity aspect of charter schools should induce state legislatures to consider management structures derived from for-profit businesses and nonprofit organizations under which such enterprises operate with advisory boards in order to provide varying perspectives from "independent" persons without potential conflicts of interest as to the entity. State legislatures might require all charter schools to appoint advisory boards composed largely of such "independent" individuals, who might serve on a volunteer basis without compensation. If unwilling to mandate this, legislatures could at least counsel and encourage the state department of education to promote the idea. Either way, state officials should stress the importance of a charter school maintaining an advisory board with a diverse racial, ethnic, gender, and religious composition and perhaps even suggest aspirational guidelines for achieving such pluralism in membership. In this regard, the profile of an advisory board might reflect the composition of the community-at-large served by the charter school. A diverse, independent advisory board could help substantially to allay concerns that a "public" charter school in fact is too "religious" in character or oriented too closely to one faith.

Third, because the economic climate and other factors have led some private, parochial schools to seek to convert to charter school status, such action has stirred considerable consternation about the blurring of the public-private and church-state lines. It is important that state legislatures adopt laws to place controls, or even perhaps prohibitions, on such conversions. As noted in Chapter 1, two states, Wisconsin and Utah, have statutes that specifically prohibit private, sectarian schools from converting to charter status; 27 states prohibit any private school conversions; but nine states and the District of Columbia permit such conversions. Without adequate controls on such conversions, possibly including mandatory advisory boards as just described, disquieting charges of government establishment of religion likely are inescapable.

Lastly, we described in Chapter 1 the expanding popularity of home schooling as one aspect of the school choice movement. Home-schooling parents increasingly rely on broadband connections to cyber-charter schools or other internet-based private education providers, and many of these are religiously affiliated. State legislatures need to be attuned to the potential constitutional hazards of providing

151 *See* Chapter 1, nn.164–68 and accompanying text.

parents financial assistance that easily can be diverted to these and other sources of religiously-oriented instruction or indoctrination in the home. Although there currently is a dearth of litigation in this area, public funding for religious instruction in home schooling situations raises especially complicated and important constitutional questions.

As we have noted repeatedly, parents certainly enjoy the right to direct the educational and religious upbringing of their children, particularly in their own homes and at their own expense. Still, to the extent possible, appropriate restrictions on use of government assistance should apply. Government tuition subsidies for enrolling in a cyber-provider's curriculum, for example, should be restricted to those aspects that are secular, not sectarian, in character. At a minimum, a state might restrict any hard copy textbooks and materials, or e-texts, software, or other online instructional resources provided to home-schooled students to those used in traditional public schools. Nonetheless, if a state's financial aid helps to provide a computer and broadband access to a home-schooled student, it might be overreaching and, at the very least, futile to attempt to limit the types of additional materials, religious or otherwise, the student could peruse. Parents should be advised periodically of the restrictions to which they should adhere. But legislators and the public-at-large ultimately must rely simply on the good faith of parents who enjoy the benefit of government assistance for their desired home schooling not to abuse the privilege. Realistically it is impossible for state legislatures to restrain all diversions of public money that home-schooling parents may direct to sectarian organizations and spend on religiously-imbued instructional materials. Even so, particularly in the secluded home schooling setting, it is incumbent upon legislators to be sensitive to, and balance, parents' and children's freedom of religious belief and practice with prohibitions against government establishment of religion under the First Amendment's Establishment Clause, state anti-establishment analogues, and state anti-funding provisions.

X. Conclusion

The importance of primary and secondary school education for this country's children and their future accomplishments and well-being, as well as for the nation's cultural, political, and economic life, cannot be over-emphasized. Nor is it an overstatement that many education experts, policymakers, parents, and other citizens have become extremely dissatisfied in recent decades with the educational experiences that traditional public schools provide and are enormously concerned that students and the country are being poorly served. There is therefore an abundant, and growing, demand for alternative educational opportunities, which is leading to an increasing proliferation of tax-supported school choice initiatives across many states. These taxpayer-funded programs aid not only students and their parents (many seeking religious as well as secular education), but often also accrue to the benefit of religiously-based culture-oriented public charter schools, and private, parochial schools and other religiously-affiliated education enterprises (such as cyber-providers). Tax revenues purportedly flow to these persons and entities only on a "neutral" basis and as a result of private, independent choices of individuals, but realistically all taxpayers are forced vicariously to financially support religious education. These developments raise grave and legitimate concerns about the wisdom of eroding separation of church and state in such a sensitive area and the constitutional propriety of doing so in the face of the First Amendment's Establishment Clause, state anti-establishment analogues, and state constitutions' anti-funding provisions.

In a final analogy to free speech values, we recall that Justice Souter once expressed the need for strict judicial scrutiny of legislative action to "keep[] the starch in the standards for those moments when the daily politics cries loudest for limiting what may be said."[152] In many ways, Justice Souter was echoing one of the classic statements of the free speech principle enshrined in the First Amendment, Justice Oliver Wendell Holmes' remarkable dissent (joined by Justice Brandeis) in *Abrams v. United States*.[153] Justice Holmes observed that when people are certain about their convictions they have no reason to allow opposing speech. But "when men have realized that time has upset many fighting faiths," they may understand that it is far better to eschew censorship and instead rely on competition in the market for ideas.[154] This is the theory of our Constitution, and so Justice Holmes warned of the need to be "eternally vigilant" against encroachments upon freedom of speech, even the "expression of opinions that we loathe and believe to be fraught with death."[155] Justice Holmes was defending freedom of expression but expressly used the language "fighting faiths" and other religious imagery to relate intolerance of political dissent to narrow-minded religious orthodoxy. So it is hard to resist applying his principle more broadly to religious convictions that for many might represent eternal and uncontestable truths.

As long as the holding in *Winn* remains good law, federal courts essentially will be removed from reviewing the constitutionality of legislative schemes that fund religious education. When it upheld in *Marsh v. Chambers* state legislative prayers over the concern that such practices lead to inappropriate establishments of religion, the Court invoked Justice Holmes' earlier retort to a claim that the power to tax is the power to destroy. The Court in *Marsh* said there is no real threat of creating establishments of religion "while this court sits."[156] But now, for all practical

---

152 Denver Area Educ. Telecom Consortium v. F.C.C., 518 U.S. 727, 774 (1996) (Souter, J., concurring).

153 250 U.S. 616 (1919). *See generally* Thomas Healy, The Great Dissent: How Oliver Wendell Holmes Changed His Mind—and Changed the History of Free Speech in America (Henry Holt 2013).

154 *Abrams*, 250 U.S. at 630 (Holmes, J., dissenting).

155 *Id.*

156 463 U.S. 783, 795 (1983) (quoting Panhandle Oil Co. v. Miss. ex rel. Knox, 277 U.S. 218, 223 (1928) (Holmes, J., dissenting)).

purposes the Court is not sitting. Therefore it falls to state legislatures, governors, and courts to take up Justice Holmes' admonition that the Constitution requires them to be "eternally vigilant" and apply it against government establishments of religion even when—perhaps especially when—these are popular among large segments of the public.

We critically explored the jurisprudence bearing on the provocative and contentious issues involved in state funding of religious education. Realizing the current state of affairs, we have made several unabashedly modest proposals for consideration by state legislatures to ameliorate the great controversy and divisiveness engendered in this area. Our proposals are certain not to please purists on either side—neither strict separationists for whom we compromise too much nor ardent proponents of school choice for whom concession is neither necessary nor warranted. In an era of stark political polarization it may be somewhat chimerical for us to urge legislative self-restraint and regard for opposing positions. But it is just when "daily politics cries loudest" that legislatures must temper the exercise of their powers to tax and spend so that they do not destroy.

Index

A Beka Academy, 59, 59n181
A Nation at Risk, 19, 19n12
Abrams v. United States, 270 & nn.153–54
Adams, John, 86n71, 88
Adler, Donna D., 166n51
Affordable Care Act (ACA)
  See Patient Protection and Affordable Care Act
Agency for International Development v. Alliance for Open Society International, Inc., 259n115
Agostini v. Felton, 128n245, 130n253, 133n268, 134–36, 139
Agudo, Sarah E., 77n31
Aguilar v. Felton, 120n220, 128, 130
Aid Clause (Arizona), 47, 235, 235n26, 236, 236n30, 238–39
Alito, Samuel, 80, 82, 204–05, 207, 254n98, 255, 262
Allen v. Wright, 187n10, 188nn17–19 & 23, 210n120
Amar, Akhil, 73n17, 74n20, 76n27, 86nn66 &69, 88n81, 89nn85 & 87
American Bar Association, United States v., 152n16
Anti-funding provision, 5, 39, 44, 47–48, 50, 55, 60–61, 61n188, 64, 66–67, 93, 94n109, 222, 228n4, 229–30, 231nn11 & 13, 234, 234nn21–22, 235, 235nn23 & 26, 236, 239, 239n48, 240–43, 268–70,
  See also Blaine Amendment, state versions; Aid Clause (Arizona)
Apple, Michael W., 19n13, 20nn15–16, 48n137
Arizona Christian School Tuition Organization v. Winn, 4–5, 5n12, 11–14, 64n197, 67, 91n98, 109, 128, 141, 145, 147, 147n322, 149n1, 150, 140n9, 160, 179–183, 186, 191, 193–94, 196, 204, 206n105, 209, 212–19, 220nn167–68, 221–24, 227–28, 232–33, 235, 237, 242, 244, 270
Arizonans for Official English v. Arizona, 187n12, 223n179
Article III of U.S. Constitution, 14, 131, 185, 188n22, 189, 189n27, 190, 190n29, 193–95, 195n50, 197, 199, 201n81, 203–04, 206–07, 214, 217, 222, 224, 227, 230
ASARCO Inc. v. Kadish, 222nn175–76, 223n179, 224nn180 &183

Baptist Association of Danbury, 83 & n55
Balkin, Jack M., 84 & n60
Barnett, Randy E., 81n51
Barrington, Tobias, 254n97
Ben Gamla Charter School, 53
Berg, Thomas C., 43n106, 44n124, 47n134, 76n26, 79n38, 92n100, 261–62 & n128, 265n142
Bill Establishing A Provision For Teachers Of The Christian Religion
  See Virginia Tax Assessment
Bittker, Boris I., 170 & nn61–62, 175n72
Black, Hugo, 1n3, 83, 109–10, 113, 115–16, 117n204, 118, 124, 128
Blackmun, Harry, 100n142, 101, 203, 258
Blackstone, 66n5, 89, 89n84
Blaine Amendment,
  Federal, 46–47, 76n26, 77n30, 113n192
  State versions, 67n214, 238n41
  See also Anti-funding provision; Aid Clause (Arizona)
Blaine, James G., 45–46
Board of Airport Commissioners v. Jews for Jesus, Inc., 211n126

Board of Education v. Allen, 1, 116–19, 122–24, 165n45, 198n61, 251n84
Board of Education of Kiryas Joel Village School District v. Grumet, 9n23, 101n146, 133–34, 246
Bob Jones University v. United States, 9n22, 253n91, 257, 261–62 & n129
Bolick, Clint, 18n7, 39n90
Bowen v. Kendrick, 105n163, 139nn293–94, 140n297, 145n314, 165n45, 204n97
Boy Scouts of America v. Dale, 242n58, 251n85, 254nn93, 96 & 98
Bradfield v. Roberts, 165n45, 194–96
Brady, Michael H., 77n32, 78nn34–36, 79n38,
Brandeis, Louis, 241–42 & n57, 270
Brennan, William J., Jr., 18 & n7, 74–76 & n26, 89–90 & n93, 97 & n121, 107, 116n200, 123, 131n257, 149, 176–77 & n79, 178 & n84, 190n31, 196, 203–04, 208, 214, 219, 221, 227 & n3, 256n104
Breyer, Stephen, 11n29, 96, 105, 137, 139, 142n304, 145–46, 191 & n35, 217
Briffault, Richard, 234n21
Brown v. Board of Education, 17n1, 27 & n42, 35–37
Brown v. Entertainment Merchants Association, 81n49
Brumfield v. Dodd, 9n22, 39n90
Buchanan, Nina K., 38n89,
Burger, Warren, 111–12, 122, 131, 131n257, 175–76, 179
Bush v. Holmes, 241nn54–56

Cain v. Horne, 228n4, 235 & nn24 & 26, 238–39 & nn42–44
Calabresi, Steven G., 77n31
Campbell, David E., 104n159
Channing, Edward, 42n99, 43n108
Charter school, 7, 15, 19–20 & n18, 21n19, 23n28, 25 & n34, 28 & n47, 29 & nn49 & 52, 32n66, 38 & n89, 49n143, 51–52 & nn149–50, 53 & nn 153 & 155, 54 & nn161 & 164, 56, 62n191, 63n195, 65 & n205, 213n130, 227, 229, 240, 243, 249, 267–69
Chemerinsky, Erwin, 212n128
Choper, Jesse H., 125n236
Christian Legal Society Chapter of the University of California v. Martinez, 250nn79 & 81–82, 251n83, 252, 253n90, 254 & nn94 & 98–100, 258 & n114, 262 & n130, 263, 265n144
Citizens United v. Federal Election Committee, 222n174
City of Erie v. Pap's A.M., 69n3, 245n64
Clapper v. Amnesty International USA, 209n117
County of Allegheny v. American Civil Liberties Union, 73n18, 99n133, 108n173, 192n37
Cochran v. Louisiana State Board of Education, 109n175
Colorado Christian University v. Weaver, 139n293, 245n66, 265n142
Committee for Public Education & Religious Liberty v. Nyquist, 93, 109n175, 120 & n221, 121 & nn222–23, 122n224, 125–26, 127n243, 143n309, 178–79 & n86, 180, 247n72, 252n87
Cooley, Thomas M., 75, 76n26
Corona, Brittany, 64n200
Coyle, Marsha, 81n51
Crimm, Nina J., 6nn15–18, 132n264, 151n14, 152n19, 169nn58–60, 171n65, 257n110, 259n115
Cutter v. Wilkinson, 71n10

DaimlerChrysler Corporation v. Cuno, 181n96, 196n57
Davis, Derek H., 85n63, 86nn69–70 & 72, 87nn75 & 78
Detached Memoranda, 73n19, 81n53, 86n73, 87n76
Dewey, John, 34 & n71
District of the City of Grand Rapids v. Ball, 106, 128–30, 133–36
Doremus v. Board of Education, 190n32, 196–98, 206

Douglas County, Colorado, 34n70, 60n184, 235, 246
Douglas, William O., 1–2, 9n23, 56n171, 112 & n187, 114 & n195, 115–19, 120n219, 123, 149, 196–97, 200 & n78
Dreisbach, Daniel L., 73n19, 83n55, 85n65, 86n71, 92n100
Duncan v. State of New Hampshire, 236n28
Dworkin, Ronald, 207 & n111, 218n156

Edwards v. Aguillard, 104n158, 125n236
Elementary and Secondary Education Act of 1965 (ESEA), 24 & nn29–30, 26n39, 198
Elk Grove Unified School District v. Newdow, 79n42, 80n44, 108n172, 188nn17–18, 20 & 22, 191n33
Employment Division, Department of Human Resources v. Smith, 245n65
Empowerment Scholarship Accounts (ESA), 31 & n61, 64–65 & n201, 66 & n208, 67, 151n10, 154–55 & n26, 156, 159–60 & n35, 163n42, 164, 167–68, 235, 246–247
Engel v. Vitale, 8n21, 48 & n138, 85n62, 86n67, 87n78, 97n124, 99, 112n187
Epstein, Richard E., 196n54
Erznoznik v. City of Jacksonville, 209n115
Esbeck, Carl H., 72n16, 73n18, 74n21, 77n31, 78n37, 88 & nn79 & 82, 197n58
Everson v. Board of Education, 69n1, 71, 83 & n56, 84 & n59, 91 & n96, 93 & n105, 109–114, 117 & n204, 118, 128, 132 & n263, 133, 145, 147, 177, 182 & n101, 200

Fabricant, Michael, 21n19, 32n66
Fallon, Richard H., Jr., 185n3, 189n28, 199n73, 211n125, 223n177
Federal Communications Commission v. League of Women Voters of California, 259n117
Federal Election Commission v. Akins, 188n22
Federal Election Commission v. Wisconsin Right to Life, Inc., 222n174
Federalist No. 1, 40n92
Feldman, Noah, 43n104, 47n134, 78n137
Fine, Michelle, 21n19, 32n66
Finkelman, Paul, 51n148
Flast v. Cohen, 1, 2n7, 14, 185n2, 186n6, 190n31, 198–201 & n82, 202–07, 209, 210n122, 211, 214 & n137, 215 & n145, 216–219 & n166, 220 & n167, 221–22, 227 & n1, 233, 243
Fleming, J. Clifford, Jr., 170nn62 & 63
Forman, James, Jr., 38n88, 48n138, 49nn140–43
Fortas, Abe, 117, 200
Fox, Robert A., 38n89
Frankfurter, Felix, 107, 112, 113n192, 115
Friedman Foundation, The, 29n54, 30n57, 31nn60 & 62, 34n70, 65n202, 66 & nn209–10
Friedman, Milton, 26n39, 35 & n75, 36 & n78, 49n142
Friends of the Earth, Inc. v. Laidlaw Environmental Services (TOC), Inc., 191n36, 208n114
Frothingham v. Mellon, 194–96, 198–206

Gajendragadkar, Suhid S., 38n89
Garnett, Nicole Steele, 48n137, 214n140
Garnett, Richard W., 211n127
Gates, Bill, 20
Gedicks, Frederick Mar, 245n66
Getchell, E. Duncan, Jr., 77n32, 78nn34–36, 79n38
Ginsburg, Ruth Bader, 139, 145, 217
Good News Club v. Milford Central School, 130n252, 263n135
Graetz, Michael J., 170n62
Grant, Ulysses S., 45 & n118
Green, Preston C. III, 54nn164–65, 61n188, 228n5
Green, Steven K., 40n93, 42nn98, 100, & 102–03, 44nn111–12 & 115–17, 45nn119–21, 46n123, 47nn129, 131 & 133–34, 74nn19 & 21, 76n26, 77n30, 83n58, 92n100, 93 & n109

Greenawalt, Kent, 46n123, 94n110
Grove City College v. Bell, 256n104, 258
Gulen, Fethulla, 54
Gunn, T. Jeremy, 73n19, 78n37, 83 & n58

Hamburger, Philip, 83 & n57
Harlan, John Marshall, 176, 200–201 & n81
Healy, Thomas, 270n153
Hein v. Freedom from Religion Foundation, Inc., 188n22, 189nn24–25, 204–10
Henry, Patrick, 4, 91–92 & nn99 & 100, 93, 147, 201n81, 215n145
Hernandez v. Commissioner, 63n193, 126n40, 152nn15 & 17
Hershkoff, Helen, 26n40, 234n21
Hibbs v. Winn, 213n132, 214n137
Hobby Lobby Stores, Inc. v. Sebelius, 70n6, 216n147, 245n65
Hollingsworth v. Perry, 187nn12–13, 188n21, 199n70, 212n128, 223n179, 224n181
Holmes, Oliver Wendell, 270–71
Home schooling, 7 & n20, 29 & n55, 30 & n56, 53n153, 56–60, 65 & n206, 268–69
Hosanna-Tabor Evangelical Lutheran Church & School v. Equal Employment Opportunity Commission, 7n19, 71n8, 72nn15–16, 119n216, 208nn112–13
Howe, Mark DeWolfe, 83n55
Hunt v. McNair, 120n221, 165n45
Hutson, James H., 87n74

Inazu, John D., 255n101
Internal Revenue Code (IRC),
§ 117, 65n203, 151n10, 155n26, 160n35
§ 170, 6, 63 & n193, 126, 151 & n14, 152 & nn18–19, 154 & n22, 156, 158 & n32, 159n33, 163n41, 168, 173 & n67, 174, 257n112, 259n117
§ 501(a), 126, 151, 156, 158–59
§ 501(c)(3), 6, 8, 30, 53, 62, 63n193, 126, 151 & n12, 152 & n19, 153–54 & n22, 156, 158–59, 163n41, 168–69 & n58, 170, 173 & n67, 180n93, 212, 216, 257nn110 & 112, 259n117

Jackson, Robert H., 100, 103n152, 110–111 & n182, 112n187, 115 & n199, 118, 196, 210n121
Jaffe, Louis L., 186n7, 189n28, 190n29, 199n73
Jefferson, Thomas, 4, 17n2, 35n75, 40 & n95, 41, 51, 79, 81n53, 83 & n55, 86 & n71, 87–92 & n103, 93–94 & n110, 105n167, 109, 111, 128, 178, 185

Kaestle, F. Carl, 40n95, 42n99, 44n109
Kagan, Elena, 11n29, 147n322, 180–81, 214n140, 215n145, 216–19, 232
Kennedy, Anthony, 80, 83, 100n142, 101, 131, 134, 145n314, 149–50, 180 & n93, 181, 205, 206n105, 207, 215 & n143, 216–17 & n149, 218–19, 233, 237
Kentucky Resolutions, 89n84
Ketcham, Ralph, 92n102
Klein, Joel, 22 & n23
Kleinbard, Edward D., 166n51
Koppelman, Andrew, 254n97
Kotterman v. Killian, 5n12, 214n136, 235 & n23, 236 & n30, 237 & nn34 & 36, 238 & nn37–41

Lee v. Weisman, 80nn44–45, 82n54, 85n62, 86n67, 87n75, 90n92, 91nn94–95, 99 & nn135–36, 100 & nn142–45, 101 & nn147 & 149, 102nn150–51, 103n155, 104n161, 105n167, 190n32
Leiter, Brian, 72n16
Lemon test or guidelines, 98 & n129, 118, 119n212, 121, 126, 129, 130n254, 134–35, 245
Lemon v. Kurtzman, 98 & nn128–29, 111–12 & n186, 118–20 & n220, 122–23, 128, 130, 179, 251n84
Levitt v. Committee for Public Education & Religious Liberty, 120n221

Levy, Leonard W., 40n94
Lewis, Anthony, 89nn83 & 86
Locke v. Davey, 71n10, 146n321, 264 & nn137–40, 265nn141–42
Lottery, 23n28, 229, 266 & n147, 267 & n149
Lukas, Carrie, 64n198
Lujan v. Defenders of Wildlife, 186 & n9, 187nn10–11 & 14, 189, 194n46, 208 & n114
Lupu, Ira C., 76n26, 211n127
Lynch v. Donnelly, 77n33, 81n50, 84n59, 85n62, 98 & nn130–32, 101, 104 & n162, 192n37

Madison, James, 4, 13 & n31, 51, 72 & nn14 & 16, 73 & n19, 74n20, 79, 81n53, 83n55, 86 & nn72–73, 87 & nn76–78, 89 & n84, 90 & nn89–90, 91–92 & n101, 93–94 & n110, 103 & n157, 111 & n182, 128, 146–147 & n322, 157, 177–78, 180n93, 189n27, 200, 203 & n92, 206 & n105, 207, 215 & n145, 255, 263
Magnet schools, 7, 27 & n42, 28, 142, 143
Maher v. Roe, 259n116
Mann, Horace, 42–43 & n108
Marsh v. Chambers, 85n62, 90n93, 97nn121 & 123, 270 & n156
Marshall, Thurgood, 123–25 & n236, 127n243, 131–132, 179, 203
Marshall, William P., 186n7, 211n127
Massachusetts v. Environmental Protection Agency, 185n4, 187n16, 189n25, 224n182
McCollum v. Board of Education, 97n126, 107n171, 112–15, 118n208, 245
McConnell, Michael W., 26n40, 72n16, 73n19, 245n66, 265n142
McConnell v. Federal Election Committee, 222n174
McCreary County, Kentucky v. American Civil Liberties Union, 15n34, 79n40, 81n53, 96n118, 103, 104n161, 191nn34–36, 210n121
McDaniel, Paul R., 166nn50–51, 167n53, 176n73
McGarvie, Mark D., 73n17, 77n31, 94n10
McGowan v. Maryland, 48n136
Mead, Julie F., 52n150, 55n165, 56n168
Means-testing, 229, 244
Meek v. Pittenger, 122–24, 137, 251n84
Memorial and Remonstrance Against Religious Assessments, 4, 92 & n101, 111, 147 & n322, 200, 206 & n105, 215
Meredith v. Pence, 231n11, 236n29, 239 & n47, 240nn49–52, 241n53
Meyer v. Nebraska, 107n169
Miami Herald Publishing Company v. Tornillo, 211n125
Mill, John Stuart, 35n75, 103n154
Milliken v. Bradley, 37 & n85
Minersville School District v. Gobitis, 100n140, 210n121
Minow, Martha, 36 & n78
Mitchell v. Helms, 10n26, 47n128, 122n225, 123n229, 136–41, 165n46, 178 & n83, 248, 253n89
Moran, Peter L., 61n188, 228n5
Morse v. Frederick, 80nn46–48, 81n49, 95nn116–17
Mueller v. Allen, 105n163, 125–28, 130, 143, 179

National Center for Education Statistics (NCES), 24n29, 28n45, 29nn49–52, 30n56, 31n63, 32nn64–65, 57n173
National Federation of Independent Business v. Sebelius, 150 & n8
Near v. Minnesota, 69n5, 89n84
New York Times Company v. Sullivan, 89 & n88
Newdow v. Lefevre, 193nn42–45
Newdow v. Rio Linda Union School District, 90n93
Nichol, Gene R., 186n7, 211n127
Niehaus v. Huppenthal, 12n30, 235 & n25, 239 & nn45–46, 246
No Child Left Behind Act (NCLB), 24 & n32, 25
Nondiscrimination, religious, *See* Religious nondiscrimination
Northwest Ordinance, 87–88

Norwood v. Harrison, 249n78, 255nn102–03, 256 & nn106–09, 257

O'Connor, Sandra Day, 15, 77, 82, 98 & n132, 99, 101, 103–05, 125, 130n254, 134, 137–39 & n297, 140n298, 143 & n311, 210, 248, 266n145

Paine, Thomas, 85 & n64
Parent trigger law, 28 & n48
Parents Involved in Community Schools v. Seattle School District, No. 1, 27n42, 37n87
Patient Protection and Affordable Care Act (ACA), 70 & n6, 128n244, 150
Payne v. Tennessee, 222nn172–73
Peroni, Robert J., 170nn62–63
Pervasively sectarian, 5n14, 11, 120nn220–21, 129–31, 139–40, 145n314, 212, 220, 251
Philanthro-capitalists, 20–21 & n19, 28
Pierce v. Society of Sisters, 5n13, 107n169
Playboy Entertainment Group, United States v., 245n63
Plyler v. Doe, 18n4, 37n83
Politics, Taxes, and the Pulpit: Provocative First Amendment Conflicts, 6nn15–18, 132n264, 151n14, 152n19, 169nn58–60, 171n65, 257n110, 259n115
Post, Robert, 95 & n112
Powell, Lewis, 125, 128, 130, 131, 178, 179n86
Program for International Student Assessment (PISA), 2n9, 23n25
Psychic Injury, 205–08, 220–21, 243
Putnam, Robert D., 104n159

Quick Bear v. Leupp, 109n175

Race to the Top (RTT), 23n28, 25 & nn33–34
Ravitch, Diane, 2n8, 19 & n11, 20nn15 & 18, 21 & n19, 24n31, 26n39, 28n48, 32n66, 36n76, 49n142, 52n149
Red River Freethinkers v. Fargo, 193nn40–41
Regan v. Taxation with Representation of Washington (TRW), 149–50 & n7, 152n18, 257n110, 259n117
Rehnquist, William, 71, 88, 122, 125n236, 130n254, 131n257, 134, 141, 143 & nn308 & 311, 149, 202–03, 264
Religious discrimination, 250n79, 253, 255 & n101, 256 & n105, 257
Religious Freedom Restoration Act (RFRA), 245 & n65, 260–61 & nn120 & 122, 262
Religious nondiscrimination, 251, 253, 261
Report on the Virginia Resolutions, 13n31, 89n84, 90n89
Resegregation, 37 & n84, 39
Richardson, United States v., 201n82, 209–10 & n120
Roberts, John G., Jr., 83, 150n8, 212 & n128
Roberts v. U.S. Jaycees, 254nn94–95
Roemer v. Board of Public Works, 120n221, 165n45
Rosenberger v. Rector & Visitors of the University of Virginia, 8n21, 10n26, 72n12, 88n80, 91n98, 93 & n107, 135n274, 139n296, 147 & n322, 166n49, 175n72, 266n145
Runyon v. McCrary, 251n85, 264n136
Rust v. Sullivan, 259n115
Rutledge, Wiley B., 91 & n96, 111 & n182, 177, 182
Ryan, James E., 29n52, 32n66, 37n86

Saiger, Aaron, 38n89, 52nn149 & 151–52, 54n164
Salazar v. Buono, 82n54
San Antonio Independent School District v. Rodriguez, 18nn4–5
Santa Fe Independent School District v. Doe, 11n27, 99 & n137, 100 & nn143–44, 101 & n149, 104n161, 105n167
Scalia, Antonin, 80–81 & nn49 & 51, 82 & n54, 100–01 & n146, 110n180, 131 & n257, 134, 145n314, 149, 186–87, 197n60, 205 & n102,

206–10 & n122, 217–18, 221n170, 222
Schenk, Deborah H., 170n62
Schlesinger v. Reservists Committee to Stop the War, 201n82, 209
Scholarship Tuition Organization (STO), 31, 62–63 & n195, 64 & n197, 65, 150–51, 154 & n22, 156 & n28, 162 & n39, 163 & nn40–41, 164, 167, 180 & n93, 181 & n98, 182 & n100, 212 & n129, 213 & n132, 214–15 & n143, 216–17 & n149, 220, 227, 235–37, 246–48, 263, 265
School choice, 1, 3, 12, 14, 22, 26 & nn39–40, 27, 29n52, 30n57, 31–32 & nn64 & 66, 34–39, 48 & n137, 49 & n142, 50–51, 61, 64, 66–67, 136–37, 147, 156, 173, 213, 222, 228 & n5, 229, 233–35, 238, 243–50, 256–57, 260–61, 263–67 & n149, 268–69, 271
School District of Abington v. Schempp, 48 & n138, 74, 97nn122, 124 & 126, 99, 103nn153 & 155, 105n167, 107n170, 116n200, 190n32
Schwartzman, Micah, 72n16, 211n127
Scott, Janelle, 20n18, 21n19
Sedition Act, 89 & nn83 & 88, 90 & n89, 94
Shekinah Learning Institute, 54
Simmons-Harris v. Goff, 234n22
Sklar v. Commissioner, 63n193, 126n241, 152n15
Sloan v. Lemon, 120n221
Snyder v. Phelps, 136n278
Sotomayor, Sonia, 217
Souter, David, 105, 131n257, 136, 138–42 & n304, 143–47 & n322, 163n40, 175n72, 178, 189, 205, 207, 228, 270
Standing, taxpayer, 11, 14, 147, 150, 180, 186, 192n37, 193–94, 196, 198, 201 & n82, 202 & n83, 204–05, 208, 210n122, 211 & n124, 212, 214, 217n149, 218–20 & n167, 221, 224, 230 & n10, 231 & nn11 & 12, 232 & nn14–16, 233 & n19, 234 & nn21–22, 235–36, 242–43
Staudt, Nancy C., 197n59
Stevens, John Paul, 105, 139, 145–46, 203, 251n83, 254, 265
Stevens, United States v., 69n2, 211n126
Stewart, Potter, 125, 200, 207
Stone, Geoffrey R., 99n134
Sugarman, Stephen D., 31n58, 181n98
Sugin, Linda, 174n69, 175n72, 219n159
Suhre v. Haywood County, 192nn38–39
Sunset provisions, 166n51, 229, 243–44
Sunstein, Cass, 189 & nn27–28, 190 & nn29–31
Surrey, Stanley S., 166 & nn50–51, 167nn52–53, 176n73
Sutherland, George, 195–96, 199
Swalwell, Katy, 19n13, 20nn15–17

Tarek ibn Ziyad Academy, 53 & n155
Tax credit, 4, 9n22, 30, 50, 58, 59n179, 61–62, 150 & n8, 153n20, 154 & n22, 156 & n29, 160–61 & n37, 181n96, 218n156, 234, 238n37, 247
  STO-tax credit, 11, 31& n58, 63 & nn194–95, 64, 156, 162, 162n39, 163nn40–41, 164, 167n55, 180 & n93, 181 & n97, 182 & n100, 183, 213 & nn130 & 133, 214nn137 & 140, 215–21 & n167, 235–37, 246, 247n70, 263
  Tuition or education tax credit, 8, 63, 145n319, 167n53, 168, 178, 234n22, 235n23
Tax deduction, 30–31, 50, 61, 125–26, 128, 151, 153 & n20, 154 & n22, 156–57, 161–63, 166n49, 167–68, 173, 174n68, 178–79 & n86, 213, 217, 234, 247 & n71
Tax expenditure, 4, 8, 11, 13–14, 125, 149, 150n8, 159n33, 164, 166n51, 167 & nn53–55, 168–70 & n62, 171nn64–65, 173–75 & n72, 176 & n73, 177–78, 180–81 & n96, 182–83, 214, 218, 220n167, 233, 236–37 & nn32 & 35

Tax mechanism, 7, 13, 61–62, 92, 128, 145, 151n10, 155, 157, 163–66, 169, 246–48
Taxing and spending, 149 & n2, 152–53, 165n47, 167, 179, 180–81, 194, 199–200, 202, 205–06, 208, 215, 228, 231n11, 233, 242
Taxpayers for Public Education v. Douglas County School District, 236n27
Texas Monthly, Inc. v. Bullock, 71n9, 149 & n6, 150, 171n65
Thanksgiving Proclamations, 85–86
Thomas, Clarence, 10 & n26, 71, 79–80 & n43, 81 & nn49 & 53, 82, 88, 131, 134, 136–39, 147 & n322, 175n72, 205, 217–18
Thomas v. Review Board of the Indiana Employment Security Division, 71n9
Tilton v. Richardson, 120n220, 165n45, 201n82
Tinker v. Des Moines Independent Community School District, 94n111, 95nn116–17
Toney v. Bower, 234n22, 235n23, 237n36
Town of Greece v. Galloway, 11n27, 80nn43–44, 93n108, 97n121, 140n300, 244n62
Tuttle, Robert W., 76n26, 211n127

Unconstitutional conditions doctrine, 258–59 & n115
United States v.
See other party's name
Urban, Wayne J., 43n108, 56n170, 57n173
Urquhart, Joshua G., 230n10, 231n12, 232n14, 233n18, 234n21, 242n59

Valley Forge Christian College v. Americans United for Separation of Church & State, Inc., 1n1, 165n145, 178 & n84, 185n1, 186n5, 188n22, 189n26, 190n31, 196n54, 200n77, 201–04, 206, 208, 214n139, 219
Van Orden v. Perry, 80n45, 81n52, 86n68, 90n91, 96n119, 104n161, 191 & nn34–35, 220–21
Village of Arlington Heights v. Metropolitan Housing Development Corporation, 197n59
Virginia Bill for Establishing Religious Freedom, 92, 111
Virginia Tax Assessment, 91 & n96, 92 & n99, 93, 109, 147, 201n81, 215n145
Virginia, Act for Establishing Religious Freedom, 81n53, 93n104
Viteritti, Joseph P., 24n31, 25n34, 32n66, 33n75, 35n75, 46nn123 & 127, 47n132, 55n166
Volokh, Eugene, 76n27, 255n101, 256n104, 260n119, 261 & nn123 & 125–27, 262, 263 & nn131–32, 265n143
Voucher, tuition, 4, 7, 9n22, 11, 20, 29n52, 30 & n57, 31n58, 32nn64–66, 33n68, 34 & n70, 39 & n90, 49n142, 50, 52n149, 54n164, 60 & n185, 61 & n188, 65, 67 & n214, 79, 105, 113n191, 137, 141–42, 143n308, 144 & n313, 145–46, 151n10, 155, 163n40, 223, 231n11, 234 & n22, 235 & n26, 236, 238–40 & nn49 & 52, 241, 246–47 & n72, 248, 252, 263–64

West Virginia State Board of Education v. Barnette, 100nn140–41, 103n152, 112n187, 210n121
Waggoner, Jennings L., 43n108, 56n170, 57n173
Waiting for "Superman", 19 & nn13–14, 20
Wallace v. Jaffrey, 76n29, 85n62, 88nn80–81, 97n127, 98n132, 99, 100n144, 101 & nn148–49, 105n167, 125n236
Wallet Injury, 205
Walton family, 20
Walz v. Tax Commission of the City of New York, 71nn7 & 10, 112n187, 132n264, 149, 171n65, 175 & n72, 176nn73–77, 177 & nn78–79, 178n84, 179n86
Warren, Earl, 17, 176n73, 198–200

Warth v. Seldin, 187n16, 188n22, 197n59, 221n171
Washington, George, 15 & n33, 17 & n2, 86, 103 & n156, 185
Widmar v. Vincent, 130n252
Williams, Roger, 83 & n55
Windsor, United States v., 131n260, 187nn15–16, 197n60, 205n102, 209n118, 212n128
Winer, Laurence H., 6nn15–18, 132n264, 151n14, 152n19, 169nn58–60, 171n65, 257n110, 259n115
Wisconsin v. Yoder, 9n23, 19n10, 56n171, 108n172
Witte, John, Jr., 40n91, 47n133, 73n19, 74n21, 78n37
Witters v. Washington Department of Services for the Blind, 129n249, 135 & nn274–75, 137–38, 140, 143, 247n72
Wolfman, Bernard, 166n51
Wolman v. Walter, 123–25, 130, 132, 137, 165n46, 252

Yudof, Mark D., 41n96

Zelinsky, Edward A., 164n44, 166n51, 174 & n70, 175n71, 197n59, 230n10, 231n12, 232n14
Zelman v. Simmons-Harris, 4, 10 & n25, 11 & nn27–29, 13, 54n164, 60n186, 61, 79, 104n158, 105 & nn164–66, 141–46, 151n10, 163n40, 223 & n178, 228, 237 & n33, 240 & n52, 246, 247n72, 248–49 & n75, 252, 257, 263
Zobrest v. Catalina Foothills School District, 106, 131–33, 135 & n274, 138, 140, 143
Zorach v. Clauson, 113–16, 245
Zuckerberg, Mark, 20